A Guide to Critical Reviews of United States Fiction, 1870-1910

Compiled by
CLAYTON L. EICHELBERGER

assisted by

Karen L. Bickley
R. Bruce Bickley, Jr.
Douglas H. Shepard
Bonnie F. Sloane
David E. E. Sloane

William P. Black
George Fortenberry
Barrie Hayne
Joyce McGowan
Ernestine Sewell

The Scarecrow Press, Inc.
Metuchen, N.J.   1971

The Library of Congress Cataloged the Original Printing of
This Title as:

Eichelberger, Clayton L   1925–
   A guide to critical reviews of United States fiction, 1870–
1910, compiled by Clayton L. Eichelberger. Assisted by
Karen L. Bickley ₍and others₎ Metuchen, N. J., Scarecrow
Press, 1971.

   415 p.   22 cm.

   1. American fiction—Book reviews—Bibliography.   2. Periodicals—
Indexes.   I. Title.

Z1225.E35   016.813′4′09   77–149998
ISBN 0–8108–0380–1   MARC

Library of Congress   71 ₍70–2₎

Contents

Preface

This index is intended as a research tool designed to guide the student and scholar to representative contemporary critical comment on fiction written by both major and minor United States writers and published during the 1870-1910 period. It is in no way comprehensive or definitive and should be interpreted simply as a preliminary contribution extending in several directions:

1) As a listing of authors and titles, it overlaps the contributions of bibliographers and indexers such as Oscar Fay Adams (A Dictionary of American Authors, 5th ed.), Jacob Blanck (Bibliography of American Literature), W. Stewart Wallace (Dictionary of North American Authors Deceased Before 1950), and Lyle H. Wright (American Fiction, 1851-1875 and American Fiction, 1876-1900), all of which were used as checklists for author and title identification; but it moves beyond them in its inclusion of some authors and many titles not previously listed in these standard sources.

2) A majority of the important critical reviews of books by authors who are conceded major rank are already known. Insofar as those reviews appear in periodicals covered by this index, they are entered here. But the index additionally includes some significant entries not well known because of the minor status of the publications in which they appeared and the relative unavailability of those publications today.

3) The chief contribution of this guide is its listing of critical comment on minor titles and on works by minor authors, items previously unlisted except as they appear in scattered form in unpublished dissertations and theses. Scholarly emphasis on major writers has dwarfed the contribution of minor writers to the foundation upon which the edifice of literary greatness stands. This index not only indicates which of the minor authors, because

v

of their popularity, may have contributed significantly to the development of United States fiction, but also directs the researcher to some of the limited published comment on their works.

4) In addition to serving as a locator index, this listing provides a bibliographic basis for a comparative study of reviews as a reflection of the many aspects of popular culture in the late-nineteenth and early-twentieth centuries and as such will be of interest to American studies specialists.

The periodicals covered here were selected with the long-range objective, not fully realized in this single volume, of representing major American and English review outlets and lesser publications reflecting regional interests. Indexers thumbed through the selected periodicals in a systematic way, noted comment in the form of reviews and critical notices of American fiction, and prepared a bibliographic entry for each item. The random critical comments which make up literary columns such as "Notes" in Nation and "Contributor's Club" in Atlantic are not included here. General essays relating to the work of an author or group of authors and formal critical articles are also omitted.

Necessarily, the boundaries of an index such as this are highly flexible because of problems of definition. What constitutes a review or critical comment? What is the difference between a sketch and a short story--judged on the basis of review comments, frequently the indexer's only guide--or between a fictional sketch and a factual sketch? Are English-American authors to be included or excluded? Without a close examination of primary works and a full knowledge of seemingly non-existent biographical information, guided only by the reviewers and typesetters who too often confused Henry with Harry and man with woman, the indexer finds many of these questions difficult to answer arbitrarily.

Critical review is interpreted here in the broadest possible way: it has nothing to do with either extent or depth of content, with either quality or quantity; it includes any effort on the part of the reviewer, be it only a single sentence, to evaluate the substantive or artistic achievement of the author. While the index focuses on adult fiction, juvenile fiction is generally included if it was not specifically labeled as juvenile by the reviewer; if it was so labeled, or if it appeared in columns devoted to children's literature, it was omitted. Travel sketches and biographies identified as such were naturally excluded; if doubt existed as to the factual or fictional nature of the material, the tendency was to include the title in the listing. No serious effort was made to distinguish between the fictional sketch and the short story, or between collections of short stories and novels.

While the attempt was made to include only United States authors, the listing does include a few English authors who served as co-authors with American writers and a number of English-American writers, inclusion generally determined by the writer's having spent a considerable portion of his life or having done a considerable body of his writing in the United States. Variant spellings of names and variant titles as reported by reviewers have been brought into conformity with Volumes II and III of Wright's bibliography whenever the names and titles in question are included in those volumes; inclusion of an author in the Wright bibliography was also accepted as authentication of nationality. W. Stewart Wallace's Dictionary of North American Authors Deceased Before 1950 and Oscar Fay Adam's Dictionary of American Authors, 5th ed., were relied upon heavily for identification of the nationality of authors not included in Wright. Other sources for identification indirectly include all those relied upon by Adams, Wallace, and Wright, especially American Authors, 1600-1900, ed. S. J. Kunitz and H. Haycraft; W. J. Burke and W. D. Howe, American Authors and Books; Dictionary of American Biography, ed. A. Johnson and D. Malone; Encyclopedia Americana, International Edition, 1964; and Who's Who in America, ed. A. N. Marquis.

Mechanics of Compilation

Arrangement of Entries. Titles are entered alphabetically under known authors' names or under identified pseudonyms or initials. Under single book titles, reviews are arranged alphabetically by the title of the periodical in which the review appeared. When a periodical carried multiple reviews, the entries are chronological beneath the periodical title.

Square brackets around the name of an author indicate editorial identification of authorship for a work published anonymously or pseudonymously. Known pseudonyms are identified by the abbreviation "pseud." in brackets, and parentheses are used to indicate the maiden name of married female authors. Because of the difficulty of establishing nationality of authorship, unidentified anonymous titles and those published under unidentified pseudonyms and initials are entered alphabetically in an appendix.

Titles. As a general rule sub-titles, used extensively during the period, are omitted if they are not necessary for distinguishing between two or more works with duplicate main titles.

Form of Bibliographic Entry. The title of the work reviewed in periodicals is followed by bibliographic detail in this sequence: the name (sometimes shortened) of the periodical in which the review appeared (followed by place of publication in parentheses when that information is necessary for accurate identification), series designation if any, volume number in Arabic form, pagination (separated from volume number by a colon), and date of the periodical number in which the review appeared (month names have been uniformly shortened to the first three letters), thus:

Bookman (London), 17:120, Jan 1900.

The only newspaper covered by this listing is the New Orleans Daily Picayune. The Louisiana State University microfilm reproduction was used as a source; actual pagination of the Picayune was not initiated until the mid-1880's, so page designation up to that time is based on the counting of microfilm frames.

Cross References. In cases of co-authorship identified pseudonyms, and name changes resulting from marriage, cross references are included in the main body of the list. Titles are listed under the author's actual name--Mark Twain appears under Clemens, Samuel--or married name--Mary E. Wilkins is entered under Freeman, Mary E. (Wilkins).

Index of Titles

The titles in shortened form of all books reviewed and an indication of the page of the guide on which the review information appears are included in the Index of Titles.

30 June 1970   Clayton L. Eichelberger

Acknowledgments

The compilation of an index of this type depends upon the assistance of many persons whose names do not appear on the title page, most of them librarians who worked anonymously and without knowledge of the project to which they were contributing.

I am particularly grateful to the Amon Carter Museum of Fort Worth, Texas, for access to the microfilm of the New Orleans Daily Picayune, and to Mrs. Margaret McLean, Microfilm Librarian, for her bracing coffee and her courteous assistance; to the staff of the Library of Congress, especially the stack assistants on Deck 47, who never made me feel in the way; to Francine Morris, Reference Librarian, University of Texas at Arlington, and her staff for continuing not only to tolerate me, but also to assist me; and to my secretary, Mrs. Geneva Ransom, for never complaining about being asked to manipulate file cards.

My special gratitude is reserved for my wife, Nancy, and for our three children, Julie, Joel, and Jon. Without their willingness to sacrifice family activity for my nights in the library, this index would not have been completed.

C. L. E.

Periodicals Covered

America (Chicago), Apr 1889 through Sep 1891

Athenaeum (London), 1870 through 1910

Atlantic Monthly, 1870 through 1910

Bookman (London), 1895 through 1910

Bookman (New York), Feb 1895 through 1910

The Bystander (Canada), 1880 through 1881, 1883, 1889 through
   1890

The Canadian Magazine, 1893 through 1910

Canadian Monthly and National Review, 1872 through 1878 (then
   becomes Rose-Belford's Magazine)

Continent (Philadelphia), Feb 1882 through Aug 1884

Cottage-Hearth (Boston), Dec 1881 through May 1894 (except for
   scattered issue omissions in Library of Congress holdings)

Daily Picayune (New Orleans), 1870 through 1900

Dixie (Baltimore), Jan 1899 through Apr 1900

Epoch (New York), Feb 1887 through Mar 1892

Godey's Lady's Book and Magazine, 1870 through Aug 1898

Good Company (Springfield, Massachusetts), Vol. 4, Nos. 3-6 (1880)
   only (brief continuation of Sunday Afternoon)

Harper's Monthly, 1870 through 1910

Library Table (New York), 1876 through 1878

Manhattan (New York), Apr 1883 through Sep 1884

The Nation, 1870 through 1910

North American Review, 1870 through 1910

Outlook, 1898 through 1910

Overland Monthly, 1870 through 1910

Poet Lore, 1889 through 1909

Quarterly Review (London), 1870 through 1910

Rose-Belford's Magazine (Canada), 1878 through 1882

The Saturday Review (London), 1870 through 1910

Sewanee Review, 1892 through 1910

South Atlantic Quarterly, 1902 through 1910

Sunday Afternoon (Springfield, Massachusetts), 1878 through Aug
   1879 (continued briefly as Good Company)

Times Literary Supplement (London), 1870 through 1910

Abarbanelle, J. R.
   The Rector's Secret
      Picayune, 4 Sep 1892,
         p. 7

Abbott, Charles Conrad
   A Colonial Wooing
      Nation, 63:180, 3 Sep 1896
      Picayune, 5 Jan 1896, p.
         13

Abbott, John S. C.
   Driven to Sea
      Harper's, 41:459, Aug
         1870

Abbott, Lyman
   Laicus
      Harper's, 45:298, Jul 1872

Abbott, Mary Perkins (Ives)
   Alexia
      America, 3:280, 28 Nov
         1889
      Nation, 50:226, 13 Mar
         1890
   The Beverleys
      Atlantic, 67:424, Mar 1891
      Epoch, 8:415, 30 Jan 1891
      Nation, 52:106-7, 6 Aug
         1891

About, Edwin
   The King of the Mountains
      Picayune, 22 Aug 1897,
         p. 24

Adams, Andy
   The Log of a Cowboy
      Athenaeum, 3972:790,
         12 Dec 1903
   The Outlet
      Nation, 80:422, 25 May
         1905
      Saturday Review, 100:630,
         11 Nov 1905
   Reed Anthony, Cowman
      Nation, 85:16, 4 Jul 1907

Adams, Frederick Upham
   John Henry Smith
      Athenaeum, 4059:202, 12
         Aug 1905

[Adams, Henry]
   Democracy
      Athenaeum, 2852:793-5, 24
         Jun 1880
      Atlantic, 46:421-2, Sep 1880
      Bookman (NY), 29:227-8,
         May 1909
      Nation, 30:312-3, 22 Apr
         1880
      Quarterly Review, 155:209,
         223, Jan 1883
      Saturday Review, 54:55-6,
         8 Jul 1882
   Esther
      By Frances Snow Compton
      [pseud.].
         Athenaeum, 3013:107-8, 25
            Jul 1885
         Saturday Review, 60:356-7,
            12 Sep 1885

Adams, Jane
   The Test
      Athenaeum, 4318:121, 30
         Jul 1910

Adams, Mrs. Leith
   Madelon Lemoine
      Godey's, 99:469, Nov
         1879
      Harper's, 60:151, Dec
         1879
      Nation, 29:279, 23 Oct
         1879
      Picayune, 21 Sep 1879,
         [p. 9]
   My Land of Beulah
      Picayune, 11 Oct 1891,
         p. 13
   Winstowe
      Picayune, 9 Sep 1877,
         [p. 9]

Adams, Mary
  Confessions of a Wife
    Athenaeum, 3917:679,
      22 Nov 1902
    Bookman (London),
      23:55-7, Nov 1902
    Nation, 75:448, 4 Dec
      1902
  An Honorable Surrender
    Continent, 4:60-1, 11 Jul
      1883
    Manhattan, 1:315-6, Apr
      1883
    Nation, 36:302, 5 Apr
      1883

Adams, Oscar Fay
  The Archbishop's Unguarded
    Moment
    Picayune, 26 Nov 1899,
      II, 8

Adams, Samuel Hopkins
  See White, Stewart Edward,
  and Samuel Hopkins Adams.

Adams, William
  Born in the Whirlwind
    Picayune, 29 Oct 1893,
      p. 16

[Adams, William Taylor]
  The Dorcas Club
    By Oliver Optic [pseud.].
    Saturday Review, 39:425,
      27 Mar 1875
  A Millionaire at Sixteen
    By Oliver Optic [pseud.].
    Godey's, 125:195-6, Aug
      1892
  On the Blockade
    By Oliver Optic [pseud.].
    Godey's, 122:96, Jan 1891
  Stand by the Union
    By Oliver Optic [pseud.].
    Epoch, 10:215, 6 Nov 1891
  The Way of the World
    By Oliver Optic [pseud.].
    Godey's, 85:187, Aug 1872;
      121:542, Dec 1890
    Picayune, 9 Jun 1872, [p. 9]

Within the Enemy's Lines
  By Oliver Optic [pseud.].
  Picayune, 15 Dec 1889,
    p. 11

Ade, George
  Artie
    Bookman (NY), 4:262, Nov
      1896
    Picayune, 18 Oct 1896,
      p. 9
    Saturday Review, 82:658,
      19 Dec 1896
  Doc' Horne
    Bookman (NY), 10:502,
      Jan 1900
  Forty Modern Fables
    Overland, 2d S, 39:731-2,
      Mar 1902
  The Girl Proposition
    North American Review,
      176:739-43, May 1903
  More Fables
    Picayune, 28 Oct 1900,
      II, 9
  The Pastures New
    Bookman (London), 32:178,
      Aug 1907
    Saturday Review, 103:624-
      25, 18 May 1907
  Pink Marsh
    Bookman (NY), 6:74, Sep
      1897
    Picayune, 20 Jun 1897,
      p. 16
  The Slim Princess
    Athenaeum, 4208:757-8,
      20 Jun 1908

Adee, David Graham
  The Blue Scarab
    Picayune, 24 Apr 1892,
      p. 12
  No. 19 State Street
    Godey's, 117:254, Sep
      1888
    North American Review,
      147:358, Sep 1888
    Picayune, 8 Jul 1888,
      p. 3

14

Adeler, Max [pseud.].
See Clark, Charles Heber.

Adler, Cyrus, and Allan Ramsay
Told in the Coffee-House
  Picayune, 17 Apr 1898,
    p. 10

Affery, Charles
Misled
  Picayune, 22 Dec 1889,
    p. 17

Afterem, George [pseud.].
See Williams, Harold.

Aitken, Robert
The Golden Horseshoe
  Athenaeum, 4199:474, 18
    Apr 1908
  Nation, 85:519, 5 Dec
    1907

Alcott, Louisa M.
Aunt Jo's Scrap Bag
  Athenaeum, 2341:303, 7
    Sep 1872
  Godey's, 86:187, Feb 1873;
    78:186, Feb 1874
  Harper's, 44:463, Feb
    1872
  Nation, 29:427, 18 Dec
    1879
Eight Cousins
  Athenaeum, 2504:538-9,
    23 Oct 1875
  Godey's, 91:570, Dec 1875
  Overland, 15:493, Nov
    1875
Little Men
  Athenaeum, 2278:781, 24
    Jun 1871
  Godey's, 73:186, Aug 1871
  Harper's, 43:458, Aug
    1871
  Overland, 7:293, Sep 1871
Little Women
  Bookman (London), 37:80,
    Christmas Suppl. , Dec
    1909

Lulu's Library
  Saturday Review, 62:26-7,
    3 Jul 1886
A Modern Mephistopheles
  Atlantic, 40:109, Jul 1877
  Godey's, 95:86, Jul 1877
  Library Table, 3:27, Sep
    1877
  North American Review,
    125:316-8, Sep 1877
An Old-Fashioned Girl
  Athenaeum, 2225:803, 18
    Jun 1870
  Atlantic, 25:752-3, Jun
    1870
  Godey's, 80:576, Jun 1870;
    81:281, Sep 1870; 81:
    472, Nov 1870
  Harper's, 41:143, Jun 1870
  Nation, 11:30, 14 Jul 1870
  Picayune, 17 Apr 1870,
    [p. 12]
Proverb Stories
  Saturday Review, 54:774,
    9 Dec 1882
Rose in Bloom
  Nation, 23:373, 21 Dec
    1876
  Picayune, 4 Feb 1877,
    [p. 6]
Shawl Straps
  Harper's, 46:616, Mar
    1873
Silver Pitchers
  Harper's, 53:629, Sep 1876
  Nation, 23:45, 25 Jul 1876
Spinning Wheel Stories
  Nation, 39:487, 4 Dec 1884
Under the Lilacs
  Picayune, 8 Dec 1878,
    [p. 5]; 16 Feb 1879,
    [p. 11]
  Rose-Belford's, 1:637,
    Nov 1878
  Saturday Review, 46:700,
    30 Nov 1878
Work
  Godey's, 87:284, Sep 1873
  Harper's, 47:618-9, Sep
    1873

Nation, 17:73, 31 Jul 1873
Saturday Review, 36:320-1,
6 Sep 1873

Alden, Mrs. G. R.
See Alden, Isabella (Mac-
donald).

[Alden, Isabella (Macdonald)]
By Way of Wilderness
By Pansy [pseud.].
Outlook, 65:87, 5 May 1900
Judge Burnham's Daughter
By Pansy [pseud.].
Cottage Hearth, 14:328,
Oct 1888
Ruth Erskine's Crosses
By Pansy [pseud.].
Nation, 29:214, 25 Sep
1879
Stephen Mitchell's Journey
By Pansy [pseud.].
Godey's, 128:106, Jan 1894

Alden, William Livingston
Among the Freaks
Picayune, 13 Apr 1896,
p. 10
Drewitt's Dream
Bookman (London), 23:214,
Feb 1903
Nation, 74:471, 12 Jun
1902
Saturday Review, 95:555,
2 May 1903
His Daughter
Saturday Review, 84:176,
14 Aug 1897
A Lost Soul
Bookman (London), 3:59-60,
Nov 1892
Told by the Colonel
Bookman (London), 4:155,
Aug 1893
Godey's, 128:105, Jan 1894
Overland, 2d S, 23:219,
Feb 1894

Aldrich, Anne Reeve
The Feet of Love

Nation, 51:293, 9 Oct 1890
Picayune, 27 Apr 1890,
p. 10

Aldrich, Thomas Bailey
Marjorie Daw, and Other
Stories
Atlantic, 32:625, Nov 1873;
46:696, Nov 1880
Overland, 11:581, Dec
1873; 2d S, 5:559, May
1885; 2d S, 28:371-2,
Sep 1896
Saturday Review, 36:606-7,
8 Nov 1873; 60:226-7,
15 Aug 1885
Sewanee Review, 11:352,
Jul 1903
Outside of Slocum's Yard
Atlantic, 46:697, Nov 1880
Père Antoine's Date Palm
Atlantic, 46:695, Nov 1880
Prudence Palfrey
Athenaeum, 2441:167, 8
Aug 1874
Atlantic, 34:227-9, Aug
1874; 46:697-8, Nov
1880
Harper's, 49:444, Aug 1874
Nation, 19:207-8, 24 Sep
1874
Saturday Review, 38:291,
29 Aug 1874; 61:304,
27 Feb 1886
The Queen of Sheba
Atlantic, 41:141-2, Jan
1878; 46:696, Nov 1880
Library Table, 4:196, 30
Mar 1878
Sunday Afternoon, 1:92-3,
Jan 1878
A Sea Turn, and Other Stories
Athenaeum, 3914:584, 1
Nov 1902
Atlantic, 92:713, Nov 1903
Nation, 75:331-2, 23 Oct
1902
Saturday Review, 95:206,
14 Feb 1903
The Stillwater Tragedy

Athenaeum, 2765:529-30,
23 Oct 1880
Atlantic, 25:124-5, Jan
1970; 46:696-7, Nov
1880
Saturday Review, 50:560,
30 Oct 1880
The Story of a Bad Boy
Overland, 4:294, Mar 1870
Two Bites at a Cherry, with
Other Tales
Atlantic, 72:849, Dec 1893
Godey's, 127:766, Dec
1893
Nation, 57:452, 14 Dec
1893
Overland, 2d S, 23:216,
Feb 1894
Picayune, 22 Oct 1893,
p. 14
Saturday Review, 76:528,
4 Nov 1893

_____, and M. O. W.
Oliphant
The Second Son
Epoch, 3:76, 2 Mar 1888
Nation, 46:304, 12 Apr
1888

Allderdice, Elizabeth Winslow
An Interesting Case
Manhattan, 4:251, Aug
1884

Allen, Grant
A Bride from the Desert
Godey's, 133:208, Aug
1896
For Mamie's Sake
Godey's, 112:537, May
1886
Hilda Wade
Nation, 71:156, 23 Aug
1900
Michael's Crag
Godey's, 128:106, Jan
1894
The Scallywag
Godey's, 127:363, Sep
1893

This Mortal Coil
Godey's, 118:180, Feb
1889

Allen, James Lane
Aftermath
Bookman (NY), 2:327-8,
Dec 1895
Picayune, 16 Feb 1896,
p. 16
Sewanee Review, 8:48, Jan
1900; 11:363, Jul 1903
South Atlantic Quarterly,
3:286, Jul 1904
The Bride of the Mistletoe
Athenaeum, 4265:91, 24
Jul 1909
Bookman (NY), 29:539-41,
Jul 1909; 29:577, Aug
1909
Nation, 89:16, 1 Jul 1909
North American Review,
190:267-8, Aug 1909
Butterflies
Bookman (NY), 1:303-5,
Jun 1895
Sewanee Review, 8:48,
Jan 1900
The Choir Invisible
Athenaeum, 3646:348, 11
Sep 1897
Bookman (London), 12:87,
Jul 1897; 12:100, Jul
1897
Bookman (NY), 5:288-90,
Jun 1897; 5:336-8, Jun
1897
Godey's, 135:[331], Sep
1897
Nation, 65:17, 1 Jul 1897
Overland, 2d S, 30:187,
Aug 1897
Picayune, 9 May 1897, p.
17; 5 Feb 1899, p. 11
Poet-Lore, 9:437-8,
Summer 1897
Sewanee Review, 5:379-80,
Jul 1897; 8:48, 53, Jan
1900; 11:356, Jul 1903;
11:363, Jul 1903

The Doctor's Christmas Eve
  Athenaeum, 4339:790,
    24 Dec 1910
Flute and Violin, and Other
  Kentucky Tales and Ro-
  mances
    Atlantic, 69:264-5, Feb
      1892
    Epoch, 9:382, 17 Jul 1891
    Harper's, 83:640-1, Sep
      1891
    Nation, 53:107, 6 Aug 1891
    Saturday Review, 73:553-4,
      May 1892
    Sewanee Review, 2:507,
      Aug 1894; 8:45, Jan
      1900; 11:363, Jul 1903
The Increasing Purpose
  Athenaeum, 3794:53, 14
    Jul 1900
  Bookman (London), 18:157,
    Aug 1900
  Saturday Review, 90:213,
    18 Aug 1900
John Gray
  Godey's, 126:769, Jun 1893
  Sewanee Review, 8:45-52,
    Jan 1900; 11:363, Jul
    1903
A Kentucky Cardinal
  Atlantic, 75:567, Apr 1895
  Saturday Review, 82:202,
    22 Aug 1896
  Sewanee Review, 5:379,
    Jul 1897; 8:47-8, Jan
    1900; 11:166-7, Apr
    1903; 11:363, Jul 1903
  South Atlantic Quarterly,
    3:286, Jul 1904
The Mettle of the Pasture
  Athenaeum, 3958:309-10,
    5 Sep 1903
  Bookman (London), 25:49,
    Oct 1903
  Bookman (NY), 18:78-80,
    Sep 1903
  Saturday Review, 96:212,
    15 Aug 1903; 96:402,
    26 Sep 1903
  Times Literary Supplement,
    25 Sep 1903, p. 273

The Reign of Law
  Atlantic, 86:419-20, Sep
    1900
  Bookman (NY), 11:510,
    Aug 1900
  Saturday Review, 91:342,
    16 Mar 1901
  Sewanee Review, 11:364,
    Jul 1903
Summer in Arcady
  Atlantic, 78:568, Oct 1896
  Bookman (NY), 3:347-9,
    Jun 1896; 5:290, Jun
    1897
  Dixie, 2:533-41, Nov 1899
  Godey's, 133:431, Oct
    1896
  Overland, 2d S, 28:607,
    Nov 1896
  Picayune, 28 Jun 1896,
    p. 14
  Sewanee Review, 8:48,
    52-3, Jan 1900; 11:166
    -7, Apr 1903; 11:363,
    Jul 1903
Under the Dragon Flag
  Saturday Review, 85:401-2,
    19 Mar 1898

[Allen, Linda Marguerite Sangrée]
  Florine
    Picayune, 28 Jun 1891,
      p. 12

Allen, Luman
  Helene Sainte Maur
    Picayune, 31 Jan 1892,
      p. 3
  Lucia Lascar
    Picayune, 22 Feb 1891,
      p. 13
  Pharoah's Treasure
    Picayune, 24 May 1891,
      p. 12

Allen, Richard
  Miss Eaton's Romance
    Nation, 52:385, 7 May
      1891
    Picayune, 15 Jun 1890,
      p. 14

Allen, Stanton P.
Down in Dixie
Picayune, 3 Dec 1893,
p. 19

Allen, Willis Boyd
Cleared for Action
Outlook, 63:510, 28 Oct
1899
The Head of Pasht
Picayune, 17 Jun 1900,
II, 12
Navy Blue
Outlook, 59:386, 11 Jun
1898
Pine Cones
Cottage Hearth, 11:394,
Dec 1885

Altsheler, Joseph Alexander
The Candidate
Outlook, 79:960, 15 Apr
1905
Guthrie of the 'Times'
Athenaeum, 4045:555,
6 May 1905
A Herald of the West
Atlantic, 83:286, Feb 1899
Bookman (NY), 8:490,
Jan 1899
Picayune, 7 Nov 1898,
p. 8
The Hidden Mine
Picayune, 27 Nov 1898,
p. 10
In Circling Camps
Bookman (NY), 12:194-5,
Oct 1900
Outlook, 65:597, 7 Jul 1900
Picayune, 15 Jul 1900,
III, 3
In Hostile Red
Picayune, 18 Nov 1900,
III, 4
The Last Rebel
Outlook, 63:651, 11 Nov
1899
Picayune, 10 Dec 1899,
III, 7
The Rainbow of Gold
Picayune, 31 Jul 1898, II, 6

A Soldier of Manhattan and
His Adventures at Ticonde-
roga and Quebec
Picayune, 31 Oct 1897,
p. 11
The Sun of Saratoga
Picayune, 27 Jun 1897,
p. 9

Ames, Lucia True
See Mead, Lucia True (Ames).

Ames, Mary (Clemmer)
Eirene
Harper's, 43:937-8, Nov
1871
Saturday Review, 32:445,
30 Sep 1871
His Two Wives
Cottage Hearth, 15:92,
Mar 1889
Nation, 20:44, 21 Jan 1875
Picayune, 20 Jan 1889,
p. 11
Saturday Review, 67:641,
25 May 1889
Outlines of Men, Women, and
Things
Overland, 11:389, Oct 1873

Anderson, Ada Woodruff
The Heart of the Red Firs
Nation, 87:56, 16 Jul 1908
Overland, 2d S, 51:582,
Jun 1908
The Strain of White
Overland, 2d S, 54:534,
Nov 1909

Anderson, Edward
Camp Fire Stories
Picayune, 24 May 1896,
p. 20

Anderson, Mrs. Finley
A Woman with a Record
Picayune, 20 Dec 1896,
p. 20

[Anderson, Olive Santa Louise]
  An American Girl and Her Four
  Years in a Boys' College.
    By Sola [pseud.].
    Nation, 26:204, 28 Mar 1898

[Andrews, Eliza Frances]
  A Family Secret
    By Elzey Hay [pseud.].
    Godey's, 93:92, Jul 1876
    Nation, 22:369, 8 Jun 1876
    Picayune, 23 Apr 1876,
      [p. 12]; 30 Apr 1876,
      [p. 2]
    Saturday Review, 42:522,
      28 Oct 1876
  A Mere Adventurer
    By Elzey Hay [pseud.].
    Nation, 29:115, 14 Aug 1879
    Picayune, 15 Jun 1879,
      [p. 10]
  Prince Hal
    Picayune, 23 Jul 1882,
      [p. 2]

Andrews, Mary Raymond
(Shipman)
  The Lifted Bandage
    Nation, 90:653, 30 Jun 1910
  The Militants
    Nation, 85:58, 18 Jul 1907

Arctander, John W.
  Guilty?
    Overland, 2d S, 55:641,
      Jun 1910

Argyle, Anna
  Olive Lacey
    Nation, 19:93, 6 Aug 1874
    Saturday Review, 38:417,
      26 Sep 1874

[Arkell, William J., and A. T.
Worden]
  Napoleon Smith
    Overland, 2d S, 12:432,
      Oct 1888
    North American Review,
      147:238, Aug 1888

Armstrong, Minnie L.
  The Modern Evil
    America, 6:483, 23 Jul
      1891
    Picayune, 19 Jul 1891,
      p. 10

_____, and George N.
Sceets
  The Social Crime
    Picayune, 21 Sep 1896,
      p. 10

Armstrong, William
  An American Nobleman
    Saturday Review, 75:525,
      13 May 1893
  Thekla
    Picayune, 16 Oct 1887,
      p. 11

Arp, Bill [pseud.].
  See Smith, Charles Henry.

Arthur, Timothy Shay
  The Bar Rooms at Brantly
    Saturday Review, 45:127,
      26 Jan 1878
  Cast Adrift
    Godey's, 87:188, Aug 1873
  Danger
    Godey's, 90:476, May 1875
  The Pitcher of Cool Water,
    and Other Stories
    Godey's, 72:98, Jan 1871
  Three Years in a Man-Trap
    Godey's, 84:576, Jun 1872
  Woman to the Rescue
    Godey's, 78:565, Jun 1874

Astor, John Jacob
  A Journey in Other Worlds
    Godey's, 128:742-4, Jun
      1894
    Nation, 59:198, 13 Sep
      1894
    Saturday Review, 78:279,
      8 Sep 1894

Astor, W. W.
  Pharaoh's Daughter, and Other

Stories
> Bookman (London), 19:130,
> Jan 1901
> Saturday Review, 91:117,
> 26 Jan 1901

Astor, William Waldorf
> Sforza: a Story of Milan
>> Atlantic, 65:123-4, Jan
>> 1890
>> Epoch, 6:759, 27 Dec 1889
>> Nation, 50:226, 13 Mar
>> 1890
>> Saturday Review, 69:153,
>> 1 Feb 1890
> Valentino
>> Atlantic, 57:270-1, Feb
>> 1886
>> Nation, 42:240, 18 Mar
>> 1886
>> Picayune, 24 Jan 1886,
>> p. 8

Atherton, Gertrude Franklin
(Horn)
> American Wives and English
> Husbands
>> Athenaeum, 3680:597, 7
>> May 1898
>> Bookman (London), 14:17,
>> Apr 1898
>> Bookman (NY), 7:251, May
>> 1898
>> Saturday Review, 85:501,
>> 9 Apr 1898
> Ancestors
>> Athenaeum, 4178:650,
>> 23 Nov 1907
>> Bookman (London), 33:148,
>> Dec 1907
>> Bookman (NY), 26:528-30,
>> Jan 1908
>> Nation, 85:377, 24 Oct
>> 1907
>> North American Review,
>> 186:607-11, Dec 1907
>> Saturday Review, 104:732,
>> 14 Dec 1907
>> Times Literary Supplement,
>> 7 Nov 1907, p. 341

The Aristocrats
> Athenaeum, 3843:784, 22
> Jun 1901
> Bookman (London), 20:123-4,
> Jul 1901
The Bell in the Fog, and Other
Stories
> Athenaeum, 4035:238, 25
> Feb 1905
> Bookman (London), 27:260,
> Mar 1905
> Saturday Review, 99:317,
> 11 Mar 1905
> Times Literary Supplement,
> 24 Feb 1905, p. 65
The Californians
> Athenaeum, 3741:62, 8 Jul
> 1899
> Bookman (London), 15:51,
> Nov 1898
> Bookman (NY), 8:253-4,
> Nov 1898
> Outlook, 60:537, 29 Oct
> 1898
> Saturday Review, 86:648,
> 12 Nov 1898
Los Cerritos
> Athenaeum, 3310:436-7,
> 4 Apr 1891
> Picayune, 11 May 1890,
> p. 9; 5 May 1895, p. 7
> Saturday Review, 71:445-6,
> 11 Apr 1891
The Conqueror
> Athenaeum, 3899:87, 19
> Jul 1902
> Bookman (London), 22:133
> -134, Jul 1902
> Bookman (NY), 15:255-6,
> May 1902
> Overland, 2d S, 39:913-4,
> May 1902
> Saturday Review, 93:776,
> 14 Jun 1902
> Times Literary Supplement,
> 30 May 1902, pp. 155-6;
> 20 Mar 1903, p. 90
A Daughter of the Vine
> Athenaeum, 3741:62, 8
> Jul 1899

Atherton, Gertrude Franklin
(Horn)
> Bookman (London), 16:83,
> Jun 1899
>
> Saturday Review, 87:729,
> 10 Jun 1899

The Doomswoman
> Athenaeum, 4234:784, 19
> Dec 1908
>
> Atlantic, 74:705, Nov 1894
>
> Godey's, 127:238, Aug
> 1893
>
> Picayune, 4 Jun 1893,
> p. 18
>
> Saturday Review, 81:437,
> 25 Apr 1896; 106:800,
> 26 Dec 1908
>
> Times Literary Supplement,
> 19 Nov 1908, p. 417

The Gorgeous Isle
> Athenaeum, 4230:640, 21
> Nov 1908
>
> Bookman (NY), 28:475,
> Jan 1909

Hermia Suydam
> Overland, 2d S, 14:100,
> Jul 1889
>
> Picayune, 14 Sep 1890,
> p. 14
>
> Saturday Review, 67:766,
> 22 Jun 1889

His Fortunate Grace
> Bookman (London), 14:17,
> Apr 1898
>
> Bookman (NY), 7:251,
> May 1898
>
> Godey's, 135:109, Jul 1897
>
> Picayune, 6 Jun 1897,
> p. 17

Patience Sparhawk and Her
Times
> Bookman (London), 12:18,
> Apr 1897
>
> Bookman (NY), 5:194,
> May 1897
>
> Saturday Review, 84:202-3,
> 21 Aug 1897; 98:585,
> 5 Nov 1904

A Question of Time
> Athenaeum, 3373:788-9,
> 18 Jun 1892

> Picayune, 16 Aug 1891,
> p. 11
>
> Saturday Review, 73:668,
> 4 Jun 1892

Rezánov
> Athenaeum, 4127:687,
> 1 Dec 1906
>
> Bookman (London), 31:154,
> Dec 1906
>
> Saturday Review, 102:712-3,
> 8 Dec 1906
>
> Times Literary Supplement,
> 23 Nov 1906, p. 394

Rulers of Kings
> Athenaeum, 3998:746, 11
> Jul 1904
>
> Bookman (London), 26:63-4,
> May 1904
>
> Bookman (NY), 19:311-3,
> May 1904
>
> Saturday Review, 97:560,
> 30 Apr 1904
>
> Times Literary Supplement,
> 15 Apr 1904, p. 116

Senator North
> Athenaeum, 3802:307, 8
> Sep 1900
>
> Bookman (NY), 11:588-9,
> Aug 1900
>
> Times Literary Supplement,
> 21 Mar 1902, p. 77

The Splendid Idle Forties
> Athenaeum, 3925:77, 17
> Jan 1903
>
> Nation, 75:468, 11 Dec
> 1902
>
> Saturday Review, 95:83,
> 17 Jan 1903

Tower of Ivory
> Athenaeum, 4304:488-9,
> 23 Apr 1910
>
> Bookman (London), 38:136,
> Jun 1910
>
> Bookman (NY), 31:85-6,
> Mar 1910
>
> Nation, 90:187-8, 24 Feb
> 1910
>
> North American Review,
> 192:136, Jul 1910
>
> Saturday Review, 109:468-9,
> 9 Apr 1910

The Travelling Thirds
    Athenaeum, 4076:793, 9
        Dec 1905
    Bookman (NY), 22:368-9,
        Dec 1905
The Valiant Runaways
    Bookman (London), 17:120,
        Jan 1900
What Dreams May Come
    By Frank Lin [pseud.].
    Saturday Review, 66:723,
        15 Dec 1888
A Whirl Asunder
    Athenaeum, 3542:351, 14
        Sep 1895
    Overland, 2d S, 27:466,
        Apr 1896
    Picayune, 31 May 1896,
        p. 27
    Saturday Review, 81:82,
        18 Jan 1896
    See also The Spinners' Book
    of Fiction.

Atkinson, William
    Western Stories
        Saturday Review, 75:526,
            13 May 1893

Augustin, George
    Romances of New Orleans
        Picayune, 19 Apr 1891,
            p. 15

Austin, Jane (Goodwin)
    Betty Alden
        Epoch, 10:370, 8 Jan 1892
        Nation, 53:395, 19 Nov
            1891
        Overland, 2d S, 19:331,
            Mar 1892
    David Alden's Daughter, and
    Other Stories of Colonial
    Times
        Cottage Hearth, 19:47, Jan
            1893
        Godey's, 126:102, Jan 1893
        Overland, 2d S, 20:661,
            Dec 1892
    The Desmond Hundred
        Continent, 2:91, 26 Jul 1882

Cottage Hearth, 8:263,
    Aug 1882
Harper's, 65:640, Sep 1882
Nation, 35:181-2, 31 Aug
    1882
Saturday Review, 54:422,
    23 Sep 1882; 67:641,
    25 May 1889
Dr. LeBaron and His Daughters
    Atlantic, 67:278, Feb 1891
    Epoch, 8:398, 23 Jan 1891
    Godey's, 122:180, Feb 1891
    Nation, 52:244, 19 Mar
        1891
    Overland, 2d S, 17:661,
        Jun 1891
Dora Darling
    Cottage Hearth, 18:363,
        Nov 1892
    Godey's, 109:210, Aug 1884
Moonfolk
    Saturday Review, 38:840,
        26 Dec 1874
Mrs. Beauchamp Brown
    Atlantic, 46:416-7, Sep
        1880
    Nation, 31:16-7, 1 Jul
        1880
    Picayune, 23 May 1880,
        [p. 5]
A Nameless Nobleman
    Atlantic, 47:862, Jun 1881
    Nation, 32:411, 9 Jul 1881
    Overland, 2d S, 10:217,
        Aug 1887
    Saturday Review, 51:829,
        25 Jun 1881; 53:422,
        31 Mar 1883
The Shadow of Molock Moun-
tain
    Godey's, 72:291, Mar 1871
    Harper's, 42:622, Mar 1871
Standish of Standish
    Atlantic, 65:286, Feb 1890
    Epoch, 6:758, 27 Dec
        1889
    Nation, 50:117, 6 Feb
        1890
    Overland, 2d S, 15:438-9,
        Apr 1890

23

Austin, John Osborne
  Philip and Philippa
    Nation, 72:437, 30 May 1901

Austin, Mary
  Isidro
    Atlantic, 97:49, Jan 1906
    Bookman (London), 29:41,
      Oct 1905
    Bookman (NY), 21:601, Aug
      1905
    Overland, 2d S, 46:81, Jul
      1905
    Saturday Review, 100:122,
      22 Jul 1905
  Lost Borders
    Nation, 89:513, 25 Nov 1909
  Santa Lucia
    Athenaeum, 4205:664, 30
      May 1908
    Bookman (NY), 27:400,
      Jun 1908
    Nation, 86:380, 23 Apr 1908
  See also The Spinners' Book
  of Fiction.

Avery, M. A.
  Shadowed Perils
    Saturday Review, 42:552,
      28 Oct 1876

Avirett, James B.
  The Old Plantation
    Outlook, 68:744, 27 Jul
      1901

Ayres, Nelson
  Adventures of Abel Blow
    Picayune, 27 Apr 1896,
      p. 10
  Adventures of an Evangelist
    Picayune, 14 Feb 1892,
      p. 14

[Babcock, John Martin Luther]
  The Dawning
    Cottage Hearth, 12:60,
      Feb 1886
    Overland, 2d S, 7:211,
      Feb 1886

Babcock, William Henry
  The Brides of the Tiger
    Picayune, 15 Jan 1893,
      p. 20
  Cypress Beach
    Picayune, 6 Jul 1890,
      p. 12
  Kent Fort Manor
    Athenaeum, 3947:780, 20
      Jun 1903
    Saturday Review, 96:241,
      22 Aug 1903
  The Tower of Wye
    Athenaeum, 3871:13, 4 Jan
      1902
    Bookman (London), 22:124,
      Jul 1901

Bache, Richard Meade
  Under the Palmetto in Peace
  and War
    Atlantic, 46:828, Dec 1880
    Picayune, 20 Jun 1880,
      [p. 6]

Bacheller, Irving
  Cricket Heron
    Saturday Review, 109:177-8,
      5 Feb 1910
  Darrel of the Blessed Isles
    Athenaeum, 3959:341, 12
      Sep 1903
    Bookman (London), 25:53,
      Oct 1903
    Bookman (NY), 17:405-6,
      Jul 1903; 17:534-5, Jul
      1903
    Overland, 2d S, 42:176,
      Aug 1903
    Saturday Review, 96:466,
      10 Oct 1903
    Times Literary Supplement,
      18 Sep 1903, p. 265
  D'ri and I
    Athenaeum, 3874:110, 25
      Jan 1902
    Bookman (London), 21:140-1,
      Jan 1902
    Bookman (NY), 14:154-5,
      Oct 1901

Canadian Magazine,
17:579, Oct 1901
Nation, 73:458, 12 Dec
1901
Outlook, 68:1028, 31
Aug 1901
Overland, 2d S, 38:315-8,
Oct 1901
Eben Holden
Athenaeum, 3832:429,
6 Apr 1901
Bookman (London), 20:25,
Apr 1901
Bookman (NY), 12:235-7,
Nov 1900
Canadian Magazine, 16:93,
Nov 1900
Nation, 71:117-8, 9 Aug
1900
Picayune, 29 Jul 1900,
II, 9
Saturday Review, 91:277,
2 Mar 1901; 91:344,
16 Mar 1901
The Hand-Made Gentleman
Nation, 88:562, 3 Jun
1909
The Master of Silence
Atlantic, 70:707, Nov
1892
Godey's, 125:409, Oct
1892
Nation, 90:64, 20 Jan
1910
Overland, 2d S, 20:445,
Oct 1892
Picayune, 10 Jul 1892,
p. 20
Silas Strong
Athenaeum, 4118:363,
29 Sep 1906
Virgilius
Athenaeum, 4023:761,
3 Dec 1904

Bacon, Alice Mabel
In the Land of the Gods
Nation, 81:510, 21 Dec
1905

Bacon, Dolores Marbourg

[pseud.].
See Bacon, Mary Schell (Hoke).

Bacon, Eugenia Jones
Lyddy
Picayune, 18 Dec 1898,
II, 8

Bacon, Josephine Dodge (Daskam)
The Biography of a Boy
Bookman (NY), 31:86-7,
Mar 1910
The Domestic Adventurers
Bookman (NY), 26:278-9,
Nov 1907
Nation, 85:307, 3 Oct 1907
Her Finance
Overland, 2d S, 45:[253],
Mar 1905
An Idyll on All Fools' Day
Nation, 88:282, 18 Mar
1909
The Imp and the Angel
Nation, 74:117, 6 Feb 1902
Memoirs of a Baby
Bookman (NY), 19:395, Jun
1904
Middle-Aged Love Stories
Nation, 76:421, 21 May 1903
Sister's Vocation and Other
Girls' Stories
Bookman (NY), 13:79-80,
Mar 1901
Nation, 72:280, 4 Apr 1901
Smith College Stories
Bookman (NY), 11:285,
May 1900
Nation, 71:55, 19 Jul 1900
Outlook, 64:840, 7 Apr 1900
Picayune, 6 May 1900, III, 8
Ten to Seventeen
Athenaeum, 4198:449, 11
Apr 1908
Nation, 86:237, 12 Mar 1908
Whom the Gods Destroyed
Nation, 75:425, 27 Nov 1902

[Bacon, Mary Schell (Hoke)]
In High Places
By Dolores Marbourg Bacon
[pseud.].

[Bacon, Mary Schell (Hoke)]
Nation, 85:497, 28 Nov 1907
See also Eggleston, George
Cary, and Dolores Marbourg
[pseud.].

[Badcock, Winnifred (Eaton)]
Daughters of Nijo
By Onoto Watanna [pseud.].
Saturday Review, 97:790,
792, 18 Jun 1904

Badeau, Adam
Conspiracy
Saturday Review, 61:444-5,
27 Mar 1886

Bailey, Alice (Ward)
Mark Heffron
Bookman (NY), 3:557,
Aug 1896
Godey's, 134:206, Feb
1897
The Sage Brush Parson
By A. B. Ward [pseud.].
Bookman (NY), 23:30,
Mar 1906
Nation, 82:183, 1 Mar
1906
Overland, 2d S, 47:385,
Apr 1906

Bailey, James Montgomery
The Danbury Boom!
Godey's, 102:183, Feb 1881
Mr. Phillips' Goneness
Godey's, 99:565, Dec 1879
Nation, 25:442, 25 Dec
1879
They All Do It
Picayune, 28 Oct 1877,
[p. 9]

Baker, Emma Eugene (Hall)
Masters and Men
Picayune, 7 Jun 1891,
p. 10
The Master of L'Estrange
By Eugene Hall [pseud.].
Cottage Hearth, 12:94,
Mar 1886

[Baker, Harriette Newell (Woods)]
Out of the Depths
Picayune, 21 Oct 1877,
[p. 9]

Baker, Julie Keim (Wetherill)
Wings
Godey's, 98:181, Feb 1879

Baker, Louise R.
Cis Martin
Picayune, 18 Dec 1898,
II, 8

Baker, William Mumford
A Blessed Ghost
Atlantic, 53:141-3, Jan
1884
Blessed Saint Certainty
Harper's, 63:315, Jul 1881
Nation, 33:98, 4 Aug 1881
Carter Quarterman
Godey's, 92:568, Jun 1876
Harper's, 52:777, Apr 1876
Colonel Dunwoddie, Millionaire
Harper's, 57:789, Oct 1878
His Majesty, Myself
Good Company, 4:573,
(No. 6) 1880
Harper's, 60:630-1, Mar
1880
Nation, 30:65, 22 Jan 1880
Mose Evans
Atlantic, 34:230, Aug 1874
Harper's, 49:593-4, Sep
1874
Saturday Review, 38:417,
26 Sep 1874
The New Timothy
Atlantic, 26:504-6, Oct
1870
Godey's, 81:474, Nov 1870
Harper's, 41:786, Oct
1870
Nation, 11:125, 25 Aug 1870
Picayune, 17 Jun 1894,
p. 15
The Virginians in Texas
Harper's, 58:310, Jan 1879
A Year Worth Living
Cottage Hearth, 5:214-5,

Jun 1878
Godey's, 97:171, Aug 1878
Library Table, 4:301, 22
   Jun 1879
Sunday Afternoon, 2:190,
   Aug 1878

[Balch, Elizabeth]
  An Author's Love
    Epoch, 6:565-6, 4 Oct
      1889
    Saturday Review, 67:733-4,
      15 Jun 1889
  Mustard Leaves
    By D. T. S. [pseud.].
    Nation, 42:40, 14 Jan
      1886
  Zorah
    Nation, 46:304, 12 Apr
      1888
    Saturday Review, 63:884,
      18 Jun 1887

Balch, Frederick Homer
  The Bridge of the Gods
    Atlantic, 67:425, Mar 1891
    Epoch, 8:415-6, 30 Jan
      1891
    Godey's, 122:180, Feb
      1891
    Overland, 2d S, 17:663,
      Jun 1891

Balch, William Stevens
  A Peculiar People
    Saturday Review, 53:679,
      27 May 1882

Baldwin, Eugene Francis, and
Maurice Eisenberg
  Doctor Cavallo
    Picayune, 1 Dec 1895,
      p. 17

Baldwin, Lydia Wood
  A Yankee School Teacher in
    Virginia
    Nation, 39:441, 20 Nov
      1884
    Picayune, 12 Oct 1884
      [p. 2]

Baldy, Alice Montgomery
  The Romance of a Spanish
    Nun
    Epoch, 9:158, 10 Apr
      1891
    Godey's, 122:373, Apr
      1891
    Saturday Review, 71:482-3,
      18 Apr 1891

Balestier, Charles Wolcott
  The Average Woman
    Athenaeum, 3376:58-9,
      9 Jul 1892
    Godey's, 125:519, Nov 1892
    Nation, 55:263, 6 Oct 1892
    Picayune, 4 Sep 1892,
      p. 7
  Benefits Forgot
    Athenaeum, 3467:440, 7
      Apr 1893
    Saturday Review, 77:446,
      28 Apr 1894
  A Victorious Defeat
    Nation, 43:142, 12 Aug
      1886
    Picayune, 23 May 1886,
      p. 14

_____, and Rudyard Kipling
  The Naulahka
    Godey's, 125:404, Oct 1892

Balfour, M. C.
  The Fall of the Sparrow
    Godey's, 136:104, Jan 1898
  White Sand
    Picayune, 18 Apr 1897,
      p. 17

Ballard, Robert E.
  Myrtle Lawn
    Atlantic, 46:828, Dec 1880

Ballou, William Hosea
  The Bachelor Girl
    Picayune, 15 Jun 1890,
      p. 14
  A Ride on a Cyclone
    Godey's, 119:258, Sep
      1889

Ballou, William Hosea
 The Upper Ten
  Epoch, 8:222-3, 7 Nov
   1890
  Picayune, 19 Oct 1890,
   p. 3

Balmer, Edwin
 Waylaid by Wireless
  Overland, 2d S, 54:534,
   Nov 1909

_____, and William Mac-
Harg
 The Achievements of Luther
 Trant
  Nation, 90:377, 14 Apr
   1910
  Overland, 2d S, 55:640,
   Jun 1910

Bangs, John Kendrick
 The Bicyclers, and Three
 Other Farces
  Atlantic, 78:137, Jul 1896
 The Booming of Acre Hill
  Picayune, 24 Jun 1900,
   II, 12
 The Enchanted Typewriter
  Bookman (NY), 10:503,
   Jan 1900
 Ghosts I Have Met, and Some
 Others
  Outlook, 59:588, 2 Jul
   1898
 The Houseboat on the Styx
  Overland, 2d S, 30:285,
   Sep 1897
 The Idiot
  Atlantic, 76:421, Sep 1895
 The Idiot at Home
  Picayune, 11 Nov 1900, II, 4
 The New Munchausen
  Atlantic, 90:417, Sep 1902
 Olympian Nights
  Atlantic, 90:417, Sep 1902
 Paste Jewels
  Athenaeum, 3656:706,
   20 Nov 1897
 The Pursuit of the House-
 Boat

  Overland, 2d S, 30:285, Sep
   1897
  Saturday Review, 84:326, 18
   Sep 1897
 A Rebellious Heroine
  Atlantic, 79:274, Feb 1897
  Bookman (NY), 5:169,
   Apr 1897
  Nation, 64:400, 27 May
   1897
  Picayune, 16 Nov 1896,
   p. 16
 Toppleton's Client
  Picayune, 18 Jun 1893,
   p. 19
 See also The Whole Family.

Banks, Charles Eugene, and
George Cram Cook
 In Hampton Roads
  Picayune, 4 Dec 1899,
   p. 10

Banks, Elizabeth
 The Luck of the Black Cat,
 and Other Stories
  Saturday Review, 109:667,
   21 May 1910
 The Mystery of Frances
 Farrington
  Athenaeum, 4256:612, 22
   May 1909

Banks, Mary Ross
 Bright Days in the Old
 Plantation Time
  Cottage Hearth, 8:295,
   Sep 1882
  Godey's, 105:284, Sep
   1882
  Picayune, 30 Jul 1882,
   [p. 6]

Banks, Nancy (Huston)
 The Little Hills
  Athenaeum, 4058:171, 5
   Aug 1905
  Bookman (NY), 21:599-
   600, Aug 1905
  Saturday Review, 100:283,
   26 Aug 1905

Oldfield
  Athenaeum, 3902:182, 9
    Aug 1902
  Bookman (NY), 15:373-4,
    Jun 1902
  Nation, 76:118, 5 Feb 1903
  Sewanee Review, 11:112,
    Jan 1903; 11:357, Jul
    1903
Round Anvil Rock
  Athenaeum, 3959:342,
    12 Sep 1903
  Bookman (London), 25:54-5,
    Oct 1903
  Bookman (NY), 17:518-9,
    Jul 1903
  Saturday Review, 96:212,
    15 Aug 1903; 96:708,
    5 Dec 1903
  Sewanee Review, 12:124-5,
    Jan 1904
Stairs of Sand
  Picayune, 23 Sep 1890,
    p. 12

Barbara [pseud.].
  See Wright, Mabel (Osgood).

[Barber, Harriet Boomer]
  Wrecked, but Not Lost
    By Faith Templeton [pseud.].
    Picayune, 28 Mar 1880,
    [p. 10]

Barbour, Ralph Henry
  The Land of Joy
    Overland, 2d S, 42:552-3,
    Dec 1903
  A Maid in Arcady
    Nation, 83:539, 20 Dec
    1906

Barclay, Florence L.
  The Rosary
    Nation, 91:444, 10 Nov
    1910
  The Wheels of Time
    Overland, 2d S, 56:436,
    Oct 1910

Bardeen, Charles William
  Roderick Hume
    Nation, 28:104, 6 Feb 1879

Barnard, Charles
  The Soprano
    By Jane Kingsford [pseud.].
    Godey's, 80:196, Feb 1870

Barnes, James
  The Clutch of Circumstance
    Nation, 86:558, 18 Jun
    1908
  A Princetonian
    Godey's, 134:542, May 1897

Barnes, Willis
  Dame Fortune Smiled
    Picayune, 27 Apr 1896,
    p. 10

Barnum, P. T.
  See His Fleeting Ideal.

Barr, Amelia Edith (Huddleston)
  The Beads of Tasmer
    Epoch, 9:237, 15 May 1891
    Picayune, 27 Sep 1891,
    p. 12
    Saturday Review, 76:633,
    2 Dec 1893
  The Belle of Bowling Green
    Athenaeum, 4093:417,
    7 Apr 1906
  Bernicia
    Bookman (NY), 3:167-8,
    Apr 1896
    Picayune, 25 Nov 1895,
    p. 10
  Between Two Loves
    Atlantic, 63:859, Jun 1889
    Nation, 44:125, 10 Feb
    1887
    Saturday Review, 64:264-5,
    20 Aug 1887
  The Black Shilling
    Saturday Review, 98:402,
    404, 24 Sep 1904
  A Border Shepherdess

Barr, Amelia Edith (Huddleston)
   Nation, 45:337, 27 Oct
      1887
   Saturday Review, 64:794-5,
      10 Dec 1887
   The Bow of Orange Ribbon
      Nation, 44:125, 10 Feb 1887
   Saturday Review, 64:264
      -65, 20 Aug 1887
   Cecilia's Lovers
      Athenaeum, 4101:662,
         2 Jun 1906
   A Daughter of Fife
      Athenaeum, 3050:486,
         10 Apr 1886
      Nation, 42:533, 24 Jun
         1886
   Feet of Clay
      Saturday Review, 68:333
         -34, 21 Sep 1889
   The Flower of Gala Water,
      and Other Stories
      Bookman (London),
         9:130-1, Jan 1896
      Saturday Review, 81:82,
         18 Jan 1896
   Friend Olivia
      Epoch, 9:11-2, 6 Feb
         1891
      Saturday Review, 71:118,
         24 Jan 1891
   The Hands of Compulsion
      Nation, 88:515, 20 May
         1909
      Outlook, 92:20, 1 May
         1909
   The Heart of Jessie Laurie
      Nation, 86:15-6, 2 Jan
         1908
   The Household of McNeil
      Athenaeum, 3195:81,
         19 Jan 1889
      Saturday Review, 67:26,
         5 Jan 1889
   I, Thou, and the Other One
      Bookman (NY), 9:281,
         May 1899
      Outlook, 61:834, 8 Apr
         1899
      Saturday Review, 88:176,
         5 Aug 1899

In Spite of Himself
   Saturday Review, 66:298
      -99, 8 Sep 1888
Jan Vedder's Wife
   Saturday Review, 60:816,
      19 Dec 1885; 66:618-9,
      24 Nov 1888
The King's Highway
   Bookman (NY), 6:561,
      Feb 1898
A Knight of the Nets
   Bookman (NY), 4:258,
      Nov 1896
The Last of the MacAllisters
   Nation, 42:533, 24 Jun
      1886
   Overland, 2d S, 7:653,
      Jun 1886
   Saturday Review, 70:299
      -300, 6 Sep 1890
The Lion's Whelp
   Athenaeum, 3890:619,
      17 May 1902
   Bookman (London), 22:110,
      Jun 1902
   Saturday Review, 93:777,
      14 Jun 1902
The Lone House
   Picayune, 20 May 1894,
      p. 1
Love for an Hour Is Love
   Forever
   Picayune, 8 May 1894,
      p. 10
   Saturday Review, 74:430,
      8 Oct 1892
The Maid of Maiden Lane
   Picayune, 30 Sep 1900,
      II, 6
Michael and Theodora
   Godey's, 125:522, Nov 1892
Paul and Christina
   Saturday Review, 64:491-2,
      8 Oct 1887
The Preacher's Daughter
   Godey's, 125:522, Nov 1892
   Saturday Review, 75:252,
      4 Mar 1893
Prisoners of Conscience
   Bookman (NY), 5:345-6,
      Jun 1897

Overland, 2d S, 29:656,
Jun 1897
Picayune, 2 May 1897,
p. 15
Saturday Review, 85:57,
8 Jan 1898
Remember the Alamo
Epoch, 4:194, 19 Oct 1888
Nation, 48:166, 21 Feb
1889
Romances and Realities
Harper's, 52:941, May
1876
Saturday Review, 41:697,
27 May 1876
She Loved a Sailor
Epoch, 10:62, 28 Aug 1891
A Singer from the Sea
Godey's, 127:494, Oct
1893
Picayune, 25 Jun 1893,
p. 22
Saturday Review, 76:633,
2 Dec 1893
A Sister to Esau
Bookman (London), 1:218,
Mar 1892
The Song of a Single Note
Athenaeum, 4031:106,
28 Jan 1905
Saturday Review, 99:182,
11 Feb 1905
The Squire of Sandal-Side
Nation, 44:300, 7 Apr
1887
Saturday Review, 63:696,
14 May 1887
Thyra Varrick
Outlook, 74:200, 16 May
1903
Saturday Review, 97:498,
16 Apr 1904
Trinity Bells
Picayune, 4 Dec 1899,
p. 10
Saturday Review, 90:728,
8 Dec 1900
Was It Right to Forgive?
Saturday Review, 89:566,
5 May 1900
Women of Love and Glory

Saturday Review, 69:244,
22 Feb 1890

Barr, Robert
See Crane, Stephen, and
Robert Barr.

Barrett, Frank
The Admirable Lady Biddy
Jane
Nation, 48:273, 28 Mar
1889
Breaking the Shackles
Picayune, 23 Dec 1900,
II, 12
Found Guilty
Picayune, 29 Apr 1894,
p. 23
His Helpmate
Epoch, 2:76-7, 2 Sep 1887
Godey's, 115:343, Oct
1887
Out of the Jaws of Death
Atlantic, 71:137, Jan 1893
Godey's, 125:521, Nov
1892
A Set of Rogues
Atlantic, 77:708, May 1896

Barrett, Wilson, and Elwyn Alfred
Barron
In Old New York
Bookman (London), 17:192,
Mar 1900
Picayune, 10 Dec 1899,
III, 7
Saturday Review, 89:338,
17 Mar 1900

Barrett, Wilson, and Robert
Hichens
The Daughters of Babylon
Outlook, 61:929, 22 Apr
1899
Picayune, 16 Apr 1899,
II, 12

Barron, Elwyn Alfred
Manders
Picayune, 26 Nov 1899,
II, 8

Barron, Elwyn Alfred
    Saturday Review, 87:121,
      28 Jan 1899
  The Triple Scar
    Athenaeum, 4146:437,
      13 Apr 1907
  See also Barrett, Wilson,
  and Elwyn Barron.

Barry, John Daniel
  The Acrobat
    Saturday Review, 89:566,
      5 May 1900
  The Congressman's Wife
    Nation, 78:134, 18 Feb
      1904
    Poet-Lore, 14:138,
      Winter 1903
  A Daughter of Thespis
    Athenaeum, 3958:310,
      5 Sep 1903
    Bookman (London), 24:221
      -22, Sep 1903
  The Intriguers
    Nation, 64:400, 27 May
      1897
  Mademoiselle Blanche
    Godey's, 135:445-6, Oct
      1897
    Outlook, 77:476, 25 Jun
      1904
    Picayune, 14 Mar 1897,
      p. 17

Barry, William
  Arden Massiter
    Nation, 70:403, 24 May
      1900
    Outlook, 65:132, 12 May
      1900
    Picayune, 3 Jun 1900,
      III, 7
  The Wizard's Knot
    Nation, 72:438, 30 May
      1901
    Outlook, 68:184, 18
      May 1901

Bartlett, Alice Elinor (Bowen)
  Until the Day Break
    Godey's, 95:437, Nov 1877

Bartlett, Frederick Orin
  The Prodigal Pro Tem
    Nation, 91:551, 8 Dec
      1910
  The Seventh Noon
    Overland, 2d S, 55:440,
      Apr 1910
  The Web of the Golden Spider
    Bookman (NY), 29:199,
      Apr 1909
    Nation, 88:338, 1 Apr
      1909

Bartlett, George Herbert
  Water Tramps
    Atlantic, 76:566, Oct 1895

Bartlett, Mrs. J. M. D.
  See Bartlett, Alice Elinor
  (Bowen).

[Barton, Samuel]
  Ask Her, Man! Ask Her!
    By A. B. Roker [pseud.].
      Epoch, 3:335-6, 1 Jun
      1888

Barton, William Eleazar
  A Hero in Homespun
    Bookman (NY), 6:360-2,
      Dec 1897
  Life in the Hills of Kentucky
    Cottage Hearth, 16:60,
      Feb 1890
  Pine Knot
    Bookman (NY), 12:193-4,
      Oct 1900
    Nation, 71:118, 9 Aug
      1900
    Outlook, 65:840, 4 Aug
      1900
    Picayune, 12 Aug 1900,
      II, 8
  Trouble at the Roundstone
    Outlook, 58:187, 15 Jan
      1898
  The Wind-Up of the Big Meetin'
  on No Bus'ness
    Cottage Hearth, 14:126,
      Apr 1888

Baskett, James Newton
  As the Light Led
    Outlook, 65:409, 16 Jun
      1900
    Picayune, 1 Jul 1900,
      II, 6
  At You-All's House
    Bookman (London), 14:140,
      Aug 1898
    Bookman (NY), 8:70,
      Sep 1898
    Nation, 67:265, 6 Oct
      1898

Bassett, Mary E. (Stone)
  A Fair Plebian
    Overland, 2d S, 2:216,
      Aug 1883
  A Riddle of Luck
    Picayune, 28 May 1895,
      p. 24

Bates, Arlo
  Albrecht
    Nation, 51:254, 25 Sep
      1890
  A Book o' Nine Tales
    Nation, 53:107, 6 Aug
      1891
    Overland, 2d S, 18:442,
      Oct 1891
  The Diary of a Saint
    Nation, 75:486, 18 Dec
      1902
  In the Bundle of Time
    Nation, 56:297, 20 Apr
      1893
  The Intoxicated Ghost
    Nation, 87:75, 23 Jul
      1908
  A Lad's Love
    Nation, 45:76, 28 Jul
      1887
  Mr. Jacobs
    Nation, 36:554, 28 Jun
      1883
  The Pagans
    Continent, 5:575, (No. 18)
      1884
    Godey's, 117:421-2,
      Nov 1888

Picayune, 9 Sep 1888,
  p. 10
Saturday Review, 66:494-5,
  27 Oct 1888
Patty's Perversities
  Cottage Hearth, 7:273,
    Sep 1881
  Nation, 33:258, 29 Sep
    1881
The Philistines
  Athenaeum, 3202:308,
    9 Mar 1889
  Cottage Hearth, 15:24,
    Jan 1889
The Puritans
  Athenaeum, 3729:463,
    15 Apr 1899
  Bookman (NY), 8:492-3,
    Jan 1899
  Outlook, 60:394, 8 Oct
    1898
  Saturday Review, 87:408,
    1 Apr 1899
A Wheel of Fire
  Atlantic, 57:258-60,
    Feb 1886
  Harper's, 72:323, Jan
    1886
  Nation, 41:428, 9 Nov
    1885
  Overland, 2d S, 6:552,
    Nov 1885
  Picayune, 1 Nov 1885,
    p. 11
  Saturday Review, 60:614-5,
    7 Nov 1885
See also Bates, Harriet
  Leonora, and Arlo Bates.

[Bates, Mrs. Fannie D.]
  Tatters
    By Beulah [pseud.].
      Picayune, 17 Apr 1892,
      p. 22

[Bates, Harriet Leonora (Vose)]
  Old Salem
    By Eleanor Putnam [pseud.].
      Overland, 2d S, 8:224,
      Aug 1886

[Bates, Harriet Leonora (Vose)]
A Woodland Wooing
By Eleanor Putnam [pseud.].
Athenaeum, 3220:61-2,
13 Jul 1898
Nation, 49:317, 17 Oct
1889
Saturday Review, 68:45
-46, 13 Jul 1889

_____, and Arlo Bates
Prince Vance
Saturday Review, 68:474,
26 Oct 1889

Bates, Harriet True
Two Men of the World
Picayune, 1 Mar 1891,
p. 10

Bates, Josephine (White)
A Blind Lead
Nation, 47:13, 5 Jul
1888
Picayune, 20 May 1888,
p. 10
Bunch-Grass Stories
Bookman (NY), 2:434-5,
Jan 1896
A Nameless Wrestler
Overland, 2d S, 15:322,
Mar 1890
Picayune, 8 Sep 1889,
p. 12

Bates, Mrs. Lindon W.
See Bates, Josephine (White).

[Bates, Lizzie]
The Gabled House
Nation, 10:79, 3 Feb
1870

Bates, Margret Holmes
(Ernsperger)
The Chamber Over the Gate
By Margret Holmes [pseud.].
Harper's, 74:827, Apr
1887
Picayune, 24 Oct 1886,
p. 10

Bates, Morgan
Martin Brook
Nation, 72:438, 30 May
1901
Outlook, 67:923, 20 Apr
1901
Saturday Review, 92:280,
31 Aug 1901

Battershall, Fletcher Williams
A Daughter of This World
Saturday Review, 78:606,
1 Dec 1894

Baxter, Katherine Schuyler
In Bamboo Lands
Picayune, 17 Jan 1897,
p. 10

Baylor, Frances Courtenay
Behind the Blue Ridge
Atlantic, 60:417-8, Sep
1887
Epoch, 1:521-2, 8 Jul
1887
Godey's, 115:180, Aug
1887
Nation, 45:236-7, 22 Sep
1887
Picayune, 26 Jun 1887,
p. 8
Claudia Hyde
Atlantic, 74:279, Aug
1894
Nation, 59:67, 26 Jul
1894
Picayune, 24 Jun 1894,
p. 15
Juan and Juanita
Epoch, 2:355, 2 Dec 1887
Saturday Review, 64:802,
10 Dec 1887
The Ladder of Fortune
Outlook, 62:84, 6 May
1899
Miss Nina Barrow
Picayune, 24 Oct 1897,
p. 9
On Both Sides
Atlantic, 57:266-8, Feb
1886

Picayune, 1 Nov 1885,
p. 11
Saturday Review, 62:592-3,
30 Oct 1886
A Shocking Example, and
Other Stories
Nation, 48:352, 25 Apr
1889

Beach, Edgar Rice
Stranded
Picayune, 2 Feb 1890,
p. 14

[Beach, Rebecca (Gibbons)]
The Puritan and the Quaker
Atlantic, 44:364, Sep
1879
Nation, 29:114, 14 Aug
1879

Beach, Rex
The Barrier
Bookman (NY), 27:282-3,
May 1908
Going Some
Athenaeum, 4315:39,
9 Jul 1910
Bookman (NY), 31:644,
Aug 1910
The Silver Horde
Bookman (NY), 30:280-1,
Nov 1909
The Spoilers
Bookman (NY), 23:433-5,
Jun 1906

Beale, Maria (Taylor)
Jack O'Doon
Atlantic, 76:421, Sep
1895
Picayune, 24 Feb 1895,
p. 23

Bean, Fannie
Colonel Judson of Alabama
Picayune, 24 Apr 1892,
p. 12
Pudney and Walp
Atlantic, 69:567, Apr
1892

Epoch, 10:110, 18 Sep
1891
Picayune, 14 Jun 1891,
p. 15
Ruth Marsh
Atlantic, 70:852, Dec
1892
Picayune, 27 Nov 1892,
p. 22
A Southerner's Experience
at the North
Atlantic, 70:708, Nov
1892

[Bean, Mrs. Helen Marr]
The Widow Wyse
Nation, 40:159, 19 Feb
1885

Beard, Daniel Carter
Moonblight, and Six Feet
of Romance
Atlantic, 70:708, Nov
1892
Picayune, 29 May 1892,
p. 13

Beard, Wolcott Le Cléar
Sand and Cactus
Nation, 69:301, 19 Oct
1899
Outlook, 62:265, 30 Sep
1899
Picayune, 8 Oct 1890,
II, 12
Saturday Review, 89:242,
24 Feb 1900

Beattie, Hans Stevenson
Joshua Wray
Godey's, 126:101, Jan
1893
Picayune, 9 Oct 1892,
p. 12; 28 Sep 1896,
p. 9

Beatty, John
The Belle o' Becket's Lane
Picayune, 4 Mar 1883,
[p. 8]

Bech-Meyer, Mrs. Nico
A Story from Pullmantown
  Overland, 2d S, 26:223,
  Aug 1895

Becke, Louis
Pacific Tales
  Bookman (NY), 6:68-70,
  Sep 1897
Sketches from Normandy
  Nation, 84:567, 20 Jun
  1907

Beckett, Charles Henry
Who Is John Norman?
  Nation, 45:57, 21 Jul
  1887
  Picayune, 12 Jun 1887,
  p. 9

[Beckwith, Anna Louise]
Constance Winter's Choice
  Nation, 29:444, 25 Dec
  1879

Beckwith, Carmelita
See Shaw, Adele Marie, and
Carmelita Beckwith.

Beckwith, Mrs. J. B.
The House Behind the Poplars
  Picayune, 15 Jan 1871,
  [p. 13]

[Beebe, Charles Washington]
Edmund Dawn
  By Ravenswood [pseud.].
  Picayune, 5 Oct 1873,
  [p. 5]

Beers, Henry Augustin
A Suburban Pastoral, and
Other Tales
  Atlantic, 76:278, Aug
  1895
  Nation, 59:198, 13 Sep
  1894
  Picayune, 3 Jun 1894,
  p. 10
The Ways of Yale
  Godey's, 131:[546]-8,

Nov 1895
  Nation, 61:69, 25 Jul
  1895

Bell, Lilian Lida
Carolina Lee
  Canadian Magazine,
  27:185, Jun 1906
  Overland, 2d S, 48:502,
  Dec 1906
The Concentration of Bee
  Nation, 90:140, 10 Feb
  1910
The Expatriates
  Athenaeum, 3888:558,
  3 May 1902
  Bookman (NY), 12:301-2,
  Nov 1900
  Nation, 71:410, 22 Nov
  1900
  Outlook, 66:469, 20 Oct
  1900
  Picayune, 4 Nov 1900,
  II, 9
  Saturday Review, 93:606,
  10 May 1902
A Home with the Jardines
  Overland, 2d S, 45:[253],
  Mar 1905
The Instinct of Step-Fatherhood
  Nation, 67:452, 15 Dec
  1898
  Outlook, 60:538, 29 Oct
  1898
A Little Sister to the Wilder-
ness
  Athenaeum, 3529:769,
  15 Jun 1895
  Atlantic, 76:707, Nov 1895
  Bookman (London), 8:89,
  Jun 1895
  Bookman (NY), 1:260-1,
  May 1895
  Godey's, 130:655, Jun 1895
  Overland, 2d S, 26:221,
  Aug 1895
  Picayune, 5 May 1895,
  p. 7
  Saturday Review, 79:703,
  25 May 1895

The Love Affairs of an Old Maid
  Atlantic, 73:279, Feb 1894
  Bookman (London), 9:30, Oct 1895
  Godey's, 127:362, Sep 1893
  Saturday Review, 80:118 -19, 27 Jul 1895
The Under Side of Things
  Atlantic, 78:849, Dec 1896
  Bookman (NY), 3:550-1, Aug 1896
  Canadian Magazine, 7:487-8, Sep 1896
  Godey's, 134:[203], Feb 1897

Bellamy, Charles Joseph
The Breton Mills
  Athenaeum, 2705:267-8, 30 Aug 1879
  Harper's, 59:792, Oct 1879
  Nation, 29:213, 25 Sep 1879
A Moment of Madness
  Picayune, 6 Jan 1889, p. 11
Were They Sinners?
  Overland, 2d S, 16:442, Oct 1890
  Picayune, 27 Jul 1890, p. 10

Bellamy, Edward
The Blindman's World, and Other Stories
  Nation, 67:433, 8 Dec 1898
  Outlook, 60:536, 29 Oct 1898
  Picayune, 24 Oct 1898, p. 8
Dr. Heidenhoff's Process
  Athenaeum, 2938:212-3, 16 Feb 1884
  Atlantic, 46:824-6, Dec 1880

Godey's, 101:294, Sep 1880
Nation, 31:17, 1 Jul 1880
Picayune, 4 Jul 1880, [p. 6]
Saturday Review, 57:285 -87, 1 Mar 1884
The Duke of Stockbridge
  Bookman (NY), 12:488-9, Jan 1901
  Outlook, 66:942, 15 Dec 1900
  North American Review, 171:947-8, Dec 1900
  Picayune, 18 Nov 1900, III, 4
Equality
  Bookman (NY), 5:505-6, Aug 1897
  Nation, 65:170-1, 26 Aug 1897
  Overland, 2d S, 30:472, Nov 1897
  Picayune, 22 Aug 1897, p. 24; 30 Jul 1899, II, 8
  Saturday Review, 84:45-6, 10 Jul 1897
Looking Backward, 2000-1887
  Atlantic, 61:845-6, Jun 1888
  Cottage Hearth, 14:262, Aug 1888
  Epoch, 3:217, 20 Apr 1888
  Harper's, 77:154-5, Jun 1888
  Nation, 46:266, 29 Mar 1888
  Outlook, 60:536, 29 Oct 1898
  Overland, 2d S, 12:214, Aug 1888
  Saturday Review, 65:356-7, 24 Mar 1888; 67:508-9, 27 Apr 1889
Miss Ludington's Sister
  Atlantic, 54:413-7, Sep 1884
  Cottage Hearth, 13:396, Dec 1887

Bellamy, Edward
    Epoch, 2:256, 4 Nov
        1887
    Godey's, 115:516, Dec
        1887
    Manhattan, 4:377-8,
        Sep 1884
    Nation, 39:182, 28 Aug
        1884
    Overland, 2d S, 4:223,
        Aug 1884
    Saturday Review, 58:231,
        16 Aug 1884
    Six to One
        Athenaeum, 2653:271-2,
            31 Aug 1878
        Harper's, 57:783, Oct
            1878
        Nation, 27:118, 22 Aug
            1878
        Overland, 2d S, 15:434
            -35, Apr 1890
        Saturday Review, 46:290,
            31 Aug 1878

[Bellamy, Elizabeth Whitfield
(Croom)]
    The Little Joanna
        By Kamba Thorpe [pseud.].
        Godey's, 92:382, Apr
            1876
        Nation, 22:213, 30 Mar
            1876
    Penny Lancaster, Farmer
        Picayune, 31 Mar 1889,
            p. 7

Belt, Harriett Pennawell
    A Mirage of Promise
        Picayune, 28 Nov 1886,
            p. 7

Bendbow, Hesper
    More Than She Could Bear
        Picayune, 28 Jan 1872,
            [p. 14]
        Saturday Review, 33:258,
            24 Feb 1872

Benedict, Frank Lee
    Her Friend Laurence

        Picayune, 27 Jul 1879,
            [p. 12]
    John Worthington's Name
        Atlantic, 34:361-2, Sep
            1874
        Godey's, 79:93, Jul 1874
        Harper's, 49:290, Jul
            1874
        Nation, 19:206-7, 24 Sep
            1874
    Miss Dorothy's Charge
        Godey's, 87:567, Dec 1873
        Harper's, 48:140, Dec
            1873
        Nation, 17:373, 4 Dec
            1873
    Miss Van Kortland
        Atlantic, 26:509-10, Oct
            1870
        Godey's, 81:183, Aug 1870
        Harper's, 40:925, May
            1870
        Nation, 11:127, 25 Aug
            1870
        Overland, 5:102, Jul 1870
        Saturday Review, 30:409,
            24 Sep 1870
    Mr. Vaughan's Heir
        Atlantic, 36:111-2, Jul
            1875
        Harper's, 51:146, Jun 1875
    The Price She Paid
        Godey's, 107:485-6, Nov
            1883
        Picayune, 16 Sep 1883,
            [p. 5]
    St. Simon's Niece
        Godey's, 91:478, Nov 1875
        Harper's, 51:754-5, Oct
            1875
        Nation, 22:32, 13 Jan 1876
        Picayune, 5 Sep 1875,
            [p. 4]

Benham, Charles
    The Fourth Napoleon
        Bookman (London), 13:161,
            Feb 1898
        Bookman (NY), 7:171,
            Apr 1898
        Saturday Review, 85:368,

12 Mar 1898

[Benham, George Chittenden]
A Year of Wreck
By a Victim.
Atlantic, 47:121, Jan
1881
Picayune, 10 Oct 1880,
[p. 5]

[Benjamin, Charles A.]
The Strike in the B--- Mill
Epoch, 1:360, 20 May
1887
Nation, 44:454, 26 May
1887

Benjamin, Elizabeth Dundas
(Bedell)
Hilda and I
Godey's, 100:374, Apr
1880

Benjamin, Lewis
Why Was It?
Picayune, 23 Sep 1888,
p. 7

Benjamin, Samuel Greene Wheeler
The Choice of Paris
Harper's, 42:142, Dec
1870
Picayune, 23 Oct 1870,
[p. 5]
Sea-Spray
Nation, 45:403, 17 Nov 1877

Bennett, Emerson P.
Clara Moreland
Godey's, 121:173, Aug
1890
Leni Leoti
Picayune, 18 Aug 1889,
p. 11
The Prairie Flower
Godey's, 119:176, Aug
1889
Picayune, 1 Jul 1883,
[p. 2]
The Orphan's Trials
Godey's, 79:280, Sep 1874

The Outlaw's Daughter
Picayune, 2 Nov 1873,
[p. 7]

Bennett, John
Master Skylark
Nation, 66:136, 17 Feb
1898
The Treasure of Peyre Gaillard
Nation, 83:485, 6 Dec
1906

[Bennett, Mary E.]
Jefferson Wildrider
By Elizabeth Glover [pseud.].
Picayune, 4 Dec 1898,
II, 4

Bennett, Robert Ames
Into the Primitive
Nation, 87:97, 30 Jul
1908
The Shogun's Daughter
Overland, 2d S, 56:613,
Dec 1910

Benrimo, Abraham
Vic
Nation, 29:442, 25 Dec
1879
Picayune, 2 Nov 1879,
[p. 12]

Benson, Blackwood Ketchum
Bayard's Courier
Athenaeum, 3936:431,
4 Apr 1903
Bookman (London), 23:214,
Feb 1903
Nation, 75:467-8, 11 Dec
1902
A Friend with a Countersign
Nation, 73:418, 28 Nov
1901
Overland, 2d S, 39:665,
Feb 1902
Old Squire
Athenaeum, 3972:789,
12 Dec 1903
Outlook, 74:139, 9 May
1903

Benson, Blackwood Ketchum
Saturday Review, 96:273,
29 Aug 1903
Who Goes There?
Nation, 72:98, 31 Jan
1901
Outlook, 66:901, 8 Dec
1900
Picayune, 9 Dec 1900,
II, 8
Saturday Review, 91:744,
8 Jun 1901

Benton, Kate A.
Geber
Nation, 70:303, 19 Apr
1900
Picayune, 22 Apr 1900,
III, 4

Bergengren, Anna (Farquhar)
The Devil's Plough
Bookman (London), 20:191,
Sep 1901
Canadian Magazine,
16:483, Mar 1901
Saturday Review, 91:711,
1 Jun 1901
An Evans of Suffolk
Atlantic, 93:852, Jun
1904
The Professor's Daughter
Picayune, 10 Apr 1899,
II, 8

Bernhard, Marie
The Household Idol
Picayune, 10 Apr 1892,
p. 15

Bernstein, Herman
Contrite Hearts
Nation, 81:510-1, 21 Dec
1905
In the Gates of Israel
Nation, 75:332, 23 Oct
1902
Overland, 2d S, 41:233
-34, Mar 1903

Berringer, Mrs. Oscar

The New Virtue
Saturday Review, 81:608,
13 Jun 1896

Berry, Edward Payson
Where the Tides Meet
Picayune, 22 Oct 1893,
p. 14

Bertron, Mrs. Ottilie
Edith
Nation, 45:403, 17 Nov
1887

Betts, Craven Langstroth
See Eaton, Arthur Wentworth,
and Craven Langstroth Betts.

Betts, Lillian W.
The Story of an East Side
Family
Bookman (NY), 17:515-6,
Jul 1903

Beulah [pseud.].
See Bates, Mrs. Fannie D.

Beynon, Mrs. Marie Edith
Saints, Sinners, and Queer
People
Picayune, 5 Jul 1897,
p. 9

Bianchi, Martha Gilbert (Dickinson)
The Cuckoo's Nest
Bookman (NY), 30:68,
Sep 1909
Nation, 89:212-3, 2 Sep
1909
A Modern Prometheus
Nation, 86:333, 9 Apr
1908

Bickford, Luther H.
Circumstances Beyond Control
Overland, 2d S, 15:323,
Mar 1890

_____, and Richard Stillman
Powell

Phyllis in Bohemia
   Picayune, 10 Oct 1897,
     p. 12

Biddle, Anthony Joseph Drexel
  Word for Word and Letter
  for Letter
   Outlook, 59:342, 4 Jun
    1898
   Saturday Review, 86:153,
    30 Jul 1898

Bien, Herman M.
  Ben Beor
   Atlantic, 69:567, Apr
    1892

Bierce, Ambrose
  Ashes of the Beacon
   Saturday Review, 108:144,
    31 Jul 1909
  Can Such Things Be?
   Athenaeum, 4311:702,
    11 Jun 1910
   Picayune, 4 Feb 1894,
    p. 16
  In the Midst of Life
   Athenaeum, 3356:240-1,
    20 Feb 1892; 4300:367,
    26 Mar 1910
   Bookman (London), 1:196,
    Mar 1892
   Bookman (NY), 7:257,
    May 1898
   Outlook, 58:731, 19 Mar
    1898
   Picayune, 1 May 1898,
    p. 25
  Tales of Soldiers and Civilians
   Atlantic, 70:136, Jul
    1892
   Picayune, 4 Aug 1895,
    p. 12

Bigelow, Edith Evelyn (Jaffray)
  Diplomatic Disenchantments
   Bookman (NY), 2:57,
    Sep 1895

Bigelow, Mrs. Poultney
  The Middle Course

Poet-Lore, 14:138,
   Winter 1903
  When Charlie Was Away
   Saturday Review, 93:239
   -40, 22 Feb 1902

Bigot, Madame [pseud.].
  See Healy, Mary.

Bill, Edward Lyman
  The Sword of the Pyramids
   Outlook, 59:184, 21 May
    1898

[Bird, Frederic Mayer]
  An Alien from the Common-
  wealth
   By Robert Timsol [pseud.].
   Nation, 49:175, 29 Aug
    1889

Bishop, Putnam Peter
  The Psychologist
   Nation, 44:18, 6 Jan
    1887
   Saturday Review, 62:844
    -45, 25 Dec 1886
  The Brown Stone Boy
   Picayune, 1 Jul 1888,
    p. 3

Bishop, William Henry
  Choy Susan and Other Stories
   Nation, 40:59, 15 Jan
    1885
   Overland, 2d S, 5:108,
    Jan 1885
  Detmold
   Atlantic, 44:264-5, Aug
    1879
   Saturday Review, 48:125,
    26 Jul 1879
  The Golden Justice
   Epoch, 1:19, 11 Feb 1887
   Harper's, 74:828-9,
    Apr 1887
   Nation, 44:278, 31 Mar
    1887
   Overland, 2d S, 9:325-6,
    Mar 1887

Bishop, William Henry
  The House of a Merchant
  Prince
    Continent, 3:478, 11
      Apr 1883
    Nation, 36:151, 15 Feb
      1883
    Overland, 2d S, 1:434,
      Apr 1883
  A Pound of Cure
    Nation, 59:199, 13 Sep
      1894
  The Yellow Snake
    Picayune, 25 Oct 1891,
      p. 3

Black, Alexander
  The Girl and the Guardsman
    Nation, 71:452, 6 Dec
      1900
  Miss Jerry
    Picayune, 23 Dec 1895,
      p. 9
  Richard Gordon
    Athenaeum, 3926:108,
      24 Jan 1903

Black, Margaret Horton (Potter)
  The Genius
    Bookman (NY), 23:283,
      May 1903
    Times Literary Supplement,
      4 May 1906, p. 158
  The Golden Ladder
    Athenaeum, 4217:204,
      22 Aug 1908
    Bookman (NY), 27:399
      -400, Jun 1908
    Nation, 86:469, 21 May
      1908
    Times Literary Supplement,
      11 Jun 1908, p. 190
  The House of De Mailly
    Athenaeum, 3849:152,
      3 Aug 1901
    Bookman (London),
      20:191, Sep 1901
  The Princess
    Nation, 84:389, 25 Apr
      1907
    North American Review,

185:549-52, 5 Jul 1907
  Uncanonized
    Outlook, 66:232, 22 Sep
      1900

Blackburn, Mrs. Margaret
Elizabeth
  Katharine Conway
    Picayune, 27 Nov 1898,
      p. 10

Blackwell, Antoinette Brown
  The Island Neighbors
    Godey's, 73:376, Oct
      1871
    Harper's, 43:623-4,
      Sep 1871
    Nation, 13:262, 19 Oct
      1871
    Picayune, 6 Aug 1871,
      [p. 9]

Blaisdell, Elijah Whittier
  The Hidden Record
    Godey's, 105:573, Dec
      1882
    Picayune, 12 Nov 1882,
      [p. 13]

Blake, Katherine (Evans)
  Hearts' Haven
    Bookman (NY), 23:30-1,
      Mar 1906
    Overland, 2d S, 46:587,
      Dec 1905

Blake, Lillie (Devereux) Umsted
  A Daring Experiment, and
  Other Stories
    Godey's, 128:234-5,
      Feb 1894
  Fettered for Life
    Harper's, 49:442-3, Aug
      1874
    Nation, 18:336, 21 May
      1874

Blakely, Elizabeth Seal
  Unto the Fourth Generation
    Picayune, 16 Sep 1894,
      p. 12

42

[Block, Rudolph]
Children of Men
By Bruno Lessing [pseud.].
Bookman (NY), 18:419,
Dec 1903

[Bloede, Gertrude]
The Story of Two Lives
By Stuart Sterne [pseud.].
Picayune, 7 Jun 1891,
p. 10

Bloomfield-Moore, Clara Sophia
(Jessup)
On Dangerous Ground
Godey's, 92:567, Jun
1876
Nation, 22:370, 8 Jun
1876
Saturday Review, 41:697,
27 May 1876

Bloomingdale, Charles
Mr. , Miss and Mrs.
Bookman (NY), 9:475,
Jul 1899
Picayune, 23 Apr 1899,
II, 8

Blossom, Henry Martyn
Checkers
Godey's, 134:94-5,
Jan 1897
Picayune, 3 Aug 1896,
p. 8
Poet-Lore, 8:619, (No. 8)
1896

Blum, Edgar C.
Bertha Laycourt
Godey's, 119:175, Aug
1889
Picayune, 7 Jul 1889,
p. 11

Bly, Nellie [pseud.].
See Seaman, Elizabeth
Cockrane.

Boggs, Martha Frye
A Romance of the New

Virginia
Picayune, 9 Aug 1896,
p. 15

Boggs, Robert [pseud.].
See Clark, Hugh A.

Bogy, Lewis Vital
A Cynic's Sacrifice
Picayune, 29 Oct 1893,
p. 16
In Office
Picayune, 23 Aug 1891,
p. 11

Boisgilbert, Edmund [pseud.].
See Donnelly, Ignatius Loyola.

Boldrewood, Rolf [pseud.].
See Brown, Thomas A.

Bolmer, W. E.
The Time Is Coming
Picayune, 6 Sep 1896,
p. 9

Bolton, Sarah (Knowles)
The Present Problem
Sunday Afternoon, 2:190,
Aug 1878
Stories from Life
Overland, 2d S, 9:559,
May 1887

Bonner, Geraldine
The Castlecourt Diamond Case
Overland, 2d S, 47:289,
Mar 1906
Hard-Pan
Picayune, 11 Nov 1900,
II, 4
Rich Men's Children
Bookman (NY), 26:78-9,
Sep 1907
Overland, 2d S, 48:501,
Dec 1906
To-morrow's Tangle
Athenaeum, 3989:458,
9 Apr 1904
Bookman (NY), 18:312-3,
Nov 1903

43

Bonner, Geraldine
See also The Spinners' Book
of Fiction.

Bonner, Sherwood [pseud.].
See McDowell, Katherine
Sherwood (Bonner).

Booth, Edward C.
The Doctor's Lass
Overland, 2d S, 56:436,
Oct 1910

Boothby, Guy
The Beautiful White Devil
Godey's, 135:333, Sep
1897

[Bosher, Kate Lee (Langley)]
Bobbie
By Kate Cairns [pseud.].
Picayune, 25 Jun 1899,
II, 12

Bouvé, Edward T.
Centuries Apart
Atlantic, 77:708, May
1896

Bouvé, Pauline Carrington (Rust)
Their Shadows Before
Picayune, 24 Dec 1899,
II, 27

Bouvet, Marie Marguerite
Tales of an Old Château
Outlook, 63:1028, 30 Dec
1899

Bowen, Helen M.
A Daughter of Cuba
Picayune, 3 Aug 1896,
p. 8

Bowyer, Edith M. (Nicholl)
The Human Touch
Athenaeum, 4067:467,
7 Oct 1905
Tales of Mountain and Mesa
Outlook, 63:74, 25 Nov
1899

Bowyer, James T.
The Pollinctor
Nation, 60:427, 30 May
1895

Boyce, Neith
See Hapgood, Neith (Boyce).

[Boyden, Emma]
Both Were Mistaken
By Arline Dare [pseud.].
Picayune, 12 Feb 1893,
p. 16

Boyesen, Hjalmar Hjorth
Against Heavy Odds
Epoch, 8:252, 21 Nov
1890
Nation, 53:107, 6 Aug
1891
Picayune, 19 Oct 1890,
p. 3
Saturday Review, 71:146,
31 Jan 1891
Boyhood in Norway
Godey's, 126:110, Jan
1893
Picayune, 4 Dec 1892,
p. 8
A Daughter of the Philistines
Athenaeum, 2908:74,
21 Jul 1883
Continent, 3:607, 9 May
1883
Falconberg
Atlantic, 44:364-6, Sep
1879
Harper's, 59:309, Jul
1879
Sewanee Review, 4:299,
May 1896
Sunday Afternoon, 3:575,
Jun 1879
The Golden Calf
Godey's, 125:405-6, Oct
1892
Sewanee Review, 4:299,
May 1896
Gunnar
Atlantic, 34:624-5, Nov
1874

Bradshaw, William Richard
The Goddess of Atvatabar
Atlantic, 70:707, Nov
1892
Picayune, 1 May 1892, p. 12

Brady, Cyrus Townsend
The Better Man
Bookman (NY), 32:295
-96, Nov 1910
The Corner in Coffee
Athenaeum, 4002:43,
9 Jul 1904
A Doctor of Philosophy
Athenaeum, 3965:544,
24 Oct 1903
Bookman (NY), 18:164-5,
Oct 1903
Nation, 77:286, 3 Oct
1903
For Love of Country
Nation, 66:407, 26 May
1898
Outlook, 58:638, 5 Mar
1898
Picayune, 10 Apr 1898, p. 25
For the Freedom of the Sea
Outlook, 63:979, 16
Dec 1899
Picayune, 31 Dec 1899,
II, 7
The Grip of Honor
Picayune, 20 May 1900,
III, 7
A Little Traitor to the South
Athenaeum, 4007:202,
13 Aug 1904
The Southerners
Overland, 2d S, 42:366,
Oct 1903
The Two Captains
Athenaeum, 4042:460,
15 Apr 1905
Times Literary Supple-
ment, 17 Mar 1905,
p. 91
Under Tops'ls and Tents
Nation, 72:477, 3 May 1901

Braganza [pseud.].
See Bragg, Henry A.

[Bragg, Henry A.]
Tekel
By Braganza [pseud.].
Saturday Review, 30:540,
22 Oct 1870

Brailsford, Henry Noel
The Broom of the War God
Picayune, 3 Apr 1898,
p. 17

Braine, Robert D.
Messages from Mars
Godey's, 126:102, Jan
1893
Picayune, 9 Oct 1892,
p. 12

Brainerd, Eleanor Hoyt
Concerning Belinda
Bookman (NY), 23:108,
Mar 1906
The Personal Conduct of
Belinda
Bookman (London), 38:268,
Sep 1910
Nation, 90:349, 7 Apr
1910

Brainerd, Thomas H. [pseud.].
See Jarboe, Mary Halsey
(Thomas).

Brazelton, Ethel Maude (Colson)
The Story of a Dream
Picayune, 26 Jan 1896,
p. 16

Brearley, William Henry
Wanted: A Copyist
Picayune, 8 Jul 1894,
p. 7
See also Kelley, Adelaide
(Skell), and William H.
Brearley.

[Brewer, Willis]
The Children of Issacher
Nation, 40:101, 29 Jan
1885
Picayune, 12 Oct 1884,

[p. 2]
Saturday Review, 60:258
-59, 22 Aug 1885

[Bridge, James Howard]
A Fortnight in Heaven
By Harold Brydges [pseud.].
Nation, 43:549, 30 Dec
1886
Saturday Review, 62:204,
7 Aug 1886
Uncle Sam at Home
By Harold Brydges [pseud.].
Overland, 2d S, 30:188,
Aug 1897
Picayune, 11 Mar 1888,
p. 12
Saturday Review, 66:278,
1 Sep 1888

Bridgman, Raymond Landon
Loyal Traitors
Outlook, 73:592, 7 Mar
1903

Bright, Mrs. A. M.
The Three Bernices
Nation, 10:112, 17 Feb
1870

Briscoe, Margaret Sutton
See Hopkins, Margaret Sutton
(Briscoe).

Bristol, Elias Leroy Macomb
Before He Was Born
Picayune, 4 Oct 1891,
p. 10

Brodhead, Eva Wilder (Mc-
Glasson)
Bound in Shallows
Nation, 64:401, 27 May
1897
Diana's Livery
Epoch, 8:384, 16 Jun
1891
An Earthly Paragon
Godey's, 126:106, Jan
1893
Nation, 55:396-7, 24 Nov

1892
Ministers of Grace
Atlantic, 76:278, Aug 1895
One of the Visconti
Atlantic, 78:850, Dec 1896
Bookman (NY), 4:373-4,
Dec 1896
Nation, 64:400-1, 27 May
1897
Picayune, 1 Nov 1896,
p. 12

Bronson, Edgar Beecher
The Red-Blooded
Overland, 2d S, 56:614,
Dec 1910

Brooks, Byron Alden
Earth Revisited
Picayune, 25 Feb 1894,
p. 25
Those Children and Their
Teachers
Nation, 35:448, 23 Nov
1882
Saturday Review, 55:422,
31 Mar 1883

Brooks, Elbridge Streeter
In Leislee's Times
Picayune, 13 Jun 1886,
p. 5
A Son of Issachar
Athenaeum, 3285:477,
11 Oct 1890
Atlantic, 66:695-8, Nov
1890
Overland, 2d S, 16:443,
Oct 1890
Picayune, 13 Jul 1890,
p. 11
Saturday Review, 70:321-2,
13 Sep 1890
A Son of the Revolution
Outlook, 59:184, 21 May
1898
With Lawton and Roberts
Outlook, 65:746, 28 Jul
1900

Brooks, Elizabeth W.
  As the World Goes By
    Outlook, 80:190, 20 May
    1905

Brooks, Henry Stanford
  A Catastrophe in Bohemia,
    and Other Stories
    Godey's, 127:236, Aug
    1893
    Overland, 2d S, 23:217,
    Feb 1894

Brooks, Hildegarde
  The Master of Caxton
    Atlantic, 90:277, Aug
    1902
    Nation, 74:411, 22 May
    1902
    Outlook, 70:1021, 26
    Apr 1902
  Without a Warrant
    Outlook, 67:925, 20
    Apr 1901

Brooks, Lilian
  See Camp, Walter Chauncey,
  and Lilian Brooks.

Brooks, Noah
  The Boy Settlers
    Saturday Review, 72:594,
    21 Nov 1891
  Tales of the Maine Coast
    Atlantic, 74:565, Oct
    1894
    Nation, 59:198-9, 13
    Sep 1894
    Picayune, 22 Jul 1894,
    p. 21

Brooks, Sarah Perot
  In the Bivouac of Life
    Picayune, 8 Oct 1899,
    II, 12

Brooks, Sarah (Warner)
  Poverty Knob
    Bookman (NY), 13:79,
    Mar 1901
    Outlook, 65:510,

23 Jun 1900

Brotherhead, Alfred P.
  Himself His Worst Enemy
    Harper's, 42:931, May
    1871
    Saturday Review, 31:384,
    25 Mar 1871

Brown, Abby Whitney
  Can She Atone?
    Nation, 31:382, 25 Nov
    1880

Brown, Alice
  By Oak and Thorn
    Godey's, 133:320, Sep
    1896
    Overland, 2d S, 28:488,
    Oct 1896
  Country Neighbors
    Bookman (London), 38:173,
    Jul 1910
    Nation, 91:12, 7 Jul 1910
    North American Review,
    192:720, Nov 1909
    Saturday Review, 110:22-3,
    2 Jul 1910
  The Country Road
    Bookman (London), 31:231
    -32, Feb 1907
    Bookman (NY), 24:598-9,
    Feb 1907
    Nation, 83:332, 18 Oct
    1906
  The Day of His Youth
    Picayune, 2 May 1897,
    p. 15
    Poet-Lore, 9:436, Summer
    1897
  Fools of Nature
    Atlantic, 98:56-65, Jul
    1906
    Nation, 45:485, 15 Dec
    1887
  High Noon
    Atlantic, 98:56-65, Jul
    1906
    Bookman (London), 26:178,
    Aug 1904
    Nation, 78:395-6, 19 May

1904
Times Literary Supplement,
1 Jul 1904, p. 204
John Winterbourne's Family
Nation, 91:550, 8 Dec
1910
Judgment
Bookman (NY), 18:302-3,
Nov 1903
Nation, 78:54, 21 Jan
1904
Poet-Lore, 14:136-7,
Winter 1903
King's End
Athenaeum, 3848:119-20,
27 Jul 1901
Bookman (London), 20:161,
Aug 1901
Bookman (NY), 13:287-8,
May 1901
Nation, 72:399, 16 May
1901
Outlook, 67:739, 30 Mar
1901
The Mannerings
Saturday Review, 96:212,
15 Aug 1903
Times Literary Supplement,
19 Jun 1903, p. 193
Margaret Warrener
Bookman (NY), 15:105,
Mar 1902
Nation, 74:117, 6 Feb
1902
Outlook, 69:1088, 28
Dec 1901
Meadow-Grass
Atlantic, 76:558-9, Oct
1895; 98:56-65, Jul
1906
Bookman (NY), 2:221-2,
Nov 1895
Poet-Lore, 8:43, (No. 1)
1896
Paradise
Athenaeum, 4080:12,
6 Jan 1906
Nation, 81:488, 14 Dec
1905
Rose MacLeod
Bookman (London), 35:56-7,

Oct 1908
Bookman (NY), 27:494-5,
Jul 1908
Nation, 86:492, 28 May
1908
North American Review,
188:136-40, Jul 1908
The Story of Thyrza
Athenaeum, 4255:581,
15 May 1909
Bookman (London), 36:157,
Jul 1909
Bookman (NY), 29:191,
Apr 1909
Nation, 88:307-8, 25
Mar 1909
Outlook, 92:19, 1 May
1909
North American Review,
190:119-20, Jul 1909
Saturday Review, 107:822,
26 Jun 1909
Stratford by the Sea
Nation, 38:449, 22 May
1884
Tiverton Tales
Atlantic, 98:56-65,
Jul 1906
Nation, 69:300, 19 Oct
1899
Outlook, 62:351, 10 Jun
1899

Brown, Anna Robeson
See Burr, Anna Robeson
(Brown).

[Brown, Mrs. C. K.]
Ethel Dutton
By Mattie May [pseud.].
Nation, 31:209, 16 Sep
1880

Brown, Caroline [pseud.].
See Krout, Carolina Virginia.

Brown, Clara Spalding
Life at Shut-in Valley, and
Other Pacific Coast Tales
Overland, 2d S, 27:240,
Feb 1896

Brown, Demetra (Vaka)
See Brown, Kenneth, and
Demetra (Vaka) Brown.

[Brown, George Douglas]
The House with the Green
Shutters
By George Douglas [pseud.].
Atlantic, 89:709, May
1902

Brown, Helen Dawes
The Petrie Estate
Atlantic, 72:849, Dec
1893
Godey's, 127:624, Nov
1893
Nation, 57:452, 14 Dec
1893
Picayune, 22 Oct 1893,
p. 14
Saturday Review, 76:720,
23 Dec 1893
Two College Girls
Athenaeum, 3067:171-2,
7 Aug 1886
Nation, 42:364-5, 29 Apr
1886
Overland, 2d S, 12:432
-33, Oct 1888
Saturday Review, 62:428
-29, 25 Sep 1886

Brown, L. Q. C.
Kenneth Cameron
Cottage Hearth, 14:295,
Sep 1888
Godey's, 117:254, Sep
1888
Picayune, 15 Jul 1888,
p. 7

Brown, Katharine Holland
Diane
Athenaeum, 4035:237,
25 Feb 1905
Nation, 79:527-8, 29 Dec
1904
Saturday Review, 99:280
-81, 4 Mar 1905
The Messenger

Nation, 90:653, 30 Jun
1910

Brown, Kenneth, and Demetra
(Vaka) Brown
The First Secretary
Bookman (NY), 26:555-6,
Jan 1908
Nation, 86:174, 20 Feb
1908

_____, and Henry B.
Booth
Eastover Courthouse
Harper's, 103:825-6,
Oct 1901

[Brown, S. A.]
Rheingrafenstein
By Ruth Dandelyon [pseud.].
Picayune, 11 Jun 1893,
p. 16
Babes in the Bush
By Rolf Boldrewood [pseud.].
Outlook, 65:409, 16 Jun
1900
Plain Living
By Rolf Boldrewood [pseud.].
Outlook, 58:1030, 23
Apr 1898
The Sealskin Cape
By Rolf Boldrewood [pseud.].
Picayune, 10 Jan 1897,
p. 11

Brown, William Garrott
A Gentleman of the South
Athenaeum, 3952:120,
25 Jul 1903
Nation, 77:118, 6 Aug
1903

Brown, William Horace
The Slaves of Folly
Picayune, 24 Mar 1889,
p. 7
A Southern Heritage
Picayune, 27 Dec 1891,
p. 11; 11 Jun 1893,
p. 16

Brown, William Perry
A Sea-Island Romance
Epoch, 6:808-9, 17
Jan 1890

Browne, George Waldo
The Young Gunbearer
Outlook, 66:949, 15 Dec
1900

Brownell, Gertrude (Hall)
Allegretto
Godey's, 128:[232],
Feb 1894
Far from To-Day
Atlantic, 70:419, Sep
1892
Cottage Hearth, 18:255,
Aug 1892
Overland, 2d S, 20:444,
Oct 1892
Foam of the Sea, and Other
Tales
Atlantic, 76:421, Sep
1895
The Hundred, and Other
Stories
Bookman (NY), 8:69,
Sep 1898
Outlook, 59:889, 6 Aug
1898

Brun, Samuel Jacques
Tales of Languedoc
Outlook, 63:512, 28 Oct
1899

[Brush, Christine (Chaplin)]
The Colonel's Opera Cloak
Harper's, 59:632, Sep
1879
Sunday Afternoon, 3:767,
Aug 1879
Inside Our Gate
Epoch, 5:422, 2 Aug
1889

[Bryan, Ella Howard]
Behind the Veil
Nation, 13:278, 26 Oct
1871

Outlook, 63:840, 2 Dec
1899

Bryan, Mary (Edwards)
Wild Work
Godey's, 103:477, Nov
1881
Harper's, 63:955, Nov
1881
Picayune, 25 Sep 1881,
[p. 3]

Bryce, Lloyd Stephens
Friends in Exile
Picayune, 2 Jul 1893,
p. 17; 21 Oct 1900,
II, 9
Lady Blanche's Salon
Outlook, 62:902, 19 Aug
1899
Picayune, 24 Sep 1899,
II, 6
Paradise
North American Review,
145:704, Dec 1887
Overland, 2d S, 11:435,
Apr 1888
Picayune, 11 Dec 1887,
p. 6
Romance of an Alter Ego
Saturday Review, 68:21-2,
6 Jul 1889

Brydges, Harold [pseud.].
See Bridge, James Howard.

Buchanan, Rachel
See Longstreet, Rachel
Abigail (Buchanan).

Buck, Charles William
Under the Sun
Overland, 2d S, 44:482,
Oct 1904

Buck, Francis Tiltou
A Fiancé and Trial
Picayune, 9 May 1897,
p. 17
A Man of Two Minds
Picayune, 29 Dec 1895,

Buck, Francis Tiltou
    p. 15

Buckingham, Emma May
  A Self-Made Woman
    Saturday Review, 37:418,
      28 Mar 1874

[Buckner, Alice Morris]
  Towards the Gulf
    Harper's, 74:827-8,
      Apr 1887
    Nation, 44:148, 17 Feb
      1887
    Picayune, 12 Dec 1886,
      p. 7

Buddington, Zadel B.
  Can the Old Love?
    Harper's, 44:780, Apr
      1872
    Nation, 14:111, 15
      Feb 1872
    Picayune, 10 Mar 1872,
      [p. 9]

Bunce, Oliver Bell
  The Adventures of Timias
  Terrystone
    Godey's, 110:669, Jun
      1885
    Overland, 2d S, 5:660,
      Jun 1885
  The Cash Value of a Book
  Review
    North American Review,
      149:223-7, Aug 1889
  The Story of Happinolande
    Epoch, 5:326, 21 Jun
      1889

Bunner, Henry Cuyler
  Jersey Street and Jersey
  Lane
    Atlantic, 78:568, Oct
      1896
    Bookman (NY), 4:162
      -63, Oct 1896
    Nation, 63:201, 10 Sep
      1896
    Picayune, 12 Jul 1896,

      p. 23
  Love in Old Clothes, and
  Other Stories
    Picayune, 8 Nov 1896,
      p. 6
  "Made in France"
    Godey's, 127:619, Nov
      1893
    Nation, 57:199, 14 Sep
      1893
  The Midge
    Atlantic, 58:267-9, Aug
      1886
    Harper's, 74:828, Apr
      1887
    Nation, 42:532-3, 24 Jun
      1886
    Picayune, 23 May 1886,
      p. 14
  The Runaway Browns
    Godey's, 125:518, Nov
      1892
  "Short Sixes"
    Cosmopolitan, 10:510-11,
      Feb 1891
  The Story of a New York
  House
    Atlantic, 60:414-5, Sep
      1887
    Epoch, 1:408, 3 Jun 1887
    Nation, 44:533, 23 Jun
      1887
    North American Review,
      145:703, Dec 1887;
      145:104-5, Jul 1887
    Overland, 2d S, 10:216,
      Aug 1887
    Picayune, 12 Jun 1887,
      p. 9
  A Woman of Honor
    Athenaeum, 2928:735-6,
      8 Dec 1883
    Continent, 4:799, 19 Dec
      1883
    Godey's, 107:583, Dec
      1883; 118:428, May 1889
    Harper's, 68:160, Dec
      1883; 68:428, May 1889
    Manhattan, 2:480, Nov
      1883
    Nation, 37:419, 15 Nov 1883

Overland, 2d S, 3:220,
Feb 1884
Picayune, 24 Feb 1889,
p. 12
Saturday Review, 57:129,
26 Jan 1884; 67:641-2,
25 May 1889
Zadoc Pine, and Other Stories
America, 6:134-5, 30
Apr 1891
Atlantic, 69:269, Feb
1892
Cosmopolitan, 11:639
-40, Sep 1891
Nation, 53:v, 9 Jul
1891
See also Matthews, Brander,
and H. C. Bunner.

Burgess, Gelett
Are You a Bromide?
Overland, 2d S, 49:185,
Feb 1907
The Heart Line
Athenaeum, 4212:65,
18 Jul 1908
Overland, 2d S,
51:[xii-xiii, xvi], Feb
1908
Little Sister of Destiny
Overland, 2d S, 48:187,
Sep 1906
Vivette
Bookman (NY), 7:169
-70, Apr 1898
Godey's, 136:[103]-4,
Jan 1898
Picayune, 12 Dec 1897,
p. 25
The White Cat
Athenaeum, 4191:222,
22 Feb 1908

_____, and Will Irwin
The Picaroons
Bookman (London),
27:48-9, Oct 1904
Nation, 78:395, 19 May
1904
Saturday Review, 97:592,
7 May 1904

Times Literary Supplement,
22 Apr 1904, p. 127

Burhaus, Viola
The Cave-Woman
Bookman (NY), 31:643,
Aug 1910

Burnett, Frances Eliza (Hodgson)
Townsend
The Dawn of To-morrow
Athenaeum, 4148:505,
27 Apr 1907
Bookman (NY), 23:299,
May 1906
Dolly
Athenaeum, 3404:84,
21 Jan 1893
Godey's, 96:83, Jan 1878
Nation, 26:66, 24 Jan
1878
Picayune, 9 Dec 1877,
[p. 9]
Saturday Review, 74:779,
31 Dec 1892
Earlier Stories
America, 6:451, 16 Jul
1891
Epoch, 10:215, 6 Nov
1891
Library Table, 4:505,
7 Dec 1878
Picayune, 5 Jul 1891,
p. 12
Editha's Burglar
Overland, 2d S, 12:434,
Oct 1888
A Fair Barbarian
Atlantic, 47:861-2, Jun
1881; 70:130-3, Jul
1892
Cottage Hearth, 7:177,
Jun 1881
Picayune, 3 Apr 1881,
[p. 6]
Saturday Review, 51:376
-77, 19 Mar 1881
The Fortunes of Philippa
Fairfax
Saturday Review, 65:697
-98, 9 Jun 1888

Burnett, Frances Eliza (Hodgson)
Townsend
Giovanni and the Other
  Picayune, 23 Oct 1892,
    p. 18
Haworth's
  Good Company, 4:287,
    (No. 3) 1879
  Harper's, 59:955, Nov
    1879
  Nation, 29:278-9, 23
    Oct 1879
His Grace of Osmonde
  Athenaeum, 3660:852,
    18 Dec 1897
  Bookman (NY), 6:355-6,
    Dec 1897
  Nation, 66:135, 17 Feb
    1898
  Overland, 2d S, 31:285,
    Mar 1898
  Picayune, 16 Jan 1898,
    p. 11
In Connection with the De
  Willoughby Claim
  Athenaeum, 3767:9,
    6 Jan 1900
  Bookman (London),
    17:119, Jan 1900
  Bookman (NY), 10:599,
    Feb 1900
  Nation, 70:245, 29 Mar
    1900
  Picayune, 7 Jan 1900,
    II, 3
  Saturday Review, 89:23,
    6 Jan 1900
Jarl's Daughter, and Other
  Stories
  Godey's, 121:173, Aug
    1890
  Nation, 28:188, 13 Mar
    1879
  Picayune, 9 Feb 1879,
    [p. 11]
Kathleen
  Atlantic, 44:367, Sep
    1879
  Godey's, 118:181, Feb
    1889
  Nation, 28:104, 6 Feb

1879
  Picayune, 17 Feb 1878,
    [p. 10]; 25 Nov 1888,
    p. 14
A Lady of Quality
  Athenaeum, 3571:440,
    4 Apr 1896
  Atlantic, 78:273-5, Aug
    1896
  Godey's, 133:95, Jul 1896
  Nation, 62:398, 21 May
    1896
  Picayune, 30 Mar 1896,
    p. 8
Lindsay's Luck
  Nation, 28:104, 6 Feb
    1879
  Picayune, 1 Jul 1883,
    [p. 2]
Little Lord Fauntleroy
  Picayune, 24 Oct 1886,
    p. 10
Little Saint Elizabeth, and
  Other Stories
  Epoch, 7:301, 13 Jun 1890
  Picayune, 27 Apr 1890,
    p. 10
Louisiana
  Atlantic, 46:414-5, Sep
    1880
  Nation, 30:313, 22 Apr
    1880
  Picayune, 20 Jun 1880,
    [p. 6]
The Making of a Marchioness
  Athenaeum, 3868:807,
    14 Dec 1901
  Bookman (London), 21:98,
    Dec 1901
  Bookman (NY), 14:632,
    Feb 1902
  Overland, 2d S, 38:315-6,
    Oct 1901
  Saturday Review, 93:115,
    25 Jan 1902
Miss Crespigny
  Godey's, 97:83, Jul 1878;
    119:86, Jul 1889
  Harper's, 59:475, Aug
    1879
  Library Table, 4:263,

25 May 1878
Nation, 29:30, 10 Jul
1879
Picayune, 7 Jul 1878,
[p. 3]
Miss Defarge
Picayune, 1 Jul 1888,
p. 3
The One I Knew the Best
of All
Nation, 57:395, 23 Nov
1893
Picayune, 12 Nov 1893,
p. 14
Sewanee Review, 2:509,
Aug 1894
Pretty Polly Pemberton
Nation, 28:104, 6 Feb
1879
The Pretty Sister of José
America, 2:151, 2 May
1889
Epoch, 5:228, 10 May
1889
Godey's, 118:508, Jun
1889
Nation, 48:530, 27 Jun
1889
Picayune, 5 May 1889,
p. 10
A Quiet Life
Cottage Hearth, 16:60,
Feb 1890
Godey's, 120:185, Feb
1890
Picayune, 24 Nov 1878,
[p. 5]
Sara Crewe
Epoch, 3:117, 16 Mar
1888
North American Review,
146:599, May 1888
Overland, 2d S, 12:216,
Aug 1888
Picayune, 11 Mar 1888,
p. 12
The Shuttle
Athenaeum, 4174:513,
26 Oct 1907
Bookman (NY), 26:272-3,
Nov 1907

Canadian Magazine,
30:196, Dec 1907
Nation, 85:474, 21 Nov
1907
Saturday Review, 104:642,
23 Nov 1907
Times Literary Supplement,
24 Oct 1907, p. 325
Surly Tim, and Other Stories
Atlantic, 41:142, Jan
1878
Library Table, 4:196,
30 Mar 1878
Nation, 26:66, 24 Jan
1878
Sunday Afternoon, 1:384,
Apr 1878
That Lass o' Lowrie's
Atlantic, 40:630-1,
Nov 1877
Nation, 25:44, 19 Jul
1877
North American Review,
125:318-9, Sep 1877;
128:108-10, Jan 1879
"Theo"
Cottage Hearth, 15:128,
Apr 1888
Godey's, 95:525, Dec
1877; 118:350, Apr
1889
Harper's, 59:475, Aug
1879
Picayune, 21 Oct 1877,
[p. 9]
Through One Administration
Athenaeum, 2898:600,
12 May 1883
Atlantic, 52:121-3, Jul
1883
Continent, 4:447, 3 Oct
1883
Manhattan, 2:92, Jul
1883
Nation, 36:552-3, 28 Jun
1883
Picayune, 27 May 1883,
[p. 13]
Vagabondia
Continent, 4:93, (No. 3)
1884

Burnett, Frances Eliza (Hodgson)
Townsend
    Cottage Hearth, 10:25,
     Jan 1884
    Nation, 38:58, 17 Jan
     1884
    Picayune, 16 Dec 1883,
     [p. 14]
    Saturday Review, 57:129,
     26 Jan 1884
  A Woman's Will
    Athenaeum, 3095:254,
     19 Feb 1887

Burnham, Clara Louise (Root)
  Dearly Bought
    Overland, 2d S, 15:435,
     Apr 1890
  Dr. Latimer
    Atlantic, 74:135, Jul
     1894
    Cottage Hearth, 19:345,
     Jul 1893
    Picayune, 28 May 1895,
     p. 24
  A Great Love
    Outlook, 60:395, 8 Oct
     1898
  Jewel
    Athenaeum, 3984:301,
     5 Mar 1904
    Bookman (London), 25:262,
     Mar 1904
    Nation, 78:134, 18 Feb
     1904
    Saturday Review, 97:497,
     16 Apr 1904
  The Leaven of Love
    Nation, 87:443, 5 Nov
     1908
  Miss Bagg's Secretary
    Epoch, 11:92, 11 Mar
     1892
  The Mistress of Beech Knoll
    Cottage Hearth, 16:294,
     Sep 1890
    Nation, 51:194, 4 Sep
     1890
    Overland, 2d S, 16:441,
     Oct 1890
  Next Door

    Athenaeum, 3060:808-9,
     19 Jun 1886
    Cottage Hearth, 14:262,
     Aug 1888
    Godey's, 117:84-5, Jul
     1888
    Nation, 43:14, 1 Jul
     1886
    Picayune, 20 May 1888,
     p. 10
  "No Gentlemen"
    Overland, 2d S, 15:435,
     Apr 1890
  The Opened Shutters
    Bookman (London), 31:274,
     Mar 1907
  The Right Princess
    Nation, 75:369, 6 Nov
     1902
  A Sane Lunatic
    Nation, 50:160, 20 Feb
     1890
    Overland, 2d S, 15:435,
     Apr 1890
  Sweet Clover
    Nation, 60:426, 30 May
     1895
  A West Point Wooing, and
  Other Stories
    Bookman (NY), 9:282-3,
     May 1899
    Outlook, 61:602, 11 Mar
     1899
  A Wise Woman
    Nation, 62:62, 16 Jan
     1896
  Young Maids and Old
    Epoch, 4:310, 30 Nov
     1888
    Nation, 48:272, 28 Nov
     1889

Burr, Anna Robeson (Brown)
  The Black Lamb
    Picayune, 9 Feb 1896,
     p. 11
  A Cosmopolitan Tragedy
    Picayune, 13 Aug 1899,
     II, 8
  The Immortal Garland
    Nation, 70:402, 24 May

1900
Picayune, 20 May 1900,
III, 7
The Jessop Bequest
  Nation, 86:62-3, 16 Jan
  1908
Sir Mark
  Godey's, 134:205, Feb
  1897
The Warriors
  Outlook, 75:424, 17 Oct
  1903
The Wine Press
  Atlantic, 97:51, Jan
  1906
  Nation, 81:123, 10 Aug
  1905
  Outlook, 80:346, 3 Jun
  1905

Burr, Katherine Douglas (King)
Off the Roll
  Picayune, 19 Dec 1875,
  [p. 4]
Our Detachment
  Harper's, 51:297-8,
  Jul 1875

Burt, Mary E.
Odysseus, the Hero of
  Ithaca
  Outlook, 59:184, 21
  May 1898

Burton, Frederick Russell
Strongheart
  Bookman (NY), 28:382
  -83, Dec 1908

Bush, G. G.
Our Choir
  Overland, 2d S, 1:654,
  Jun 1883

Butler, Ellis Parker
The Confessions of a Daddy
  Nation, 85:122, 8 Aug
  1907
The Incubator Baby
  Overland, 2d S, 48:502,
  Dec 1906

That Pup
  Nation, 87:656, 31 Dec
  1908

Butler, William Allen
Domesticus
  Nation, 42:240, 18 Mar
  1886

Butterworth, Hezekiah
The Wampum Belt
  Bookman (NY), 4:572,
  Feb 1897

Bynner, Edwin Lasseter
Agnes Surriage
  Godey's, 117:169, Aug
  1888
  Nation, 44:18, 6 Jan
  1881
  Overland, 2d S, 9:322-4,
  Mar 1887
The Begum's Daughter
  Athenaeum, 3316:632,
  16 May 1891
  Nation, 51:486, 18 Dec
  1890
Damen's Ghost
  Nation, 33:337, 27 Oct
  1881
  Overland, 2d S, 11:438,
  Apr 1888
Nimport
  Atlantic, 40:508-9, Oct
  1877
  Library Table, 3:22,
  10 Nov 1877
  Nation, 25:183, 20 Sep
  1877
  North American Review,
  125:321, Sep 1877
  Picayune, 14 Oct 1877,
  [p. 11]
Penelope's Suitors
  Epoch, 2:58, 26 Aug 1887
  Nation, 45:237, 22 Sep
  1887
Tritons
  Harper's, 57:941, Nov 1878
  Library Table, 4:385,
  31 Aug 1878

Bynner, Edwin Lasseter
    Nation, 27:118-9, 22 Aug
      1878
    Sunday Afternoon, 2:384,
      Oct 1878
    Zachary Phips
      Cottage Heart, 19:47,
        Jan 1893
      Godey's, 126:104, Jan
        1893
      Nation, 55:437, 8 Dec
        1892

Byrd, Ella Billingsley
    Marston Hall
      By Beryl Carr [pseud.].
      Picayune, 24 Oct 1880,
        [p. 2]

C. and C. [pseud.].
    See Cabot, Arthur Winslow.

Cabell, James Branch
    The Cords of Vanity
      Athenaeum, 4274:357,
        25 Sep 1909
      Nation, 88:563, 10 Jun
        1909
    The Eagle's Shadow
      Athenaeum, 4025:838,
        17 Dec 1904
    Gallantry
      Nation, 85:423, 7 Nov
        1907

Cable, George Washington
    Bonaventure
      Atlantic, 61:841-3, Jun
        1888
      Epoch, 3:197, 13 Apr
        1888
      Harper's, 77:801, Oct
        1888
      Nation, 46:529, 28 Jun
        1888
      North American Review,
        146:718, Jun 1888
      Picayune, 25 Mar 1888,
        p. 11
    Bylow Hill
      Athenaeum, 3912:516,

      18 Oct 1902
      Nation, 75:332, 23 Oct
        1902
      Saturday Review, 94:524,
        25 Oct 1902
      Times Literary Supplement,
        25 Jul 1902, p. 221
    The Cavalier
      Athenaeum, 3864:658,
        16 Nov 1901
      Atlantic, 88:847-8, Dec
        1901
      Bookman (NY), 14:386-7,
        Dec 1901
      Canadian Magazine, 17:291,
        Jan 1902
      Nation, 73:458, 12 Dec
        1901
      Overland, 2d S, 38:508-9,
        Dec 1901
      Saturday Review, 92:746,
        14 Dec 1901
      Saturday Review, 93:405,
        29 Mar 1902
      Sewanee Review, 10:245-6,
        Apr 1902; 11:357, Jul
        1903
    The Creoles of Louisiana
      Godey's, 110:111, Jan
        1885
      Picayune, 11 Jan 1885,
        [p. 5]
    Dr. Sevier
      Athenaeum, 2978:656-7,
        22 Nov 1884
      Atlantic, 55:121-2, Jan
        1885
      Harper's, 70:493, Feb
        1885
      Nation, 39:441, 20 Nov
        1884
      Picayune, 12 Oct 1884,
        [p. 2]
      Saturday Review, 59:61-2,
        10 Jan 1885
    The Grandissimes
      Atlantic, 46:829-31, Dec
        1880; 101:855, Jun
        1908
      Bookman (London), 14:72
        -73, Jun 1898

Bookman (NY), 7:401-3,
Jul 1898
Harper's, 62:153, Dec
1880
Nation, 31:415-6, 9 Dec
1880
Picayune, 26 Sep 1880,
[p. 12]
Sewanee Review, 6:303,
Jul 1898; 11:354, Jul
1903; 11:360, Jul
1903; 11:362, Jul 1903
John March, Southerner
Atlantic, 75:821-3,
Jun 1895
Bookman (London), 8:56,
May 1895
Nation, 60:206, 14 Mar
1895
Picayune, 23 Dec 1894,
p. 12
Kincaid's Battery
Bookman (London), 36:39,
Apr 1909
Canadian Magazine, 33:280,
Jul 1909
Nation, 88:19-20, 7 Jan
1909
Madame Delphine
Athenaeum, 2807:203,
13 Aug 1881
Nation, 33:54-5, 21 Jul
1881
Picayune, 24 Jul 1881,
[p. 2]
Saturday Review, 52:237
-38, 20 Aug 1881
Sewanee Review, 11:354,
Jul 1903; 11:360, Jul
1903
Old Creole Days
Continent, 4:96, 18 Jul
1883
Picayune, 1 Jun 1879,
[p. 10]; 6 Feb 1898,
p. 17
Sewanee Review, 11:354,
Jul 1903
"Posson Jone"
Bookman (London),
14:64-5, Jun 1898

Nation, 89:600, 16 Dec
1909
The Silent South
Picayune, 20 Dec 1885,
p. 14
Strange True Stories of
Louisiana
Athenaeum, 3254:305,
8 Mar 1890
Atlantic, 65:286, Feb
1890
Nation, 51:136, 14 Aug
1890
Picayune, 5 Jan 1890,
p. 16
Saturday Review, 69:117,
25 Jan 1890
Strong Hearts
Athenaeum, 3742:96,
15 Jul 1899
Bookman (London), 16:77,
Jun 1899
Bookman (NY), 9:473,
Jul 1899
Nation, 68:441-2, 8 Jun
1899
Picayune, 9 Apr 1899,
II, 4

[Cabot, Arthur Winslow]
Two Gentlemen of Gotham
By C. and C. [pseud.].
Nation, 44:454, 26 May
1887

Cabot, Elisabeth Lyman
In Plain Air
Picayune, 6 Jun 1897,
p. 17
Sewanee Review, 5:383,
Jul 1897

Cahan, Abraham
The Imported Bridgegroom,
and Other Stories
Bookman (NY), 7:513-4,
Aug 1898
Outlook, 58:1078, 30 Apr
1898
The White Terror and the Red
Athenaeum, 4046:588,

Cahan, Abraham
    13 May 1905
    Bookman (NY), 20:415-7,
      Jan 1905; 21:186-8,
      Apr 1905
  Yekl
    Bookman (NY), 4:157-8,
      Oct 1896
    Godey's, 133:544, Nov
      1896

Cahill, Mabel Esmonde
  Her Playthings, Men
    Picayune, 10 May 1891,
      p. 12

Cairns, Kate [pseud.].
  See Bosher, Kate Lee
  (Langley).

Calder, Alma
  See Johnston, Alma (Calder).

Calhoun, Alfred C.
  See His Fleeting Ideal.

Calkins, Frank Welles
  The Cougar-Tamer, and
  Other Stories of Adventure
    Outlook, 62:171, 20 May
      1899
    Picayune, 30 Jul 1899,
      II, 8
  The Wooing of Tokala
    Nation, 84:591, 27 Jun
      1907

Camera, Cara [pseud.].
  Sifting Matrimony
    Godey's, 121:347, Oct
      1890
    Picayune, 21 Sep 1890,
      p. 12

Cameron, Margaret
  The Involuntary Chaperon
    Saturday Review,
      109:698, 28 May 1910

Camp, Walter Chauncey, and
  Lilian Brooks

Drives and Puts
    Nation, 69:300, 19 Oct
      1899

Campbell, Helen (Stuart)
  His Grandmothers
    Nation, 25:274, 1 Nov
      1877
  Miss Melinda's Opportunity
    Nation, 43:398, 11 Nov
      1886
    Overland, 2d S, 8:327,
      Sep 1886
  Mrs. Herndon's Income
    Nation, 42:40, 14 Jan
      1886
    Overland, 2d S, 7:213,
      Feb 1886
  Roger Berkeley's Probation
    Nation, 47:274, 4 Oct
      1888
  Six Sinners
    By Campbell Wheaton [pseud.].
    Library Table, 3:75,
      22 Dec 1877
  Under Green Apple Boughs
    Cottage Hearth, 15:164,
      May 1889
    Godey's, 118:429, May
      1889
    Nation, 35:447-8, 23 Nov
      1882
    Saturday Review, 67:641,
      25 May 1889
  Unto the Third and Fourth
  Generation
    Atlantic, 46:417-8, Sep
      1880
    Continent, 2:188, 16 Aug
      1882
    Nation, 31:208, 16 Sep
      1880
    Picayune, 4 Jul 1880,
      [p. 6]
  White and Red
    Saturday Review, 29:130,
      22 Jan 1870

Campbell, Scott [pseud.].
  See Davis, Frederick
  William.

Canfield, Dorothy.
    See Fisher, Dorothy
    (Canfield).

Canfield, Henry Spofford
    Fergy the Guide
        Athenaeum, 4039:364-5,
        25 Mar 1905

Canfield, William Walker
    Along the Way
        Nation, 89:433-4, 4 Nov
        1909
    The Spotter
        Nation, 85:401, 31 Oct
        1907

Capers, Henry Dickson
    Belleview
        Picayune, 7 Nov 1880,
        [p. 8]

Capsadell, Louisa [pseud.].
    See Hammond, Henrietta
    (Hardy).

Carew, Rachel
    Tangled
        Nation, 26:66, 24 Jan
        1878
        Picayune, 12 Aug 1877,
        [p. 7]

Carey, Alice V.
    Paradise World
        Picayune, 22 Mar 1896,
        p. 10

Carleton, Will
    The Old Infant, and Similar
    Stories
        Bookman (NY), 4:167-8,
        Oct 1896
        Nation, 64:400, 27 May
        1897

Carpenter, Edith
    Your Money or Your Life
        Athenaeum, 3591:253,
        22 Aug 1896
        Atlantic, 78:137, Jul 1896

Bookman (NY), 3:455,
    Jul 1896
Picayune, 27 Apr 1896,
    p. 10
Saturday Review, 82:402,
    10 Oct 1896

Carpenter, Edmund Janes
    A Woman of Shawmut
        Picayune, 25 Oct 1891,
        p. 3
        Saturday Review, 74:207,
        13 Aug 1892

Carpenter, Edward Childs
    Captain Courtesy
        Overland, 2d S, 49:96,
        Jan 1907

Carpenter, Esther Bernon
    South-County Neighbors
        Harper's, 75:321, Jan
        1888
        Overland, 2d S, 11:435,
        Apr 1888

Carpenter, Frank DeYeaux
    Ride About Rio
        Manhattan, 3:188, Feb
        1884

[Carpenter, Wheeler Andrew]
    The Conquering of Kate
        By J. P. Mowbray [pseud.].
        Nation, 76:479, 11 Jun
        1903
    Tangled Up in Beulah Land
        By J. P. Mowbray [pseud.].
        Saturday Review, 95:21,
        3 Jan 1903

Carr, Beryl [pseud.].
    See Byrd, Ella Billingsley.

[Carrington, Kate]
    Aschenbroedel
        Continent, 2:91, 26 Jul
        1882
        Nation, 35:182-3, 31 Aug
        1882

[Carroll, John]
St. Maur
    Picayune, 30 Nov 1879,
      [p. 13]

Carruth, Frances Weston
Those Dale Girls
    Bookman (NY), 9:559,
      Aug 1899
    Outlook, 62:172, 20 May
      1899
The Way of Belinda
    Bookman (NY), 13:286
      -87, May 1901

Carruth, Fred Hayden
The Adventures of Jones
    Atlantic, 77:280, Feb
      1896
Mrs. Milo Bush, and Other
Worthies
    Outlook, 62:720, 29 Jul
      1899

Carruth, Hayden
See Carruth, Fred Hayden.

Carruthers, William A.
The Knights of the Horseshoe
    Nation, 35:448, 23 Nov
      1882

Carryl, Charles Edward
The River Syndicate, and
Other Stories
    Bookman (London), 17:153,
      Feb 1900
    Outlook, 61:833, 8 Apr
      1899

Carryl, Guy Wetmore
Fables for the Frivolous
    Outlook, 60:537, 29 Oct
      1898
The Lieutenant-Governor
    Nation, 76:358, 30 Apr
      1903
The Transgression of Andrew
Vane
    Athenaeum, 4025:838,
      17 Dec 1904

    Bookman (London), 28:136
      -37, Jul 1905
Zut, and Other Parisians
    Nation, 78:54, 21 Jan
      1904

Carter, John Henton
Thomas Rutherton
    Atlantic, 67:128, Jan
      1891

Carter, Mary Nelson
North Carolina Sketches
    Nation, 71:410, 22 Nov
      1900

Carter, Ruth [pseud.].
See Robertson, Sarah Franklin
(Davis).

Carus, Paul
Nirvâna
    Outlook, 58:83, 1 Jan
      1898
Truth in Fiction
    Picayune, 22 Jan 1893,
      p. 20
    Poet-Lore, 5:163-4,
      (No. 3) 1893

Cary, Gillie
See McCabe, Gillie (Cary).

Case, William Scoville
Forward House
    Atlantic, 76:708, Nov
      1895
    Nation, 62:61, 16 Jan
      1896

Caskoden, Edwin [pseud.].
See Major, Charles.

Cassedy, Frank H.
The Milton Tragedy
    Picayune, 25 Oct 1891,
      p. 3

Castlemon, Harry
The Mail Carrier
    Picayune, 25 May 1879,

[p. 6]

Castleton, D. R. [pseud.].
See Derby, Caroline Rosine.

Cather, George R.
Dora's Device
Picayune, 1 Nov 1885,
p. 11

Cather, Willa Sibert
The Troll Garden
Atlantic, 97:48, Jan
1906
Bookman (NY), 21:612
-14, Aug 1905

Catherwood, Mary (Hartwell)
The Chase of Saint-Castin,
and Other Stories
Atlantic, 75:423, Mar
1895
Nation, 60:206, 14 Mar
1895
Craque-o'Doon
Picayune, 20 Nov 1881,
[p. 2]
The Days of Jeanne d'Arc
Bookman (NY), 6:247
-50, Nov 1897
Nation, 66:136, 17 Feb
1898
Picayune, 17 Oct 1897,
p. 10
The Lady of Fort St. John
Athenaeum, 3373:788-9,
18 Jun 1892
Atlantic, 69:705-6,
May 1892
Nation, 54:153-4, 25 Feb
1892
Overland, 2d S, 19:330
-31, Mar 1892
Lazarre
Athenaeum, 3890:619-20,
17 May 1902
Bookman (London), 22:30,
Apr 1902
Bookman (NY), 14:259
-60, Nov 1902
Old Kaskaskia

Atlantic, 72:697, Nov
1893
Cottage Hearth, 19:345,
Jul 1893
Godey's, 127:106, Jul
1893
Overland, 2d S, 23:219,
Feb 1894
Picayune, 11 Jun 1893,
p. 16
The Queen of the Swamp, and
Other Plain Americans
Outlook, 62:314, 3 Jun
1899
Rocky Fork
Nation, 34:505-6, 15 Jun
1882
The Romance of Dollard
Athenaeum, 3240:740,
30 Nov 1889
Atlantic, 65:124-6,
Jan 1890
Epoch, 6:678-9, 22 Nov
1889
Nation, 50:226, 13 Mar
1890
Picayune, 20 Oct 1889,
p. 8
Spanish Peggy
Picayune, 31 Dec 1899,
II, 7
The Spirit of an Illinois
Town
Godey's, 134:669, Jun
1897
The Story of Tonty
America, 3:598, 6 Feb
1890
Athenaeum, 3987:396,
26 Mar 1904
Nation, 50:492, 19 Jun
1890
The White Islander
Atlantic, 73:557-8,
Apr 1894
Nation, 57:452-3, 14 Dec
1893
Picayune, 22 Oct 1893,
p. 14
Saturday Review, 77:106,
27 Jan 1894

Catherwood, Mary (Hartwell)
  A Woman in Armor
    Godey's, 91:190, Aug
      1875
    Picayune, 20 Jun 1875,
      [p. 6]

Catlin, Henry Guy
  Yellow Pine Basin
    Bookman (NY), 5:514-5,
      Aug 1897

Cavazza, Elisabeth
  See Pullen, Elisabeth (Jones)
  Cavazza.

Caxton, Laura [pseud.].
  See Comins, Elizabeth
  Barker.

Cervus, G. L. [pseud.].
  See Roe, William James.

Chadwick, Julia Halstead
  The Whole Truth
    Godey's, 115:260, Sep
      1887
    Nation, 44:454, 26 May
      1887

Chamberlain, Henry Richardson
  6,000 Tons of Gold
    Saturday Review, 78:366,
      29 Sep 1894

Chamberlain, Nathan Henry
  The Sphinx in Aubrey Parish
    Epoch, 5:228, 10 May
      1889

[Chamberlain, William Mellen]
  Manuela Parédes
    Nation, 32:411, 9 Jun
      1881

[Chambers, Julius]
  On a Margin
    Nation, 39:508, 11 Dec
      1884
    Picayune, 23 Nov 1884,
      [p. 7]

The Rascal Club
  Saturday Review, 85:825,
    18 Jun 1898

Chambers, Robert William
  Ailsa Page
    Bookman (NY), 32:80-1,
      Sep 1910
    Nation, 91:145, 18 Aug
      1910
  Ashes of Empire
    Bookman (NY), 9:185,
      Apr 1899
  The Cambric Mask
    Athenaeum, 3776:302,
      10 Mar 1900
    Bookman (London), 17:192,
      Mar 1900
    Bookman (NY), 11:190,
      Apr 1900
    Picayune, 22 Apr 1900,
      III, 4
    Saturday Review, 89:338,
      17 Mar 1900
  Cardigan
    Athenaeum, 3856:382,
      21 Sep 1901
    Nation, 74:195, 6 Mar
      1902
    Saturday Review, 92:435,
      5 Oct 1901
  The Conspirators
    Outlook, 65:87, 5 May
      1900
    Picayune, 13 May 1900,
      III, 3
  The Danger Mark
    Athenaeum, 4298:304,
      12 Mar 1910
    Bookman (London), 37:8,
      Oct 1909; 38:56, Spring
      Suppl., Apr 1910
    Bookman (NY), 30:264-5,
      Nov 1909
    Outlook, 93:515, 30 Oct
      1909
    Saturday Review, 109:666
      -67, 21 May 1910
  The Fighting Chance
    Athenaeum, 4138:193,
      16 Feb 1907

Bookman (NY), 24:157
-58, Oct 1906
Nation, 83:246, 20 Sep
1906
The Firing Line
Athenaeum, 4249:403,
3 Apr 1909
Bookman (London), 36:44
-45, Apr 1909
Bookman (NY), 28:151-3,
Oct 1908
Nation, 87:235, 10 Sep
1908
Saturday Review, 107:694
-95, 29 May 1909
A Gay Conspiracy
Athenaeum, 3786:618,
19 May 1900
Saturday Review, 90:245,
25 Aug 1900
The Green Mouse
Athenaeum, 4328:416,
8 Oct 1910
Nation, 90:435, 28 Apr
1910
Saturday Review, 110:489,
15 Oct 1910
The Haunts of Men
Athenaeum, 3765:862,
23 Dec 1899; 4082:75,
20 Jan 1906
Outlook, 59:789, 30 Jul
1898
In Search of the Unknown
Athenaeum, 4045:555,
6 May 1905
Atlantic, 95:690, May
1905
In the Quarter
Bookman (London), 9:65,
Nov 1895
Godey's, 134:[667]-9,
Jun 1897
Saturday Review, 80:881,
28 Dec 1895
Iole
Atlantic, 97:50, Jan
1906
A King and a Few Dukes
Atlantic, 78:426, Sep
1896

Bookman (London), 10:87,
Jun 1896
Godey's, 134:[667]-9,
Jun 1897
Saturday Review, 82:121,
1 Aug 1896
The King in Yellow
Bookman (London), 9:29
-30, Oct 1895
Godey's, 130:[654], Jun
1895; 134:[667]-9, Jun
1897
Saturday Review, 80:695,
23 Nov 1895
Lorraine
Athenaeum, 3688:32,
2 Jul 1898
Bookman (NY), 7:167,
Apr 1898
Overland, 2d S, 31:86-7,
Jan 1898
Saturday Review, 86:53,
9 Jul 1898
The Maid-at-Arms
Athenaeum, 3912:516,
18 Oct 1902
Bookman (London), 23:69,
Nov 1902
Saturday Review, 94:679,
29 Nov 1902
The Maids of Paradise
Athenaeum, 3957:281,
29 Aug 1903
Bookman (London), 24:223,
Sep 1903
Poet-Lore, 14:137,
Winter 1903
The Maker of Moons
Athenaeum, 3611:46,
9 Jan 1897
Godey's, 134:[667]-9, Jun
1897
The Mystery of Choice
Godey's, 136:329, Mar
1898
Overland, 2d S, 31:86-7,
Jan 1898
Picayune, 26 Dec 1897,
p. 9
Outsiders
Athenaeum, 3798:184-5

Chambers, Robert William
11 Aug 1900
Bookman (NY), 9:471-2,
Jul 1899
Saturday Review, 89:786,
23 Jun 1900
The Reckoning
Athenaeum, 4068:504,
14 Oct 1905
Atlantic, 97:50, Jan
1906
Bookman (London), 29:255,
Feb 1906
Bookman (NY), 22:374,
Dec 1905
The Red Republic
Atlantic, 78:426,
Sep 1896
Bookman (NY), 3:168,
Apr 1896
Godey's, 134:[667]-9,
Jun 1897
Some Ladies in Haste
Saturday Review, 107:48,
9 Jan 1909
Special Messenger
Athenaeum, 4279:522,
30 Oct 1909
Bookman (London), 37:105,
Nov 1909
Bookman (NY), 29:310-1,
May 1909
The Tracer of Lost Persons
Athenaeum, 4150:574,
11 May 1907
Bookman (London),
32:212-3, Sep 1907
The Tree of Heaven
Bookman (London), 34:117,
Jun 1908
Bookman (NY), 25:603-4,
Aug 1907
Nation, 84:544, 13 Jun
1907
With the Band
Godey's, 134:[667]-9,
Jun 1897
The Younger Set
Athenaeum, 4176:580,
9 Nov 1907
Bookman (London), 33:97,

Nov 1907
Bookman (NY), 26:163-4,
Oct 1907
Nation, 85:188, 29 Aug
1907
Saturday Review, 104:549,
2 Nov 1907
A Young Man in a Hurry, and
Other Stories
Bookman (London), 31:48,
Oct 1906

Champney, Elizabeth (Williams)
Bourbon Lilies
Harper's, 56:941, May
1878
Nation, 26:264, 18 Apr
1878
Great Grandmother's Girls
Epoch, 5:85-6, 8 May
1899
Margarita
Outlook, 72:375, 11 Oct
1902
Romance of Imperial Rome
Nation, 91:579, 15 Dec
1910
Rosemary and Rue
Nation, 33:437, 1 Dec
1881
Three Vassar Girls Abroad
Nation, 36:41, 11 Jan
1883
Witch Winnie's Studio
Picayune, 4 Dec 1892,
p. 8

Chandler, Bessie
A Woman Who Failed, and
Others
Nation, 56:476, 29 Jun
1893

Channing, Grace Ellery
See Stetson, Grace Ellery
(Channing).

Chapin, Anna Alice, and Glen
MacDonough
Babes in Toyland
Poet-Lore, 15:142,

Winter 1904

[Chaplin, Heman White]
Five Hundred Dollars, and
Other Stories of New Eng-
land Life
By C. H. W. [pseud.].
Nation, 47:14, 5 Jul
1888
Picayune, 18 Dec 1887,
p. 14; 16 Mar 1890,
p. 16

Charles, Elizabeth (Rundle)
The Bartram Family
Godey's, 92:190, Feb
1876
Conquering and to Conquer
Godey's, 90:570, Feb
1875
Joan the Maid
Harper's, 59:148, Jun
1879
Sunday Afternoon, 3:575,
Jun 1879
The Victory of the Vanquished
Harper's, 42:623, Mar
1871

Charles, Frances (Asa)
In the Country God Forgot
Nation, 74:448, 5 Jun
1902
Pardner of Blossom Ranch
Overland, 2d S, 48:502,
Dec 1906

Chatfield-Taylor, Hobart
Charfield
An American Peeress
Picayune, 11 Mar 1894,
p. 25
Saturday Review, 77:641,
16 Jun 1894
Two Women & a Fool
Godey's, 130:655, Jun
1895
Saturday Review,
80:118-9, 27 Jul 1895

Chauncey, Shelton [pseud.].

See Nicholls, Charles Wilbur
de Lyon.

Cheney, Ednah Dow (Littlehale)
Nora's Return
Godey's, 120:517, Jun
1890
Picayune, 4 May 1890,
p. 7
Saturday Review, 69:584,
10 May 1890

Cheney, John Vance
The Old Doctor
Overland, 2d S, 8:439,
Oct 1886

Cheney, Warren
The Challenge
Outlook, 82:762, 31 Mar
1906
His Wife
Overland, 2d S, 51:[xii],
Feb 1908

Chesebro', Caroline
The Foe in the Household
Atlantic, 28:126, Jul
1871
Harper's, 43:623, Sep
1871

Chesnutt, Charles Waddell
The Colonel's Dream
Athenaeum, 4081:43,
13 Jan 1906
Outlook, 81:278, 30 Sep
1905
The Conjure Woman
Atlantic, 85:699-701,
May 1900
Bookman (NY), 9:295-6,
Jun 1899; 9:372-3, Jun
1899
Nation, 68:421, 1 Jun
1899
Outlook, 61:884, 15 Apr
1899
Picayune, 9 Apr 1899,
II, 4

Chesnutt, Charles Waddell
The House Behind the
Cedars
Nation, 72:182, 28 Feb
1901
Saturday Review, 91:342
-43, 16 Mar 1901
The Marrow of Tradition
Bookman (NY), 14:533,
Jan 1902
Nation, 74:232, 20 Mar
1902
North American Review,
173:883-5, Dec 1901
The Wife of His Youth,
and Other Stories
Atlantic, 85:699-701,
May 1900
Bookman (NY), 10:597-8,
Feb 1900
Picayune, 24 Dec 1899,
II, 27

Chester, Evelyn
Miss Derrick
Picayune, 26 Aug 1894,
p. 16

Chester, George Randolph
Get-Rich-Quick Wallingford
Overland, 2d S, 52:90,
Jul 1908
The Making of Bobby Burnit
Bookman (NY), 29:642,
Aug 1909

Child, Frank Samuel
The Colonial Parson
Picayune, 6 Dec 1896,
p. 15
A Colonial Witch
Picayune, 7 Nov 1897,
p. 6
A Puritan Wooing
Picayune, 4 Dec 1898,
II, 4
Saturday Review, 89:114,
27 Jan 1900

Childs, Eleanor Stuart (Patterson)

Averages
By Eleanor Stuart [pseud.].
Bookman (NY), 10:502,
Jan 1900
Picayune, 26 Nov 1899,
II, 8
The Postscript
By Eleanor Stuart [pseud.].
Nation, 86:558, 18 Jun
1908
Overland, 2d S, 52:90,
Jul 1908

Choate, Lowell [pseud.].
See Hopkins, Mrs. Alice
Kimball

Chopin, Kate (O'Flaherty)
At Fault
Nation, 53:264, 1 Oct
1891
Picayune, 12 Oct 1890,
p. 15
The Awakening
Nation, 69:96, 3 Aug
1899
Outlook, 62:314, 3 Jun
1899
Bayou Folk
Atlantic, 73:558-9,
Apr 1894
Cottage Hearth, 20:250,
May 1894
Godey's, 130:432, Apr
1895
Nation, 58:488, 28 Jun
1894
Picayune, 15 Apr 1894,
p. 14
A Night in Acadie
Nation, 66:447, 9 Jun
1898
Picayune, 26 Dec 1897,
p. 9

Chopin, Sallie F. (Moore)
Fitz-Hugh St. Clair
Picayune, 28 Jul 1872,
[p. 11]

Chiles, Rosa Pendleton

Down Among the Crackers
Picayune, 18 Nov 1900,
III, 6

Chittendon, Lucius Eugene
An Unknown Heroine
Picayune, 26 Nov 1893,
p. 16

Christopher, E. Earl
The Invisibles
Outlook, 72:420, 18 Oct
1902

Church, Samuel Harden
John Marmaduke
Athenaeum, 3661:883,
25 Dec 1897
Outlook, 61:602, 11 Mar
1899

Churchill, Winston
The Celebrity
Athenaeum, 3680:597,
7 May 1898
Bookman (NY), 7:254
-55, May 1898
Godey's, 137:106-7,
Jul 1898
Nation, 66:447, 9 Jun
1898
Outlook, 58:639, 5 Mar
1898
Overland, 2d S, 31:477,
May 1898
Picayune, 20 Mar 1898,
p. 17
Sewanee Review, 6:377
-78, Jul 1898
Coniston
Athenaeum, 4109:97,
28 Jul 1906
Atlantic, 99:123, Jan
1907; 101:855, Jun
1908
Bookman (London), 31:48,
Oct 1906
Bookman (NY), 31:251-2,
May 1910
Nation, 83:38-9, 12 Jul
1906

Overland, 2d S, 48:187,
Sep 1906
Saturday Review, 102:305,
8 Sep 1906
Times Literary Supplement,
13 Jul 1906, p. 249
The Crisis
Athenaeum, 3843:784,
22 Jun 1901
Bookman (NY), 13:345-7,
Jun 1901
Nation, 72:513, 27 Jun
1901
Overland, 2d S, 38:152-3,
Aug 1901
Saturday Review, 91:808-9,
22 Jun 1901; 92:280,
31 Aug 1901
Sewanee Review, 9:375-8,
Jul 1901; 9:496, Oct
1901; 11:356, Jul 1903
Times Literary Supplement,
25 Jul 1902, p. 221
The Crossing
Athenaeum, 4009:266,
27 Aug 1904
Atlantic, 94:707, Nov
1904
Bookman (London), 26:176,
Aug 1904
Bookman (NY), 19:607-8,
Aug 1904; 31:250-1,
May 1910
Nation, 79:121, 11 Aug
1904
Saturday Review, 98:115-6,
23 Jul 1904; 98:276,
27 Aug 1904
Times Literary Supplement,
15 Jul 1904, p. 220
Mr. Crewe's Career
Athenaeum, 4207:723,
13 Jun 1908
Bookman (London), 34:152
-53, Jul 1908
Nation, 86:447-8, 14 May
1908
Saturday Review, 105:698,
30 May 1908
South Atlantic Quarterly,
7:391-2, Oct 1908

[Clark, Charlotte (Moon)]
Baby Rue
  Athenaeum, 2814:425-6,
   1 Oct 1881
  Picayune, 7 Aug 1881,
   [p. 2]
The Daughter of the Gods
  By Charles M. Clay
  [pseud.].
  Continent, 5:574,
   (No. 18) 1884
  Manhattan, 3:286-7,
   Mar 1884
How She Came Into Her
  Kingdom
  By Charles M. Clay
  [pseud.].
  Sunday Afternoon, 2:96,
   Jul 1878
The Modern Hagar
  By Charles M. Clay
  [pseud.].
  Atlantic, 51:412-3, Mar
   1883
  Godey's, 106:92, Jan
   1883
  Overland, 2d S, 1:202,
   Feb 1883
  Picayune, 7 Jan 1883,
   [p. 17]; 13 May 1883,
   [p. 15]

Clark, Felicia (Buttz)
Schwester Anna
  Outlook, 58:883, 2 Apr
   1898
  Picayune, 10 Apr 1898,
   p. 25

Clark, Frederick Thickstun
In the Valley of Havilah
  Picayune, 25 May 1890,
   p. 14
A Mexican Girl
  By Frederick Thickstun
  [pseud.].
  Godey's, 117:339, Oct
   1888
  Saturday Review, 66:409
   -10, 6 Oct 1888
The Mistress of the Ranch

  Athenaeum, 3675:434,
   2 Apr 1898
  Saturday Review, 83:588,
   22 May 1897
On Cloud Mountain
  Atlantic, 75:567, Apr
   1895
  Nation, 60:426, 30 May
   1895

[Clark, Hugh A.]
After Many Years
  By Robert Boggs [pseud.].
  Picayune, 26 Sep 1880,
   [p. 12]
A Stepdaughter of Israel
  By Robert Boggs [pseud.].
  Overland, 2d S, 38:155,
   Aug 1901

Clark, Imogen
A Charming Humbug
  Nation, 89:256, 16 Sep
   1909
The Domine's Garden
  Athenaeum, 3848:120,
   27 Jul 1901
  Saturday Review, 92:373,
   21 Sep 1901
God's Puppets
  Canadian Magazine, 17:198,
   Jun 1901
The Victory of Ezry Gardner
  Picayune, 31 May 1896,
   p. 27

Clark, Kate Elizabeth
The Dominant Seventh
  Epoch, 7:174, 18 Apr
   1890
  Nation, 51:195, 4 Sep
   1890
  Saturday Review, 70:425
   -26, 11 Oct 1890

Clark, Kate (Upson)
Up the Witch Brook Road
  Nation, 75:271, 2 Oct
   1902
White Butterflies, and Other
  Stories

Clark, Kate (Upson)
Nation, 70:402, 24 May
1900
Outlook, 65:365, 9 Jun
1900
Picayune, 3 Jun 1900,
III, 7

Clark, Mrs. S. R. Graham
Achor
Picayune, 27 Jul 1884,
[p. 8]

Clark, Susie Champney
Pilate's Query
Picayune, 30 Jun 1895,
p. 21

Clarke, James Freeman
The Legend of Thomas
Didymus
Harper's, 63:315, Jul
1881

[Clarke, Rebecca Sophia]
The Doctor's Daughter
By Sophie May [pseud.].
Harper's, 44:780, Apr
1872
Drone's Honey
By Sophie May [pseud.].
Epoch, 1:541, 15 Jul
1887
Overland, 2d S, 10:328
-29, Sep 1887
Saturday Review, 64:574,
22 Oct 1887
Pauline Wyman
By Sophie May [pseud.].
Picayune, 4 Dec 1898,
II, 4
Wee Lucy's Secret
By Sophie May [pseud.].
Outlook, 63:421, 14 Oct
1899

[Clarke, Sarah J.]
Little Miss Weezy's Sister
By Penn Shirley [pseud.].
Godey's, 120:96, Jan
1890

Clarkson, L. [pseud.].
See Whitelock, Louise
(Clarkson).

Clay, Charles M. [pseud.].
See Clark, Charlotte Moon.

Clay, Grover
Hester of the Hills
Nation, 86:515, 4 Jun
1908
Overland, 2d S, 51:[xii],
Feb 1908

Claytor, Graham
Pleasant Waters
Godey's, 116:394, Apr
1888
Wheat and Tares
Epoch, 5:406, 26 Jul
1889
Godey's, 119:176, Aug
1889
Picayune, 7 Jul 1889,
p. 11

Cleghorn, Sarah N.
A Turnpike Lady
Nation, 85:423, 7 Nov
1907

Clemens, Jere
An American Colonel
Overland, 2d S, 36:88,
Jul 1900

[Clemens, Samuel Langhorne]
The Adventures of Huckle-
berry Finn
By Mark Twain [pseud.].
Athenaeum, 2983:854-5,
27 Dec 1884
Cosmopolitan, 12:638,
Mar 1891
Saturday Review, 59:153
-54, 31 Jan 1885
The Adventures of Tom Sawyer
By Mark Twain [pseud.].
Athenaeum, 2539:851,
24 Jun 1876
Atlantic, 37:621-2, May

1876
Sewanee Review, 11:354,
Jul 1903

The American Claimant
By Mark Twain [pseud.].
Athenaeum, 3407:184,
11 Feb 1893
Bookman (London), 3:60,
Nov 1892

Captain Stormfield's Visit
to Heaven
By Mark Twain [pseud.].
Bookman (NY), 30:323
-24, Dec 1909

A Connecticut Yankee in
King Arthur's Court
By Mark Twain [pseud.].
Athenaeum, 3251:211,
15 Feb 1890
Atlantic, 65:286, Feb
1890
Epoch, 6:840, 31 Jan
1890
Harper's, 80:319-20,
Jan 1890
North American Review,
171:946, Dec 1900

A Dog's Tale
By Mark Twain [pseud.].
Saturday Review, 99:425,
1 Apr 1905

A Double-Barrelled Detective
Story
By Mark Twain [pseud.].
Athenaeum, 3901:152,
2 Aug 1902
Atlantic, 90:415, Sep
1902
Nation, 74:448, 5 Jun
1902
Saturday Review, 94:147,
2 Aug 1902
Times Literary Supplement,
25 Jun 1902, pp. 188-9

Following the Equator
By Mark Twain [pseud.].
Picayune, 30 Jan 1898,
p. 17

A Horse's Tale
By Mark Twain [pseud.].
Bookman (London), 33:74,

Christmas Suppl. ,
Dec 1907
Nation, 85:519, 5 Dec
1907

The Innocents Abroad
By Mark Twain [pseud.].
Athenaeum, 2239:395,
24 Sep 1870
Bookman (NY), 31:374-9,
Jun 1910
Overland, 4:100-1, Jan
1870
Picayune, 16 Jan 1870,
[p. 12]
Saturday Review, 30:467-8,
8 Oct 1870; 63:495,
2 Apr 1887

The Jumping Frog
By Mark Twain [pseud.].
Times Literary Supplement,
16 Sep 1904, p. 283

Life on the Mississippi
By Mark Twain [pseud.].
Athenaeum, 2901:694-5,
2 Jun 1883
Atlantic, 52:406-8, Sep
1883
Harper's, 67:799, Oct
1883
Nation, 37:192, 30 Aug
1883

The Man That Corrupted
Hadleyburg, and Other
Stories and Essays
By Mark Twain [pseud.].
Athenaeum, 3805:410,
29 Sep 1900
Picayune, 8 Jul 1900,
II, 8
Saturday Review, 90:464,
13 Oct 1900

Mark Twain's (Burlesque)
Autobiography
Godey's, 72:575, Jun
1871

Mark Twain's Sketches, New
and Old
Atlantic, 36:749-51, Dec
1875
Saturday Review, 41:154,
29 Jan 1876

[Clemens, Samuel Langhorne]
  Merry Tales
    By Mark Twain [pseud.].
    Atlantic, 70:563, Oct
      1892
    Overland, 2d S, 19:666,
      Jun 1892
  More Tramps Abroad
    By Mark Twain [pseud.].
    Athenaeum, 3661:883-4,
      25 Dec 1897
    Bookman (London),
      13:164, Feb 1898
    Saturday Review, 85:153,
      29 Jan 1898
  The Ł1,000,000 Bank Note,
    and Other Stories
    By Mark Twain [pseud.].
    Athenaeum, 3432:191,
      5 Aug 1893
    Saturday Review, 76:130,
      29 Jul 1893
  Personal Recollections of
    Joan of Arc
    By the Sieur Louis de
    Conte [pseud.].
    Athenaeum, 3589:192,
      8 Aug 1896
    Bookman (London), 10:71,
      Jun 1896
    Bookman (NY), 3:207
      -10, May 1896
  The Prince and the Pauper
    By Mark Twain [pseud.].
    Athenaeum, 2826:849,
      24 Dec 1881
    Atlantic, 48:843-5,
      Dec 1881
    Harper's, 64:634-5,
      Mar 1882
    Rose-Belford's, 8:106-7,
      Jan 1882
    Saturday Review, 52:801,
      24 Dec 1881
  Roughing It
    By Mark Twain [pseud.].
    Sewanee Review, 11:352,
      Jul 1903
  The Stolen White Elephant
    By Mark Twain [pseud.].
    Athenaeum, 2852:793-5,

    24 Jun 1882
    Continent, 2:59, 19 Jul
      1882
    Cottage Hearth, 8:263,
      Aug 1882
    Nation, 35:119, 10 Aug
      1882
  Tom Sawyer Abroad
    By Huck Finn. Ed. Mark
    Twain [pseud.].
    Athenaeum, 3474:676,
      26 May 1894
    Bookman (London), 6:89
      -90, Jun 1894
    Saturday Review, 77:535
      -36, 19 May 1894
  Tom Sawyer, Detective . . .
    and Other Stories
    By Mark Twain [pseud.].
    Athenaeum, 3617:244,
      20 Feb 1897
    Bookman (London), 11:151
      -52, Feb 1897
    Saturday Review, 84:125,
      31 Jul 1897
  The Tragedy of Pudd'nhead
    Wilson
    By Mark Twain [pseud.].
    Athenaeum, 3508:83-4,
      19 Jan 1895
    Bookman (London), 7:122,
      Jan 1895
    Saturday Review, 78:722,
      29 Dec 1894
  A Tramp Abroad
    By Mark Twain [pseud.].
    Athenaeum, 2739:529-30,
      24 Apr 1880
    Atlantic, 45:686-8, May
      1880
    Saturday Review, 49:514
      -15, 17 Apr 1880

  _____, and Charles Warner
    The Gilded Age
    Athenaeum, 2411:53,
      10 Jan 1874
    Saturday Review, 37:223
      -24, 14 Feb 1874

Clement, Clara (Erskine)

See Waters, Clara (Erskine)
Clement.

Clemmer, Mary
See Hudson, Mary (Clemmer).

Cleveland, Cynthia Eloise
His Honor
Picayune, 26 Jan 1890,
p. 10

Cleveland, Rose Elizabeth
The Long Run
Picayune, 18 Jul 1886,
p. 5

Clews, James Blanchard
Fortuna
Picayune, 11 Sep 1898,
II, 3

Clifford, Josephine
See McCrackin, Josephine
(Woempner) Clifford.

Clingham, Clarice Irene
That Girl from Bogata
Godey's, 133:[206],
Aug 1896

Clodfelter, Noah J.
Snatched from the Poor-
House
Cottage Hearth, 14:226,
Jul 1888
Godey's, 116:295, Mar
1888

Clyde, Alton [pseud.].
See Jeffreys, Mrs. Arnold.

[Coates, Joseph Hornor]
The Counterpart
By Hornor Cotes [pseud.].
Nation, 90:289, 24 Mar
1910

Cobb, Sylvanus
Bion, the Wanderer
Picayune, 21 Feb 1892,
p. 10

The Gunmaker of Moscow
Picayune, 23 Sep 1888,
p. 7; 30 Sep 1888,
p. 7

Cody, Sherwin
In the Heart of the Hills
Saturday Review, 82:262
-63, 5 Sep 1896

Coffin, Charles Carleton
Caleb Krinkle
Godey's, 90:287, Mar
1875
Nation, 20:140, 25 Feb
1873

Coffin, Roland Folger
An Old Sailor's Yarns
Saturday Review, 59:26,
3 Jan 1885

Cogswell, Frederick Hull
The Regicides
Picayune, 11 Oct 1896,
p. 11

Cohen, Alfred J.
Conscience on Ice
By Alan Dale [pseud.].
Picayune, 25 Sep 1892,
p. 13
Miss Innocence
By Alan Dale [pseud.].
Picayune, 4 Oct 1891,
p. 10
Wanted: A Cook
By Alan Dale [pseud.].
Overland, 2d S, 45:87,
Jan 1905

[Colburn, Frona Eunice Wait
(Smith)]
Yermah, the Dorado
By Frona Eunice Wait
[pseud.].
Bookman (NY), 7:168,
Apr 1898

Cole, Cyrus
The Auroraphone

Cole, Cyrus
    America, 6:304-5,
      11 Jun 1891

[Cole, William Morse]
    An Old Man's Romance
    By Christopher Craigie
    [pseud.].
      Atlantic, 76:566, Oct
        1895
      Poet-Lore, 8:41, (No. 1)
        1896

Colestock, Henry Thomas
    The Ministry of David Bald-
    win
      Nation, 84:341, 11 Apr
        1907
      Overland, 2d S, 49:xx,
        Jun 1907

Collier, Price
    See McVickar, Henry Goelet,
    and Price Collier.

Collingwood, Herbert Winslow
    Andersonville Violets
      Cottage Hearth, 15:56,
        Feb 1889
      Overland, 2d S, 13:215
        -16, Feb 1889

Collins, Mrs. E. Burke
    A Modern Heathen
      Picayune, 17 May 1896,
        p. 15

Colson, Ethel Maude
    See Brazelton, Ethel Maude
    (Colson).

Coltharp, Mrs. Jeannette
Downes
    Burrill Coleman, Colored
      Picayune, 20 Dec 1896,
        p. 20

Colton, Arthur Willis
    The Belted Seas
      Atlantic, 97:46, Jan
        1906

      Nation, 80:442, 1 Jun
        1905
      Sewanee Review, 14:107,
        Jan 1906
    The Cruise of the Violetta
      Nation, 83:396, 8 Nov
        1906
      Sewanee Review, 15:249
        -50, Apr 1907
    Port Argent
      Sewanee Review, 13:119,
        Jan 1905
    Tioba
      Bookman (NY), 17:259,
        May 1903

Comer, Cornelia Atwood (Pratt)
    A Book of Martyrs
      Picayune, 8 Nov 1896,
        p. 6
    The Daughter of a Stoic
      Picayune, 21 Jun 1896,
        p. 16
      Overland, 2d S, 28:605,
        Nov 1896

Comfort, Will Levington
    Routledge Rides Alone
      Nation, 91:242, 15 Sep
        1910

[Comins, Elizabeth Barker]
    The Hartwell Farm
    By Laura Caxton [pseud.].
      Godey's, 84:385, Apr
        1872

Compton, Frances Snow [pseud.].
    See Adams, Henry.

Comstock, Harriet Theresa
(Nichols)
    Janet of the Dunes
      Bookman (NY), 27:101,
        Mar 1908
      Nation, 86:129, 6 Feb
        1908

Connelley, Celia (Logan)
Kellogg
    Her Strange Fate

Atlantic, 64:143-4,
Jul 1889

Connelly, Emma Mary
Under the Surface
Godey's, 87:476, Nov
1873
Picayune, 14 Sep 1873,
[p. 3]

Connelly, James H.
Neila Sen
Picayune, 26 Oct 1890,
p. 10

Connery, Thomas Bernard
Joseph
All the Dog's Fault
Godey's, 127:234, Aug
1893
In the Mafia's Clutches
Picayune, 31 May 1891,
p. 12
That Noble Mexican
Overland, 2d S, 31:383,
Apr 1898

Connor, Ralph [pseud.].
See Gordon, Charles William.

Conrad, Stephen [pseud.].
See Stimtz, Stephen Conrad.

Conrad, Thomas N.
A Confederate Spy
Godey's, 126:100, Jan
1893

Converse, Florence
The Burdens of Christopher
Picayune, 27 May 1900,
III, 7
Diana Victrix
Picayune, 24 Oct 1897,
p. 9
Long Will
Saturday Review, 97:52
-53, 9 Jan 1904

Conway, Clara L.
Life's Promise to Pay

Picayune, 25 Jun 1876,
[p. 3]

Conway, Moncure Daniel
Pine and Palm
Athenaeum, 3135:707,
26 Nov 1887
Epoch, 2:375, 16 Dec
1887
Nation, 46:219, 15 Mar
1888
North American Review,
146:479-80, Apr 1888
Saturday Review, 65:19,
7 Jan 1888
Prisons of Air
Nation, 54:154, 25 Feb
1892
Picayune, 26 Jul 1891,
p. 11

Conyngham, Dane [pseud.].
See Curran, Mrs. L. P. M.

Cook, George Cram
Roderick Taliaferro
Athenaeum, 3977:77,
16 Jan 1904
Overland, 2d S, 41:472-3,
Jun 1903
Sewanee Review, 12:125,
Jan 1904

Cook, Grace Louise
Wellesley Stories
Nation, 72:280, 4 Apr
1901

Cook, Mary Louise (Redd)
A Woman's Perils
Godey's, 105:284, Sep
1882
Picayune, 23 Jul 1882,
[p. 2]

Cook, Mrs. James C.
See Cook, Mary Louise (Redd).

Cooke, Grace (McGowan)
The Grapple
Outlook, 81:279, 30 Sep

Cooke, Grace (McGowan)
1905
Overland, 2d S, 46:589,
Dec 1905
The Power and the Glory
Nation, 91:241, 15 Sep
1910

_____, and Alice McGowan
Aunt Huldah
Bookman (London), 27:91
-92, Nov 1904
Overland, 2d S, 44:385,
Sep 1904
Return
Athenaeum, 4071:607,
4 Nov 1905
Canadian Magazine,
25:89-90, May 1905
Nation, 80:378-9, 11
May 1905
Overland, 2d S, 45:565,
Jun 1905
Times Literary Supplement,
6 Oct 1905, p. 329

_____, and Annie Booth
McKinney
Mistress Joy
Overland, 2d S, 39:733,
Mar 1902
Sewanee Review, 10:117
-18, Jan 1902; 11:364,
Jul 1903

Cooke, John Esten
Beatrice Hallam
Picayune, 12 Feb 1893,
p. 16
Bonnybell Vane
Harper's, 68:975,
May 1884
Canolles
Atlantic, 40:631-2,
Nov 1877
Nation, 25:185, 20 Sep
1877
Doctor Vandyke
Godey's, 85:467, Nov
1872
Fanchette

By One of Her Admirers.
Continent, 3:700, 30 May
1883
Cottage Hearth, 9:189,
Jun 1883
Nation, 36:406, 10 May
1883
Saturday Review, 55:678,
26 May 1883
Heir of Graymount
Harper's, 41:787, Oct
1870
Her Majesty the Queen
Godey's, 87:188, Aug
1873
Picayune, 1 Jun 1873,
[p. 2]
Justin Harley
Saturday Review, 38:840,
26 Dec 1874
The Maurice Mystery
Godey's, 111:403, Oct
1885
Overland, 2d S, 6:549,
Nov 1885
Mr. Grantley's Idea
Harper's, 59:475, Aug
1879
Mohun
Picayune, 9 Feb 1890,
p. 11
My Lady Pokahontas
By Anas Todkill [pseud.].
Nation, 40:266, 26 Mar
1885
Overland, 2d S, 5:431,
Apr 1885
Out of the Foam
Godey's, 72:479, May
1871
Overland, 6:388, Apr
1871
Pretty Mrs. Gaston, and
Other Stories
Atlantic, 34:231, Aug
1874
Nation, 18:336, 21 May
1874
Professor Pressensee
Picayune, 22 Sep 1878,
[p. 2]

The Virginia Bohemian
  Atlantic, 46:827-8,
    Dec 1880
  Rose-Belford's, 5:217
    -18, Aug 1880
The Virginia Comedians
  Godey's, 106:574, Jun
    1883
  Nation, 36:406, 10 May
    1883

Cooke, Rose Terry
  Huckleberries Gathered from
    New England Hills
    Atlantic, 69:268-9,
      Feb 1892
    Epoch, 10:356, 1 Jan
      1892
    Harper's, 84:479, Feb
      1892
    Nation, 53:512, 31 Dec
      1891
    Overland, 2d S, 20:660,
      Dec 1892
  Somebody's Neighbors
    Nation, 33:257-8, 29 Sep
      1881
  The Sphinx's Children, and
    Other People's
    Nation, 43:15, 1 Jul
      1886
    Saturday Review, 61:890,
      26 Jun 1886
  Steadfast
    Atlantic, 63:720, May
      1889
    Epoch, 5:180-1, 19 Apr
      1889
    Harper's, 78:986-7,
      May 1889
    Nation, 48:472, 6 Jun
      1889
    Saturday Review, 68:383
      -84, 15 Oct 1889

Cooley, Alice (Kingsbury)
  Asaph
    Epoch, 9:286, 5 Jun
      1891
    Picayune, 19 Apr 1891,
      p. 15

Cooley, William Forbes
  Emmanuel
    Atlantic, 65:576, Apr
      1890; 66:698-9, Nov
      1890

Coolidge, Erwin L.
  A Maine Girl
    Picayune, 7 Aug 1892,
      p. 11

Coolidge, Susan [pseud.].
  See Woolsey, Mrs. Sarah C.

[Coombs, Anne (Sheldon)]
  As Common Mortals
    Athenaeum, 3086:822,
      18 Dec 1886
    Picayune, 1 Aug 1886,
      p. 15
    Saturday Review, 63:230,
      12 Feb 1887
  A Game of Chance
    Godey's, 115:261, Sep
      1887
    Nation, 45:403, 17 Nov
      1877
  The Garden of Armida
    Picayune, 15 Dec 1889,
      p. 11

Cooper, Samuel Williams
  Think and Thank
    Picayune, 28 Sep 1890,
      p. 13
  Three Days
    Epoch, 5:406, 26 Jul
      1889
    Godey's, 119:258, Sep
      1889
    Picayune, 11 Aug 1889,
      p. 11

Corbin, Caroline (Fairfield)
  His Marriage Vow
    Godey's, 78:91, Jan
      1874
    Harper's, 48:450, Feb
      1874
    Nation, 18:79, 29 Jan
      1874

Corbin, Caroline (Fairfield)
Picayune, 25 Oct 1891,
p. 3
Saturday Review, 37:286,
28 Feb 1874
Rebecca
Nation, 26:66, 24 Jan
1878

Corbin, John
The Cave Man
Nation, 84:457, 16 May
1907

Cornell, Hughes
Kenelm's Desire
Overland, 2d S, 49:[276],
Mar 1907; 49:xxvi,
May 1907

Cornish, William W. M.
Behind Plastered Walls
Picayune, 6 Sep 1896,
p. 9

Cornwall, C. M. [pseud.].
See Roe, Mary Abigail.

Cornwallis, Kinahan
Adrift with a Vengeance
Godey's, 72:193, Feb
1871
Picayune, 27 Nov 1870,
[p. 11]
A Marvellous Coincidence
Picayune, 25 Oct 1891,
p. 3

Cory, Charles Barney
Montezuma's Castle, and
Other Weird Tales
Outlook, 63:934, 16 Dec
1899

Cotes, Hornor [pseud.].
See Coates, Joseph Hornor.

[Coulson, George James Atkin-
son]
The Clifton Picture
Godey's, 97:171, Aug

1878
The Ghost of Redbrook
Godey's, 99:182, Aug
1879
Picayune, 15 Jun 1879,
[p. 10]
The Odd Trump
Nation, 21:107, 12 Aug
1875
Picayune, 20 Jun 1875,
[p. 6]

Coulter, John
Mr. Desmond, U. S. A.
Nation, 43:272, 30 Sep
1886

Coventry, John [pseud.].
See Palmer, John Williamson.

Cowan, John Franklin
Endeavor Doin's Down to the
Corners
Atlantic, 74:848, Dec
1894

[Cowdrey, Robert H.]
Foiled
By a Lawyer.
Cottage Hearth, 12:60,
Feb 1886
A Tramp in Society
By a Lawyer.
Picayune, 31 May 1891,
p. 12

[Cowles, M. L.]
Redbank
Picayune, 16 Apr 1893,
p. 21

[Cozzens, Samuel Woodworth]
Nobody's Husband
By Nobody Knows Who.
Rose-Belford's, 1:384,
Sep 1878
Sunday Afternoon, 2:384,
Oct 1878

Crabtrie, N. Warrington [pseud.].
See James, Samuel Humphreys.

Craddock, Charles Egbert
[pseud.].
See Murfree, Mary Noailles.

Craddock, Florence Nightingale
Edgar Fairfax
Picayune, 6 Sep 1896,
p. 9
The Twin Sisters
Picayune, 8 Mar 1896,
p. 25

Craigie, Christopher [pseud.].
See Cole, William Morse.

Cram, George
Minette
Overland, 2d S, 39:665,
Feb 1902

Cram, Ralph Adams
Black Spirits & White
Atlantic, 78:847, Dec
1896
Bookman (London),
10:57-8, May 1896
Nation, 62:182, 27 Feb
1896

Crane, James Lyons
The Two Circuits
Atlantic, 41:404, Mar
1878

Crane, Stephen
Active Service
Athenaeum, 3759:650-1,
11 Nov 1899
Bookman (London), 17:89,
Dec 1899
Bookman (NY), 10:501,
Jan 1900
Nation, 69:413, 30 Nov
1899
Outlook, 63:463, 21 Oct
1899
Picayune, 4 Dec 1899,
p. 10
Saturday Review, 88:xii,
Suppl. , 9 Dec 1899
Bowery Tales

Saturday Review, 90:213
-14, 18 Aug 1900
George's Mother
Athenaeum, 3583:842,
27 Jun 1896
Bookman (NY), 3:446-7,
Jul 1896
Godey's, 133:[317]-9,
Sep 1896
Nation, 63:15, 2 Jul
1896
North American Review,
171:235-6, Aug 1900
Picayune, 14 Jun 1896,
p. 19
Saturday Review, 82:262
-63, 5 Sep 1896
The Little Regiment, and
Other Episodes of the
American Civil War
Athenaeum, 3617:245,
20 Feb 1897
Bookman (London),
11:179-80, Mar 1897
Maggie, a Girl of the Streets
Athenaeum, 3600:562,
24 Oct 1896
Bookman (London),
11:19-20, Oct 1896
Bookman (NY), 1:229,
May 1895
Godey's, 131:[430]-2,
Oct 1895; 133:[317]-9,
Sep 1896
Nation, 63:15, 2 Jul
1896
North American Review,
171:235-6, Aug 1900
Quarterly Review,
196:411-2, Oct 1902
Saturday Review, 82:655,
19 Dec 1896
The Monster, and Other
Stories
Athenaeum, 3829:334,
16 Mar 1901
Bookman (London), 20:26,
Apr 1901
Picayune, 31 Dec 1899,
II, 7
Saturday Review, 91:308-9,

Crane, Stephen
9 Mar 1901
The Open Boat, and Other
Tales of Adventure
Athenaeum, 3680:597,
7 May 1898
Outlook, 59:134, 14 May
1898
Saturday Review, 85:785,
11 Jun 1898
Pictures of War
Saturday Review, 86:280,
27 Aug 1898
The Red Badge of Courage
Atlantic, 77:422, Mar
1896
Bookman (London), 9:131,
Jan 1896
Bookman (NY), 2:219-
20, Nov 1895
Godey's, 133:[317]-9,
Sep 1896
Nation, 63:15, 2 Jul
1896
North American Review,
171:234-6, Aug 1900
Overland, 2d S, 28:235,
Aug 1896
Saturday Review, 81:44-
45, 11 Jan 1896
The Third Violet
Athenaeum, 3630:678,
22 May 1897
Bookman (London), 12:72,
Jun 1897
Bookman (NY), 5:436,
Jul 1897
Godey's, 135:[331], Sep
1897
Picayune, 20 Jun 1897,
p. 16
Whilomville Stories
Athenaeum, 3814:722,
1 Dec 1900
Bookman (NY), 12:165,
Oct 1900
Nation, 72:182, 28 Feb
1901
Picayune, 9 Sep 1900,
II, 8
Wounds in the Rain

Athenaeum, 3805:410,
29 Sep 1900
Nation, 71:430, 29 Nov
1900
Outlook, 66:519, 27 Oct
1900
Picayune, 14 Oct 1900,
II, 8
Saturday Review, 90:831,
29 Dec 1900

_____, and Robert Barr
The O'Ruddy
Athenaeum, 4007:200,
13 Aug 1904
Saturday Review, 98:177,
6 Aug 1904

Crane, Walter Beverley
Odd Tales
Outlook, 66:182, 15 Sep
1900

Crawford, Francis Marion
Adam Johnstone's Son
Athenaeum, 3579:709-10,
30 May 1896
Bookman (London), 10:87,
Jun 1896
Bookman (NY), 3:456-7,
Jul 1896
Godey's, 133:96, Jul
1896
Overland, 2d S, 28:233,
Aug 1896
Picayune, 17 May 1896,
p. 15
Saturday Review, 81:608,
13 Jun 1896
An American Politician
Athenaeum, 2980:730-1,
6 Dec 1884
Atlantic, 55:130-2, Jan
1885
Nation, 40:58-9, 15 Jan
1885
Overland, 2d S, 5:107,
Jan 1885
Picayune, 14 Dec 1884,
[p. 9]
Saturday Review, 59:217,

14 Feb 1885
Sewanee Review, 2:239,
Feb 1894
Arethusa
Athenaeum, 4177:613,
16 Nov 1907
Bookman (London), 33:91-
92, Nov 1907
Bookman (NY), 26:268-9,
Nov 1907
Nation, 85:496, 28 Nov
1907
Saturday Review, 104:vii-
viii, Suppl., 19 Oct
1907
Times Literary Supple-
ment, 10 Oct 1907,
p. 309
Casa Braccio
Athenaeum, 3556:866,
21 Dec 1895
Atlantic, 78:426, Sep
1896
Bookman (NY), 2:318-20,
Dec 1895
Overland, 2d S, 27:238,
Feb 1896
Picayune, 22 Nov 1895,
p. 9
Cecilia
Athenaeum, 3917:679,
22 Nov 1902
Bookman (NY), 16:378-80,
Dec 1902
Saturday Review, 95:i-ii,
Suppl., 10 Jan 1903
Sewanee Review, 11:111,
Jan 1903
Times Literary Supple-
ment, 7 Nov 1903,
p. 331
The Children of the King
Athenaeum, 3410:277,
4 Mar 1893
Atlantic, 71:849, Jun
1893
Bookman (London), 3:190,
Mar 1893
Cottage Hearth, 19:195,
Apr 1893
Godey's, 126:500, Apr

1893
Nation, 56:297, 20 Apr 1893
Picayune, 5 Mar 1893,
p. 16
Saturday Review, 75:381,
8 Apr 1893
Sewanee Review, 2:239,
Feb 1894
A Cigarette-Maker's Romance
Athenaeum, 3287:539, 25
Oct 1890
Atlantic, 67:126, Jan 1891
Bookman (NY), 26:134-5,
Oct 1907
Nation, 51:506, 25 Dec 1890
Saturday Review, 70:563-4,
15 Nov 1890
Sewanee Review, 2:239,
Feb 1894
Corleone
Athenaeum, 3659:817, 11
Dec 1897
Atlantic, 83:130-1, Jan 1899
Bookman (NY), 6:243-4,
Nov 1897
Godey's, 136:104, Jan 1898
Nation, 66:53, 20 Jan 1898
Overland, 2d S, 31:474-5,
May 1898
Saturday Review, 84:527-8,
13 Nov 1897
The Diva's Ruby
Athenaeum, 4229:602, 14
Nov 1908
Bookman (NY), 28:261-2,
Nov 1908
Nation, 87:466, 12 Nov 1908
Times Literary Supplement,
19 Nov 1908, p. 417
Doctor Claudius
Athenaeum, 2902:727, 9
Jun 1883
Continent, 4:254, 22 Aug
1883
Harper's, 67:641, Sep 1883
Manhattan, 2:91-2, Jul 1883
Nation, 36:553-4, 28 Jun
1883
Saturday Review, 55:844-5,
30 Jun 1883
Sewanee Review, 2:239,

Crawford, Francis Marion
Feb 1894
Don Orsino
Athenaeum, 3395:699,
19 Nov 1892
Bookman (London), 3:90-1,
Dec 1892
Cottage Hearth, 18:411,
Dec 1892
Godey's, 126:100, Jan
1893
Nation, 56:15-6, 5 Jan
1893
Picayune, 4 Dec 1892,
p. 8
Poet-Lore, 5:165, (No. 1)
1893
Sewanee Review, 1:254,
Feb 1893; 2:239, Feb
1894
Fair Margaret
Bookman (NY), 22:373,
Dec 1905
Greifenstein
Athenaeum, 3208:501,
20 Apr 1889
Epoch, 5:212, 3 May
1889
Nation, 48:529-30, 27
Jun 1889
Picayune, 28 Apr 1889,
p. 10
Saturday Review, 67:539,
4 May 1889
Sewanee Review, 2:239,
Feb 1894
The Heart of Rome
Athenaeum, 3968:646,
14 Nov 1903
Bookman (NY), 18:412-3,
Dec 1903
Nation, 77:391, 12 Nov
1903
Saturday Review, 96:582,
7 Nov 1903
Times Literary Supple-
ment, 16 Oct 1903,
p. 297
In the Palace of the King
Athenaeum, 3810:577,
3 Nov 1900

Bookman (London), 19:91,
Dec 1900
Bookman (NY), 12:347-8,
Dec 1900
Nation, 72:97, 31 Jan 1901
Picayune, 2 Dec 1900, II,
9
Saturday Review, 91:84-5,
19 Jan 1901; 91:344, 16
Mar 1901
Katharine Lauderdale
Athenaeum, 3469:505-6,
21 Apr 1894
Atlantic, 74:416, Sep 1894
Canadian Magazine, 3:196,
Jun 1894
Godey's, 129:221-2, Aug
1894
Nation, 58:488, 28 Jun 1894
Overland, 2d S, 23:665,
Jun 1894
Saturday Review, 78:300,
15 Sep 1894
Khaled
Athenaeum, 3319:728, 6
Jun 1891
Atlantic, 68:709-10, Nov
1891
Epoch, 9:382, 17 Jul 1891
Nation, 53:264, 1 Oct 1891
Overland, 2d S, 19:332,
Mar 1892
Picayune, 21 Jun 1891, p.
12
Saturday Review, 71:748,
20 Jun 1891
Sewanee Review, 2:239,
Feb 1894
A Lady of Rome
Athenaeum, 4124:577-8,
10 Nov 1906
Bookman (NY), 24:388-9,
Dec 1906
Nation, 83:417, 15 Nov
1906
Saturday Review, 102:522,
27 Oct 1906
Times Literary Supplement,
26 Oct 1906, p. 360
The Little City of Hope
Bookman (NY), 26:556,

Jan 1908

Love in Idleness

Atlantic, 76:707, Nov 1895

Bookman (London), 7:56, Nov 1894

Nation, 60:96, 31 Jan 1895

Picayune, 11 Nov 1894, p. 11

Saturday Review, 78:419, 13 Oct 1894

Marietta

Athenaeum, 3865:695, 23 Nov 1901

Bookman (London), 21:98, Dec 1901

Bookman (NY), 15:198, Apr 1902

Canadian Magazine, 17:582, Oct 1901; 17:290-291, Jan 1902

Nation, 74:117, 6 Feb 1902

Marion Darche

Athenaeum, 3446:658, 11 Nov 1893

Atlantic, 74:278, Aug 1894

Bookman (London), 5:88, Dec 1893

Godey's, 128:107, Jan 1894

Nation, 58:277, 12 Apr 1894

Picayune, 19 Nov 1893, p. 14

Saturday Review, 77:16-7, 6 Jan 1894

Sewanee Review, 2:239, Feb 1894

Marzio's Crucifix

Athenaeum, 3131:565, 29 Oct 1887

Atlantic, 61:847-8, Jun 1888

Nation, 46:142, 16 Feb 1888

North American Review, 145:700-1, Dec 1887

Picayune, 20 Nov 1887,

p. 15

Saturday Review, 64:632-3, 5 Nov 1887

Sewanee Review, 2:239, Feb 1894

Mr. Isaacs

Athenaeum, 2877:809-10, 16 Dec 1882

Atlantic, 51:408-11, Mar 1883

Continent, 3:188, 7 Feb 1883

Nation, 36:152, 15 Feb 1883

Picayune, 22 Sep 1895, p. 8

Saturday Review, 55:215-7, 17 Feb 1883

Paul Patoff

Athenaeum, 3138:821, 17 Dec 1887

Cottage Hearth, 14:24, Jan 1888

Epoch, 2:456, 13 Jan 1888

Godey's, 116:191, Feb 1888

Nation, 46:141, 16 Feb 1888

Overland, 2d S, 11:440-1, Apr 1888

Saturday Review, 65:77, 21 Jan 1888

Sewanee Review, 2:239, Feb 1894

Pietro Ghisleri

Athenaeum, 3430:125, 22 Jul 1893

Atlantic, 72:693-5, Nov 1893

Bookman (London), 4:153-4, Aug 1893

Cottage Hearth, 19:397, Aug 1893

Godey's, 127:618, Nov 1893

Nation, 57:374, 16 Nov 1893

Picayune, 16 Jul 1893, p. 19

Saturday Review, 76:242-3, 26 Aug 1893

Sewanee Review, 2:239, Feb 1894

The Primadonna

Crawford, Francis Marion
    Athenaeum, 4200:505,
      25 Apr 1908
    Bookman (NY), 27:396,
      Jun 1908
    Nation, 86:536, 11 Jun
      1908
    Saturday Review, 105:601,
      9 May 1908
    Times Literary Supple-
      ment, 19 Mar 1908,
      pp. 93-4
The Ralstons
    Athenaeum, 3510:146,
      2 Feb 1895
    Bookman (London), 7:155,
      Feb 1895
    Bookman (NY), 1:50,
      Feb 1895
    Overland, 2d S, 25:687-8,
      Jun 1895
    Picayune, 15 Oct 1899,
      II, 7
    Saturday Review, 79:195,
      9 Feb 1895
A Roman Singer
    Atlantic, 54:421-2, Sep
      1884
    Continent, 5:831, (No. 26)
      1884
    Cottage Hearth, 19:195,
      Apr 1893
    Manhattan, 4:375-7,
      Sep 1884
    Nation, 38:531-2, 19 Jun
      1884
    Overland, 2d S, 4:105,
      Jul 1884
    Picayune, 8 Jun 1884,
      [p. 5]; 9 Apr 1893,
      p. 24
    Saturday Review, 58:118-9,
      26 Jul 1884
    Sewanee Review, 2:239,
      Feb 1894
A Rose of Yesterday
    Athenaeum, 3633:772,
      12 Jun 1897
    Bookman (London), 12:99-
      100, Jul 1897
    Bookman (NY), 5:523-4,

      Aug 1897
    Godey's, 135:445, Oct 1897
    Nation, 66:53, 20 Jan 1898
    Picayune, 5 Jul 1897, p.
      9
The Rulers of the South
    Bookman (NY), 12:579-80,
      Feb 1901
Sant' Ilario
    America, 2:791, 19 Sep
      1889
    Athenaeum, 3225:218, 17
      Aug 1889
    Atlantic, 65:122-3, Jan
      1890
    Epoch, 6:646, 8 Nov 1889
    Godey's, 119:444, Nov
      1889
    Nation, 50:16, 2 Jan 1890
    Overland, 2d S, 26:223,
      Aug 1895
    Picayune, 1 Sep 1889, p.
      7; 26 May 1895, p. 16
    Saturday Review, 68:246-7,
      31 Aug 1889
    Sewanee Review, 2:239, Feb
      1894
Saracinesca
    Athenaeum, 3104:542, 23
      Apr 1887
    Atlantic, 60:413-4, Sep
      1887
    Cottage Hearth, 18:287,
      Sep 1892
    Epoch, 1:456-7, 17 Jun
      1887
    Nation, 44:532-3, 23 Jun
      1887
    North American Review,
      145:220, Aug 1887
    Picayune, 15 May 1887, p.
      15; 3 Jul 1892, p. 19
    Saturday Review, 63:589,
      23 Apr 1887
    Sewanee Review, 2:239,
      Feb 1894
Soprano: a Portrait
    Athenaeum, 4075:758, 2
      Dec 1905
    Times Literary Supplement,
      17 Nov 1905, p. 396

Stradella
 Athenaeum, 4275:388,
  2 Oct 1909
 Bookman (London), 37:160,
  Dec 1909
 Bookman (NY), 30:281,
  Nov 1909
 Nation, 89:329, 7 Oct
  1909
 Outlook, 93:317, 9 Oct
  1909
 Saturday Review, 108:636,
  20 Nov 1909
 Times Literary Supple-
  ment, 23 Sep 1909,
  p. 346
A Tale of a Lonely Parish
 Athenaeum, 3048:421,
  27 Mar 1886
 Atlantic, 57:850-7, Jun
  1886
 Godey's, 133:96, Jul 1896
 Nation, 43:15, 1 Jul 1886
 Picayune, 11 Apr 1886,
  p. 14; 2 Mar 1896,
  p. 6
 Saturday Review, 61:621,
  1 May 1886
 Sewanee Review, 2:239,
  Feb 1894
Taquisara
 Athenaeum, 3604:712,
  21 Nov 1896
 Bookman (London), 11:96-7,
  Dec 1896
 Bookman (NY), 4:460-1,
  Jan 1897
 Godey's, 134:204, Feb
  1897
 Nation, 66:53, 20 Jan
  1898
 Overland, 2d S, 29:107,
  Jan 1897
 Picayune, 20 Dec 1896,
  p. 20
The Three Fates
 Athenaeum, 3367:598,
  7 May 1892
 Atlantic, 69:848, Jun
  1892
 Bookman (London), 2:58-9,

 May 1892
 Cottage Hearth, 18:255,
  Aug 1892
 Nation, 54:451, 16 Jun 1892
 Overland, 2d S, 20:441,
  Oct 1892
 Picayune, 1 May 1892, p.
  12
 Saturday Review, 73:542,
  7 May 1892
 Sewanee Review, 2:239,
  Feb 1894
To Leeward
 Athenaeum, 2930:812, 22
  Dec 1883
 Atlantic, 53:277-9, Feb
  1884
 Continent, 5:381, (No. 12)
  1884
 Cottage Hearth, 10:62, Feb
  1884; 19:295, Jun 1893
 Nation, 38:193, 28 Feb 1884
 Picayune, 30 Apr 1893, p.
  21
 Saturday Review, 57:87, 19
  Jan 1884
 Sewanee Review, 2:239,
  Feb 1894
The Undesirable Governess
 Athenaeum, 4309:635, 28
  May 1910
 Bookman (NY), 31:523-4,
  Jul 1910
 Nation, 90:483-4, 12 May
  1910
The Upper Berth
 Atlantic, 74:278-9, Aug
  1894
Via Crucis
 Athenaeum, 3765:861, 23
  Dec 1899
 Bookman (London), 17:119,
  Jan 1900
 Bookman (NY), 11:92-3,
  Mar 1900
 Nation, 69:396, 23 Nov
  1899
 Outlook, 63:742, 25 Nov
  1899
 Picayune, 10 Dec 1899, III,
  7

Crawford, Francis Marion
  Saturday Review, 89:23,
    6 Jan 1900
  Sewanee Review, 14:157,
    Apr 1906
  The White Sister
    Athenaeum, 4255:581,
      15 May 1909
    Atlantic, 104:679, Nov
      1909
    Bookman (London), 36:139-
      140, Jun 1909
    Bookman (NY), 29:401,
      Jun 1909
    Canadian Magazine, 33:376,
      Aug 1909
    Nation, 88:514, 20 May
      1909
    North American Review,
      190:120-1, Jul 1909
    Saturday Review, 107:757,
      12 Jun 1909
  Whosoever Shall Offend
    Athenaeum, 4020:653,
      12 Nov 1904
    Atlantic, 95:695, May
      1905
    Bookman (London), 27:91,
      Nov 1904
    Bookman (NY), 20:364,
      Dec 1904
    Nation, 80:98, 2 Feb
      1905
    Poet-Lore, 15:143, Winter
      1904
    Saturday Review, 98:673,
      26 Nov 1904
    Times Literary Supple-
      ment, 14 Oct 1904,
      p. 312
  The Witch of Prague
    Athenaeum, 3330:251-2,
      22 Aug 1891
    Bookman, 1:37, Oct 1891
    Epoch, 10:370, 8 Jan
      1892
    Nation, 53:395, 19 Nov
      1891
    Overland, 2d S, 19:332,
      Mar 1892
    Picayune, 4 Oct 1891,

      p. 10
    Saturday Review, 72:364-5,
      26 Sep 1891
    Sewanee Review, 2:239,
      Feb 1894
  With the Immortals
    Athenaeum, 3170:126-7,
      28 Jul 1888
    Nation, 47:459, 6 Dec 1888
    Saturday Review, 66:149,
      4 Aug 1888
    Sewanee Review, 2:239,
      Feb 1894
  Zoroaster
    Athenaeum, 3006:723, 6
      Jun 1885
    Atlantic, 56:561-2, Oct
      1885
    Nation, 41:158, 2 Aug 1885
    Overland, 2d S, 6:323-6,
      Sep 1885
    Picayune, 26 Jul 1885,
      [p. 10]
    Saturday Review, 60:325,
      5 Sep 1885
    Sewanee Review, 2:239,
      Feb 1894

Crawford, Oswald [pseud.].
  See Harris, William Richard.

Creelman, James
  Eagle Blood
    Bookman (NY), 16:500-1,
      Jan 1903

[Crim, Martha Jane]
  Adventures of a Fair Rebel
    By Matt Crim [pseud.].
    Atlantic, 69:711, May
      1892
    Nation, 53:512, 31 Dec
      1891
    Picayune, 15 Nov 1891,
      p. 10
  Elizabeth, Christian Scientist
    By Matt Crim [pseud.].
    Atlantic, 72:704, Nov 1893
    Godey's, 127:105-6, Jul
      1893
    Nation, 56:408, 1 Jun 1893

Overland, 2d S, 23:219,
Feb 1894
Picayune, 16 Apr 1893,
p. 21
In Beaver Cove and Else-
where
By Matt Crim [pseud.].
Picayune, 3 Apr 1892,
p. 13

Crim, Matt [pseud.].
See Crim, Martha Jane.

Crinkle, Nym [pseud.].
See Wheeler, Andrew Car-
penter.

Crockett, R. D.
Love Idylls
Bookman (NY), 14:532-3,
Jan 1902

Crockett, S. R.
See Tales of Our Coast.

Crosby, Ernest
Captain Jinks, Hero
Overland, 2d S, 39:918,
May 1902

Crosby, George S.
The Mystery
Godey's, 91:284, Sep
1875

Crouch, Julia
Three Successful Girls
Overland, 7:101, Jul
1871
Picayune, 30 Apr 1871,
[p. 9]

Crowninshield, Mary (Bradford)
Among the Lighthouses
Godey's, 115:515, Dec
1887
The Archbishop and the Lady
Athenaeum, 3843:784,
22 Jun 1901
Bookman (London), 20:125,
Jul 1901

Bookman (NY), 13:78,
Mar 1901
Nation, 72:280, 4 Apr 1901
Latitude 19°
Nation, 68:358, 11 May
1899
San Isidro
Bookman (NY), 10:599,
Feb 1900
Nation, 70:77, 25 Jan 1900
Picayune, 17 Dec 1899, III,
8
Valencia's Garden
Bookman (NY), 14:97, Sep
1901
Nation, 73:15, 4 Jul 1901
Where the Trade-Wind Blows
Bookman (NY), 7:352, Jun
1898
Outlook, 58:489, 19 Feb
1898

Crowninshield, Mrs. Schuyler
See Crowninshield, Mary
(Bradford).

[Cruger, Julie Grinnell (Storrow)]
A Diplomat's Diary
By Julien Gordon [pseud.].
Athenaeum, 3295:850, 20
Dec 1890
Cosmopolitan, 10:766, Apr
1891
Picayune, 7 Sep 1890, p.
13
Saturday Review, 70:740,
27 Dec 1890
His Letters
By Julien Gordon [pseud.].
Godey's, 127:105, Jul 1893
Picayune, 21 May 1893, p.
23; 13 Jun 1897, p. 22
Mademoiselle Réséda
By Julien Gordon [pseud.].
Cosmopolitan, 10:766-7,
Apr 1891
Epoch, 11:13, 5 Feb 1892
Marionettes
By Julien Gordon [pseud.].
Athenaeum, 3406:150, 4
Feb 1893

[Cruger, Julie Grinnell (Storrow)]
Atlantic, 70:419-20,
Sep 1892
Mrs. Clyde
By Julien Gordon [pseud.].
Athenaeum, 3904:250,
23 Aug 1902
Poppaea
By Julien Gordon [pseud.].
Athenaeum, 3542:351,
14 Sep 1895
Saturday Review, 80:322,
7 Sep 1895
A Puritan Pagan
By Julien Gordon [pseud.].
America, 6:640-1, 27
Aug 1891
Saturday Review, 78:102,
28 Jul 1894
A Successful Man
By Julien Gordon [pseud.].
Athenaeum, 3311:470-1,
11 Apr 1891
Cosmopolitan, 10:766,
Apr 1891
Epoch, 8:384, 16 Jan
1891
Picayune, 4 Jan 1891,
p. 11
Vampires
By Julien Gordon [pseud.].
Epoch, 11:13, 5 Feb
1892
A Wedding, and Other Stories
By Julien Gordon [pseud.].
Picayune, 22 Nov 1895,
p. 9
Saturday Review, 81:461,
2 May 1896
World's People
By Julien Gordon [pseud.].
Athenaeum, 3932:302,
7 Mar 1903
Bookman (London), 23:248,
Mar 1903
Saturday Review, 95:493,
18 Apr 1903

Cruger, Mrs. Van Rensselaer
See Cruger, Julie Grinnell
(Storrow).

Cullen, Clarence Louis
More Ex-Tank Tales
Overland, 2d S, 40:86,
Jul 1902
Tales of the Ex-Tanks
Picayune, 14 Oct 1900,
II, 8

Cunningham, Mrs. B. Sim
For Honor's Sake
Picayune, 25 May 1879,
[p. 6]

Curran, John Elliott
Miss Frances Merley
Picayune, 15 Jul 1888,
p. 7

[Curran, Mrs. L. P. M.]
Eunice Quince
By Dane Conyngham [pseud.].
Picayune, 8 Dec 1895,
p. 4; 23 Aug 1896,
p. 15

Currier, Mrs. Sophronia
By the Sea and Shiloh
Harper's, 42:622, Mar
1871

Curry, Lily
A Bohemian Tragedy
Godey's, 112:638, Jun 1886
Picayune, 25 Apr 1886,
p. 8
Drops of Blood
Picayune, 24 Apr 1887,
p. 7

[Curtis, Caroline Gardiner (Cary)]
From Madge to Margaret
By Carroll Winchester
[pseud.].
Atlantic, 46:421, Sep 1880
Nation, 31:83, 29 Jul 1880

[Curtis, George Ticknor]
John Charáxes
By Peter Boylston [pseud.].
Atlantic, 63:859, Jun 1889

Curtis, George William
  Prue and I
    Atlantic, 71:124, Jan
      1893

Curwood, James Oliver
  The Danger Trail
    Bookman (NY), 31:202,
      Apr 1910

Cushing, Frank Hamilton
  Zuni Folk Tales
    Times Literary Supple-
      ment, 7 Feb 1902,
      p. 30

Cushing, Paul [pseud.].
  See Wood-Seys, Roland
  Alexander.

Cutting, Mary Stewart (Double-
  day)
  Little Stories of Courtship
    Bookman (NY), 21:545,
      Jul 1905
    Nation, 80:380, 11 May
      1905
  Little Stories of Married Life
    Saturday Review, 102:276,
      1 Sep 1906
  The Suburban Whirl
    Bookman (NY), 26:406-8,
      Dec 1907
  The Wayfarers
    Bookman (NY), 27:576-7,
      Aug 1908
    Nation, 87:289-90, 24 Sep
      1908
    Overland, 2d S, 52:[579]-
      80, Dec 1908

D., S. E.
  See Douglas, Sarah E.

Dabney, Virginius
  Gold That Did Not Glitter
    Picayune, 22 Sep 1889,
      p. 7
  The Story of Don Miff
    Nation, 43:14, 1 Jul
      1886

Overland, 2d S, 8:326,
  Sep 1886
Picayune, 2 May 1886,
  p. 14
Saturday Review, 63:451,
  26 Mar 1887

Daggett, Mrs. Charles Stewart
  See Daggett, Mary (Stewart).

Daggett, Mary (Stewart)
  Mariposilla
    Overland, 2d S, 27:351,
      Mar 1896

Dahlgren, Madeleine (Vinton)
  Divorced
    Picayune, 4 Sep 1887,
      p. 8
  Lights and Shadows of a Life
    Godey's, 115:81, Jul 1887
    Nation, 45:57, 21 Jul 1887
  The Lost Name
    Cottage Hearth, 12:196,
      Jun 1886
    Saturday Review, 61:889-90,
      26 Jun 1886
  South Mountain Magic
    Saturday Review, 54:161,
      29 Jul 1882
  A Washington Winter
    Continent, 4:381-2, 19 Sep
      1883
    Saturday Review, 56:418,
      29 Sep 1883
  The Woodly Lane Ghost
    Outlook, 60:1021, 24 Dec
      1898

Daintrey, Laura
  Actaeon
    Picayune, 14 Aug 1892,
      p. 17
  Eros
    Saturday Review, 66:723,
      15 Dec 1888
  Gold
    Picayune, 6 Aug 1893, p.
      17
  The King of Alberia
    Bookman (London), 9:164,

Daintrey, Laura
Feb 1896
Picayune, 5 Jun 1896,
p. 13
Miss Varian of New York
North American Review,
146:598, May 1888

Dale, Alan [pseud.].
See Cohen, Alfred J.

Dale, J. S. of [pseud.].
See Stimson, Frederic Jesup.

Daley, Pearl
Jerd Cless
Overland, 2d S, 55:220,
Feb 1910

Dall, Caroline H.
My First Holiday
Saturday Review, 52:839,
31 Dec 1881

Dallas, Richard [pseud.].
See Williams, Nathan Win-
slow.

Damon, Sophie M. (Buckman)
Old New-England Days
Nation, 46:219, 15 Mar
1888

Dana, Francis
The Decoy
Athenaeum, 3884:427,
5 Apr 1902
Bookman (London), 22:66-
67, May 1902
Leonora of the Yawmish
Bookman (NY), 6:73-4,
Sep 1897

Dana, Katharine Floyd
Our Phil, and Other Stories
Nation, 48:142, 14 Feb
1889
Overland, 2d S, 13:212-3,
Feb 1889

Dana, Olive E.

Under Friendly Eaves
Atlantic, 76:135, Jul
1895

Dande, Leon [pseud.].
Blue Blood
Nation, 25:184, 20 Sep 1877

Dandelyon, Ruth [pseud.].
See Brown, S. A.

Danforth, Parke [pseud.].
See Talbot, Hannah Lincoln.

Daniel, Charles S.
AI: a Social Vision
Picayune, 9 Apr 1893, p.
24; 18 Mar 1894, p. 27

Daniel, Cora Linn (Morrison)
The Bronze Buddah
Picayune, 12 Nov 1899, II,
3
Sardia
America, 6:106-7, 23 Apr
1891
Cottage Hearth, 17:119,
Apr 1891
Epoch, 9:158, 10 Apr 1891
Picayune, 22 Mar 1891, p.
12

Daniels, Gertrude Potter
The Warners
Nation, 72:438, 30 May
1901

Danziger, Gustav Adolph
See DeCastro, Adolphe Danziger.

Dare, Arline [pseud.].
See Boyden, Emma.

Darling, Mary G.
We Four Girls
Outlook, 63:607, 4 Nov
1899

Darrow, Clarence Seward
An Eye for an Eye

Bookman (NY), 22:629,
Feb 1906

Daskam, Josephine Dodge
See Bacon, Josephine Dodge
(Daskam).

Daugé, Henri [pseud.].
See Hammond, Henrietta
(Hardy).

Daughters of Aesculapius:
Stories Written by Alumnae
and Students of the Woman's
Medical College of Pennsyl-
vania
Nation, 66:53, 20 Jan
1898

Daulton, Mrs.
Fritzi
Overland, 2d S, 52:193,
Aug 1908

Davenport, Benjamin Rush
"Uncle Sam's" Cabins
Picayune, 3 Mar 1895,
p. 14

Davis, Charles Belmont
The Lodger Overhead
Nation, 89:101-2, 29 Jul
1909
The Stage Door
Nation, 86:515, 4 Jun
1908

Davis, Edith Smith
Whether White or Black, a
Man
Outlook, 58:782, 26 Mar
1898

Davis, Ethel
When Love Is Done
Atlantic, 77:131, Jan
1896
Nation, 62:61-2, 16 Jan
1896

[Davis, Frederick William]

Union Down
By Scott Campbell [pseud.].
Picayune, 15 Apr 1894, p.
14

Davis, Harriet Riddle
Gilbert Elgar's Son
Atlantic, 67:127-8, Jan
1891
Epoch, 8:238, 14 Nov 1890
Nation, 52:141, 12 Feb
1891
Overland, 2d S, 17:662,
Jun 1891
In Sight of the Goddess
Picayune, 21 Jun 1896, p.
16

Davis, John E.
Belleview
Picayune, 7 Aug 1892, p.
11

Davis, L. Clarke
A Stranded Ship
Atlantic, 46:419, Sep 1880
Nation, 31:208-9, 16 Sep
1880
Picayune, 4 Jul 1880,
[p. 6]

Davis, Leela B.
A Modern Argonaut
Picayune, 28 Jun 1896, p.
14

Davis, Mary Evelyn (Moore)
An Elephant's Track, and
Other Stories
Picayune, 13 Dec 1896, p.
16
In War Times at La Rose
Blanche
Nation, 47:503, 20 Dec 1888
The Little Chevalier
Outlook, 75:759, 28 Nov
1903
The Price of Silence
Athenaeum, 4157:786, 29
Jun 1907
Bookman (London), 32:177-8,

Davis, Mary Evelyn (Moore)
Aug 1907
Nation, 84:544, 13 Jun
1907
Saturday Review, 104:369,
21 Sep 1907
The Queen's Garden
Outlook, 64:926, 21 Apr
1900
Picayune, 15 Apr 1900,
III, 7
Under the Man-Fig
Atlantic, 76:134, Jul 1895
Godey's, 131:207, Aug
1895
Overland, 2d S, 26:218,
Aug 1895
The Wire Cutters
Nation, 68:359, 11 May
1899

Davis, Norah
The Northerner
Atlantic, 97:49, Jan 1906
Nation, 81:510, 21 Dec
1905
Wallace Rhodes
Nation, 89:77-8, 22 Jul
1909
The World's Warrant
Nation, 84:501, 30 May
1907

Davis, Rebecca (Harding)
Doctor Warrick's Daughters
Bookman (NY), 3:166-7,
Apr 1896
Nation, 62:459, 11 Jun
1896
Frances Waldeaux
Bookman (NY), 5:167-8,
Apr 1897
John Andross
Atlantic, 34:115, Jul 1874
Harper's, 49:290, Jul
1874
Nation, 18:336, 21 May
1874
Saturday Review, 37:698,
30 May 1874
Kent Hampden

Picayune, 16 Oct 1892, p.
15
Kitty's Choice
Godey's, 78:184, Feb 1874
Picayune, 23 Nov 1873,
[p. 8]
A Law Unto Herself
Godey's, 96:435, May 1878
Nation, 26:264, 18 Apr 1878
Natasqua
Nation, 43:14, 1 Jul 1886
Picayune, 25 Apr 1886, p.
8
Silhouettes of American Life
Nation, 55:262, 6 Oct 1892
See also Stories of the South.

Davis, Richard Harding
About Paris
Bookman (NY), 2:149, Oct
1895
Captain Macklin
Athenaeum, 3921:821, 20
Dec 1902
Bookman (NY), 16:175-8,
Oct 1902
Nation, 75:425, 27 Nov
1902
Overland, 2d S, 40:483-4,
Nov 1902
Saturday Review, 94:496,
18 Oct 1902
Cinderella, and Other Stories
Atlantic, 78:426, Sep 1896
Picayune, 17 May 1896, p.
15
The Confessions of a Wife
Saturday Review, 95:207,
14 Feb 1903
Dr. Jameson's Raiders
Picayune, 17 Jan 1897, p.
10
The Exiles, and Other Stories
Athenaeum, 3481:63, 14 Jul
1894
Godey's, 128:[741], Jun
1894
Nation, 59:199, 13 Sep 1894
Saturday Review, 78:542-3,
17 Nov 1894
Gallagher, and Other Stories

America, 6:248, 28 May
1891
Atlantic, 69:266-8, Feb
1892
Harper's, 83:640, Sep
1891
Nation, 52:484, 11 Jun
1891; 53:v, 9 Jul 1891
Saturday Review, 72:21-2,
4 Jul 1891
In the Fog
Athenaeum, 3890:619,
17 May 1902
Bookman (London), 22:110,
Jun 1902
Overland, 2d S, 39:733,
Mar 1902
The King's Jackal
Athenaeum, 371 4:928,
31 Dec 1898
Bookman (NY), 7:521-3,
Aug 1898
Outlook, 59:690, 16 Jul
1898
Picayune, 10 Jul 1898,
II, 6
Saturday Review, 86:387,
17 Sep 1898
Sewanee Review, 6:510,
Oct 1898
The Lion and the Unicorn
Athenaeum, 3765:862,
23 Dec 1899
Bookman (London), 17:120,
Jan 1900
Nation, 69:300, 19 Oct
1899
Outlook, 62:265, 30 Sep
1899
Picayune, 1 Oct 1899,
II, 4
Saturday Review, 89:23,
6 Jan 1900
Once Upon a Time
Bookman (NY), 32:179,
Oct 1910
Nation, 91:392, 27 Oct
1910
The Princess Aline
Bookman (NY), 1:191,
Apr 1895

Saturday Review, 80:694-5,
23 Nov 1895
Ransom's Folly, and Other
Stories
Athenaeum, 3939:529, 25
Apr 1903
Nation, 75:134, 14 Aug
1902
Overland, 2d S, 40:336,
Sep 1902
Saturday Review, 95:427-8,
4 Apr 1903
Times Literary Supplement,
25 Jul 1902, p. 221
The Scarlet Car
Nation, 85:102, 1 Aug 1907
Soldiers of Fortune
Athenaeum, 3635:838, 26
Jul 1897
Atlantic, 80:859-60, Dec
1897
Bookman (London), 12:99,
Jul 1897
Canadian Magazine, 9:266-
77, Jul 1897
Nation 66:54, 20 Jan 1898
Overland, 2d S, 30:186-7,
Aug 1897
Picayune, 20 Jun 1897, p.
16
Saturday Review, 84:427,
16 Oct 1897
Van Bibber, and Others
Athenaeum, 3376:58-60,
9 Jul 1892
Bookman (NY), 5:466-7,
Aug 1897
Nation, 54:451, 16 Jun 1892
Picayune, 8 Jul 1894, p. 7
Vera the Medium
Nation, 86:579, 25 Jun 1908
The West from a Car Window
Godey's, 125:644, Dec 1892
The White Mice
Atlantic, 104:680, Nov 1909
Bookman (NY), 29:541-3,
Jul 1909
Nation, 89:77, 22 Jul 1909

[Davis, Robert S.]
As It May Happen

[Davis, Robert S.]
  By Trebor [pseud.].
    Godey's, 98:278, Mar
      1879
    Library Table, 5:28, 18
      Jan 1879
    Saturday Review, 47:379,
      22 Mar 1879

Davis, Samuel Post
  Short Stories
    Overland, 2d S, 7:212,
      Feb 1886

Davis, Varina Anne Jefferson
  The Veiled Doctor
    Bookman (NY), 2:54-5,
      Sep 1895
    Picayune, 4 Aug 1895,
      p. 12

Davis, William Stearns
  Falaise of the Blessed Voice
    Outlook, 78:633, 5 Nov
      1904
  A Friend of Caesar
    Bookman (London), 19:26,
      Oct 1900
    Nation, 71:55, 19 Jul
      1900
    Saturday Review, 90:368,
      22 Sep 1900
  God Wills It
    Overland, 2d S, 39:664-5,
      Feb 1902
    Saturday Review, 93:148,
      1 Feb 1902

Dawson, Emma Frances
  An Itinerant House, and Other
  Stories
    Overland, 2d S, 30:188,
      Aug 1897

Dawson, Francis Warrington
  The Scar
    Athenaeum, 4084:132,
      3 Feb 1906
    Outlook, 94:956, 23 Apr
      1910
    Overland, 2d S, 55:537,

      May 1910
    Saturday Review, 101:561,
      5 May 1906
  The Scourge
    Athenaeum, 4198:444-5,
      11 Apr 1908
    Nation, 91:551, 8 Dec 1910
    Saturday Review, 105:537,
      25 Apr 1908

Day, Holman Francis
  King Spruce
    Nation, 86:557, 18 Jun
      1908
  The Ramrodders
    Nation, 91:55-6, 21 Jul
      1910
  Squire Phin
    Nation, 81:488, 14 Dec
      1905

Day, Oscar Fayette Gaines
  A Crown of Shame
    Picayune, 28 May 1893,
      p. 24
  The Devil's Gold
    Overland, 2d S, 21:661,
      Jun 1893
    Picayune, 4 Dec 1892, p.
      8
  A Mistaken Identity
    Picayune, 20 Sep 1891, p.
      10

Dazey, Charles
  See Marshall, Edward, and
    Charles Dazey.

Dearborn, Laura [pseud.].
  See Picton, Nina.

DeCastro, Adolphe Danziger
  In the Confessional and The
  Following
    Overland, 2d S, 23:217,
      Feb 1894

Deering, Mary S.
  An Average Boy's Vacation
    Saturday Review, 43:245,
      24 Feb 1877

De Forest, John William
The Bloody Chasm
  Atlantic, 48:860, Dec
    1881
  Godey's, 103:573, Dec
    1881
  Nation, 33:376-7, 10
    Nov 1881
Honest John Vane
  Atlantic, 35:238, Feb
    1875
  Nation, 19:441-2, 31
    Dec 1874
Irene the Missionary
  Atlantic, 45:680-1, May
    1880
  Good Company, 4:480,
    (No. 5) 1880
  Nation, 29:442, 25 Dec
    1879
Justine's Lovers
  Harper's, 57:468, Aug
    1878
Kate Beaumont
  Atlantic, 29:363-5,
    Mar 1872
  Harper's, 44:936, May
    1872
  Nation, 14:189-90, 21
    Mar 1872
  Picayune, 24 Mar 1872,
    [p. 9]
  Saturday Review, 34:260,
    24 Aug 1872
A Lover's Revolt
  Bookman (NY), 8:588,
    Feb 1899
  Nation, 67:453, 15 Dec
    1898
  North American Review,
    171:947, Dec 1900
  Picayune, 20 Nov 1898,
    III, 3
Overland
  Atlantic, 29:110-1, Jan
    1872
  Godey's, 84:98, Jan 1872
  Harper's, 44:936, May
    1872
  Nation, 13:423, 28 Dec
    1871

Picayune, 5 Nov 1871
  [p. 12]
Playing the Mischief
  Atlantic, 37:238-9, Feb
    1876
  Godey's, 91:380, Oct 1875
  Harper's, 51:602, Sep 1875
  Nation, 21:106, 12 Aug 1875
  Picayune, 1 Aug 1875,
    [p. 10]
The Wetherel Affair
  Atlantic, 34:229-30, Aug
    1874
  Nation, 18:336, 21 May 1874
See also Not Pretty, but Pre-
  cious.

Dejeans, Elizabeth
The Heart of Desire
  Bookman (NY), 31:435-6,
    Jun 1910

DeKay, Charles
The Bohemian
  Nation, 28:188, 13 Mar
    1879
  Sunday Afternoon, 3:286-7,
    Mar 1879

DeKoven, Anna (Farwell)
A Sawdust Doll
  Atlantic, 76:708, Nov 1895
  Godey's, 130:655, Jun 1895
  Picayune, 21 Apr 1895, p.
    20
  Saturday Review, 80:55, 13
    Jul 1895

DeKoven, Mrs. Reginald
See DeKoven, Anna (Farwell).

Deland, Ellen Douglas
Alan Ransford
  Nation, 66:54, 20 Jan 1898
Miss Betty of New York
  Nation, 88:255, 11 Mar
    1909

Deland, Margaret Wade (Campbell)
The Awakening of Helena Richie

Deland, Margaret Wade (Campbell)

Athenaeum, 4111:153,
11 Aug 1906
Atlantic, 99:124-5, Jan
1907
Bookman (NY), 24:57-9,
Sep 1906
Harper's, 113:801-2,
Nov 1906
Nation, 83:83, 26 Jul
1906
North American Review,
183:547-50, 21 Sep
1906
Dr. Lavendar's People
Athenaeum, 3973:823,
19 Dec 1903
Saturday Review, 97:21-2,
2 Jan 1904; 98:276,
27 Aug 1904
An Encore
Nation, 85:423, 7 Nov
1907
Florida Days
Athenaeum, 3286:510,
18 Oct 1890
John Ward, Preacher
Athenaeum, 3168:61, 14
Jul 1888
Atlantic, 62:704-6, Nov
1888
Bookman (London), 1:201,
Mar 1892
Nation, 46:530, 28 Jun
1888
Saturday Review, 66:56-7,
14 Jul 1888
Mr. Tommy Dove, and Other
Stories
Athenaeum, 3432:188,
5 Aug 1893
Atlantic, 72:698-9, Nov
1893
Bookman (London), 4:123,
Jul 1893
Cottage Hearth, 19:345,
Jul 1893
Nation, 56:476, 29 Jun
1893
Saturday Review, 76:75-6,

15 Jul 1893
Old Chester Tales
Atlantic, 83:518-9, Apr
1899
Nation, 68:358, 11 May
1899
Outlook, 60:972, 17 Dec
1898
Philip and His Wife
Athenaeum, 3504:858, 22
Dec 1894
Nation, 61:243, 3 Oct 1895
Overland, 2d S, 25:441,
Apr 1895
Saturday Review, 79:55-6,
12 Jan 1895
R. J. 's Mother, and Some
Other People
Bookman (London), 34:155,
Jul 1908
Bookman (NY), 27:577-8,
Aug 1908
Nation, 86:580, 25 Jun 1908
Sidney
Athenaeum, 3293:773, 6
Dec 1890
Atlantic, 67:127, Jan 1891
Cottage Hearth, 16:385,
Dec 1890
Epoch, 8:285, 5 Dec 1890
Nation, 53:107, 6 Aug 1891
Overland, 2d S, 17:662,
Jun 1891
Saturday Review, 70:649-50,
6 Dec 1890
The Story of a Child
Athenaeum, 3397:773-5, 3
Dec 1892
Bookman (London), 3:91-2,
Dec 1892
Cottage Hearth, 19:95, Feb
1893
Nation, 56:16, 5 Jan 1893
Saturday Review, 75:211,
25 Feb 1893
The Wisdom of Fools
Athenaeum, 3675:434, 2
Apr 1898
Bookman (NY), 5:437, Jul
1897

DeLeon, Edwin
  Askaros Kassis, the Captain
    Harper's, 40:925, May
      1870
    Saturday Review, 31:221-
      22, 18 Feb 1871
  A Romance of Modern Egypt
    Godey's, 80:383, Apr
      1870

DeLeon, Thomas Cooper
  A Bachelor's Box
    Overland, 2d S, 31:476,
      May 1898
  Crag-Nest
    Picayune, 20 Jun 1897,
      p. 16
  Creole Carnival
    Picayune, 16 Feb 1890,
      p. 10
  John Holden, Unionist
    Picayune, 23 Apr 1893,
      p. 21
  Juny
    Picayune, 16 Mar 1890,
      p. 16; 11 Jun 1893,
      p. 16
    Saturday Review, 69:541,
      3 May 1890
  The Puritan's Daughter
    Picayune, 9 Aug 1891,
      p. 10
  The Rock or the Rye
    Picayune, 29 Apr 1888,
      p. 7
  Sybilla
    Picayune, 13 Dec 1891,
      p. 12

DeMille, James
  The American Baron
    Godey's, 84:384, Apr
      1872
  The Cryptogram
    Godey's, 72:382, Apr
      1871
  The Lily and the Cross
    Godey's, 79:567, Dec
      1874
  The Living Link
    Godey's, 79:281, Sep

      1874

Deming, Philander
  Adirondack Stories
    Atlantic, 47:281-3, Feb
      1881
  The Story of a Pathfinder
    Nation, 84:568, 20 Jun
      1907
  Tompkins, and Other Folks
    Nation, 40:159, 19 Feb
      1885
    Picayune, 11 Jan 1885,
      [p. 5]

Denison, Mary (Andrews)
  Captain Molly
    Overland, 2d S, 29:659,
      Jun 1897
  Cracker Joe
    Epoch, 1:541, 15 Jul 1887
    Nation, 45:236, 22 Sep 1887
  Hannah's Triumphs
    Godey's, 80:97, Jan 1870
  His Triumph
    Continent, 4:607, 7 Nov
      1883
    Godey's, 107:584, Dec 1883
  If She Will She Will
    America, 6:107, 23 Apr
      1891
    Cottage Hearth, 17:182,
      Jun 1891
    Epoch, 9:237, 15 May 1891
  Like a Gentleman
    Godey's, 104:93, Jan 1882
  Mr. Peter Crewitt
    Sunday Afternoon, 2:384,
      Oct 1878
  Old Slip Warehouse
    Atlantic, 43:172, Feb 1879
    Harper's, 57:941, Nov 1878
    Library Table, 4:449, 26
      Oct 1878
  Rothmell
    Harper's, 57:468, Aug 1878
  Tell Your Wife
    Cottage Hearth, 11:394, Dec
      1885
  That Husband of Mine
    Picayune, 26 Aug 1877,

Denison, Mary (Andrews)
  [p. 9]
  Library Table, 3:157,
    30 Aug 1877
  Nation, 25:273, 1 Nov
    1877
  That Wife of Mine
    Cottage Hearth, 4:316,
      Dec 1877
  Victor Norman, Rector
    Godey's, 86:87, Jan 1873
    Nation, 15:319, 14 Nov
      1872
    Saturday Review, 34:837,
      28 Dec 1872

[Denison, Thomas Stewart]
  The Iron Crown
    Overland, 2d S, 7:320,
      Mar 1886
    Picayune, 20 Dec 1885,
      p. 14
  The Man Behind
    Godey's, 116:395, Apr
      1888
    Harper's, 77:800-1,
      Oct 1888
    Overland, 2d S, 12:215,
      Aug 1888

Denton, Lyman W.
  Under the Magnolias
    Overland, 2d S, 13:215,
      Feb 1889
    Picayune, 23 Dec 1888,
      p. 14

[Derby, Caroline Rosina]
  Salem
    By D. R. Castleton [pseud.].
    Atlantic, 35:108-9,
      Jan 1875
    Godey's, 90:93, Jan 1875
    Harper's, 50:140, Dec
      1874

Derrick, Francis [pseud.].
  See Motley, Mrs. Francis E.

Deslonde, Mrs. Maria Darring-
ton

John Maribel
  Picayune, 17 Dec 1876,
    [p. 11]

Despard, Matilda (Pratt)
  Kilrogan Cottage
    Harper's, 57:788-9, Oct
      1878
    Library Table, 4:385, 31
      Aug 1878
    Picayune, 8 Sep 1878,
      [p. 4]

Dessommes, George
  Tante Cydette
    Picayune, 13 May 1888,
    p. 7

Devereux, George Humphrey
  Sam Shirk
    Nation, 12:31, 12 Jan
      1871

Devereux, Mary
  From Kingdom to Colony
    Athenaeum, 3771:143, 3
      Feb 1900
    Outlook, 63:1029, 30 Dec
      1899
    Picayune, 17 Dec 1899,
      III, 8
  Up and Down the Sands of
  Gold
    Overland, 2d S, 38:509,
      Dec 1901

Devoore, Ann
  Oliver Iverson
    Outlook, 62:314, 3 Jun
      1899

Dey, Frederic Van Rensselaer
  A Gentleman of Quality
    Nation, 89:142, 12 Aug
      1909

Diaz, Abby (Morton)
  Bybury to Beacon Street
    North American Review,
      147:118, Jul 1888
  Lucy Maria

Harper's, 48:748, Apr
1874
Saturday Review, 36:827,
27 Dec 1873
Only a Flock of Women
Atlantic, 72:704, Nov
1893
The Schoolmaster's Trunk
Saturday Review, 39:162-3,
30 Jan 1875

di Brazzà, Countess
See Slocomb, Cora.

Dick, Herbert G. [pseud.].
See Morgan, Carrie A.

[Dickinson, Edith May]
So Runs the World Away
By Ansley May [pseud.].
Picayune, 29 Mar 1891,
p. 3

Dickinson, Mrs. Ellen E.
The King's Daughters
Picayune, 23 Aug 1896,
p. 15

Dickson, Capers
John Ashton
Picayune, 22 Feb 1897,
p. 12

Dickson, Harris
The Black Wolf's Breed
Bookman (NY), 11:93,
Mar 1900
Outlook, 64:462, 24 Feb
1900
Picayune, 5 Nov 1899,
II, 7
The Siege of Lady Resolute
Athenaeum, 3891:653,
24 May 1902
Overland, 2d S, 39:917,
May 1902

Didier, Charles Peale
Would Any Man?
Picayune, 22 May 1898,
II, 2

Dillingham, Lucy
The Missing Chord
Picayune, 20 Jan 1895,
p. 15

Dillon, Mary C. (Johnson)
In Old Bellaire
Outlook, 82:476, 24 Feb
1906
The Leader
Bookman (NY), 24:158-60,
Oct 1906
Nation, 83:246, 20 Sep 1906
The Patience of John Morland
Bookman (London), 37:162,
Dec 1909
Bookman (NY), 30:69, Sep
1909
Nation, 89:256, 16 Sep 1909

Diltz, Hanson Penn
The Duchesse Undine
Picayune, 28 Jan 1882,
[p. 12]

Disosway, Ella Taylor
South Meadows
Nation, 20:137-8, 25 Feb
1875

Ditson, Lina Bartlett
The Soul and the Hammer
Nation, 70:402, 24 May
1900

Dix, Beulah Marie
The Beau's Comedy
Outlook, 70:926, 12 Apr
1902
The Fair Maid of Graystones
Athenaeum, 4076:794, 9
Dec 1905
Nation, 81:488, 14 Dec 1905
Hugh Gwyeth
Bookman (NY), 9:559-60,
Aug 1899
Outlook, 61:833, 8 Apr 1899
Saturday Review, 88:53, 8
Jul 1899
The Life, Treason, and Death
of Blount of Breckenhow

Dix, Beulah Marie
  Saturday Review, 97:272-
    73, 27 Feb 1904
  Soldier Rigdale
    Athenaeum, 3771:143,
      3 Feb 1900
    Bookman (NY), 10:598,
      Feb 1900
    Picayune, 10 Dec 1899,
      III, 7
    Saturday Review, 89:147,
      3 Feb 1900

Dix, Edwin Asa
  Deacon Bradbury
    Athenaeum, 3820:45,
      12 Jan 1901
    Bookman (NY), 11:399,
      Jun 1900
    Nation, 70:304, 19 Apr
      1900
    Outlook, 64:838, 7 Apr
      1900
    Picayune, 6 May 1900,
      III, 8
  Old Bowen's Legacy
    Bookman (NY), 13:616,
      Aug 1901
    Nation, 72:438, 30 May
      1901
    Outlook, 67:969, 27 Apr
      1901
  Prophet's Landing
    Nation, 84:523, 6 Jun
      1907

Dix, Gertrude
  The Girl from the Farm
    Saturday Review, 80:55,
      13 Jul 1895
  The Image Breakers
    Bookman (London), 19:27-
      28, Oct 1900
    Outlook, 66:370, 6 Oct
      1900
    Saturday Review, 90:524,
      27 Oct 1900

Dixon, Clarissa
  Janet and Her Dear Phebe
    Overland, 2d S, 53:252,
      Mar 1909

Dixon, Thomas, Jr.
  The Clansman
    Athenaeum, 4037:303-4, 11
      Mar 1905
    Bookman (NY), 20:559-60,
      Feb 1905; 21:407-11, Jun
      1905
    Saturday Review, 99:636,
      13 May 1905
    South Atlantic Quarterly,
      4:192-5, Apr 1905
  The Leopard's Spots
    Bookman (NY), 15:472-4,
      Jul 1902
    Overland, 2d S, 39:983-4,
      Jun 1902
    Saturday Review, 94:274,
      30 Aug 1902
    South Atlantic Quarterly,
      1:188-9, Apr 1902; 2:344,
      Oct 1903
  The Life Worth Living
    Bookman (NY), 22:70-1,
      Sep 1905
  The One Woman
    Bookman (NY), 18:161-2,
      Oct 1903
    South Atlantic Quarterly,
      2:344, Oct 1903
  The Traitor
    Bookman (NY), 26:83-5,
      Sep 1907

Dod, Samuel Bayard
  A Highland Chronicle
    Bookman (London), 2:185,
      Sep 1892
  Stubble or Wheat?
    North American Review,
      147:597-8, Nov 1888

Dodd, Anna Bowman (Blake)
  On the Knees of the Gods
    Nation, 86:236-7, 12 Mar
      1908
  Struthers, and the Comedy of
    the Masked Musicians
    Picayune, 24 Jun 1894, p.
      15

Dodd, Ira Seymour
The Song of the Rappahannock
Outlook, 61:832, 8 Apr
1899

[Dodge, Louis Preston, and
H. W. Preston]
The Question of Identity
Nation, 44:300, 7 Apr
1887

[Dodge, Mary Abigail]
First Love Is Best
By Gail Hamilton [pseud.].
Atlantic, 40:111-2, Jul
1877
Continent, 3:445, 4 Apr
1883
Harper's, 55:788-9,
Oct 1877
Library Table, 3:56,
7 Jun 1877
Nation, 25:185, 20 Sep
1877
North American Review,
125:321, Sep 1877
Picayune, 8 Jul 1877,
[p. 3]

Dodge, Mary Mapes
Theophilus and Others
Athenaeum, 2556:525-6,
21 Oct 1876
Nation, 23:304, 16 Nov
1876

Dodge, Walter Phelps
A Strong Man Armed, and
Other Tales
Saturday Review, 83:725-
26, 26 Jun 1897

Doe, Charles H.
Buffets
Nation, 22:32, 13 Jan
1876

Dole, Edmund Pearson
Hiwa
Outlook, 65:324, 2 Jun
1900

Dole, Nathan Haskell
Not Angels Quite
Athenaeum, 3463:310, 10
Mar 1894
Godey's, 127:620, Nov 1893
Nation, 57:374, 16 Nov 1893
Picayune, 27 Aug 1893, p.
20
Saturday Review, 78:277, 8
Sep 1894
Omar the Tentmaker
Bookman (London), 17:24,
Apr 1899
Saturday Review, 87:343-4,
18 Mar 1899
On the Point
Bookman (NY), 2:55, Sep
1895
Nation, 62:61, 16 Jan 1896
Overland, 2d S, 27:351,
Mar 1896
Poet-Lore, 8:43, (No. 1)
1896

Donelson, Katharine
Rodger Latimer's Mistake
Picayune, 17 Jan 1892, p.
2

Donnell, Annie (Hamilton)
Rebecca Mary
Athenaeum, 4092:388, 31
Mar 1906

[Donnelly, Ignatius Loyola]
Caesar's Column
By Edmund Boisgilbert
[pseud.].
Saturday Review, 71:141, 1
Aug 1891
Doctor Huguet
Picayune, 20 Sep 1891, p.
10
Saturday Review, 73:155-6,
6 Feb 1892
The Golden Bottle
Godey's, 126:643, May 1893
Picayune, 23 Oct 1892, p.
18

Donnelly, Joseph Gordon
Jesus Delaney
  Nation, 69:300, 19 Oct
    1899
  Outlook, 62:128, 13 May
    1899

Donworth, Grace
Down Home with Jennie Allen
  Overland, 2d S, 56:528,
    Nov 1910
The Letters of Jennie Allen
to Her Friend Miss Musgrove
  Nation, 88:93, 28 Jan
    1909

Doran, James
In the Depths of the First
Degree
  Outlook, 58:979, 16 Apr
    1898
  Picayune, 17 Apr 1898,
    p. 16

Dorr, Julia Caroline (Ripley)
Expiation
  Godey's, 86:281, Mar
    1873
  Harper's, 47:301, Jul
    1873
  Picayune, 12 Jan 1873,
    [p. 9]
In Kings' Houses
  Saturday Review, 88:337,
    9 Sep 1899
Sibyl Huntington
  Godey's, 86:561, Jun
    1873

Dorsey, Anna Hanson (McKenney)
Mona, the Vestal
  Picayune, 9 May 1880,
    [p. 7]
Nora Brady's Vow
  Picayune, 9 May 1880,
    [p. 7]
Tangled Paths
  Nation, 29:115, 14 Aug
    1879

Dorsey, Anna Vernon

See Williams, Anna Vernon
(Dorsey).

Dorsey, Sarah Anne (Ellis)
Agnes Graham
  Picayune, 6 Jun 1880,
    [p. 10]
Athalie
  By "Filia" [pseud.].
  Picayune, 11 Feb 1872,
    [p. 7]
The Creole Beauty
  Picayune, 4 Jul 1880,
    [p. 6]
Panola
  Godey's, 95:925, Dec 1877
  Library Table, 3:8, 27
    Oct 1877
  Picayune, 30 Sep 1877,
    [p. 7]

Doubleday, Roman [pseud.].
See Long, Lily Augusta.

Douglas, Amanda Minnie
Bethia Wray's New Name
  Cottage Hearth, 19:397,
    Aug 1893
Drifted Asunder
  Nation, 22:213, 30 Mar
    1876
Floyd Grandson's Honor
  Continent, 5:448, (No. 14)
    1884
  Godey's, 108:199, Feb 1884
  Overland, 2d S, 3:556,
    May 1884
  Picayune, 6 Jan 1884,
    [p. 11]
The Fortunes of the Faradays
  Cottage Hearth, 14:58,
    Feb 1888
From Hand to Mouth
  Harper's, 56:629, Mar
    1878
  Library Table, 4:127, 2
    Feb 1878
  Picayune, 27 Jan 1878,
    [p. 11]
The Heirs of Bradley House
  Epoch, 11:13, 5 Feb 1892

Picayune, 4 Oct 1891,
p. 10
Heroes of the Crusades
Cottage Hearth, 15:416,
Dec 1889
Hope Mills
Atlantic, 45:679-80, May
1880
Nation, 30:65, 22 Jan
1880
In Trust
Cottage Hearth, 16:359,
Nov 1890
In Wild Rose Time
Bookman (NY), 1:51,
Feb 1895
Larry
Cottage Hearth, 19:397,
Aug 1893
Picayune, 18 Jun 1893,
p. 19
A Little Girl in Old Phila-
delphia
Picayune, 21 Jan 1900,
II, 7
A Little Girl in Old San
Francisco
Overland, 2d S, 46:591,
Dec 1905
Lost in a Great City
Cottage Hearth, 7:145,
May 1881
Godey's, 102:381, Apr
1881; 117:85, Jul 1888
Lucia
Godey's, 84:289, Mar
1872
Harper's, 44:463, Feb
1872
Nation, 14:207, 28 Mar
1872
A Modern Adam and Eve in
a Garden
Overland, 2d S, 13:209-
10, Feb 1889
Nelly Kinnard's Kingdom
Cottage Hearth, 3:315,
Dec 1876; 18:411,
Dec 1892
Godey's, 94:189, Feb
1877

Library Table, 2:29, Apr
1877
Picayune, 25 Sep 1892, p.
13
Osborne of Arrochar
Epoch, 11:13, 5 Feb 1892
Godey's, 120:94, Jan 1890
Overland, 2d S, 15:435-6,
Apr 1890
Picayune, 15 Dec 1889, p.
11
Out of the Wreck
Cottage Hearth, 11:58,
Feb 1885
Overland, 2d S, 5:214,
Feb 1885
Picayune, 28 Dec 1884,
[p. 10]
A Question of Silence
Outlook, 67:740, 30 Mar
1901
Whom Kathie Married
Godey's, 107:94, Jul 1883
Picayune, 27 May 1883,
[p. 13]
With Fate Against Him
Godey's, 72:194, Feb 1871
Harper's, 42:460, Feb 1871
A Woman's Inheritance
Cottage Hearth, 12:26, Jan
1886
Overland, 2d S, 7:210, Feb
1886

Douglas, George [pseud.].
See Brown, George Douglas.

Douglas, Mark [pseud.].
Can Love Sin?
Picayune, 23 Jun 1889, p.
11; 29 Jun 1890, p. 13

Douglas, Matilda
Doings in Maryland
Godey's, 73:570, Dec 1871

[Douglas, Sarah E.]
Mahaly Sawyer
By S. E. D.
Nation, 46:121, 9 Feb 1888

[Dow, Joy Wheeler]
  Miss Polly Playfair
    Picayune, 27 May 1900,
    III, 7
  Two Days
    By W. Newport [pseud.].
    Picayune, 30 Jul 1882,
    [p. 6]

Dowd, Freeman Benjamin
  The Double Man
    Picayune, 22 Nov 1895,
    p. 9

Dowling, George Thomas
  The Wreckers
    Nation, 42:409, 13 May
    1886

Downing, Robert L.
  See Hall, A. D. , and Robert
  L. Downing.

[Downs, Sarah Elizabeth (For-
bush)]
  Love and Beauty
    By Mrs. Georgie Sheldon
    [pseud.].
    Picayune, 17 May 1896,
    p. 15
  That Dowdy
    By Mrs. Georgie Sheldon
    [pseud.].
    Picayune, 15 Dec 1889,
    p. 11

Doyle, Charles William
  The Shadow of Quong Lung
    Outlook, 63:890, 9 Dec
    1899
    Saturday Review, 90:337,
    15 Sep 1900

Drake, Jeanie
  In Old St. Stephen's
    Godey's, 126:101, Jan
    1893
    Nation, 55:437, 8 Dec
    1892
  The Metropolitans
    Bookman (NY), 4:372-3,

Dec 1896
    Nation, 64:71, 28 Jan 1897

Drake, Samuel Adams
  The Border Wars of New
  England
    Picayune, 31 Oct 1897, p.
    11
  Captain Nelson
    Harper's, 58:786, Apr
    1879
    Picayune, 9 Feb 1879,
    [p. 11]
  The Heart of the White Moun-
  tains
    Cottage Hearth, 10:218, Jul
    1884

Dreiser, Theodore
  Sister Carrie
    Athenaeum, 3854:312-3, 7
    Sep 1901
    Bookman (NY), 25:287, Apr
    1907; 25:298-9, Apr 1907
    North American Review,
    186:288-91, Oct 1907
    Picayune, 23 Dec 1900, II,
    12

Driscoll, Clara
  The Girl of La Gloria
    Athenaeum, 4045:556, 6
    May 1905
    Bookman (NY), 21:601-2,
    Aug 1905

Dromgoole, Miss Will Allen
  Cinch, and Other Stories
    Picayune, 20 Nov 1898, III,
    3
  The Heart of Old Hickory, and
  Other Stories of Tennessee
    Picayune, 1 Dec 1895, p.
    17; 6 Apr 1896, p. 11;
    19 Sep 1897, p. 8
  The Valley Path
    Outlook, 58:1078, 30 Apr
    1898

Drysdale, William
  The Princess of Montserrat

Nation, 51:293, 9 Oct 1890

DuBois, Constance Goddard
Columbus and Beatriz
Atlantic, 70:706, Nov 1892
Cottage Hearth, 18:255, Aug 1892
Martha Corey
Atlantic, 67:424, Mar 1891
Epoch, 8:416, 30 Jan 1891
Godey's, 122:98, Jan 1891
Nation, 52:244, 19 Mar 1891
A Soul in Bronze
Picayune, 9 Dec 1900, II, 8

Duer, Catherine King
Unconscious Comedians
Nation, 73:459, 12 Dec 1901

[Duffell, Annie]
In the Meshes
By Christine McKenzie [pseud.].
Picayune, 30 Dec 1877, [p. 15]

Dunbar, Alice
See Nelson, Alice Ruth (Moore) Dunbar.

Dunbar, Paul Laurence
The Fanatics
Bookman (NY), 13:502-3, Jul 1901
Nation, 72:437-8, 30 May 1901
Outlook, 67:878, 13 Apr 1901
Folks from Dixie
Bookman (NY), 7:348-9, Jun 1898
Nation, 67:54, 21 Jul 1898

Outlook, 59:86, 7 May 1898
The Heart of Happy Hollow
Nation, 80:98, 2 Feb 1905
In Old Plantation Days
Nation, 78:134, 18 Feb 1904
The Jest of Fate
Athenaeum, 3918:717-8, 29 Nov 1902
Saturday Review, 95:113, 24 Jan 1903
The Love of Landry
Bookman (NY), 12:512-3, Jan 1901
The Sport of the Gods
Nation, 74:448-9, 5 Jun 1902
The Strength of Gideon, and Other Stories
Nation, 70:461, 14 Jun 1900
The Uncalled
Bookman (London), 16:82-3, Jun 1899
Bookman (NY), 8:338-41, Dec 1898
Nation, 67:491, 29 Dec 1891

Duncan, Florence I.
My Intimate Friend
Picayune, 3 Mar 1878, [p. 11]

Duncan, Norman
The Cruise of the Shining Light
Canadian Magazine, 29:192-3, Jun 1907
Nation, 84:478, 23 May 1907
North American Review, 185:328-31, 7 Jun 1907
Doctor Luke of the Labrador
Bookman (London), 27:128-29, Dec 1904
Canadian Magazine, 24:190, Dec 1904
Nation, 80:97-8, 2 Feb 1905
Every Man for Himself
Nation, 87:364, 15 Oct 1908
The Mother
Canadian Magazine, 26:86-8, Nov 1905

Duncan, Norman
The Soul of the Street
Bookman (NY), 12:583-4,
Feb 1901
Nation, 72:280, 4 Apr
1901
The Way of the Sea
Bookman (London), 26:102,
Jun 1904
Bookman (NY), 18:270-1,
Nov 1903
Nation, 78:55, 21 Jan
1904

Dunn, Martha (Baker)
Memory Street
Athenaeum, 3857:410,
28 Sep 1901
Picayune, 22 Jul 1900,
II, 8

Dunne, Finley Peter
Mr. Dooley in Peace and War
Atlantic, 83:288, Feb
1899
Bookman (NY), 8:574-6,
Feb 1899
North American Review,
176:743-6, May 1903
Picayune, 4 Dec 1898,
II, 4
Saturday Review, 87:409,
1 Apr 1899
Mr. Dooley in the Hearts of
His Countrymen
Bookman (NY), 10:378-9,
Dec 1899
Picayune, 29 Oct 1899,
II, 12
Mr. Dooley Says
Saturday Review, 110:396-7,
24 Sep 1910
Mr. Dooley's Opinions
Atlantic, 90:419, Sep 1902
Overland, 2d S, 39:731-2,
Mar 1902
Mr. Dooley's Philosophy
Picayune, 18 Nov 1900,
III, 4

Dunning, Charlotte [pseud.].

See Wood, Charlotte Dunning.

Dupuy, Eliza A.
All for Love
Picayune, 1 Jun 1873,
[p. 2]
The Cancelled Will
Godey's, 85:89, Jul 1872
Picayune, 19 May 1872,
[p. 9]
The Clandestine Marriage
Godey's, 90:380, Apr 1875
The Dethroned Heiress
Godey's, 78:473, May 1874
The Discarded Wife
Godey's, 90:569, Jun 1875
The Gipsy's Warning
Godey's, 87:476, Nov 1873
Picayune, 14 Sep 1873,
[p. 3]
The Hidden Sin
Godey's, 78:565, Jun 1874
How He Did It
Godey's, 73:89, Jul 1871
Michael Rudolph
Godey's, 81:558, Dec 1870
Picayune, 23 Oct 1870,
[p. 5]; 27 Nov 1870,
[p. 11]
The Mysterious Guest
Godey's, 86:468, May 1873
A New Way to Win a Fortune
Godey's, 92:189, Feb 1876
Who Shall Be Victor?
Picayune, 26 May 1872,
[p. 9]
Why Did He Marry Her?
Godey's, 80:480, May 1870

Durham, Robert Lee
The Call of the South
Canadian Magazine, 31:186,
Jun 1908

Duval, John Crittenden
Early Times in Texas
Picayune, 17 Apr 1892, p.
22

Duysters, George F.
A Senator at Sea

Picayune, 11 Mar 1894,
p. 25

Dye, Eva (Emery)
The Conquest
Athenaeum, 3977:77,
16 Jan 1904

Earle, Alice (Morse)
Colonial Dames and Good
Wives
Saturday Review, 81:357,
4 Apr 1896
Colonial Days in Old New
York
Picayune, 16 Nov 1896,
p. 6
In Old Narragansett
Outlook, 59:87, 7 May
1898
Picayune, 8 May 1898,
p. 7
Margaret Winthrop
Saturday Review, 81:357,
4 Apr 1896

Earle, Anne Richardson
Her Great Ambition
Atlantic, 67:127, Jan
1891
Epoch, 8:252, 21 Nov
1890
Nation, 52:141, 12 Feb
1891

Earle, Mary Tracy
The Man Who Worked for
Collister
Atlantic, 83:287, Feb
1899
Nation, 68:357, 11 May
1899
Outlook, 60:731, 19
Nov 1898
Picayune, 20 Nov 1898,
III, 2
Through Old Rose Glasses,
and Other Stories
Nation, 72:399, 16 May
1901
Picayune, 18 Nov 1900,

III, 4
The Wonderful Wheel
Bookman (NY), 4:367-8,
Dec 1896
Picayune, 16 Nov 1896,
p. 6

Eastman, Charlotte Whitney
The Evolution of Dodd's Sister
Picayune, 22 Aug 1897, p.
24

Eastman, Elaine (Goodale)
Journal of a Farmer's Daugh-
ter
Harper's, 63:475, Aug 1881
Little Brother o' Dreams
Nation, 90:263-4, 17 Mar
1910

Eaton, Arthur Wentworth, and
Craven Langstroth Betts
Tales of a Garrison Town
Overland, 2d S, 20:661,
Dec 1892

Eaton, Frances [pseud.].
See Flint, Sargent.

Eckstorm, Fannie (Hardy)
The Penobscot Man
Nation, 79:62-3, 21 Jul
1904

Eddy, Arthur Jerome
Ganton and Co.
Bookman (NY), 28:380-1,
Dec 1908
Nation, 87:580-1, 10 Dec
1908

[Edes, Robert Thaxter]
The Story of Rodman Heath
By One of Them.
Nation, 60:32-3, 10 Jan
1895

Edwards, George Wharton
P'tit Matinic', and Other
Monotones
Nation, 59:483-4, 27 Dec 1894

Edwards, George Wharton
1894

Edwards, Harry Stillwell
His Defense, and Other
Stories
Picayune, 17 Dec 1899,
III, 8
Sons and Fathers
Picayune, 20 Dec 1896,
p. 20
Two Runaways, and Other
Stories
Nation, 50:57, 16 Jan
1890
Picayune, 20 Oct 1889,
p. 8
Saturday Review, 68:691,
14 Dec 1889

Edwards, James Alexander
In the Court Circle
Picayune, 24 Jan 1896,
p. 9

Edwards, Rollin
Twice Defeated
Nation, 24:282, 10 May
1877

[Egan, Maurice Francis]
That Girl of Mine
Godey's, 96:83, Jan
1878
Picayune, 11 Nov 1877,
[p. 11]
That Lover of Mine
Picayune, 3 Mar 1878,
[p. 11]
The Wiles of Sexton Ma-
ginnis
Outlook, 92:20, 1 May
1909

Eggleston, Edward
The Circuit Rider
Atlantic, 33:745-7, Jun
1874
Nation, 19:207, 24 Sep
1874
Duffels

Cottage Hearth, 19:advert
11, Dec 1893
Godey's, 127:766, Dec 1893
Nation, 57:395, 23 Nov 1893
The End of the World
Atlantic, 30:746-7, Dec 1872
Godey's, 86:89, Jan 1873
Harper's, 46:140, Dec 1872
Nation, 15:222, 3 Oct 1872
Sewanee, 11:352, Jul 1903
The Faith Doctor
Athenaeum, 3345:758-9, 5
Dec 1891
Cosmopolitan, 12:640, Mar
1891
Harper's, 85:317, Jul 1892
Nation, 53:395, 19 Nov 1891
The Graysons
Athenaeum, 3194:48-9, 12
Jan 1889
Atlantic, 63:274-80, Feb
1889
Epoch, 4:193-4, 19 Oct 1888
Nation, 48:142, 14 Feb 1889
The Hoosier Schoolboy
Continent, 4:735, 5 Dec
1883
Picayune, 7 Oct 1883,
[p. 7]
The Hoosier Schoolmaster
Atlantic, 29:363-5, Mar
1872
Godey's, 84:289-90, Mar
1872
Nation, 14:44-6, 18 Jan
1872
Overland, 2d S, 27:238,
Feb 1896
Picayune, 20 Nov 1892,
p. 18
Quarterly Review, 155:227-
28, Jan 1883
Sewanee Review, 11:352,
Jul 1903
The Mystery of Metropolis-
ville
Godey's, 87:91, Jul 1873
Nation, 16:503, 12 Jun 1873
Roxy
Athenaeum, 2655:336, 14
Sep 1878

Harper's, 58:146, Dec
1878
Library Table, 4:416,
28 Sep 1878
Nation, 27:244, 17 Oct
1878
Sunday Afternoon, 2:574,
Dec 1878
Saturday Review, 46:600-1,
9 Nov 1878

Eggleston, George Cary
The Big Brother
Saturday Review, 40:821,
25 Dec 1875
Daughter of the South
Outlook, 81:44, 2 Sep
1905
Evelyn Byrd
Poet-Lore, 15:142-3,
Winter 1904
The Last of the Flatboats
Picayune, 24 Jun 1900,
II, 12
A Rebel's Recollections
Atlantic, 35:237-8, Feb
1875
Running the River
Atlantic, 93:852, Jun
1904
Southern Soldier Stories
Bookman (NY), 7:250-1,
May 1898
Nation, 66:273, 7 Apr
1898
Outlook, 58:678, 12 Mar
1898
Overland, 2d S, 31:382,
Apr 1898
Picayune, 20 Feb 1898,
p. 22
Westover of Wanalah
Nation, 91:579, 15 Dec
1910
The Wreck of the Red Bird
Picayune, 15 Oct 1882,
[p. 8]

_____, and Dolores Mar-
bourg [pseud.].
Juggernaut

America, 6:51, 9 Apr 1891
Epoch, 9:397-8, 24 Jul 1891
Nation, 52:384, 7 May 1891
Saturday Review, 71:780,
27 Jun 1891

Eisenberg, Maurice
See Baldwin, Eugene F. , and
Maurice Eisenberg.

Elbon, Barbara [pseud.].
See Halsted, Leonora B.

Eldridge, George Dyre
In the Potter's House
Nation, 86:402, 30 Apr 1908
Saturday Review, 107:278,
27 Feb 1909
The Millbank Case
Nation, 81:123, 10 Aug 1905

Eliot, Annie
See Trumbull, Annie Eliot.

Elivas, Knarf [pseud.].
See Savile, Frank MacKenzie.

Elliott, Henry Rutherford
The Bassett Claim
Nation, 39:509, 11 Dec 1884
Overland, 2d S, 5:213, Feb
1885

Elliott, Maud (Howe)
Atalanta in the South
Nation, 43:15, 1 Jul 1886
Overland, 2d S, 8:107, Jul
1886
Honor
Picayune, 13 Aug 1893, p.
16
A Newport Aquarelle
Continent, 4:670, 21 Nov
1883
Manhattan, 2:480-1, Nov
1883
Nation, 37:256-7, 20 Sep
1883
Phillida
Nation, 53:471, 17 Dec 1891
Picayune, 4 Oct 1891,

Elliott, Maud (Howe)
p. 10
The San Rosario Ranch
  Continent, 6:126, (No. 4)
  1884
  Nation, 38:531, 19 Jun
  1884
  Overland, 2d S, 4:107,
  Jul 1884
  Saturday Review, 58:315-
  16, 6 Sep 1884
Two in Italy
  Nation, 82:21-2, 4 Jan
  1906

Elliott, Mrs. Sarah Barnwell
The Durket Sperret
  Bookman (NY), 8:69-70,
  Sep 1898
  Nation, 66:389, 19 May
  1898
  Outlook, 58:1030, 23
  Apr 1898
  Overland, 2d S, 31:576,
  Jun 1898
  Picayune, 1 May 1898,
  p. 25
The Felmeres
  Godey's, 99:279, Sep
  1879
  Nation, 29:114-5, 14
  Aug 1879
  Picayune, 13 Jul 1879,
  [p. 9]
An Incident, and Other
Happenings
  Nation, 69:96, 3 Aug
  1899
  Sewanee Review, 7:245-7,
  Apr 1899
Jerry
  Epoch, 9:382, 17 Jul
  1891
  Saturday Review, 72:53-4,
  11 Jul 1891
  Sewanee Review, 2:509,
  Aug 1894
John Paget
  Atlantic, 72:420, Sep
  1893
  Godey's, 127:235, Aug

1893
The Making of Jane
  Nation, 73:477, 19 Dec 1901
  Sewanee Review, 10:118-9,
  Jan 1902; 11:364, Jul
  1903

Ellis, Edward S.
Camp Fire and Wigwam
  Picayune, 29 Nov 1885, p.
  10
The Eye of the Sun
  Picayune, 30 May 1897, p.
  16
The Great Cattle Trail
  Saturday Review, 78:690,
  22 Dec 1894
Klondike Nuggets
  Outlook, 60:188, 17 Sep
  1898
The Young Ranchers
  Overland, 2d S, 27:240,
  Feb 1896

Ellis, John Breckenridge
Arkinsaw Cousins
  Nation, 86:354, 16 Apr 1908
The Soul of a Serf
  Nation, 91:339, 13 Oct 1910
Stork's Nest
  Bookman (NY), 23:30, Mar
  1906
  Overland, 2d S, 46:585,
  Dec 1905

Ellison, Edith Nicholl
The Blossoming of the Waste
  Overland, 2d S, 52:192,
  Aug 1908

[Ellsworth, Mrs. Louise C.]
A Little Worlding
  By Ellis Worth [pseud.].
  Epoch, 7:413, 1 Aug 1890
  Nation, 51:293, 9 Oct 1890

Embree, Charles Fleming
A Dream of a Throne
  Outlook, 65:362, 9 Jun 1900
  Picayune, 17 Jun 1900, II,
  12

For the Love of Tonita, &
Other Tales of the Mesa
  Picayune, 17 Oct 1897,
    p. 10
A Heart of Flame
  Saturday Review, 93:642,
    17 May 1902

Emersie, John
Allisto
  Picayune, 15 Mar 1885,
    [p. 11]

[Emerson, Mary S.]
Among the Chosen
  Nation, 39:314-5, 9
    Oct 1884

Emerson, Willis George
The Builders
  Athenaeum, 4139:222,
    23 Feb 1907

Emery, E. B.
Queens
  Nation, 16:220, 27 Mar
    1873
  Picayune, 13 Apr 1873,
    [p. 10]

Emery, Sarah Anna
Three Generations
  Harper's, 45:624, Sep
    1872
  Nation, 15:170, 12 Sep
    1872

Emory, A. M. [pseud.].
See Watrous, Charles.

Emory, Frederic
A Maryland Manor
  Nation, 72:514, 27 Jun
    1901

[English, Thomas Dunn]
Jacob Schuyler's Millions
  Nation, 42:198, 4 Mar
    1886
  Overland, 2d S, 7:652,
    Jun 1886

Eric, Allan [pseud.].
See Willis, Charles W.

Evans, Augusta Jane
See Wilson, Augusta Jane
  (Evans).

Evans, Elizabeth Edson (Gibson)
Confession
  Nation, 63:179-80, 3 Sep
    1896
Laura
  Picayune, 23 Dec 1883,
    [p. 9]
  Saturday Review, 57:423,
    29 Mar 1884
Transplanted Manners
  Nation, 60:426-7, 30 May
    1895
  Saturday Review, 79:488,
    13 Apr 1895

Evans, Florence (Wilkinson)
The Lady of the Flag-Flower
  Outlook, 62:400, 17 Jun
    1899
The Silent Door
  Atlantic, 100:132, Jul 1907
  Bookman (NY), 25:284-5,
    Apr 1907
The Strength of the Hills
  Bookman (NY), 14:257-9,
    Nov 1902

Evans, George S.
Wylackie Jake
  Overland, 2d S, 45:254,
    Mar 1905

Everett, Edith Townsend
A Duel with Destiny, and
Other Stories
  Outlook, 59:342, 4 Jun 1898

Everett, Ruth
That Man from Wall Street
  Overland, 2d S, 53:56,
    Jan 1909

Everett, William
Thine Is Mine

Everett, William
    Epoch, 8:366, 9 Jan
        1891

Ewell, Alice Maude
    A White Guard to Satan
        South Atlantic Quarterly,
        1:86-8, Jan 1902

Ewing, Hugh Boyle
    A Castle in the Air
        Nation, 46:530, 28 Jun
        1888
        Picayune, 13 May 1888,
        p. 7

Ewing, Juliana Horatia
    Jackanapes
        Nation, 39:182, 28 Aug
        1884
        Overland, 2d S, 7:322,
        Mar 1886
    Jan of the Windmill
        Picayune, 4 Feb 1877,
        [p. 6]

Eyster, Nellie (Blessing)
    A Colonial Boy
        Overland, 2d S, 15:323,
        Mar 1890

Eytinge, Rose, and S. Ada
Fisher
    It Happened This Way
        Epoch, 8:384, 16 Jan
        1891

Faber, Christine [pseud.].
    See Smith, Mary E.

"Fadette" [pseud.].
    See Reeves, Marian Calhoun
    Legaré.

Fairfield, Caroline Elizabeth
    See Corbin, Caroline (Fair-
    field).

Fairman, Henry Clay
    The Third World
        Picayune, 9 Feb 1896,

        p. 11

Falkner, W. C.
    Lady Olivia
        Picayune, 19 May 1895,
        p. 8

Farman, Ella
    See Pratt, Ella (Farman).

Farmer, James Eugene
    Brinton Eliot
        Athenaeum, 3910:447, 4
        Oct 1902
        Saturday Review, 94:177,
        9 Aug 1902

Farmer, Lydia (Hoyt)
    Aunt Belindy, Point of View,
    and A Modern Mrs. Mala-
    prop
        Picayune, 2 Jun 1895, p.
        16
    A Knight of Faith
        Picayune, 24 Nov 1889, p.
        12

Farquhar, Anna
    See Bergengren, Anna (Far-
    quhar).

Farquharson, Martha Finley
    Elsie's Children
        Godey's, 95:526, Dec 1877
    Elsie's Motherhood
        Godey's, 94:92, Jan 1877
        Nation, 24:62, 25 Jan 1877
        Saturday Review, 42:675,
        25 Nov 1876
    Elsie's Womanhood
        Godey's, 91:570, Dec 1875
        Saturday Review, 40:821,
        25 Dec 1875
    Lilian
        Godey's, 73:474, Nov 1871
    An Old-Fashioned Boy
        Picayune, 18 Jun 1871,
        [p. 9]

Farrar, Charles Alden John
    Eastward, Ho!

Saturday Review, 49:837, 26 Jun 1880

Up the North Branch
Epoch, 4:193, 19 Oct 1888

Farrington, Margaret Vere
See Livingston, Margaret Vere (Farrington).

Fawcett, Edgar
The Adopted Daughter
Godey's, 126:236, Feb 1893

The Adventures of a Widow
Cottage Hearth, 14:160, May 1888
Godey's, 109:530, Nov 1884
Nation, 39:314, 9 Oct 1884
Saturday Review, 59:151, 31 Jan 1885

An Ambitious Woman
Atlantic, 53:710-1, May 1884
Continent, 5:222, (No. 7) 1884
Manhattan, 3:287, Mar 1884
Nation, 38:194, 28 Feb 1884
Overland, 2d S, 3:219, Feb 1884
Picayune, 20 Jan 1884, [p. 10]

American Push
Athenaeum, 3422:670, 27 May 1893
Saturday Review, 75:633, 10 Jun 1893

The Confessions of Claud
Epoch, 1:559-60, 22 Jul 1887
Picayune, 16 Dec 1888, p. 14

A Demoralizing Marriage
Godey's, 118:429-30, May 1889
Picayune, 31 Mar 1889, p. 7

Divided Lives
Epoch, 4:463, 25 Jan 1889
Picayune, 2 Dec 1888, p. 15
Saturday Review, 68:560, 16 Nov 1889

Ellen Story
Harper's, 53:629, Sep 1876

The Evil That Men Do
Picayune, 23 Feb 1890, p. 14

Fabian Dimitry
America, 4:525-6, 7 Aug 1890

A Gentleman of Leisure
Athenaeum, 2805:141-2, 30 Jul 1881; 2829:54-5, 14 Jan 1882
Atlantic, 48:561-6, Oct 1881
Cottage Hearth, 7:241, Aug 1881
Saturday Review, 52:282, 27 Aug 1881

Hartmann, the Anarchist
Bookman (London), 5:160, Feb 1894
Picayune, 3 Dec 1893, p. 19

An Heir to Millions
Athenaeum, 3422:670, 27 May 1893

Her Fair Fame
Athenaeum, 3489:317, 8 Sep 1894
Overland, 2d S, 24:448, Oct 1894
Saturday Review, 78:242, 1 Sep 1894

A Hopeless Case
Atlantic, 46:415-6, Sep 1880
Saturday Review, 50:124, 24 Jul 1880

The House at High Bridge
Cottage Hearth, 13:329, Sep 1887
Epoch, 1:263-4, 22 Apr 1887
Overland, 2d S, 9:219-20, Feb 1887

A Man's Will
Epoch, 3:516-7, 3 Aug 1888

Fawcett, Edgar
  Nation, 46:530, 28 Jun
      1888
  Overland, 2d S, 12:215,
      Aug 1888
  Picayune, 3 Jun 1888,
      p. 10
  Miriam Balestier
  Picayune, 17 Feb 1889,
      p. 7
  Saturday Review, 68:305-6,
      14 Sep 1889
  A New York Family
  Picayune, 29 May 1892,
      p. 13
  Olivia Delaplaine
  Cottage Hearth, 14:295,
      Sep 1888
  Epoch, 3:476-7, 20 Jul
      1888
  Outrageous Fortune
  Picayune, 3 Jun 1894,
      p. 10
  Purple and Fine Linen
  Nation, 17:27, 10 Jul
      1873
  Picayune, 6 Jul 1873,
      [p. 2]
  A Romance of Old New York
  Athenaeum, 3848:120,
      27 Jul 1901
  Godey's, 134:670, Jun
      1897
  Picayune, 11 Apr 1897,
      p. 25
  Rutherford
  Athenaeum, 2985:49, 10
      Jan 1885
  Saturday Review, 59:151,
      31 Jan 1885
  Social Silhouettes
  Athenaeum, 3037:64, 9
      Jan 1886
  Harper's, 72:323-4, Jan
      1886
  Tinkling Cymbals
  Athenaeum, 2985:49, 10
      Jan 1885
  Continent, 5:735, (No. 23)
      1884
  Nation, 39:20, 31 Jul 1884

  Picayune, 13 Jul 1884,
      [p. 9]
  Saturday Review, 60:258-9,
      22 Aug 1885
  The Vulgarians
  Outlook, 74:432, 13 Jun
      1903
  Overland, 2d S, 42:366,
      Oct 1903
  Where the Battle Was Fought
  Nation, 39:314, 9 Oct 1884
  Women Must Weep
  Picayune, 31 Jan 1892, p.
      3

[Fearing, Lilian Blanche]
  Roberta
  Picayune, 30 Mar 1896, p.
      8

Featherstone, William
  It's a Way Love Has
  Picayune, 26 Jun 1887, p.
      8

Fenollosa, Mary (McNeil)
  The Dragon Painter
  Nation, 83:396, 8 Nov 1906
  Red Horse Hill
  By Sidney McCall [pseud.].
      Atlantic, 104:683, Nov 1909
  Truth Dexter
  By Sidney McCall [pseud.].
      Outlook, 67:882, 13 Apr
      1901; 83:387, 16 Jun
      1906
  Saturday Review, 93:304,
      8 Mar 1902

Ferguson, Kate Lee
  Cliquot
  Picayune, 3 Nov 1889, p.
      10; 10 Nov 1889, p. 16

Fernald, Chester Bailey
  The Cat and the Cherub, and
  Other Stories
  Bookman (NY), 4:568-9, Feb
      1897
  Overland, 2d S, 29:229, Feb
      1897

Picayune, 29 Nov 1896,
p. 18
Chinatown Stories
Bookman (London), 17:155,
Feb 1900
Saturday Review, 89:211,
17 Feb 1900
John Kendry's Idea
Nation, 85:143, 15 Aug
1907

[Field, Caroline C. (Alden)]
Two Gentlemen of Boston
Nation, 44:453-4, 26
May 1887
Picayune, 25 Nov 1888,
p. 14

[Field, Caroline Leslie (Whit-
ney)]
High-Lights
Cottage Hearth, 11:394,
Dec 1885
Nation, 42:241, 18 Mar
1886
Overland, 2d S, 7:212,
Feb 1886

Field, Eugene
The Holy Cross, and Other
Tales
Nation, 58:488, 28 Jun
1894
Overland, 2d S, 23:666,
Jun 1894
Picayune, 11 Mar 1894,
p. 25
Sewanee Review, 5:153,
Jan 1897
The House
Picayune, 27 Apr 1896,
p. 10
Sewanee Review, 5:153,
Jan 1897
A Little Book of Profitable
Tales
Sewanee Review, 5:153,
Jan 1897
Second Book of Tales
Sewanee Review, 5:153,
Jan 1897

Sharps and Flats
Bookman (NY), 13:72-3,
Mar 1901

Field, Margaret
See Not Pretty, but Pre-
cious.

"Filia" [pseud.].
See Dorsey, Mrs. Sarah
Anne.

Finerty, John Frederick
War Path and Bivouac
Picayune, 4 May 1890,
p. 7

Finley, Martha
Elsie and the Raymonds
Picayune, 8 Dec 1889,
p. 14
Elsie at Viamede
Picayune, 4 Dec 1892,
p. 8
Elsie in the South
Outlook, 63:605, 4 Nov
1899
Elsie's Widowhood
Nation, 31:209, 16 Sep
1880
Signing the Contract and
What It Cost
Nation, 28:391, 5 Jun
1879
The Tragedy of Wild River
Valley
Picayune, 11 Jun 1893,
p. 16

Fischer, George Alexander
This Labyrinthine Life
Nation, 84:246-7, 14
Mar 1907

Fisguill, Richard [pseud.].
See Wilson, Richard Henry.

Fish, Williston
Short Rations
Outlook, 61:602, 11 Mar
1899

Fisher, Dorothy (Canfield)
Gunhild
Nation, 85:568, 19 Dec
1907
Sewanee Review, 16:509,
Oct 1908

Fisher, George P. , Jr.
Out of the Woods
Nation, 64:400, 27 May
1897

Fisher, S. Ada
See Eytinge, Rose, and S.
Ada Fisher.

Fisk, May Isabel
The Repentant Magdalen,
and Other Stories
Picayune, 12 Aug 1900,
II, 8

Fiske, Amos Kidder
Beyond the Bourn
America, 6:275-6, 4
Jun 1891

Fiske, Stephen Ryder
Holiday Stories
Picayune, 6 Dec 1891,
p. 12
Jack's Partner, and Other
Stories
Bookman (London), 6:121,
Jul 1894
Saturday Review, 78:139,
4 Aug 1894

Fitch, Anna (Mariska)
Bound Down
Saturday Review, 30:851,
31 Dec 1870

Fitch, Clyde
Barbara Frietchie, the
Frederick Girl
Outlook, 64:922, 21 Apr
1900

Flagg, William Joseph
A Good Investment

Atlantic, 30:487-8, Oct 1872
Godey's, 85:274, Sep 1872
Harper's, 45:464, Aug 1872
Nation, 15:126, 22 Aug 1872

Flandrau, Charles Macomb
The Diary of a Freshman
Athenaeum, 3868:808, 14
Dec 1901
Harvard Episodes
Sewanee Review, 6:252, Apr
1898

Flattery, Maurice Douglas
A Pair of Knaves and a Few
Trumps
Picayune, 9 Sep 1900, II, 8

Fleming, George [pseud.].
See Fletcher, Julia Constance.

Fleming, May Agnes (Early)
The Heir of Charlton
Picayune, 12 Feb 1893, p.
16
Lost for a Woman
Picayune, 26 Aug 1894, p.
16
A Mad Marriage
Saturday Review, 60:281, 28
Aug 1875
Norine's Revenge, and Sir
Noel's Heir
Picayune, 31 Oct 1875,
[p. 10]
A Terrible Secret
Godey's, 90:93, Jan 1875
The Virginia Heiress
Picayune, 25 Nov 1888, p.
14
A Wonderful Woman
Godey's, 87:568, Dec 1873
A Wronged Wife
Picayune, 26 Apr 1891, p.
15

Flemming, Harford [pseud.].
See McClellan, Harriet (Hare).

Fletcher, Coyne
The Bachelor's Baby

Picayune, 27 Sep 1891,
p. 12

Me and Chummy
Picayune, 5 Oct 1890,
p. 13

[Fletcher, Julia Constance]
Andromeda
By George Fleming [pseud.].
Nation, 41:429, 19 Nov
1885
Overland, 2d S, 6:552,
Nov 1885
Saturday Review, 60:547-
48, 24 Oct 1885

The Head of Medusa
By George Fleming [pseud.].
Atlantic, 47:707-9, May
1881
Harper's, 62:474, Feb
1881
Nation, 32:16, 6 Jan
1881
Saturday Review, 50:551-
52, 30 Oct 1880

Kismet
Atlantic, 39:500-1, Apr
1877
Godey's, 94:284, Mar
1877
Harper's, 54:771, Apr
1877
Library Table, 3:109,
19 Jul 1877

Little Stories About Women
By George Fleming [pseud.].
Athenaeum, 3637:63-4,
10 Jul 1897
Bookman (London), 12:97,
Jul 1897
Saturday Review, 83:641,
5 Jun 1897

Mirage
Harper's, 56:941, May
1878
Library Table, 4:196,
30 Mar 1878
Picayune, 24 Mar 1878,
[p. 3]
Sunday Afternoon, 1:480,
May 1878

The Truth About Clement Ker
By George Fleming [pseud.].
Epoch, 5:389, 19 Jul 1889
Saturday Review, 68:21,
6 Jul 1889

Vestigia
By George Fleming [pseud.].
Atlantic, 53:707-8, May
1884
Continent, 5:542-3, (No. 17)
1884
Godey's, 108:589, Jun 1884
Manhattan, 3:516-7, May
1884
Nation, 38:302, 3 Apr 1884
Saturday Review, 57:449,
5 Apr 1884

Fletchér, Robert Howe
The Johnstown Stage, and
Other Stories
Bookman (London), 2:91,
Jun 1892
Nation, 54:114-5, 11 Feb
1892

The Mystery of a Studio, and
Other Stories
Saturday Review, 74:21, 2
Jul 1892

Flewellyn, Juliette (Colliton)
Hill-Crest
Picayune, 15 Dec 1895 p.
15

Flint, Annie
A Girl of Ideas
Saturday Review, 96:ix-x,
Suppl., 17 Oct 1903

Flint, Joseph Frederick
His Perpetual Adoration
Picayune, 24 Jan 1896, p.
9

[Flint, Sargent]
Dollikins and the Miser
By Frances Eaton [pseud.].
Epoch, 8:366, 9 Jan 1891

A Queer Little Princess
By Francis Eaton [pseud.].

30 Jun 1883

The Prodigal
Outlook, 66:856, 1 Dec
1900
Picayune, 18 Nov 1900,
III, 4

The Royal Americans
Nation, 90:539, 26 May
1910
Saturday Review, 110:viii,
Suppl. , 8 Oct 1910

A Touch of Sun, and Other
Stories
Nation, 77:508, 24 Dec
1903

See also The Spinners' Book
of Fiction.

Ford, James Lane
The Literary Shop, and
Other Tales
Bookman (NY), 1:40-2,
Feb 1895

Ford, James Lauren
The Brazen Calf
Athenaeum, 3989:459,
9 Apr 1904
Bookman (London), 25:263,
Mar 1904
Dolly Dillenbeck
Nation, 62:458, 11 Jun
1896

Ford, Mary Hanford (Finney)
Which Wins?
America, 6:304, 11 Jun
1891
Epoch, 9:414-5, 31 Jul
1891
Nation, 53:264, 1 Oct
1891

Ford, Paul Leicester
The Great K. & A. Robbery
Canadian Magazine,
9:90, May 1897
Nation, 66:53, 20 Jan
1898
Picayune, 23 May 1897,
p. 22

The Honorable Peter Stirling
Athenaeum, 3702:489, 8
Oct 1898
Atlantic, 75:824-6, Jun
1895; 101:854, Jun 1908
Bookman (London), 14:48-9,
May 1898
Nation, 60:32, 10 Jan 1895

House Party
Sewanee Review, 10:246,
Apr 1902

Janice Meredith
Athenaeum, 3768:45, 13
Jan 1900
Atlantic, 85:408-10, Mar
1900
Bookman (London), 17:187-
88, Mar 1900
Bookman (NY), 10:563-6,
Feb 1900
Nation, 69:412, 30 Nov 1899
Outlook, 63:511, 28 Oct
1899
Saturday Review, 89:147-8,
3 Feb 1900
Sewanee Review, 11:356,
Jul 1903

The Story of an Untold Love
Athenaeum, 3695:252, 20
Aug 1898
Bookman (NY), 6:253-4,
Nov 1897
Godey's, 136:216, Feb 1898
Nation, 66:136, 17 Feb
1898
Picayune, 7 Nov 1897, p.
6
Saturday Review, 86:418,
17 Sep 1898

Tattle-Tales of Cupid
Outlook, 60:777, 26 Nov
1898

Wanted--A Chaperon
Bookman (NY), 16:501-2,
Jan 1903
Nation, 75:468, 11 Dec 1902

Ford, Sallie (Rochester)
Ernest Quest
Picayune, 17 Mar 1878,
[p. 11]

Ford, Sewell
  Horses Nine
    Overland, 2d S, 42:366-
      67, Oct 1903
    Sewanee Review, 11:503,
      Oct 1903
  Shorty McCabe
    Athenaeum, 4190:187,
      15 Feb 1908
  Side-Stepping with Shorty
    Nation, 87:97, 30 Jul
      1908

Forman, Justus Miles
  Bianca's Daughter
    Athenaeum, 4310:670,
      4 Jun 1910
    Nation, 91:11, 7 Jul
      1910
  The Garden of Lies
    Outlook, 72:466, 25
      Oct 1902
  Jason
    North American Review,
      192:720, Nov 1909
  Journey's End
    Athenaeum, 3969:681,
      21 Nov 1903
    Bookman (London), 25:149,
      Dec 1903
    Outlook, 73:645, 14 Mar
      1903
    Overland, 2d S, 42:271-2,
      Sep 1903
  Monsigny
    Outlook, 75:136, 12 Sep
      1903
  The Stumbling-Block
    Athenaeum, 4170:362,
      28 Sep 1907
    Nation, 85:102-3, 1 Aug
      1907
  Tommy Carteret
    Athenaeum, 4062:298,
      2 Sep 1905

Forney, John Wien
  The New Nobility
    Godey's, 102:477, May
      1881

Forsslund, Mary Louise
  Old Lady Number 31
    Nation, 88:419, 22 Apr 1909
  The Ship of Dreams
    Bookman (NY), 16:181-2,
      Oct 1902
  The Story of Sarah
    Athenaeum, 3866:731, 30
      Nov 1901
    Nation, 72:399, 16 May 1901

Forth, George [pseud.].
  See Frederic, Harold.

Fosdick, James William
  The Honor of the Braxtons
    Outlook, 71:134, 10 May
      1902

Foster, Charles J.
  The White Horse of Wootton
    Godey's, 98:181, Feb 1879
    Nation, 27:319, 21 Nov
      1878

Foster, David Skaats
  Elinor Fenton
    Picayune, 15 Oct 1893, p.
      18
    Saturday Review, 77:151,
      10 Feb 1894
  Prince Timoteo
    Picayune, 8 Oct 1899, II,
      12

Foster, Mabel G.
  The Heart of the Doctor
    Nation, 75:369, 6 Nov 1902

Foster, Mary Farrington
  Doty Dontcare
    Nation, 62:61, 16 Jan 1896

Foster, Maximilian
  Corrie Who?
    Overland, 2d S, 52:580,
      Dec 1908

[Fowles, Mary A.]
  A Hero's Last Days
    Nation, 38:194, 28 Feb 1884

Saturday Review, 57:294,
1 Mar 1884

Fox, John William, Jr.
Blue-Grass and Rhododen-
dron
Nation, 73:476, 19 Dec
1901
Christmas Eve on Lonesome,
and Other Stories
Athenaeum, 4026:870,
24 Dec 1904
Atlantic, 95:690, May
1905
Nation, 80:98, 2 Feb
1905
South Atlantic Quarterly,
4:96-7, Jan 1905
Crittenden
Athenaeum, 4042:459,
15 Apr 1905
Bookman (London),
28:170-1, Aug 1905
Nation, 72:362, 2 May
1901
Picayune, 16 Dec 1900,
III, 5
Saturday Review, 99:564,
29 Apr 1905
A Cumberland Vendetta,
and Other Stories
Bookman (London),
29:144-5, Dec 1905
Bookman (NY), 2:435,
Jan 1896; 12:440-1,
Jan 1901
Outlook, 65:323, 2 Jun
1900
Picayune, 17 Jun 1900,
II, 12
Following the Sun-Flag
Nation, 81:42, 13 Jul
1905
"Hell-fer-Sartain, " and
Other Stories
Bookman (NY), 6:56-7,
Sep 1897
Nation, 65:363, 4 Nov
1897
The Kentuckians
Godey's, 136:[215]-6,

Feb 1898
Saturday Review, 85:336-7,
5 Mar 1898
A Knight of the Cumberland
Nation, 83:441, 22 Nov 1906
Overland, 2d S, 49:96, Jan
1907
Saturday Review, 103:244,
23 Feb 1907
The Little Shepherd of King-
dom Come
Athenaeum, 3963:477, 10
Oct 1903
Bookman (London), 25:104,
Nov 1903
Bookman (NY), 18:158-9,
Oct 1903
Nation, 77:390-1, 12 Nov
1903
Overland, 2d S, 42:553,
Dec 1903
Poet-Lore, 14:136, Winter
1903
Saturday Review, 98:276,
27 Aug 1904
South Atlantic Quarterly,
3:288, Jul 1904
A Mountain Europa
Bookman (London), 29:256,
Mar 1906
Nation, 69:300, 19 Oct 1899
Outlook, 62:265, 30 Sep
1899
Saturday Review, 101:273,
3 Mar 1906
The Trail of the Lonesome
Pine
Athenaeum, 4233:758, 12
Dec 1908
Bookman (NY), 28:364-5,
Dec 1908
Nation, 87:466, 12 Nov 1908
Saturday Review, 107:82,
16 Jan 1909

[Fox, Mrs. Emily]
Gemini
Cottage Hearth, 5:214-5,
Jun 1878
Library Table, 4:262, 25
May 1878

[Fox, Mrs. Emily]
  Picayune, 12 May 1878,
    [p. 8]
  Sunday Afternoon, 2:96,
    Jul 1878

France, Lewis Browne
  Pine Valley
    Atlantic, 70:281, Aug
    1892
  Picayune, 2 May 1897,
    p. 15

Frances, Margaret
  Rose Carleton's Reward
    Picayune, 4 Aug 1872,
    [p. 9]

Frances, Mary [pseud.].
  See Mason, Fanny Wither-
  spoon.

Frank, Henry
  His Bold Experiment
    Atlantic, 70:564, Oct
    1892

Frankel, A. H.
  In Gold We Trust
    Picayune, 10 Jul 1898,
    II, 6

Frazar, Douglas
  The Log of the Maryland
    Overland, 2d S, 18:440-
    41, Oct 1891

Frederic, Harold
  The Copperhead, and Other
  Stories
    Athenaeum, 3467:442-3,
    7 Apr 1894
    Atlantic, 73:568-9, Apr
    1894
    Bookman (London), 6:57,
    May 1894
    Godey's, 128:[104], Jan
    1894
    Nation, 58:277, 12 Apr
    1894
    Picayune, 12 Nov 1893,

p. 14
    Saturday Review, 77:313,
    24 Mar 1894
The Damnation of Theron Ware
  Illumination
    Athenaeum, 3569:378, 21
    Mar 1896
    Atlantic, 78:270-2, Aug 1896
    Bookman (London), 10:136-8,
    Aug 1896
    Bookman (NY), 3:200, May
    1896; 3:351-2, Jun 1896
    Godey's, 133:95, Jul 1896
    Nation, 63:180-1, 3 Sep 1896
    Overland, 2d S, 28:234,
    Aug 1896
    Picayune, 13 Apr 1896, p.
    10
    Poet-Lore, 8:459-61, (No.
    7) 1896
The Deserter, and Other
  Stories
    Nation, 67:453, 15 Dec 1898
    Outlook, 60:639, 5 Nov 1898
    Picayune, 24 Oct 1898, I, 8
Gloria Mundi
    Athenaeum, 3706:637-8, 5
    Nov 1898
    Atlantic, 83:522-4, Apr 1899
    Bookman (London), 15:83,
    Dec 1898
    Bookman (NY), 8:586, Feb
    1899
    Saturday Review, 86:645-6,
    12 Nov 1898
In the Valley
    Athenaeum, 3291:696, 22
    Nov 1890
    Epoch, 8:238, 14 Nov 1890
    Harper's, 81:800, Oct 1890
    Nation, 52:483, 11 Jun 1891
    Picayune, 2 Nov 1890, p.
    14
    Saturday Review, 71:108,
    24 Jan 1891
The Lawton Girl
    Athenaeum, 3265:669-70, 24
    May 1890
    Epoch, 7:269, 30 May 1890
    Harper's, 81:800-1, Oct
    1890

Nation, 51:195, 4 Sep
   1890
Picayune, 27 Apr 1890,
   p. 10
March Hares
   By George Forth [pseud.].
   Athenaeum, 3584:32,
      4 Jul 1896
   Godey's, 133:654, Dec
      1896
   Nation, 64:399-400, 27
      May 1897
The Market-Place
   Athenaeum, 3740:31, 1
      Jul 1899
   Bookman (London), 16:136,
      Aug 1899
   Bookman (NY), 10:91,
      Sep 1899
   Nation, 69:95, 3 Aug
      1899
   Outlook, 62:314, 3 Jun
      1899
   Picayune, 10 Dec 1899,
      III, 7
Marsena, and Other Stories
   of Wartime
   Athenaeum, 3574:543,
      25 Apr 1896
   Atlantic, 75:709, May
      1895
   Bookman (London), 10:121,
      Jul 1896
   Nation, 60:426, 30 May
      1895
   Saturday Review, 81:562,
      30 May 1896
Mrs. Albert Grundy
   Athenaeum, 3578:679,
      23 May 1896
   Bookman (London), 10:57,
      May 1896
The Return of the O'Mahony
   Bookman (London), 4:58,
      May 1893
   Godey's, 126:103, Jan
      1893
   Picayune, 27 Nov 1892,
      p. 22
Seth's Brother's Wife
   Athenaeum, 3136:743-4,

3 Dec 1887
Harper's, 81:800-1, Oct
   1890
Nation, 46:219, 15 Mar
   1888
North American Review,
   145:703-4, Dec 1887
Overland, 2d S, 11:440,
   Apr 1888
Picayune, 27 Nov 1887,
   p. 6
Saturday Review, 65:202-3,
   18 Feb 1888
See also Tales of Our Coast.

[Freeman, Mrs. A. M.]
Somebody's Ned
   Nation, 29:214, 25 Sep
      1879

Freeman, Mary Eleanor (Wil-
kins)
By the Light of the Soul
   Athenaeum, 4137:160-1,
      9 Feb 1907
   Atlantic, 100:132-3, Jul
      1907
   Bookman (London), 31:269,
      Mar 1907
   Bookman (NY), 25:81-3,
      Mar 1907
   Nation, 84:110, 31 Jan
      1907
   Times Literary Supplement,
      25 Jan 1907, p. 30
The Debtor
   Athenaeum, 4078:860, 23
      Dec 1905
   Nation, 81:488, 14 Dec
      1905
   Times Literary Supplement,
      17 Nov 1905, p. 396
Doctor Gordon
   Bookman (London), 32:212,
      Sep 1907
   Saturday Review, 103:498,
      20 Apr 1907
   Times Literary Supplement,
      12 Apr 1907, p. 119
The Fair Lavinia, and Others
   Athenaeum, 4179:686, 30

Stories
  Athenaeum, 3325:92-4,
    18 Jul 1891
  Atlantic, 67:847-8, Jun
    1891
  Epoch, 9:188-9, 24 Apr
    1891
  Godey's, 134:[316]-8,
    Mar 1897
  Nation, 52:484, 11 Jun
    1891
  Saturday Review, 71:656-
    57, 30 May 1891
The Other Woman
  Cosmopolitan, 11:638-9,
    Sep 1891
Pembroke
  Athenaeum, 3476:739,
    9 Jun 1894
  Atlantic, 74:272-4, Aug
    1894
  Godey's, 129:223-4, Aug
    1894; 134:[316]-8,
    Mar 1897
  Nation, 58:488-9, 28
    Jun 1894
  Saturday Review, 77:667-
    68, 23 Jun 1894
The People of Our Neigh-
borhood
  Outlook, 60:188, 17 Sep
    1898
The Portion of Labor
  Athenaeum, 3871:12, 4
    Jan 1902
  Bookman (NY), 15:70-1,
    Mar 1902
  Harper's, 102:647, Mar
    1901
  Saturday Review, 93:405,
    29 Mar 1902
A Pot of Gold, and Other
Stories
  Bookman (London), 2:42,
    May 1892
  Nation, 54:451, 16 Jun
    1892
The Shoulders of Atlas
  Athenaeum, 4211:38,
    11 Jul 1908
  Nation, 87:35-6, 9 Jul

1908
  Times Literary Supplement,
    26 Jun 1908, p. 206
Silence, and Other Stories
  Athenaeum, 3696:287, 27
    Aug 1898
  Bookman (London), 14:138,
    Aug 1898
  Bookman (NY), 8:70, Sep
    1898
  Outlook, 59:588, 2 Jul 1898
  Saturday Review, 85:854,
    25 Jun 1898
Six Trees
  Nation, 76:276, 2 Apr 1903
  Saturday Review, 96:20, 4
    Jul 1903
  Times Literary Supplement,
    17 Apr 1903, p. 121
Understudies
  Bookman (NY), 14:306, Nov
    1901
The Wind in the Rose Bush
  Bookman (London), 24:150,
    Jul 1903
  Nation, 76:359, 30 Apr 1903
  Saturday Review, 95:784,
    20 Jun 1903
  Times Literary Supplement,
    22 May 1903, p. 160
The Winning Lady, and Others
  Nation, 90:36-7, 13 Jan 1910
Young Lucretia, and Other
Stories
  Athenaeum, 3394:660-2, 12
    Nov 1892
  Bookman (London), 3:60,
    Nov 1892
  Cottage Hearth, 18:287, Sep
    1892
  Godey's, 134:[316]-8, Mar
    1897
See also The Whole Family.

[French, Alice]
  A Book of True Lovers
    By Octave Thanet [pseud.].
    Bookman (NY), 7:170, Apr
      1898
    Overland, 2d S, 31:478,
      May 1898

127

[French, Alice]
Picayune, 12 Dec 1897,
p. 25
Expiation
By Octave Thanet [pseud.].
Athenaeum, 3276:189,
9 Aug 1890
Epoch, 7:189-90, 25
Apr 1890
Nation, 51:136, 14 Aug
1890
The Heart of Toil
By Octave Thanet [pseud.].
Athenaeum, 3745:189,
5 Aug 1899
Nation, 67:432-3, 8 Dec
1898
Picayune, 27 Nov 1898,
p. 10
Saturday Review, 88:368-
69, 16 Sep 1899
Knitters in the Sun
By Octave Thanet [pseud.].
Epoch, 3:158, 30 Mar
1888
Overland, 2d S, 11:436,
Apr 1888 ·
The Lion's Share
By Octave Thanet [pseud.].
Bookman (NY), 26:532,
Jan 1908
The Man of the Hour
By Octave Thanet [pseud.].
Bookman (NY), 22:133-4,
Oct 1905
The Missionary Sheriff
By Octave Thanet [pseud.].
Bookman (NY), 5:522,
Aug 1893
Nation, 65:17, 1 Jul
1897
Otto the Knight, and Other
Trans-Mississippi Stories
By Octave Thanet [pseud.].
Athenaeum, 3356:240-1,
20 Feb 1892
Atlantic, 68:710, Nov
1891; 69:265, Feb
1892
Bookman (London), 1:149,
Jan 1892

Epoch, 9:302, 12 Jun 1891
Nation, 53:264, 1 Oct 1891
Overland, 2d S, 18:441-2,
Oct 1891
Picayune, 31 May 1891, p.
12
Stories of a Western Town
By Octave Thanet [pseud.].
Atlantic, 72:698, Nov 1893
Godey's, 126:774, Jun 1893
Nation, 57:32, 13 Jul 1893
Picayune, 23 Apr 1893, p.
21
Saturday Review, 77:127,
3 Feb 1894
Whitsun Harp, Regulator
Harper's, 75:321, Jan 1888

French, Allen
The Colonials
Atlantic, 89:707, May 1902
Outlook, 70:440, 15 Feb
1902
Saturday Review, 94:523-4,
25 Oct 1902

French, Anne (Warner)
The Diary of a Bride
Overland, 2d S, 46:593,
Dec 1905
Just Between Themselves
Athenaeum, 4329:454, 15
Oct 1910
Bookman (NY), 31:427,
Jun 1910
The Panther
Overland, 2d S, 52:[579],
Dec 1908
Seeing England with Uncle
John
Nation, 86:402, 30 Apr
1908
Susan Clegg and a Man in
the House
Nation, 85:423, 7 Nov 1907
Susan Clegg and Her Friend
Mrs. Lathrop
Bookman (London), 28:172,
Aug 1905

French, Harry W. [pseud.].

See French, Henry Willard.

French, Henry Willard
Castle Foam
Nation, 29:443, 25 Dec
1879
Ego
By Harry W. French
[pseud.].
Atlantic, 47:713, May
1881
Godey's, 102:183, Feb
1881
Nation, 32:172, 10 Mar
1881
The Only One
Overland, 2d S, 4:223-4,
Aug 1884
Oscar Peterson
Cottage Hearth, 19:ad-
vert 28, Nov 1893
Out of the Night
Picayune, 26 Oct 1890,
p. 10

French, Lucy Virginia (Smith)
My Roses
Picayune, 10 Sep 1871,
[p. 5]

Friedman, Isaac Kahn
By Bread Alone
Athenaeum, 3887:526,
26 Apr 1902
Bookman (London), 22:109,
Jun 1902
The Lucky Number
Bookman (NY), 4:468,
Jan 1897
Poor People
Nation, 70:304, 19 Apr
1900
Picayune, 25 Mar 1900,
III, 5
The Radical
Nation, 85:474, 21 Nov
1907

Frost, Arthur Burdett
The Bull Calf, and Other
Tales

Saturday Review, 74:778-9,
31 Dec 1892

Frost, Thomas Gold
The Man of Destiny
Nation, 89:381, 21 Oct 1909

Frothingham, Eugenia Brooks
The Evasion
Bookman (London), 30:186,
Aug 1906
Bookman (NY), 23:415-6,
Jun 1906
North American Review,
182:927-8, Jun 1906
The Turn of the Road
Bookman (NY), 13:389, Jun
1901

Fuller, Anna
One of the Pilgrims
Outlook, 60:538, 29 Oct
1898
Peak and Prairie
Atlantic, 74:848, Dec 1894
Nation, 61:244, 3 Oct 1895
Pratt Portraits
Atlantic, 70:564, Oct 1892
Godey's, 125:407-8, Oct
1892
Nation, 56:475, 29 Jun 1893
A Venetian June
Atlantic, 78:848, Dec 1896
Bookman (NY), 4:76, Sep
1896

Fuller, Caroline Macomber
Across the Campus
Picayune, 18 Jun 1899, III,
1
Brunhilde's Paying Guest
Nation, 85:260, 19 Sep 1907

Fuller, Edward
The Complaining Millions of
Men
Atlantic, 73:418, Mar 1894
Godey's, 127:493, Oct 1893
Nation, 57:374, 16 Nov 1893
Fellow Travellers
Nation, 43:102, 29 Jul 1886

Fuller, Edward
　Saturday Review, 62:299,
　　28 Aug 1886
　Forever and a Day
　　Picayune, 11 Jun 1882,
　　　[p. 3]
　John Malcolm
　　Nation, 75:368, 6 Nov
　　1902

Fuller, Henry Blake
　The Cliff-Dwellers
　　Atlantic, 73:555-7, Apr
　　1894
　　Godey's, 127:764, Dec
　　1893; 131:[318]-20,
　　Sep 1895
　From the Other Side
　　Bookman (NY), 7:352-3,
　　Jun 1898
　　Outlook, 58:782, 26 Mar
　　1898
　　Picayune, 10 Apr 1898,
　　　p. 25
　The Last Refuge
　　Picayune, 4 Nov 1900,
　　　II, 9
　　Harper's, 103:824, Oct
　　1901
　　Nation, 72:182, 28 Feb
　　1901
　　Outlook, 66:665, 10
　　Nov 1900
　Under the Skylights
　　Nation, 74:232, 20 Mar
　　1902
　With the Procession
　　Atlantic, 76:555-6, Oct
　　1895
　　Godey's, 131:97, Jul
　　1895; 131:[318]-20,
　　Sep 1895

Fuller, Hulbert
　God's Rebel
　　Outlook, 61:791, 1 Apr
　　1899
　Vivian of Virginia
　　Bookman (NY), 7:170-1,
　　Apr 1898
　　Outlook, 58:82, 1 Jan

　1898
　Picayune, 8 Oct 1899, II,
　　12

Fuller, Jane Gay
　Bending Willow
　　Godey's, 89:98, Jan 1872
　Hearts and Coronets
　　Picayune, 2 Jul 1893, p.
　　17

Fuller, Lydia
　Mistaken
　　Saturday Review, 30:851,
　　31 Dec 1870

Fuller, Robert H.
　The Golden Hope
　　Athenaeum, 4051:746, 17
　　Jun 1905

Fulton, Chandos
　An Unusual Husband
　　Picayune, 29 May 1898,
　　II, 3

Furman, Lucy S.
　Stories of a Sanctified Town
　　Picayune, 6 Dec 1896, p.
　　15

Futrelle, Jacques
　The Simple Case of Susan
　　Nation, 86:580, 25 Jun
　　1908
　The Thinking Machine
　　Nation, 84:457, 16 May
　　1907

Gage, Mrs. Frances Dana
　Steps Upward
　　Picayune, 26 Feb 1871, [p. 5]
　　Saturday Review, 31:256,
　　25 Feb 1871

Gale, Zona
　Friendship Village Love
　Stories
　　Bookman (NY), 28:476,
　　Jan 1909; 31:79, Mar 1910
　　Nation, 87:655, 31 Dec

1908; 90:37, 13 Jan
1910
Saturday Review, 109:602,
7 May 1910
The Loves of Pelleas and
Etarre
  Nation, 86:38-9, 9 Jan
  1908

Gallagher, George Washington
One Man's Struggle
  Atlantic, 66:857, Dec
  1890

Gallizier, Nathan
The Court of Lucifer
  Nation, 91:551, 8 Dec
  1910

Gardener, Helen Hamilton
Is This Your Son, My
Lord?
  Picayune, 11 Jan 1891,
  p. 10
Pushed by Unseen Hands
  Nation, 54:451, 16 Jun
  1892
  Picayune, 8 May 1892,
  p. 10
An Unofficial Patriot
  Picayune, 27 May 1894,
  p. 16

Gardenhire, Samuel Major
Purple and Homespun
  Athenaeum, 4208:758,
  20 Jun 1908
  Nation, 86:580, 25 Jun
  1908
The Silence of Mrs. Harrold
  Athenaeum, 4051:746,
  17 Jun 1905

Gardner, Celia Emmeline
Her Last Lover
  Picayune, 23 Apr 1893,
  p. 21
Rich Medway's Two Loves
  Godey's, 90:570, Jun
  1875
Tested

Godey's, 79:473, Nov 1874
A Woman's Wiles
  Saturday Review, 42:675,
  25 Nov 1876
Won Under Protest
  Picayune, 22 Nov 1896, p.
  10

Gardner, Mrs. Sarah M. H.
The Fortunes of Margaret
Weld
  Picayune, 3 Jun 1894, p.
  10
Quaker Idyls
  Atlantic, 74:565, Oct 1894
  Sewanee Review, 3:102-4,
  Nov 1894

Garland, Hamlin
Boy Life on the Prairie
  Athenaeum, 3774:235, 24
  Feb 1900
The Captain of the Gray-
Horse Troop
  Athenaeum, 3913:547-8,
  25 Oct 1902
  Bookman (London), 23:109,
  Dec 1902
  Bookman (NY), 17:101,
  Mar 1903
  Saturday Review, 94:274,
  30 Aug 1902
Cavanagh
  Bookman (NY), 31:309-10,
  May 1910
  Nation, 90:484, 12 May
  1910
The Eagle's Heart
  Athenaeum, 3811:613, 10
  Nov 1900
  Bookman (NY), 12:351-2,
  Dec 1900
  Picayune, 16 Dec 1900,
  III, 5
Her Mountain Lover
  Athenaeum, 3841:722, 8
  Jun 1901
  Canadian Magazine, 17:90,
  May 1901
  Outlook, 67:922, 20 Apr
  1901

Garland, Hamlin
Overland, 2d S, 38:235,
Sep 1901
Hesper
Athenaeum, 3970:714,
28 Nov 1903
Outlook, 75:609, 7 Nov
1903
Jason Edwards
Bookman (London), 14:138,
Aug 1898
Godey's, 125:408, Oct
1892
Picayune, 28 Feb 1892,
p. 11
Saturday Review, 86:448,
1 Oct 1898
The Light of the Star
Athenaeum, 4002:43,
3 Jul 1904
A Little Norsk
Bookman (London), 14:138,
Aug 1898
Godey's, 125:408, Oct
1892
Nation, 55:262, 6 Oct
1892
The Long Trail
Athenaeum, 4152:634,
25 May 1907
Nation, 84:435, 9 May
1907
Main-Travelled Roads
America, 6:332-3, 18
Jun 1891
Atlantic, 69:266, Feb
1892
Cosmopolitan, 12:638-9,
Mar 1891
Harper's, 83:639-40,
Sep 1891
Nation, 53:125, 13 Aug
1891
Outlook, 63:464, 21 Oct
1899
Overland, 2d S, 19:332,
Mar 1892
Saturday Review, 73:103,
23 Jan 1892
Sewanee Review, 11:355,
Jul 1903

A Member of the Third House
Godey's, 125:644, Dec 1892
Nation, 54:362-3, 12 May
1892
The Moccasin Ranch
Nation, 89:433, 4 Nov 1909
Money Magic
Athenaeum, 4175:546, 2
Nov 1907
Bookman (NY), 26:417-8,
Dec 1907
Nation, 85:446, 14 Nov
1907
Outlook, 87:744, 30 Nov
1907
Other Main-Travelled Roads
Athenaeum, 4339:793, 24
Dec 1910
Bookman (NY), 32:305-6,
Nov 1910
Nation, 91:391-2, 27 Oct
1910
Prairie Folks
Athenaeum, 3439:416, 23
Sep 1893; 3774:235, 24
Feb 1900
Nation, 56:408, 1 Jun 1893
Saturday Review, 76:83, 15
Jul 1893
Rose of Dutcher's Coolly
Athenaeum, 3643:253, 21
Aug 1897
Bookman (NY), 2:512-4,
Feb 1896
Outlook, 62:129, 13 May
1899
Picayune, 23 Dec 1895, p.
9; 18 Jun 1899, III, 1
Saturday Review, 83:128,
30 Jan 1897; 83:615-6,
29 May 1897
The Shadow World
Nation, 87:631-2, 24 Dec
1908
North American Review,
189:455-8, Mar 1909
The Spirit of Sweetwater
Outlook, 58:980, 16 Apr
1898
A Spoil of Office
Nation, 55:262, 6 Oct 1892

Picayune, 4 Sep 1892,
p. 7
The Trail of the Goldseekers
Athenaeum, 3767:13,
6 Jan 1900
Picayune, 2 Jul 1899,
II, 12
The Tyranny of the Dark
Athenaeum, 4049:685,
3 Jun 1905
Nation, 81:122, 10 Aug
1905
Times Literary Supple-
ment, 19 May 1905,
p. 163
Wayside Courtships
Athenaeum, 3675:434,
2 Apr 1898
Picayune, 22 Aug 1897,
p. 24
Saturday Review, 85:370,
12 Mar 1898
Witches' Gold
Nation, 83:228, 13 Sep
1906

Garland, Will A.
The Broken Locket
Picayune, 28 Aug 1898,
II, 4

Garrigues, Mrs. Adéle M.
Summer Boarders
Picayune, 1 Aug 1880,
[p. 10]

Gasch, Marie (Manning)
Lord Alingham, Bankrupt
Bookman (NY), 15:475-7,
Jul 1902

Gash, Abram Dale
The False Star
Picayune, 2 Jul 1899,
II, 12

[Gatchell, Charles]
Haschisch
By Thorold King [pseud.].
Nation, 43:14, 1 Jul
1886

Gates, Eleanor
The Biography of a Prairie
Girl
Nation, 75:487, 18 Dec
1902
Cupid the Cowpunch
Nation, 86:62, 16 Jan 1908
The Plow Woman
Athenaeum, 4142:317, 16
Mar 1907
Nation, 83:374-5, 1 Nov
1906
A Prairie Child's Biography
Overland, 2d S, 40:552-3,
Dec 1902
See also The Spinners' Book
of Fiction.

Gayarré, Charles Etienne Arthur
Aubert Dubayet
Saturday Review, 55:422,
31 Mar 1883
Fernando de Lemos
Saturday Review, 34:260,
24 Aug 1872

[Gazzam, Anna Reading]
A Sketch in the Ideal
Picayune, 30 Aug 1891, p.
3

Genone, Hudor [pseud.].
See Roe, William James.

Geppert, Dora (Higbee)
In "God's Country"
By D. Higbee.
Picayune, 7 Nov 1897, p.
12

Gestefeid, Ursula Newell
The Woman Who Dares
Picayune, 9 Oct 1892, p.
6

Gibbs, George Fort
In Search of Mademoiselle
Athenaeum, 3866:731, 30
Nov 1901
The Love of Monsieur
Athenaeum, 3947:780, 20

Gibbs, George Fort
Jun 1903
The Medusa Emerald
Outlook, 87:828, 14 Dec
1907
Pike and Cutlass
Picayune, 26 Nov 1899,
II, 8

[Gibson, Eva Katherine (Clapp)]
Her Bright Future
Picayune, 9 May 1880,
[p. 7]
Saturday Review, 49:837,
26 Jun 1880

Gielow, Martha (Sawyer)
Mammy's Reminiscences,
and Other Stories
Bookman (NY), 9:281-2,
May 1899
Outlook, 61:371, 11 Feb
1899
Picayune, 10 Dec 1899,
III, 7

Gilchrist, Annie (Somers)
Harcourt
Picayune, 8 May 1887,
p. 7

Gilder, Jeannette Leonard
The Autobiography of a
Tom-Boy
Bookman (NY), 12:523-4,
Jan 1901
Taken by Siege
Picayune, 10 Apr 1887,
p. 10
Nation, 44:300, 7 Apr
1887

Giles, Ella A.
See Ruddy, Ella Augusta
(Giles).

[Gill, J. Thompson]
Within and Without
Overland, 2d S, 12:213-4,
Aug 1888

Gill, William
The Woman Who Didn't
Picayune, 19 May 1895, p.
8

Gilliam, Edward Winslow
1791: A Tale of San Domingo
Picayune, 4 May 1890, p.
7

Gillman, Henry
Hassan, A Fellah
Athenaeum, 3696:285, 27
Aug 1898
Picayune, 29 May 1898, II,
2

Gilman, Bradley
The Parsonage Porch
Outlook, 65:135, 12 May
1900
Ronald Carnaquay
Athenaeum, 3947:779, 20
Jun 1903

Gilman, Charlotte (Perkins)
Stetson
The Yellow Wall Paper
Picayune, 9 Jul 1899, III,
3

Gilman, Mrs. Stella Lucile
That Dakota Girl
Picayune, 7 Aug 1892, p.
11

Gilman, Wenona [pseud.].
See Schoeffel, Florence Blackburn (White).

Gilmore, James Robert
The Last of the Thorndikes
Overland, 2d S, 15:320-1,
Mar 1890
A Mountain-White Heroine
Picayune, 16 Feb 1890, p.
10; 23 Feb 1890, p. 14

Gilmore, Minnie L.
A Son of Esau
Godey's, 125:518, Nov 1892

Picayune, 15 Jan 1893,
p. 20; 7 Aug 1892,
p. 11
The Woman Who Stood Be-
tween
Saturday Review, 80:481,
12 Oct 1895

Gilson, Roy Rolfe
In the Morning Glow
Athenaeum, 3952:120,
25 Jul 1903
Katrina
Bookman (NY), 24:247-8,
Nov 1906

[Gladwin, William Zachary]
Maggie MacLanehan
By Gulielma Zollinger
[pseud.].
Nation, 73:476, 19 Dec
1901

Glasgow, Ellen Anderson Ghol-
son
The Ancient Law
Athenaeum, 4196:380,
28 Mar 1908
Bookman (NY), 27:59-60,
Mar 1908
Nation, 86:152-3, 13
Feb 1908
North American Review,
187:445-7, Mar 1908
Saturday Review, 105:760,
13 Jun 1908
South Atlantic Quarterly,
7:200-1, Apr 1908
The Battleground
Athenaeum, 3896:812,
28 Jun 1902
Bookman (NY), 15:258-9,
May 1902
Nation, 74:294, 10 Apr
1902
Saturday Review, 94:274,
30 Aug 1902
South Atlantic Quarterly,
5:254-60, Jul 1906
The Deliverance
Athenaeum, 4007:201-2,

13 Aug 1904
Atlantic, 93:852, Jun 1904
Bookman (London), 26:27,
Apr 1904
Bookman (NY), 19:43-4,
Mar 1904; 19:73-4, Mar
1904
Nation, 78:234-5, 24 Mar
1904
Sewanee Review, 12:456,
462, 464, Oct 1904
South Atlantic Quarterly,
3:288, Jul 1904; 5:254-
60, Jul 1906
Times Literary Supplement,
15 Apr 1904, p. 116
The Descendent
Bookman (NY), 5:368-9, Jul
1893
Phases of an Inferior Planet
Atlantic, 83:284-5, Feb
1899
Bookman (London), 15:121,
Jan 1899
Bookman (NY), 8:483, Jan
1899
Nation, 67:452, 15 Dec 1898
Outlook, 60:395, 8 Oct 1898
The Romance of a Plain Man
Athenaeum, 4276:424, 9
Oct 1908
Atlantic, 104:682, Nov 1909
Bookman (London), 36:234,
Aug 1909
Nation, 89:37, 8 Jul 1909
North American Review,
190:118, Jul 1909
Saturday Review, 108:173,
7 Aug 1909
The Voice of the People
Athenaeum, 3798:179, 11
Aug 1900
Atlantic, 86:416-8, Sep 1900
Bookman (London), 19:29,
Oct 1900
Bookman (NY), 11:397-8,
Jun 1900
Nation, 70:402, 24 May 1900
Picayune, 6 May 1900, III,
8
Saturday Review, 90:180,

Glasgow, Ellen Anderson Ghol-
son
    11 Aug 1900
    South Atlantic Quarterly,
      5:254-60, Jul 1906
    The Wheel of Life
      Athenaeum, 4093:416,
      7 Apr 1906
      Bookman (NY), 23:91-3,
      Mar 1906
      North American Review,
      182:922-4, Jun 1906
      Saturday Review, 101:625,
      19 May 1906
      South Atlantic Quarterly,
      5:254-60, Jul 1906

Glaspell, Susan
    The Glory of the Conquered
      Athenaeum, 4274:358,
      25 Sep 1909
      Bookman (NY), 29:317-8,
      May 1909
      Nation, 88:489-90, 13
      May 1909

Glass, Montague Marsden
    Potash & Perlmutter
      Bookman (NY), 31:630-1,
      Aug 1910

Glover, Elizabeth [pseud.].
See Bennett, Mary E.

[Goff, Harriet Newell (Knee-
land)]
    Other Fools and Their Doings
      Picayune, 18 Jul 1880,
      [p. 8]
    Who Cares?
      Godey's, 116:191, Feb
      1888

Goldsborough, Edmund Kennedy
    Ole Mars an' Ole Miss
      Nation, 72:362, 2 May
      1901

Goldsmith, Christabel [pseud.].
See Smith, Fannie N.

Goodale, Elaine
See Eastman, Elaine (Goodale).

Goodell, Charles L.
    The Old Darnman
      Overland, 2d S, 49:183-4,
      Feb 1907

Goodloe, Abbe Carter
    College Girls
      Athenaeum, 3619:311, 6
      Mar 1897
      Atlantic, 77:572, Apr 1896

Goodrich, Arthur Frederick
    The Balance of Power
      Athenaeum, 4151:601, 18
      May 1907
      Bookman (NY), 24:249,
      Nov 1906
      North American Review,
      184:188-90, 18 Jan 1907
    Gleam o' Dawn
      Nation, 87:120, 6 Aug 1908
    The Yardstick Man
      Nation, 91:473, 17 Nov 1910

Goodwin, Maud (Wilder)
    The Colonial Cavalier
      Picayune, 2 Dec 1894, p.
      10
    Flint, His Faults, His Friend-
    ships, and His Fortunes
      Bookman (NY), 6:473-4,
      Jan 1898
    The Head of a Hundred
      Godey's, 131:[206], Aug
      1895
    Veronica Playfair
      Nation, 90:87-8, 27 Jan
      1910
    White Aprons
      Bookman (NY), 3:455-6,
      Jul 1896
      Godey's, 133:96, Jul 1896

Goodwin, Mrs. H. B.
See Talcott, Hannah Elizabeth
(Bradbury) Goodwin.

Gordon, Armistead Churchill

Gift of the Morning Star
　Outlook, 80:192, 20
　　May 1905
　Overland, 2d S, 46:84,
　　Jul 1905

[Gordon, Charles William]
　The Doctor
　　By Ralph Connor [pseud.].
　　Outlook, 84:1081, 29
　　　Dec 1906
　The Prospector
　　By Ralph Connor [pseud.].
　　Saturday Review, 99:149,
　　　4 Feb 1905

[Gordon, Clarence]
　Two Lives in One
　　By "Vieux Moustache"
　　[pseud.].
　　Saturday Review, 29:426,
　　　26 Mar 1870

Gordon, Henri
　Alva Vine
　　Nation, 31:17, 1 Jul
　　　1880
　　Picayune, 23 May 1880,
　　　[p. 5]
　　Saturday Review, 50:124,
　　　24 Jul 1880

Gordon, Julien [pseud.].
　See Cruger, Julie Grinnell
　(Storrow).

Goss, Charles Frederic
　The Redemption of David
　　Corson
　　Athenaeum, 3830:365,
　　　23 Mar 1901
　　Bookman (London), 20:194,
　　　Sep 1901
　　Outlook, 64:926, 21 Apr
　　　1900
　　Picayune, 22 Apr 1900,
　　　III, 4

Goss, Warren Lee
　Jed
　　Overland, 2d S, 15:323-4,

Mar 1890

Gould, Anthony
　A Woman of Sorek
　　Overland, 2d S, 14:100, Jul
　　　1889

Gould, Jeanie T.
　Marjorie's Quest
　　Athenaeum, 2356:807, 21
　　　Dec 1872
　　Harper's, 46:140, Dec 1872
　　Saturday Review, 34:837,
　　　28 Dec 1872

Graham, Margaret (Collier)
　Stories of the Foot-Hills
　　Atlantic, 75:844, Jun 1895
　　Overland, 2d S, 25:443,
　　　Apr 1895

Graham, Mary
　Margaret Ellison
　　Overland, 2d S, 15:324,
　　　Mar 1890

Grant, Allen [pseud.].
　See Wilson, James Grant.

Grant, Robert
　The Art of Living
　　Picayune, 23 Dec 1895, p.
　　　9
　An Average Man
　　Cottage Hearth, 10:218, Jul
　　　1884
　　Nation, 38:531, 19 Jun 1884
　　Overland, 2d S, 4:105, Jul
　　　1884
　The Bachelor's Christmas, and
　　Other Stories
　　Nation, 63:180, 3 Sep 1896
　The Carletons
　　Picayune, 30 Aug 1891, p. 3
　The Chippendales
　　Bookman (NY), 29:309-10,
　　　May 1909
　　Nation, 88:338-9, 1 Apr 1909
　The Confessions of a Frivolous
　　Girl
　　Athenaeum, 2779:161, 29 Jan

Grant, Robert
1881
Nation, 31:83-4, 29 Jul
1880
Face to Face
Nation, 43:201, 2 Sep
1886
Jack Hall
Cottage Hearth, 13:396,
Dec 1887
Overland, 2d S, 11:112,
Jan 1888
Jack in the Bush
Overland, 2d S, 12:434,
Oct 1888
The Lawbreakers
Bookman (NY), 23:435-6,
Jun 1906
Opinions of a Philosopher
Atlantic, 72:850, Dec
1893
Picayune, 17 Sep 1893,
p. 23
The Orchid
Atlantic, 97:52, Jan 1906
Bookman (NY), 21:365-6,
Jun 1905
The Reflections of a Married
Man
Atlantic, 70:419, Sep
1892
Saturday Review, 74:548,
5 Nov 1892
A Romantic Young Lady
Cottage Hearth, 12:369,
Nov 1886
Godey's, 113:495, Nov
1886
The Undercurrent
Athenaeum, 4022:729,
26 Nov 1904
Atlantic, 95:692, May
1905
Bookman (London), 27:136,
Dec 1904
Bookman (NY), 20:362-3,
Dec 1904
Nation, 79:441-2, 1 Dec
1904
Sewanee Review, 13:122,
Jan 1905

South Atlantic Quarterly,
4:96, Jan 1905
Unleavened Bread
Athenaeum, 3790:745, 16
Jun 1900
Atlantic, 86:415-6, Sep 1900
Bookman (London), 18:157,
Aug 1900
Bookman (NY), 11:463-7,
Jul 1900; 20:56, Sep 1904
Nation, 70:462, 14 Jun 1900
Outlook, 65:229, 26 May
1900
Picayune, 17 Jun 1900, II,
12
Saturday Review, 91:342,
16 Mar 1901
See also The King's Men.

Gray, David
Gallops
Picayune, 9 Oct 1898, p. 6

Gray, Patrick Leopold
The Book of Ruth
Picayune, 27 Mar 1892, p.
13

Gray, Robertson
Brave Hearts
Atlantic, 33:110-1, Jan
1874
Harper's, 48:139, Dec 1873
Nation, 17:373, 4 Dec 1873

Grayson, Pauline
Kreutzer Sonata Bearing Fruit
Picayune, 23 Sep 1890, p.
12
Pyrrha
Picayune, 23 Mar 1890, p.
12

Green, Anna Katharine
See Rohlfs, Anna Katharine
(Green).

[Green, Miss M. P.]
The Fight for Dominion
By Gay Parker [pseud.].
Picayune, 6 Aug 1899, II, 3

Green, Mason Arnold
Bitterwood
　　Sunday Afternoon, 3:95,
　　Jan 1879

Greene, Belle C. [pseud.].
　See Greene, Isabel Cather-
　ine (Colton).

Greene, Homer
The Blind Brother
　　Epoch, 1:541, 15 Jul
　　1887
　　Overland, 2d S, 10:329,
　　Sep 1887
　　Picayune, 15 May 1887,
　　p. 15
Burnham Breaker
　　Overland, 2d S, 11:112,
　　Jan 1888

[Greene, Isabel Catherine
(Colton)]
　Adventures of an Old Maid
　By Aunt Ruth [pseud.].
　　Godey's, 113:391, Oct
　　1886
　A New England Conscience
　By Belle C. Greene
　[pseud.].
　　Harper's, 72:323-4, Jan
　　1886
　　Nation, 41:327, 15 Oct
　　1885
　　Overland, 2d S, 6:329,
　　Sep 1885
　　Saturday Review, 60:580-1,
　　31 Oct 1885
　A New England Idyl
　By Belle C. Greene
　[pseud.].
　　Nation, 44:431, 19 May
　　1887

Greene, Sarah Pratt (McLean)
Cape Cod Folks
　　Athenaeum, 2931:862-3,
　　29 Dec 1883
　　Continent, 2:733, 13
　　Dec 1882
　　Cottage Hearth, 7:305,

Oct 1881
　　Harper's, 63:954, Nov 1881
　　Nation, 33:236, 22 Sep 1881
　　Picayune, 8 Jan 1882, [p.
　　2]
Flood-Tide
　　Bookman (NY), 14:434-5,
　　Dec 1901
　　Nation, 73:476, 19 Dec 1901
Lastchance Junction, Far, Far
West
　　Nation, 48:352, 25 Apr 1889
The Moral Imbeciles
　　Outlook, 60:89, 3 Sep 1898
Some Other Folks
　　Continent, 5:512, (No. 16)
　　1884
Towhead
　　Continent, 2:733, 13 Dec
　　1882
　　Nation, 36:41-2, 11 Jan
　　1883
Vesty of the Basins
　　Atlantic, 71:418, Mar 1893
　　Godey's, 125:406, Oct 1892
　　Nation, 55:34, 14 Jul 1892
　　Picayune, 4 Jun 1893, p.
　　18

[Greenough, Mrs. Frances Boott]
　Annals of Brookdale
　　Nation, 33:99-100, 4 Aug
　　1881

Greenough, Mrs. Richard
　See Greenough, Sarah Dana
　(Loring).

Greenough, Sarah Dana (Loring)
Arabesques
　　Godey's, 84:194, Feb 1872
　　Picayune, 7 Jan 1872, [p.
　　16]
In Extremis
　　Harper's, 46:616, Mar 1873
Treason at Home
　　Overland, 10:582, Jun 1873

Greey, Edward
Blue Jackets
　　Harper's, 42:931, May 1871

Greey, Edward
  Overland, 7:103, Jul
    1871
  A Captive of Love
    Cottage Hearth, 12:26,
      Jan 1886

Grendel, M. R.
  Contrasts
    Harper's, 63:635, Sep
      1881

Grey, Zane
  The Heritage of the Desert
    Bookman (NY), 32:295,
      Nov 1910
  Last of the Plainsmen
    Overland, 2d S, 52:581,
      Dec 1908
    Times Literary Supple-
      ment, 6 May 1909, p.
      173

Grierson, Francis
  The Valley of Shadows
    Bookman (London), 36:187-
      88, Jul 1909

[Griffen, Annie M.]
  All Wrong
    Picayune, 3 Jun 1877,
      [p. 12]

Griffin, La Roy Freese
  The Abduction of the Prin-
    cess Chriemhild
    Outlook, 59:184, 21 May
      1898

Griswold, Hattie (Tyng)
  Fencing with Shadows
    Picayune, 15 Jan 1893,
      p. 20

Griswold, Mrs. John Alsop
  The Lost Wedding Ring
    Godey's, 115:515, Dec
      1887

[Griswold, Lorenzo]
  Priest and Puritan

  Overland, 2d S, 15:321,
    Mar 1890
  Saturday Review, 58:663,
    7 Dec 1889

Guernsey, Clara F.
  See Not Pretty, but Precious.

Guiney, Louise Imogen
  Lovers' Saint Ruth's, and
    Three Other Tales
    Bookman (NY), 3:65-6,
      Mar 1896
    Nation, 62:182, 27 Feb
      1896
    Poet-Lore, 8:617-8, (No.
      8) 1896

Gunsaulus, Frank Wakeley
  Monk and Knight
    Atlantic, 69:138, Jan 1892

Gunter, Archibald Clavering
  Baron Montez of Panama and
    Paris
    Athenaeum, 3431:156, 29
      Jul 1893
    Atlantic, 74:705, Nov 1894
    Overland, 2d S, 23:219,
      Feb 1894
    Picayune, 23 May 1893, p.
      23
    Saturday Review, 76:479,
      21 Oct 1893
  Billy Hamilton
    Saturday Review, 86:53, 9
      Jul 1898
  The Fighting Troubadour
    Athenaeum, 3857:410, 29
      Sep 1901
  A Florida Enchantment
    Athenaeum, 3745:189, 5
      Aug 1899
    Saturday Review, 88:462,
      7 Oct 1899
  Her Senator
    Godey's, 133:208, Aug 1896
    Picayune, 13 Apr 1896, p.
      10
  Jack Curzon
    Athenaeum, 3733:592-3,

Habberton, John
1877
Library Table, 2:32,
Apr 1877
Nation, 24:181-2, 22
Mar 1877
North American Review,
125:319-21, Sep 1877
Picayune, 6 May 1877,
[p. 5]
Saturday Review, 43:531,
28 Apr 1877
Just One Day
Cottage Hearth, 12:400,
Dec 1886
Godey's, 113:593, Dec
1886
Nation, 29:30, 10 Jul
1879
Mrs. Mayburn's Twins
America, 6:162, 7 May
1891
Other People's Children
Nation, 25:184, 20 Sep
1877
Out at Twinnett's
Saturday Review, 69:541,
3 May 1890
The Scripture Club of
Valley Rest
Library Table, 3:124,
2 Aug 1877
Nation, 25:184, 20 Sep
1877
North American Review,
125:319-21, Sep 1877
Some Boys' Doings
Athenaeum, 3914:584,
1 Nov 1902
Some Folks
Athenaeum, 2602:302,
8 Sep 1877
The Tiger and the Insect
Athenaeum, 3920:792,
13 Dec 1902
Well Out of It
Cottage Hearth, 18:255,
Aug 1892
Picayune, 12 Jun 1892,
p. 12
Where Were the Boys?

Picayune, 4 Aug 1895, p.
12
The Worst Boy in Town
Picayune, 3 Oct 1880, [p.
4]

Hadermann, Jeannette R.
See Walworth, Jeannette Ritchie (Hadermann).

Hadley, John Vestal
Seven Months a Prisoner
Picayune, 5 Jun 1898, II,
7

Hague, Parthena Antoinette (Vard-
aman)
A Blockaded Family
Picayune, 23 Dec 1888, p.
14; 17 Feb 1889, p. 7

Hains, Thornton Jenkins
Bahama Bill
Overland, 2d S, 52:[89]-90,
Jul 1908
The Black Barque
Athenaeum, 4063:331, 9 Sep
1905
Bookman (London), 29:39,
Oct 1905
Saturday Review, 100:600,
4 Nov 1905
Mr. Trunnell, Mate of the
Ship Pirate
Picayune, 15 Apr 1900, III,
7
The Voyage of the Arrow
Overland, 2d S, 48:410,
Nov 1906

Hale, Edward Everett
Back to Back
Harper's, 56:941, May 1878
Picayune, 17 Mar 1878, [p.
11]
The Brick Moon, and Other
Stories
Outlook, 63:694, 18 Nov
1899
Christmas Eve and Christmas
Day

Hale, Edward Everett
Atlantic, 70:851, Dec
1892
Bookman (London), 2:28,
Apr 1892
Nation, 55:34, 14 Jul
1892
Saturday Review, 73:577,
14 May 1892
Ten Times One Is Ten,
and Other Stories
By Colonel Frederic Ing-
ham [pseud.].
Nation, 11:335, 17 Nov
1870
Outlook, 63:421, 14 Oct
1899
Ups and Downs
Godey's, 87:91-2, Jul
1873
Harper's, 47:301, Jul
1873
Overland, 11:196, Aug
1873
Picayune, 1 Jun 1873,
[p. 2]
Saturday Review, 34:545-
46, 25 Oct 1873
See also Six of One by Half
a Dozen of the Other.

Hale, Louise (Closser)
The Actress
Bookman (NY), 29:191-2,
Apr 1909
Nation, 88:467, 6 May
1909
North American Review,
189:782-3, May 1909
Saturday Review, 108:264,
28 Aug 1909
See also Six of One by Half
a Dozen of the Other.

Hall, A. D.
Lady Clancarty
Picayune, 9 Feb 1890,
p. 11

_____, and Robert L.
Downing

A True Knight
Picayune, 24 Apr 1892,
p. 12

Hall, Eliza Calvert [pseud.].
See Obenchain, Eliza Caroline
(Calvert).

Hall, Eugene [pseud.].
See Baker, Emma Eugene
(Hall).

Hall, Gertrude
See Brownell, Gertrude (Hall).

Hall, Mary Lucy
Preparation
Godey's, 107:300, Sep 1883
Picayune, 1 Jul 1883, [p.
6]

Hall, Owen
Hernando
Athenaeum, 3922:850, 27
Dec 1902

Hall, Ruth
The Black Gown
Outlook, 66:369, 6 Oct 1900
A Downrenter's Son
Nation, 75:271-2, 2 Oct
1902
The Golden Arrow
Outlook, 69:608, 2 Nov 1901
The Pine Grove House
Nation, 77:390, 12 Nov 1903

Hall, Thomas Winthrop
Tales
Picayune, 20 Aug 1899, II,
12

Hall, Violette
Chanticleer
Overland, 2d S, 40:406,
Oct 1902

Halpin, Will R.
Juan Pico
Picayune, 14 May 1899, II,
12

Halsey, Calista
　Two of Us
　　Picayune, 27 Jul 1879,
　　[p. 12]

Halstead, Ada L. [pseud.].
　See Newhall, Mrs. Laura
　Eugenia.

[Halstead, Leonora B.]
　Bethesda
　　By Barbara Elbon [pseud.].
　　Athenaeum, 2947:501-2,
　　19 Apr 1884
　　Nation, 38:449, 22 May
　　1884
　　Saturday Review, 57:616-
　　17, 10 May 1884

Hamblen, Herbert Elliott
　The General Manager's Story
　　Bookman (NY), 7:425-7,
　　Jul 1898
　　Picayune, 22 May 1898,
　　II, 2
　On Many Seas
　　Picayune, 14 Mar 1897,
　　p. 17
　Tom Benton's Luck
　　Nation, 67:490-1, 29
　　Dec 1898
　　Saturday Review, 88:431,
　　30 Sep 1899
　The Yarn of a Bucko Mate
　　Picayune, 29 Oct 1899,
　　II, 12

Hamilton, Alice King
　Mildred's Cadet
　　Godey's, 103:284, Aug
　　1881
　　Picayune, 24 Jul 1881,
　　[p. 2]
　One of the Duanes
　　Epoch, 1:541, 15 Jul
　　1887
　　Godey's, 115:179, Aug
　　1887
　　Picayune, 12 Jun 1887,
　　p. 9

Hamilton, Mrs. C. V.
　See Jamison, Cecilia Viets
　(Dakin) Hamilton.

Hamilton, Gail [pseud.].
　See Dodge, Mary Abigail.

Hamilton, Kate Waterman
　The Parson's Proxy
　　Saturday Review, 86:54, 9
　　Jul 1898
　Rachel's Share of the Road
　　Continent, 3:317, 7 Mar
　　1883
　　Cottage Hearth, 8:401,
　　Dec 1882
　　Nation, 36:42, 11 Jan 1883
　　Saturday Review, 54:872,
　　30 Dec 1882

Hamilton, Mrs. M. J. R.
　Cachet
　　Picayune, 6 Jul 1873, [p.
　　2]; 13 Jul 1873, [p. 11]

Hamilton, Samuel A.
　The Vengeance of the Mob
　　Nation, 72:438, 30 May
　　1901

Hamlin, Myra Louisa (Sawyer)
　A Politician's Daughter
　　Godey's, 113:495, Nov 1886
　　Nation, 43:272, 30 Sep
　　1886

Hammond, Mrs. Adelaide F.
　Josephine Eloise
　　Nation, 15:126, 22 Aug
　　1872

Hammond, Clement Milton
　See Montague, Charles
　Howard, and Clement Milton
　Hammond.

[Hammond, Henrietta (Hardy)]
　A Fair Philosopher
　　By Henri Daugé [pseud.].
　　Continent, 2:413, 4 Oct
　　1882

[Hammond, Henrietta (Hardy)]
Her Waiting Heart
By Lou Capsadell [pseud.].
Saturday Review, 41:154,
29 Jan 1876
The Georgians
Cottage Hearth, 7:273,
Sep 1881
Nation, 33:99, 4 Aug 1881
Saturday Review, 52:282,
27 Aug 1881

Hammond, Lily (Hardy)
The Master Word
Atlantic, 97:50, Jan 1906
South Atlantic Quarterly,
4:298-300, Jul 1905

Hammond, William Alexander
Doctor Grattan
Athenaeum, 3013:107-8,
25 Jul 1885
Harper's, 70:816, Apr
1885
Nation, 40:266, 26 Mar
1885
Picayune, 11 Jan 1885,
[p. 5]
Saturday Review, 59:85,
17 Jan 1885
Lal
Harper's, 69:798-9, Oct
1884
Nation, 39:182, 28 Aug
1884
Picayune, 7 Sep, 1884, [p. 6]
Saturday Review, 59:85,
17 Jan 1885
Mr. Oldmixon
Athenaeum, 3019:299-300,
5 Sep 1885
Nation, 41:155, 20 Aug
1885
On the Susquehanna
Epoch, 1:21, 11 Feb
1887
Godey's, 114:407, Apr
1887
North American Review,
145:587, Nov 1887
A Son of Perdition

Nation, 68:167, 2 Mar 1899
A Strong-Minded Woman
Godey's, 112:103, Jan 1886
Saturday Review, 61:446,
27 Mar 1886

_____, and Clara Hammond
Lanza
Tales of Eccentric Life
Overland, 2d S, 8:325, Sep
1886

Hancock, Albert Elmer
Henry Bourland
Athenaeum, 3861:554, 26
Oct 1901
Nation, 72:514, 27 Jun 1901
Sewanee Review, 9:496-7,
Oct 1901

Hancock, Anson Uriel
Old Abraham Jackson
Picayune, 19 Jul 1891, p.
10

Hapgood, Hutchins
An Anarchist Woman
Bookman (NY), 29:636-41,
Aug 1909
The Autobiography of a Thief
Bookman (NY), 17:514-5,
Jul 1903
The Spirit of Labor
Bookman (NY), 25:294-6,
Apr 1907
The Spirit of the Ghetto
Bookman (NY), 17:97-8,
Mar 1903
Overland, 2d S, 41:233-4,
Mar 1903
Types from City Streets
Bookman (NY), 31:468-9,
Jul 1910

Hapgood, Mrs. Hutchins
See Hapgood, Neith (Boyce).

Hapgood, Neith (Boyce)
The Bond
Nation, 86:427, 7 May 1908
The Eternal Spring

Bookman (NY), 23:190-1,
  Apr 1906
The Forerunner
  Athenaeum, 3999:782,
    18 Jun 1904
  Bookman (NY), 18:411-2,
    Dec 1903
  Nation, 78:134, 18 Feb
    1904
  Outlook, 75:1007, 26 Dec
    1903
A Pioneer of To-day
  Athenaeum, 4160:65, 20
    Jul 1907

Harben, Will N.
  See Harben, William Nathan-
    iel.

Harben, William Nathaniel
  Abner Daniel
    Bookman (NY), 16:55,
      Sep 1902
  Almost Persuaded
    Picayune, 1 Feb 1891,
      p. 10
  The Georgians
    Athenaeum, 4015:480,
      8 Oct 1904
    Nation, 79:440, 1 Dec
      1904
    Outlook, 78:387, 8 Oct
      1904
  Gilbert Neal
    Nation, 87:442, 5 Nov
      1908
  The Land of the Changing
  Sun
    Picayune, 18 Nov 1894,
      p. 15
  Mam Linda
    Times Literary Supple-
      ment, 3 Oct 1907,
      p. 301
  A Mute Confessor
    Picayune, 12 Feb 1893,
      p. 16
  Northern Georgia Sketches
    Nation, 71:410, 22 Nov
      1900
    Outlook, 66:617, 3 Nov

1900
  Sewanee Review, 9:105, Jan
    1901
Pole Baker
  Sewanee Review, 14:110,
    Jan 1906
The Redemption of Kenneth
Galt
  Nation, 89:407, 28 Oct 1909
The Substitute
  Bookman (London), 24:112,
    Jun 1903
  Nation, 76:359, 30 Apr 1903
Westerfelt
  Harper's, 103:826, Oct 1901
White Marie
  Epoch, 6:808, 17 Jan 1890
  Nation, 51:136, 14 Aug 1890
  Picayune, 15 Dec 1889, p.
    11

Harding, John William
  An Art Failure
    Picayune, 17 May 1896, p.
      15

Hardy, Albert H.
  The Maid of Bethany
    Overland, 2d S, 14:101, Jul
      1889

Hardy, Arthur Sherburne
  But Yet a Woman
    Atlantic, 51:707-9, May
      1883
    Continent, 4:606, 7 Nov 1883
    Manhattan, 1:507-8, Jun
      1883
    Nation, 36:406, 10 May 1883
    Overland, 2d S, 1:653, Jun
      1883
    Picayune, 17 Jun 1883, [p.
      8]
  His Daughter First
    Athenaeum, 3948:809, 27
      Jun 1903
    Nation, 76:479, 11 Jun 1903
    Saturday Review, 96:212,
      15 Aug 1903
  Passe Rose
    Atlantic, 64:125-6, Jul 1889

Hardy, Arthur Sherburne
　Cottage Hearth, 15:164,
　　May 1889
　Nation, 48:529, 27 Jun
　　1889
　Overland, 2d S, 14:210-1,
　　Aug 1889
　Saturday Review, 68:107,
　　27 Jul 1889
　The Wind of Destiny
　　Athenaeum, 3063:44-5,
　　　10 Jul 1886
　　Atlantic, 58:131-3, Jul
　　　1886
　　Cottage Hearth, 12:264,
　　　Aug 1886
　　Nation, 43:272, 30 Sep
　　　1886
　　Overland, 2d S, 8:107-8,
　　　Jul 1886
　　Picayune, 6 Jun 1886,
　　　p. 14
　　Saturday Review, 61:889,
　　　26 Jun 1886

Harlan, Caleb
　The Fate of Marcel
　　Picayune, 16 Sep 1883,
　　　[p. 5]

[Harland, Henry]
　As It Was Written
　　By Sidney Luska [pseud.].
　　Atlantic, 57:260-1, Feb
　　　1886
　　Nation, 41:469-70, 3
　　　Dec 1885
　　Overland, 2d S, 6:551,
　　　Nov 1885
　The Cardinal's Snuff-Box
　　Athenaeum, 3786:618,
　　　19 May 1900
　　Bookman (London), 18:127,
　　　Jul 1900
　　Bookman (NY), 12:88,
　　　Sep 1900
　　Canadian Magazine, 16:187,
　　　Dec 1900
　　Saturday Review, 89:624,
　　　19 May 1900
　　Sewanee Review, 12:121-2,

　　　Jan 1904
　Comedies and Errors
　　Athenaeum, 3679:564, 30
　　　Apr 1898
　　Bookman (London), 14:75-6,
　　　Jun 1898
　　Bookman (NY), 7:525-6,
　　　Aug 1898
　　Nation, 67:299, 20 Oct 1898
　　Saturday Review, 85:600,
　　　30 Apr 1898
　Grandison Mather
　　Athenaeum, 3253:273-4,
　　　1 Mar 1890
　　Harper's, 78:987, May
　　　1889
　　Nation, 49:76, 25 Jul 1889
　　Picayune, 12 May 1889, p.
　　　12; 10 May 1891, p. 12
　　Saturday Review, 70:82,
　　　19 Jul 1890
　Gray Roses
　　Athenaeum, 3533:64, 13
　　　Jul 1895
　　Bookman (NY), 2:143-4,
　　　Oct 1895
　　Nation, 62:61, 16 Jan 1896
　The Lady Paramount
　　Athenaeum, 3887:524-5,
　　　26 Apr 1902
　　Atlantic, 90:276, Aug 1902
　　Bookman (NY), 15:376-7,
　　　Jun 1902
　　Nation, 74:469-70, 12 Jun
　　　1902
　　Overland, 2d S, 39:985-6,
　　　Jun 1902
　　Saturday Review, 93:563,
　　　3 May 1902
　　South Atlantic Quarterly,
　　　1:290-1, Jul 1902
　　Times Literary Supplement,
　　　25 Jul 1902, p. 221
　A Latin-Quarter Courtship,
　　and Other Stories
　　By Sidney Luska [pseud.].
　　Harper's, 78:987, May
　　　1889
　　Nation, 48:352, 25 Apr
　　　1889
　　Saturday Review, 70:82,

19 Jul 1890

Mademoiselle Miss, ...
  Athenaeum, 3446:659,
    11 Nov 1893
  Godey's, 128:235, Feb
    1894

Mea Culpa
  Athenaeum, 3316:632,
    16 May 1891
  Epoch, 10:109, 18 Sep
    1891
  Nation, 53:72, 23 Jul
    1891
  Picayune, 21 Jun 1891,
    p. 12; 6 Nov 1892,
    p. 15
  Saturday Review, 61:626-7,
    23 May 1891

Mrs. Peixada
  By Sidney Luska [pseud.].
  Harper's, 73:314, Jul
    1886
  Nation, 42:409, 13 May
    1886

My Friend Prospero
  Athenaeum, 3981:203-4,
    13 Feb 1904
  Bookman (London), 25:259,
    Mar 1904
  Bookman (NY), 19:74-5,
    Mar 1904
  Sewanee Review, 12:456-
    58, Oct 1904

The Royal End
  Athenaeum, 4246:312,
    13 Mar 1909
  Bookman (London), 36:96,
    May 1909
  Bookman (NY), 29:409-
    10, Jun 1909
  Nation, 88:539, 27 May
    1909
  Times Literary Supple-
    ment, 25 Feb 1909,
    p. 73

Two Voices
  Epoch, 7:77, 7 Mar 1890

Two Women or One?
  America, 4:272, 5 Jun
    1890
  Epoch, 7:382, 18 Jul

1890
  Nation, 51:252, 25 Sep 1890

The Yoke of Thorah
  By Sidney Luska [pseud.].
  Atlantic, 60:415-7, Sep 1887
  Nation, 45:56-7, 21 Jul 1887
  North American Review,
    145:104-5, Jul 1887

Harland, Marion [pseud.].
  See Terhune, Mary Virginia
  (Hawes).

Harper, Frances Ellen (Watkins)
Iola Leroy
  Nation, 56:146-7, 23 Feb
    1893

Harriman, Karl Edwin
Sadie
  Canadian Magazine, 30:487,
    Mar 1908

Harris, Corra
A Circuit Rider's Wife
  Bookman (NY), 32:175-6,
    Oct 1910

Harris, Frank
The Bomb
  Bookman (London), 35:198,
    Jan 1909
Elder Conklin, and Other
  Stories
  Bookman (London), 7:119,
    Jan 1895
  Nation, 60:32, 10 Jan 1895
  Picayune, 25 Nov 1894, p.
    10
Montes the Matador, and Other
  Stories
  Saturday Review, 90:758-9,
    15 Dec 1900
The Road to Ridgeby's
  Nation, 73:458, 12 Dec 1901

Harris, Joel Chandler
Aaron in the Wildwoods
  Athenaeum, 3695:252, 20
    Aug 1898
  Picayune, 31 Oct 1897, p.

[Harris, William Richard]
By Oswald Crawford
[pseud.].
Picayune, 21 Sep 1884,
[p. 2]

Harrison, Agnes
Martin's Vineyard
Athenaeum, 2349:558-9,
2 Nov 1872

Harrison, Mrs. Burton
See Harrison, Constance
(Cary).

Harrison, Constance (Cary)
The Anglomaniacs
Athenaeum, 3308:372-3,
21 Mar 1891
Cosmopolitan, 10:765,
Apr 1891
Nation, 51:506, 25 Dec
1890
Picayune, 30 Nov 1890,
p. 13; 24 May 1891,
p. 12
Saturday Review, 71:475-
76, 18 Apr 1891
A Bachelor Maid
Bookman (London), 8:25,
Apr 1895
Overland, 2d S, 25:443,
Apr 1895
Picayune, 18 Nov 1894,
p. 15
Bar Harbor Days
Epoch, 1:602, 5 Aug
1887
Belhaven Tales, Crow's Nest,
Una and King David
Atlantic, 72:697, Nov
1893
Godey's, 125:670, Dec
1892
Nation, 55:437, 8 Dec
1892
Picayune, 16 Oct 1892,
p. 15
The Carcellini Emerald,
with Other Tales
Outlook, 62:581, 8 Jul

1899
The Carlyles
Nation, 81:510, 21 Dec
1905
The Circle of the Century
Outlook, 63:694, 18 Nov
1899
Picayune, 26 Nov 1899, II,
8
A Daughter of the South, and
Shorter Stories
Nation, 55:34, 14 Jul 1892
Picayune, 8 May 1892, p.
10; 27 Apr 1896, p. 10
An Edelweiss of the Sierras,
Golden-Rod, and Other
Stories
Atlantic, 72:697-8, Nov
1893
Nation, 55:34, 14 Jul 1892
An Errant Wooing
Atlantic, 76:556, Oct 1895
Bookman (NY), 2:53, Sep
1895
Nation, 61:278, 17 Oct 1895
Overland, 2d S, 26:674,
Dec 1895
Flower de Hundred
Athenaeum, 3308:372-3, 21
Mar 1891
Godey's, 122:181, Feb 1891
Picayune, 3 Jul 1892, p.
19
Folk and Fairy Tales
Saturday Review, 60:817,
19 Dec 1885
Golden-Rod
Harper's, 60:632, Mar
1880
Nation, 30:240, 25 Mar
1880
Good Americans
Bookman (NY), 8:493, Jan
1899
Outlook, 60:394, 8 Oct
1898
Picayune, 16 Oct 1898, II,
2
Helen Troy
Nation, 33:99, 4 Aug 1881
Latter-day Sweethearts

Saturday Review, 102:86,
21 Jul 1906
The Merry Maid of Arcady,
His Lordship, and Other
Stories
Bookman (NY), 5:351-2,
Jun 1897
Nation, 65:17, 1 Jul
1897
A Princess of the Hills
Athenaeum, 3905:280,
30 Aug 1902
Bookman (London), 23:32,
Oct 1902
Saturday Review, 95:ii,
Suppl., 10 Jan 1903
A Son of the Old Dominion
Bookman (NY), 6:63-4,
Sep 1897
Sweet Bells Out of Tune
Atlantic, 74:564, Oct
1894
Godey's, 128:234, Feb
1894
Nation, 57:452, 14 Dec
1893
Saturday Review, 77:44,
13 Jan 1894
Transplanted Daughters
Saturday Review, 107:502,
17 Apr 1909
A Triple Entanglement
Bookman (NY), 9:474-5,
Jul 1899
Picayune, 23 Apr 1899,
II, 8
Saturday Review, 87:344,
18 Mar 1899
A Virginia Cousin & Bar
Harbor Tales
Bookman (NY), 2:530,
Feb 1896

Harrison, James Albert
Autrefois
Picayune, 7 Sep 1890,
p. 13

Harrison, Jennie
Whose Fault?
Epoch, 7:381, 18 Jul

1890

Harrison, Lewis [pseud.].
See Watson, Lewis H.

Harrison, Louis Reeves
Rothermal
Godey's, 120:353, Apr 1890
Overland, 2d S, 15:434,
Apr 1890
Picayune, 2 Mar 1890, p.
10

[Harsha, William Justin]
Ploughed Under
Nation, 32:226, 31 Mar 1881
Saturday Review, 51:701-2,
28 May 1881
A Timid Brave
Picayune, 9 May 1886, p. 8

Hart, Joseph C.
Miriam Coffin
Overland, 9:387, Oct 1872

Harte, Bret
The Argonauts of North Liber-
ty
Nation, 46:529, 28 Jun 1888
Overland, 2d S, 12:216-7,
Aug 1888
Barker's Luck, and Other
Stories
Athenaeum, 3609:900-1, 26
Dec 1896
Overland, 2d S, 28:717,
Dec 1896
The Bell-Ringer of Angel's,
and Other Stories
Athenaeum, 3505:889, 29
Dec 1894
Bookman (London), 7:122,
Jan 1895
Nation, 60:206, 14 Mar
1895
Overland, 2d S, 25:106-7,
Jan 1895
Saturday Review, 78:689,
22 Dec 1894
By Shore and Sedge
Athenaeum, 3013:111, 25

Athenaeum, 2861:269,
26 Aug 1882
Cottage Hearth, 8:365,
Nov 1882
From Sand Hill to Pine
Athenaeum, 3789:716,
9 Jun 1900
Bookman (NY), 11:507,
Aug 1900
Outlook, 65:323, 2 Jun
1900
Overland, 2d S, 36:191,
Aug 1900
Saturday Review, 89:624-
25, 19 May 1900
Gabriel Conroy
Athenaeum, 2536:762-3,
3 Jun 1876
North American Review,
124:81-90, Jan 1877
Gold Stories of '49
By a Californian.
Picayune, 3 Jan 1897,
p. 17
An Heiress of Red Dog,
and Other Tales
Athenaeum, 2682:375,
22 Mar 1879
The Heritage of Dedlow
Marsh, and Other Tales
Athenaeum, 3238:667-8,
16 Nov 1889
Atlantic, 64:720, Nov
1889
Cottage Hearth, 15:381,
Nov 1889
Epoch, 6:598, 18 Oct
1889
Overland, 2d S, 15:321-2,
Mar 1890
Picayune, 3 Nov 1889,
p. 10
Saturday Review, 70:621-2,
29 Nov 1890
In the Carquinez Woods
Atlantic, 52:705-6, Nov
1883
Continent, 4:607-8, 7
Nov 1883
Cottage Hearth, 10:25,
Jan 1884

Harper's, 68:158, Dec 1883
Nation, 37:255-6, 20 Sep
1883
Overland, 2d S, 2:553-4,
Nov 1883
In a Hollow of the Hills
Athenaeum, 3558:14, 4
Jan 1896
Bookman (London), 9:98,
Dec 1895
Overland, 2d S, 27:127,
Jan 1896
Jeff Briggs's Love Story
Athenaeum, 2733:342, 13
Mar 1880
The Luck of Roaring Camp,
and Other Sketches
Atlantic, 25:633-5, May
·1870
North American Review,
124:81-90, Jan 1877
Picayune, 8 May 1870,
[p. 13]
Saturday Review, 31:89-90,
21 Jan 1871
Sewanee Review, 11:352,
Jul 1903; 12:164, Apr
1904
Maruja
Godey's, 112:103, Jan 1886
Nation, 41:469, 3 Dec 1885
Overland, 2d S, 6:550,
Nov 1885
Saturday Review, 60:614-5,
7 Nov 1885
A Millionaire of Rough-and-
Ready, and Devil's Ford
Nation, 44:278, 31 Mar
1887
Mr. Jack Hamlin's Mediation,
and Other Stories
Athenaeum, 3768:45, 13
Jan 1900
Bookman (London), 17:88-
89, Dec 1899
Saturday Review, 88:iv,
Suppl. , 4 Nov 1899
Mrs. Skaggs's Husbands, and
Other Sketches
Harper's, 46:776, Apr 1873
Overland, 10:390-1, Apr

Harte, Bret
   1873
      Picayune, 9 Feb 1873,
         [p. 6]
      Saturday Review, 35:260-
         61, 22 Feb 1873
   On the Frontier
      Nation, 39:315, 9 Oct
         1884
      Overland, 2d S, 4:447,
         Oct 1884
      Picayune, 7 Sep 1884,
         [p. 6]
      Saturday Review, 58:413-
         14, 27 Sep 1884
   Openings in the Old Trail
      Atlantic, 90:278, Aug
         1902
      Bookman (London),
         22:144-5, Jul 1902
      Overland, 2d S, 39:983,
         Jun 1902
   The Outcasts of Poker Flat
      Sewanee Review, 11:352,
         Jul 1903
   A Phyllis of the Sierras,
      and A Drift from Redwood
      Camp
      Athenaeum, 3148:240,
         25 Feb 1888
      Epoch, 3:77, 2 Mar
         1888
      Godey's, 116:393, Apr
         1888
      Nation, 46:529, 28 Jun
         1888
   A Protégée of Jack Ham-
      lin's, and Other Stories
      Athenaeum, 3471:575,
         5 May 1894
      Atlantic, 74:705-6, Nov
         1894
      Bookman (London), 6:25,
         Apr 1894
      Cottage Hearth, 20:250,
         May 1894
      Nation, 59:68, 26 Jul
         1894
      Overland, 2d S, 23:665,
         Jun 1894
      Saturday Review, 77:312,

      24 Mar 1894
   Sally Dows, and Other Stories
      Atlantic, 73:278, Feb 1894
      Bookman (London), 4:59,
         May 1893
      Cottage Hearth, 19:295, Jun
         1893
      Godey's, 127:107, Jul 1893
      Nation, 57:32, 13 Jul 1893
      Overland, 2d S, 21:660,
         Jun 1893
      Saturday Review, 75:526,
         13 May 1893
   A Sappho of Green Springs,
      and Other Stories
      Athenaeum, 3304:244-5, 21
         Feb 1891
      Cosmopolitan, 11:637, Sep
         1891
      Cottage Hearth, 17:119, Apr
         1891
      Godey's, 122:461, May 1891
      Overland, 2d S, 18:441, Oct
         1891
      Saturday Review, 71:231, 21
         Feb 1891
   Snow-Bound at Eagle's
      Athenaeum, 3046:355-6, 13
         Mar 1886
      Godey's, 112:536, May 1886
      Nation, 42:303-4, 8 Apr
         1886
      Overland, 2d S, 7:654, Jun
         1886
      Picayune, 21 Mar 1886, p.
         4
   Stories in Light and Shadow
      Athenaeum, 3714:928, 31
         Dec 1898
      Saturday Review, 87:24, 7
         Jan 1899
   The Story of a Mine
      Cottage Hearth, 5:178-9,
         May 1878
   Susy
      Athenaeum, 3410:277, 4
         Mar 1893
      Atlantic, 72:420, Sep 1893
      Bookman (London), 3:162,
         Feb 1893
      Cottage Hearth, 19:195, Apr

1893

Godey's, 126:500, Apr
1893

Nation, 56:201, 16 Mar
1893

Overland, 2d S, 21:659,
Jun 1893

Saturday Review, 75:242,
4 Mar 1893

Tales of the Argonauts, and
Other Sketches

Overland, 15:593, Dec
1875

Saturday Review, 40:821,
25 Dec 1875

Tales of Trail and Town

Athenaeum, 3689:63,
9 Jul 1898

Bookman (London), 14:21,
Apr 1898

Bookman (NY), 7:356,
Jun 1898

Nation, 66:407, 26 May
1898

Outlook, 58:782, 26 Mar
1898

Thankful Blossom

Atlantic, 39:500, Apr
1877

Three Partners

Athenaeum, 3650:486,
9 Oct 1897

Bookman (London), 13:23,
Oct 1897; 13:87, Dec
1897

Bookman (NY), 6:246-7,
Nov 1897

Nation, 66:407, 26 May
1898

Picayune, 17 Oct 1897,
p. 10

Saturday Review, 84:373-
74, 2 Oct 1897

Trent's Trust, and Other
Stories

Athenaeum, 3943:653,
23 May 1903

Nation, 77:118, 6 Aug
1903

Times Literary Supple-
ment, 8 May 1903, p.

144

The Twins of Table Mountain,
and Other Stories

Athenaeum, 2706:301-2, 6
Sep 1879

Two Men of Sandy Bar

Cottage Hearth, 4:118, May
1877

Under the Redwoods

Athenaeum, 3841:724, 8
Jun 1901

Overland, 2d S, 37:1140,
Jun 1901

Saturday Review, 91:574,
4 May 1901

A Waif of the Plains

Athenaeum, 3257:401-2, 29
Mar 1890

Atlantic, 66:429, Sep 1890

Cottage Hearth, 16:225, Jul
1890

Epoch, 7:286, 6 Jun 1890

Nation, 50:492, 19 Jun 1890

Overland, 2d S, 16:437-8,
Oct 1890

A Ward of the Golden Gate

Athenaeum, 3290:661, 15
Nov 1890

Atlantic, 67:127, Jan 1891

Cottage Hearth, 17:25, Jan
1891

Godey's, 122:98, Jan 1891

Overland, 2d S, 17:663-4,
Jun 1891

Saturday Review, 70:92, 19
Jul 1890

Hartwell, Mary
See Catherwood, Mary (Hartwell).

Harvey, George Cockburn
The Light That Lies
Picayune, 6 Apr 1896, p. 11

Hassaurek, Friedrich
The Secret of the Andes
Atlantic, 44:361-4, Sep 1879
Harper's, 59:308-9, Jul 1879
Nation, 28:391, 5 Jun 1879
Saturday Review, 47:689, 31

Hassaurek, Friedrich
  May 1879

Hastings, Elizabeth [pseud.].
  See Sherwood, Margaret
    (Pollock).

Hatch, Mary R. (Platt)
  The Bank Tragedy
    Epoch, 7:413, 1 Aug
      1890
    Overland, 2d S, 16:442,
      Oct 1890

Haven, Gilbert
  Our Next-Door Neighbors
    Godey's, 91:189, Aug
      1875

Hawthorne, Julian
  An American Monte Cristo
    Athenaeum, 3401:914,
      31 Dec 1892
    Saturday Review, 74:652-
      53, 3 Dec 1892
  An American Penman
    Nation, 46:530, 28 Jun
      1888
  Archibald Malmaison
    Athenaeum, 2701:142,
      2 Aug 1879
    Continent, 5:831, (No. 26)
      1884
    Manhattan, 4:121, Jul
      1884
    Nation, 38:450, 22 May
      1884
    Outlook, 63:932, 16
      Dec 1899
    Picayune, 10 Dec 1899,
      III, 7
    Saturday Review, 48:213-
      14, 16 Aug 1879
  Beatrix Randolph
    Athenaeum, 2936:149,
      2 Feb 1884
    Atlantic, 53:711-2, May
      1884
    Continent, 5:448, (No. 14)
      1884
    Cottage Hearth, 10:122,

  Mar 1884
    Nation, 38:194, 28 Feb 1884
    Overland, 2d S, 3:555, May
      1884
  Bressant
    Athenaeum, 2377:626-7, 17
      May 1873
    Godey's, 87:284, Sep 1873
    Nation, 17:27, 10 Jul 1873
    Picayune, 22 Jun 1873, [p.
      2]; 11 Jun 1876, [p. 6]
    Saturday Review, 35:854-5,
      28 Jun 1873
  The Confessions of a Convict
    Godey's, 127:233, Aug 1893
  Constance, and Calbot's Rival
    Epoch, 5:212, 3 May 1889
  David Poindexter's Disappear-
    ance, and Other Tales
    Nation, 47:14, 5 Jul 1888
    North American Review,
      147:117, Jul 1888
    Saturday Review, 66:48-9,
      14 Jul 1888
  A Dream and a Forgetting
    Picayune, 1 Jul 1888, p. 3
    Saturday Review, 66:149-50,
      4 Aug 1888
  Dust
    Athenaeum, 2891:371-2, 24
      Mar 1883
    Atlantic, 51:704-6, May 1883
    Nation, 36:405, 10 May 1883
    Overland, 2d S, 1:653, Jun
      1883
    Picayune, 4 Mar 1883, [p.
      8]
    Saturday Review, 55:381-2,
      24 Mar 1883
  Ellice Quentin
    Athenaeum, 2762:431-2, 2
      Oct 1880
  A Fool of Nature
    Bookman, 3:364-5, Jun 1896
    Picayune, 27 Apr 1896, p.
      10
  Fortune's Fool
    Athenaeum, 2918:398-9, 29
      Sep 1883
    Godey's, 117:422, Nov 1888
    Harper's, 68:325-6, Jan 1884

Picayune, 5 Feb 1899,
p. 11
Kokoro
Picayune, 22 Mar 1896,
p. 10
Kotto
Nation, 76:254-5, 26
Mar 1903
Kwaidan
Atlantic, 93:852, Jun
1904
Bookman (NY), 20:159-
60, Oct 1904
Saturday Review, 97:757-
58, 11 Jun 1904
Letters from the Raven
Bookman (London), 35:48,
Oct 1908
Out of the East
Bookman (NY), 1:261-2,
May 1895
Overland, 2d S, 26:218,
Aug 1895
Picayune, 26 May 1895,
p. 16
The Romance of the Milky
Way, and Other Studies
and Sketches
Nation, 81:510, 21 Dec
1905
Shadowings
Bookman (NY), 12:582-3,
Feb 1901
Nation, 71:372, 8 Nov
1900
Some Chinese Ghosts
Epoch, 1:217, 8 Apr
1887
Overland, 2d S, 10:104-5,
Jul 1887
Picayune, 20 Mar 1887,
p. 10
Two Years in the French
West Indies
Epoch, 7:222-3, 9 May
1890
Youma
Athenaeum, 3279:284,
30 Aug 1890
Atlantic, 66:857, Dec
1890

Epoch, 7:302, 13 Jun 1890
Nation, 52:385, 7 May 1891
Saturday Review, 70:295,
6 Sep 1890

Heaton, Augustus Goodyear
Heart of David
Overland, 2d S, 37:727,
Feb 1901

[Heaton, Ellen Marvin]
The Octagon Club
By E. M. H. [pseud.].
Atlantic, 46:836, Dec 1880
Nation, 31:208, 16 Sep
1880

Heaven, Louise Palmer
Chata and Chinita
Overland, 2d S, 15:318,
Mar 1890
An Idol of Bronze
Athenaeum, 3871:13, 4 Jan
1902

Hedd, Luke A.
Philip Meyer's Scheme
Godey's, 125:649-70, Dec
1892

Heermans, Forbes
Thirteen Stories of the Far
West
Nation, 45:402, 17 Nov
1887
Overland, 2d S, 10:330,
Sep 1887

Hegan, Alice Caldwell
See Rice, Alice Caldwell
(Hegan).

Helm, Flora
Between Two Forces
Picayune, 8 Jul 1894, p. 7

Helmbold, Masson Peel
Althea St. John
Picayune, 18 Apr 1886, p.
8

Hemenway, Crabtree [pseud.].
See Hemenway, Myles.

[Hemenway, Myles]
Doomsday
By Crabtree Hemenway
[pseud.].
Outlook, 60:1021, 24
Dec 1898
Passengers, Doomsday,
April
Picayune, 22 Apr 1900,
III, 4

Hempstead, Junius Lackland
After Many Days
Picayune, 16 Jan 1898,
p. 11

Henderson, Charles Hanford
John Percyfield
Nation, 76:275, 2 Apr
1903
Outlook, 73:836, 4 Apr
1903
The Lighted Lamp
Nation, 87:497, 19 Nov
1908

Henderson, Isaac
Agatha Page
Epoch, 3:336, 1 Jun
1888
Nation, 47:13, 5 Jul
1888
Picayune, 29 Apr 1888,
p. 7
The Prelate
Nation, 42:409, 13 May
1886
Saturday Review, 62:428-
29, 25 Sep 1886

Henry, Arthur
An Island Cabin
Bookman (NY), 15:478-
80, Jul 1902
Outlook, 70:928, 12 Apr
1902
Nicholas Blood, Candidate
Picayune, 7 Aug 1892,

p. 11
Saturday Review, 71:209,
14 Feb 1891
A Princess of Arcady
Athenaeum, 3822:107-8,
26 Jan 1901
The Unwritten Law
Athenaeum, 4052:778, 24
Jun 1905
Bookman (NY), 21:267-8,
May 1905
Saturday Review, 100:218-9,
12 Aug 1905

Henry, Edgar [pseud.].
See Tourgee, Albion Winegar.

Henry, O. [pseud.].
See Porter, William Sydney.

Henshaw, Nevil G.
Aline of the Grand Woods
Nation, 88:337-8, 1 Apr
1909

Hentz, Caroline Lee
Aunt Patty's Scrap-Bag
Godey's, 97:347, Oct 1878
Library Table, 4:433, 12
Oct 1878
Picayune, 21 Apr 1872,
[p. 13]
The Banished Son and Other
Stories
Picayune, 1 May 1870, [p.
6]
Courtship and Marriage
Picayune, 11 Mar 1894, p.
25
Eloine
Godey's, 121:173, Aug 1890
Ernest Linwood
Picayune, 29 Apr 1894, p.
23
Helen and Arthur
Godey's, 122:278, Mar 1891
Picayune, 6 Mar 1870, [p.
14]
Linda
Godey's, 102:476, May 1881
Picayune, 27 Mar 1881,

[p. 6]
Marcus Warland
Picayune, 23 Jan 1870,
[p. 10]
Reva
Picayune, 23 Jan 1870,
[p. 10]

Hepworth, George Hughes
! ! !
Nation, 33:99, 4 Aug
1881
The Queerest Man Alive,
and Other Stories
Picayune, 10 Apr 1898,
p. 25

Herbert, Henry William
The Fair Puritan
Picayune, 21 May 1875,
[p. 3]

Herbert, Will [pseud.].
Not His Daughter
Godey's, 113:93, Jul
1886
Picayune, 9 May 1886,
p. 8

Hereford, William Richard
The Demagog
Bookman (NY), 30:521-2,
Jan 1910
Nation, 90:112-3, 3 Feb
1910

Herrick, Robert
The Common Lot
Athenaeum, 4028:11,
7 Jan 1905
Atlantic, 95:693, May
1905
Bookman (NY), 20:220,
Nov 1904
Nation, 79:380-1, 10 Nov
1904
The Gospel of Freedom
Athenaeum, 3688:32, 2
Jul 1898
Bookman (London), 14:168,
Sep 1898

Bookman (NY), 7:337-9,
Jun 1898
Picayune, 15 May 1898,
III, 2
Hesperides
Picayune, 8 Oct 1899, II,
12
A Life for a Life
Athenaeum, 4316:64, 16 Jul
1910
Bookman (NY), 31:351-4,
Jun 1910; 31:640-2, Aug
1910
Nation, 90:586, 9 Jun 1910
Saturday Review, 110:53-4,
9 Jul 1910
Love's Dilemmas
Outlook, 62:171, 20 May
1899
Master of the Inn
Outlook, 89:85, 9 May 1908
The Memoirs of an American
Citizen
Atlantic, 97:43-4, Jan 1906
Bookman (NY), 22:132-3,
Oct 1905
Nation, 81:205, 7 Sep 1905
Saturday Review, 101:308,
10 Mar 1906
The Real World
Athenaeum, 3871:12, 4 Jan
1902
Bookman (NY), 14:531-2,
Jan 1902
Their Child
Bookman (NY), 18:623-4,
Feb 1904
Together
Athenaeum, 4225:469, 17
Oct 1908
Bookman (NY), 27:580, Aug
1908
Nation, 87:96-7, 30 Jul 1908
Saturday Review, 106:704,
5 Dec 1908
Sewanee Review, 16:495-
504, Oct 1908
The Web of Life
Bookman (NY), 12:90-1,
Sep 1900
Picayune, 5 Aug 1900, III, 3

Herrick, Robert
Saturday Review, 90:337,
15 Sep 1900; 91:343,
16 Mar 1901; 93:405,
29 Mar 1902

Heywood, Joseph Converse
How Will It End?
Godey's, 84:383, Apr
1872
Overland, 8:485, May
1872
Saturday Review, 33:386,
23 Mar 1872

Hibbard, George Abiah
The Dark Horse
Harper's, 84:479, Feb
1892
The Governor, and Other
Stories
Athenaeum, 3394:660-2,
12 Nov 1892
Atlantic, 70:136, Jul
1892
Nation, 54:363, 12 May
1892
Picayune, 8 May 1892,
p. 10
Saturday Review, 75:299,
18 Mar 1893
Iduna, and Other Stories
Atlantic, 69:269, Feb
1892
Nation, 53:125, 13 Aug
1891
Picayune, 6 Sep 1891,
p. 10
Saturday Review, 72:561,
14 Nov 1891
Nowadays, and Other Stories
Atlantic, 73:137, Jan
1894
Nation, 57:292, 19 Oct
1893

Hickox, Chauncey
See Not Pretty, but Pre-
cious.

Hicks, John

The Man from Oshkosh
Saturday Review, 79:519, 20
Apr 1895
Something About Singlefoot
Overland, 2d S, 55:538, May
1910

Higbee, D.
See Geppert, Dora (Higbee).

Higginson, Ella Rhoads
The Flower That Grew in the
Sand, and Other Stories
Bookman (NY), 5:167, Apr
1897
Overland, 2d S, 29:653, Jun
1897
Picayune, 13 Dec 1896, p.
16
A Forest Orchid, and Other
Stories
Bookman (NY), 6:560-1, Feb
1898
Godey's, 136:328, Mar 1898
From the Land of the Snow-
Pearls
Godey's, 135:446, Oct 1897
Nation, 65:363, 4 Nov 1897
Mariella of Out West
Bookman (London), 23:168-9,
Jan 1903

Higginson, Mrs. S. J.
See Higginson, Sara Jane (Hatfield).

Higginson, Sarah Jane (Hatfield)
A Princess of Java
Cottage Hearth, 13:396, Dec
1887
Epoch, 2:235-6, 28 Oct 1887
Godey's, 115:429, Nov 1887
Overland, 2d S, 11:438, Apr
1888
Picayune, 30 Oct 1887, p.
14
Saturday Review, 64:526, 15
Oct 1887

Higginson, Thomas Wentworth
Army Life in a Black Regiment

Saturday Review, 29:128,
22 Jan 1870
Cheerful Yesterdays
Poet-Lore, 10:440-3,
(No. 3) 1898
Contemporaries
Poet-Lore, 12:311-4,
(No. 2) 1900
The Monarch of Dreams
Nation, 44:300, 7 Apr
1887
Oldport Days
Overland, 12:99, Jan
1874
Tales of the Enchanted
Islands of the Atlantic
Outlook, 60:677, 12 Nov
1898

Higham, Mrs. Mary R.
The Other House
Harper's, 57:788, Oct
1878

Hill, Beveridge
The Story of a Cañon
Picayune, 28 Apr 1895,
p. 22

Hill, Frederic Stanhope
Twenty Years at Sea
Atlantic, 73:568, Apr
1894

Hill, Frederick Trevor
The Accomplice
Nation, 81:122, 10 Aug
1905
The Minority
Bookman (NY), 15:567,
Aug 1902
The Web
Athenaeum, 3985:334,
12 Mar 1904
Bookman (NY), 18:650-1,
Feb 1904
Outlook, 75:864, 5 Dec
1903

Hill, John Alexander
Stories of the Railroad

Outlook, 63:465, 21 Oct 1899

Hilles, Lewis Baker
Chickens Come Home to Roost
Picayune, 6 May 1900, III,
8

Hillyer, Shaler Granby
The Marable Family
Nation, 29:279, 23 Oct 1879

Hilton, Alice Howard
A Blonde Creole
Godey's, 126:364, Mar 1893

Hinman, Lillian
Don Luis' Wife
Bookman (NY), 7:171, Apr
1898

Hinman, Walter N.
Under the Maples
Picayune, 25 Nov 1888, p.
14

His Fleeting Ideal
By P. T. Barnum, John L. Sulli-
van, Bill Nye, Ella Wheeler
Wilcox, Alfred C. Calhoun, et
al.
Godey's, 121:262, Sep 1890

Hitchcock, Thomas
The Unhappy Loves of a Man
of Genius
Epoch, 10:62, 28 Aug 1891

Hobart, George Vere
Dinkelspiel--His Gonversation-
ings
Picayune, 8 Apr 1900, III, 7

Hodder, Alfred
The New Americans
Athenaeum, 3881:329, 15
Mar 1902
Nation, 74:231-2, 20 Mar
1902
Overland, 2d S, 39:577-8,
Jan 1902
Saturday Review, 93:405,

Hodder, Alfred
29 Mar 1902; 94:19,
5 Jul 1902
See also Willard, Josiah
Flynt, and Francis Wal-
ton [pseud. of Alfred
Hodder].

Hogbin, Alfred C.
Elsa
Nation, 29:115, 14 Aug
1879

Holbrook, Richard Thayer
Boys and Men
Picayune, 15 Apr 1900,
III, 7
Nation, 71:55, 19 Jul
1900

Holcombe, William Henry
A Mystery of New Orleans
Solved by New Methods
Picayune, 4 Jan 1891,
p. 11

[Holden, E. Goodman]
A Famous Victory
Atlantic, 46:831-2, Dec
1880

Holford, Castello N.
Aristopia
Picayune, 16 Jun 1895,
p. 28

Holland, Mrs. Annie Jefferson
The Refugees
Picayune, 6 Apr 1896,
p. 11

Holland, Josiah Gilbert
Arthur Bonnicastle
Athenaeum, 2393:301-2,
6 Sep 1873
Godey's, 87:568, Dec
1873
Harper's, 47:776-7,
Oct 1873
Nation, 17:277, 23 Oct
1873

Overland, 11:484, Nov 1873
Picayune, 28 Sep 1873, [p.
3]
The Mystery of the Manse
Godey's, 90:93, Jan 1875
Nicholas Minturn
Athenaeum, 2614:696-7, 1
Dec 1877
North American Review,
125:588-9, Nov 1877
Sunday Afternoon, 1:91-2,
Jan 1878
Sevenoaks
Atlantic, 37:117-8, Jan 1876
Godey's, 92:93, Jan 1876
Harper's, 52:467, Feb 1876
Nation, 21:374, 9 Dec 1875

Hollister, Gideon Hiram
Kinley Hollow
Nation, 36:41, 11 Jan 1883

[Holloway, Mrs. Anna]
Kate Comerford
By Teresa A. Thornet
[pseud.].
Manhattan, 2:481, Nov
1883
Picayune, 26 Dec 1880,
[p. 5]

[Holly, Marietta]
Miss Jones' Quilting
Picayune, 3 Apr 1887, p.
13; 24 Apr 1887, p. 7
Samantha Among the Brethren
Saturday Review, 71:387-8,
28 Mar 1891
Samantha Among the Colored
Folks
By Josiah Allen's Wife
[pseud.].
Picayune, 16 Dec 1894, p.
2
Samantha at Saratoga
Godey's, 115:430, Nov 1887
Picayune, 4 Sep 1887, p. 8
Saturday Review, 65:85, 21
Jan 1888
Samantha vs. Josiah
Canadian Magazine, 27:281,

Jul 1906

Sweet Cicely
<u>Overland</u>, 2d S, 7:336, Mar
1886
<u>Picayune</u>, 13 Dec 1885, p.
8

Holm, Saxe [pseud.].
See Jackson, Helen Maria
(Fiske) Hunt.

Holmes, Margret [pseud.].
See Bates, Margret Holmes
(Ernsperger).

Holmes, Mary Jane (Hawes)
Common Pride
<u>Picayune</u>, 28 Jun 1891,
p. 12
Edith Lyle
<u>Canadian Monthly</u>,
10:273, Sep 1876
<u>Picayune</u>, 29 Apr 1894,
p. 23
Edna Browning
<u>Godey's</u>, 85:186, Aug
1872
Ethelyn's Mistake
<u>Picayune</u>, 2 Jul 1893,
p. 17
Mrs. Hallam's Companion,
and The Spring Farm, and
Other Tales
<u>Picayune</u>, 22 Nov 1896,
p. 10
Rose Mather
<u>Picayune</u>, 17 Jul 1892,
p. 13
West Lawn, and The Rector
of St. Mark's
<u>Godey's</u>, 79:567, Dec
1874

Holmes, Oliver Wendell
A Mortal Antipathy
<u>Athenaeum</u>, 3038:96,
16 Jan 1886
<u>Harper's</u>, 72:646, Mar
1886
<u>Overland</u>, 2d S, 7:324,
Mar 1886

<u>Saturday Review</u>, 61:239, 13
Feb 1886
Over the Teacups
<u>Athenaeum</u>, 3296:888, 27
Dec 1890
The Poet of the Breakfast Table
<u>Athenaeum</u>, 2349:555, 2
Nov 1872
<u>Overland</u>, 10:101, Jan 1873
The Story of Iris
<u>Saturday Review</u>, 44:531, 27
Oct 1877
The Writings of Oliver Wendell
Holmes
<u>Athenaeum</u>, 3374:818-9, 25
Jun 1892

Holt, Henry
Calmire
<u>Athenaeum</u>, 3400:881, 24
Dec 1892
<u>Atlantic</u>, 70:707, Nov 1892
<u>Nation</u>, 82:389, 10 May 1893
<u>Sewanee Review</u>, 1:266, May
1893
Sturmsee
<u>Bookman</u> (London), 28:210,
Sep 1905
<u>Nation</u>, 82:389, 10 May 1906
<u>North American Review</u>,
182:924-5, Jun 1906

[Holt, John Saunders]
Abraham Page, Esq.
<u>Athenaeum</u>, 2234:238-9, 20
Aug 1870
What I Know About Ben Eccles
By Abraham Page [pseud.].
<u>Athenaeum</u>, 2234:238-9, 20
Aug 1870

Holt, Tilbury
Miss Beck
<u>Picayune</u>, 5 Mar 1882, [p.
14]

Hooker, Brian
The Right Man
<u>Bookman</u> (NY), 28:260-1,
Nov 1908

Hooker, LeRoy
Baldoon
  Picayune, 13 Aug 1899,
    II, 8

[Hooper, George W.]
Down the River
  Saturday Review, 37:698,
    30 May 1874

Hooper, Henry
The Lost Model
  Nation, 20:44, 21 Jan
    1875
  Picayune, 27 Sep 1874,
    [p. 6]
  Saturday Review, 38:551,
    24 Oct 1874

[Hooper, Lucy Hamilton (Jones)]
The Tsar's Window
  Atlantic, 47:861, Jun
    1881
  Harper's, 63:154, Jun
    1881
  Nation, 32:303, 28 Apr
    1881
Under the Tricolor
  Nation, 30:140-1, 19
    Feb 1880
See also Not Pretty, but
  Precious.

Hoover, Bessie R.
Pa Flickinger's Folks
  Nation, 89:381, 21 Oct
    1909

Hoover, Francis Trout
Enemies in the Rear
  Picayune, 12 May 1895,
    p. 7

[Hopkins, Mrs. Alice Kimball]
The Romance of a Letter
  By Lowell Choate [pseud.].
  Nation, 45:57, 21 Jul
    1887
  Picayune, 22 May 1887,
    p. 16

Hopkins, Alphonso Alva
John Bremm
  Continent, 3:478, 11 Apr
    1883
Saint and Sinner
  Cottage Hearth, 8:365, Nov
    1882

Hopkins, Mrs. Herbert Müller
See Hopkins, Pauline Bradford (Mackie).

Hopkins, Herbert Müller
The Fighting Bishop
  Bookman (NY), 15:259-60,
    May 1902
  Nation, 74:411, 22 May
    1902
Priest and Pagan
  Bookman (NY), 27:280-1,
    May 1908
  Nation, 86:354-5, 16 Apr
    1908
The Torch
  Bookman (NY), 18:651-2,
    Feb 1904

Hopkins, Margaret Sutton (Bris-
  coe)
Jimty, and Others
  Outlook, 58:82, 1 Jan 1898
Links in a Chain
  Nation, 58:412-3, 31 May
    1894
  Picayune, 20 May 1894, p.
    9
"Perchance to Dream," and
Other Stories
  Nation, 56:146, 23 Feb
    1893
  Poet-Lore, 5:164-5, (No.
    3) 1893
The Sixth Sense, and Other
Stories
  Nation, 69:96, 3 Aug 1899
  Outlook, 62:624, 15 Jul
    1899

Hopkins, Mark
The World's Verdict
  Cottage Hearth, 14:160,

May 1888
Epoch, 3:97, 9 Mar
1888
Nation, 46:530, 28 Jun
1888
Overland, 2d S, 11:438,
Apr 1888
Picayune, 11 Mar 1888,
p. 12
Saturday Review, 65:798-
99, 30 Jun 1888

Hopkins, Pauline Bradford
(Mackie)
Mademoiselle DeBerny
Bookman (NY), 7:166,
Apr 1898
Outlook, 58:82, 1 Jan
1898
The Voice in the Desert
Saturday Review, 98:586,
5 Nov 1904
The Washingtonians
Athenaeum, 3993:587,
7 May 1904
Bookman (NY), 14:433,
Dec 1901
Saturday Review, 96:369,
19 Sep 1903
Ye Little Salem Maide
Bookman (NY), 8:165-6,
Oct 1898
Outlook, 59:789, 30 Jul
1898

Hopkins, William John
The Clammer
Atlantic, 99:125, Jan
1907
North American Review,
182:928, Jun 1906
The Meddlings of Eve
Nation, 91:444-5, 10
Nov 1910
Old Harbor
Nation, 90:163, 17 Feb
1910
Saturday Review, 109:533,
23 Apr 1910

Hopper, James

See The Spinner's Book of
Fiction.

Hoppin, Emily Howland
From Out of the Past
Picayune, 11 Jun 1893, p.
16

Hornaday, William Temple
The Man Who Became a Sa-
vage
Athenaeum, 3569:378, 21
Mar 1896

Horsley, Reginald
Stonewall's Scout
Athenaeum, 3601:598, 31
Oct 1896

Horton, George
Aphroessa
Picayune, 24 Oct 1897, p. 9
Constantine
Athenaeum, 3585:60, 11 Jul
1896
Bookman (NY), 6:74, Sep
1897
Nation, 65:282, 7 Oct 1897
The Edge of Hazard
Bookman (NY), 23:284-5,
May 1906
A Fair Brigand
Athenaeum, 3781:461, 14
Apr 1900
Outlook, 62:400, 17 Jun
1899
In Argolis
Outlook, 72:953, 20 Dec
1902
Like Another Helen
Bookman (NY), 13:188, Apr
1901
Canadian Magazine, 17:391-
92, Aug 1901
The Long Straight Road
Bookman (NY), 16:375-6,
Dec 1902

[Hosea, Lucy (Klinck) Rice]
Eastward
Godey's, 125:409, Oct 1892

Hosmer, George Washington
"As We Went Marching On"
Godey's, 112:104, Jan
1886
Picayune, 8 Nov 1885,
p. 11

Hosmer, James Kendall
How Thankful Was Bewitched
Atlantic, 75:133, Jan
1895
Nation, 61:244, 3 Oct
1895

Hosmer, Margaret (Kerr)
Blanche Gilroy
Godey's, 73:184, Aug
1871
Overland, 7:292, Sep
1871
The Subtle Spell
Godey's, 86:185, Feb
1873
See also Not Pretty, but
Precious.

Hotchkiss, Chauncey Crafts
A Colonial Free-Lance
Godey's, 135:557, Nov
1897
Overland, 2d S, 30:474,
Nov 1897
Picayune, 26 Sep 1897,
p. 15

Hough, Emerson
54-40 or Fight
Bookman (NY), 29:78-9,
Mar 1909
The Girl at the Halfway
House
Athenaeum, 3829:332,
16 Mar 1901
Nation, 71:410, 22 Nov
1900
Outlook, 65:982, 25 Aug
1900
Picayune, 9 Sep 1900,
II, 8
Heart's Desire
Bookman (NY), 22:367-8,

Dec 1905
Overland, 2d S, 46:590, Dec
1905
The Law of the Land
Atlantic, 95:692, May 1905
The Mississippi Bubble
Bookman (London), 25:57,
Oct 1903
Bookman (NY), 15:374-6,
Jun 1902
The Purchase Price
Nation, 91:606, 22 Dec 1910
The Story of a Cowboy
Godey's, 135:[666]-7, Dec
1897
Overland, 2d S, 30:470,
Nov 1897
Picayune, 31 Oct 1897, p.
11
The Way of a Man
Nation, 85:377-8, 24 Oct
1907

House, Edward Howard
Japanese Episodes
Saturday Review, 53:124, 28
Jan 1882
Yone Santo
Harper's, 78:987, May 1889
Saturday Review, 68:305-6,
14 Sep 1889

Houston, A. C.
Huge Harrison
Picayune, 10 Jan 1892, p.
14

How, Louis
The Penitentes
Picayune, 7 Oct 1900, II, 12

Howard, Blanche Willis
See Teuffel, Blanche Willis
(Howard) von.

Howe, Edgar Watson
An Ante-Mortem Statement
Picayune, 21 Jun 1891, p.
12
The Confessions of John Whit-
lock

170

Howells, William Dean

Atlantic, 48:402-5, Sep 1881

Cottage Hearth, 7:273, Sep 1881

Nation, 33:54, 21 Jul 1881

Rose-Belford's, 7:59-80, Jul 1881; 7:134-65, Aug 1881

Fennel and Rue

Athenaeum, 4201:537-8, 2 May 1908

Bookman (NY), 27:281-2, May 1908

Nation, 86:309, 2 Apr 1908

Outlook, 88:838, 11 Apr 1908

Times Literary Supplement, 16 Apr 1908, p. 126

A Foregone Conclusion

Harper's, 50:598, Mar 1875

Nation, 19:12-3, 7 Jan 1875

North American Review, 120:207-14, Jan 1875

A Hazard of New Fortunes

Athenaeum, 3244:889-90, 28 Dec 1889

Atlantic, 65:563-7, Apr 1890

Epoch, 7:158, 11 Apr 1890

Nation, 50:454-5, 5 Jun 1890

Picayune, 1 Dec 1889, p. 13; 5 Apr 1891, p. 12

Saturday Review, 68:684, 14 Dec 1889

Idyls in Drab

Saturday Review, 83:68, 16 Jan 1897

Imaginary Interviews

Times Literary Supplement, 24 Nov 1910, p. 465

An Imperative Duty

Athenaeum, 3355:210-1, 13 Feb 1892

Epoch, 10:370, 8 Jan 1892

Nation, 54:154, 25 Feb 1892

Indian Summer

Athenaeum, 3049:453-4, 3 Apr 1886

Atlantic, 57:850-7, Jun 1886

Cottage Hearth, 12:128, Apr 1886; 14:160, May 1888

Godey's, 116:479, May 1888

Nation, 42:408, 13 May 1886

Saturday Review, 61:481, 3 Apr 1886

The Kentons

Athenaeum, 3894:748, 14 Jun 1902

Atlantic, 111:77-82, Jan 1903

Bookman (London), 22:144, Jul 1902

Nation, 74:470, 12 Jun 1902

Outlook, 71:135, 10 May 1902

Saturday Review, 94:175, 9 Aug 1902

Times Literary Supplement, 16 May 1902, p. 139

The Lady of the Aroostook

Athenaeum, 2687:535, 26 Apr 1879

Harper's, 58:941, May 1879

North American Review, 128:691-4, Jun 1879

Rose-Belford's, 2:511, Apr 1879

Sunday Afternoon, 3:480, May 1879

The Landlord at Lion's Head

Athenaeum, 3630:678, 22 May 1897

Harper's, 95:961-2, Nov 1897

Nation, 65:16-7, 1 Jul 1897

London Films

Athenaeum, 4074:717-8, 25 Nov 1905

The Minister's Charge

Athenaeum, 3086:822, 18 Dec 1886

Cottage Hearth, 14:262, Aug

Howells, William Dean
  America, 4:386, 388,
    3 Jul 1890
  Athenaeum, 3270:828,
    28 Jun 1890
  Atlantic, 66:720, Nov
    1880
  Epoch, 7:397-8, 25 Jul
    1890
  Nation, 51:252-3, 25
    Sep 1890
  Picayune, 8 Jun 1890,
    p. 14
  Saturday Review, 70:18-9,
    5 Jul 1890
  Their Silver Wedding Journey
    Athenaeum, 3780:428,
      7 Apr 1900
    Nation, 70:245, 29 Mar
      1900
    Picayune, 14 Jan 1900,
      II, 7; 13 May 1900,
      III, 3
    Saturday Review, 89:466,
      14 Apr 1900
  Their Wedding Journey
    Athenaeum, 2315:303-4,
      9 Mar 1872
    North American Review,
      114:444-5, Apr 1872
    Overland, 8:481, May
      1872
    Overland, 2d S, 28:608,
      Nov 1896
    Saturday Review, 33:385,
      23 Mar 1872; 78:689,
      22 Dec 1894
  Three Villages
    Manhattan, 4:251, Aug
      1884
  Through the Eye of the
  Needle
    Athenaeum, 4157:786,
      29 Jun 1907
    Bookman (NY), 25:434-5,
      Jun 1907
    Nation, 84:434-5, 9
      May 1907
    North American Review,
      186:127-30, Sep 1907
    Times Literary Supple-

      ment, 24 May 1907, p.
      165
  A Traveller from Altruria
    Athenaeum, 3480:29, 7 Jul
      1894
    Atlantic, 74:701-4, Nov
      1894
    Nation, 59:107, 9 Aug 1894
    Picayune, 10 Sep 1893, p.
      16
    Saturday Review, 78:129, 4
      Aug 1894
  The Undiscovered Country
    Nation, 30:474, 24 Jun
      1880; 31:49-51, 15 Jul
      1880
    Saturday Review, 50:124,
      24 Jul 1880; 50:433-4,
      2 Oct 1880
  A Woman's Reason
    Atlantic, 52:704-5, Nov 1883
    Continent, 4:733-4, 5 Dec
      1883
    Cottage Hearth, 14:24, Jan
      1883
    Harper's, 68:158-9, Dec
      1883
    Nation, 37:420, 15 Nov 1883
    Saturday Review, 56:604-5,
      10 Nov 1883
  The World of Chance
    Athenaeum, 3417:502, 22
      Apr 1893
    Atlantic, 72:420, Sep 1893
    Cottage Hearth, 19: advert
      28, Nov 1893
    Godey's, 127:361, Sep 1893
    Nation, 57:31, 13 Jul 1893
    Picayune, 16 Jul 1893, p.
      19
    Saturday Review, 75:408,
      15 Apr 1893
  See also The Whole Family.

Howland, Mrs. Marie
  Papa's Own Girl
    Godey's, 79:190, Aug 1874
    Harper's, 49:443, Aug 1874
    Picayune, 14 Jun 1874, [p.
      9]; 26 Aug 1894, p. 16
    Saturday Review, 38:291,

29 Aug 1874

Hubard, Sue W.
"As Thyself!"
 Nation, 32:16, 6 Jan
  1881
 Picayune, 9 Jan 1881,
  [p. 10]

Hubbard, Elbert
 Forbes of Harvard
  Picayune, 22 Apr 1894,
  p. 25
 No Enemy (but Himself)
  Athenaeum, 3503:824-5,
  15 Dec 1894
  Atlantic, 75:424, Mar
  1895

Hubbell, Walter
 The Curse of Marriage
  Overland, 2d S, 15:434,
  Apr 1890
  Picayune, 15 Dec 1889,
  p. 11

Hucker, Annie M.
 Nearly Lost
  Picayune, 13 Jul 1890,
  p. 11

Hudson, Mary (Clemmer) Ames
 See Ames, Mary (Clemmer)
  Hudson.

Hudson, William Cadwalader
 An American Cavalier
  Picayune, 5 Jul 1897,
  p. 9
 Jack Gordon
  Picayune, 16 Mar 1890,
  p. 16
 J. P. Dunbar
  Nation, 83:539, 20 Dec
  1906
 A Man with a Thumb
  Picayune, 1 Mar 1891,
  p. 10
  Saturday Review, 72:336-
  37, 19 Sep 1891
 Vivier of Vivier, Longman

& Company, Bankers
 Picayune, 8 Jun 1890, p. 16

Hudspeth, Rosa
 The Juggernaut of the Moderns
  Picayune, 18 Oct 1896, p. 9

[Hughes, Mrs. Reginald]
 Oxley
  By Lyndon [pseud.].
  Godey's, 87:91, Jul 1873
  Harper's, 47:301, Jul 1873
 Sybil Trevyllian
  Atlantic, 71:849, Jun 1893

Hughes, Rupert
 The Dozen from Lakerim
  Outlook, 63:510, 28 Oct 1899
 The Gift Wife
  Bookman (NY), 32:431, Dec
  1910

Huling, Caroline Alden
 The Courage of Her Convictions
  Picayune, 26 Jan 1896, p.
  16

[Hume, John Ferguson]
 Five Hundred Majority
  By Willys Niles [pseud.].
  Harper's, 45:298-9, Jul 1872
  Nation, 14:410, 20 Jun 1872
  Picayune, 12 May 1872, [p.
  10]

Hume, Robert W.
 My Lodger's Legacy
  Overland, 2d S, 9:219, Feb
  1887

Humphrey, Mrs. Frank Pope
 A New England Cactus
  Bookman (London), 2:156,
  Aug 1892
  Saturday Review, 74:179,
  6 Aug 1892
 Phoebe Tilson
  Athenaeum, 3698:348, 10
  Sep 1898

Humphrey, Zephine
Over Against the Green
Peak
Sewanee Review, 17:502,
Oct 1909

Huneker, James
Visionaries
Athenaeum, 4087:228-9,
24 Feb 1906
Atlantic, 97:47-8, Jan
1906
Bookman (NY), 22:360-1,
Dec 1905

Hunt, Belle
Held in Trust
Picayune, 21 Feb 1892,
p. 10

Hunter, William C.
Frozen Dog Tales, and
Other Things
Sewanee Review, 14:379,
Jul 1906

Hurd, Grace Marguerite
The Bennett Twins
Bookman (NY), 12:303,
Nov 1900
Picayune, 28 Oct 1900,
II, 9

Hurlbut, Ella Childs
Mrs. Clift-Crosby's Niece
Picayune, 16 Jul 1893,
p. 19

Hutton, Laurence
A Boy and Four Dogs
Outlook, 59:134, 14
May 1898

Hyde, Henry M.
The Buccaneers
Outlook, 79:94, 7 Jan
1905

Hyde-Vogl, V. D.
Echoes and Prophecies
Overland, 2d S, 55:441,

Apr 1910

I., J. T.
See Irving, John Treat.

[Ide, Francis Otis (Ogden)]
A Loyal Little Red-Coat
By Ruth Ogden [pseud.].
Epoch, 8:366, 9 Jan 1891
Godey's, 121:98, Jan 1891

Iliowizi, Henry
In the Tale
Picayune, 2 May 1897, p.
15

Ingham, Colonel Frederic
[pseud.].
See Hale, Edward Everett.

Inman, Henry
The Ranch on the Oxhide
Overland, 2d S, 33:94, Jan
1899

Ireland, Mary Eliza (Haines)
What I Told Dorcas
Picayune, 8 Mar 1896, p.
25

[Irving, John Treat]
The Van Gelder Papers, and
Other Sketches
Ed. J. T. I.
Nation, 45:237, 22 Sep 1887
Saturday Review, 64:230-1,
13 Aug 1887

Irwin, Wallace
Letters of a Japanese School-
boy
Bookman (NY), 29:311-3,
May 1909

Irwin, Will
The House of Mystery
Overland, 2d S, 55:537,
May 1910

J. S. of Dale [pseud.].
See Stimson, Frederic Jesup.

Jackson, Charles Tenney
　Loser's Luck
　　Sewanee Review, 14:105-
　　　106, Jan 1906
　My Brother's Keeper
　　Bookman (NY), 32:303-4,
　　　Nov 1910

[Jackson, Edward Payson]
　A Demigod
　　Nation, 44:125, 10 Feb
　　　1887
　　Picayune, 21 Nov 1886,
　　　p. 11

Jackson, Helen Maria (Fiske)
　Hunt
　Between Whiles
　　Epoch, 1:407, 3 Jun
　　　1887
　　Nation, 45:57, 21 Jul
　　　1887
　　Overland, 2d S, 10:104-5,
　　　Jul 1887
　Hetty's Strange History
　　Godey's, 95:437, Nov
　　　1877
　　Harper's, 55:939, Nov
　　　1877
　　Library Table, 3:27-8,
　　　Sep 1877
　　Overland, 2d S, 8:109,
　　　Jul 1886
　　Picayune, 25 Apr 1886,
　　　p. 8
　　Saturday Review, 44:531,
　　　27 Oct 1877
　Mercy Philbrick's Choice
　　Athenaeum, 2554:462-3,
　　　7 Oct 1876
　　Atlantic, 39:243-4, Feb
　　　1877
　　Godey's, 93:569, Dec
　　　1876
　　Harper's, 54:149, Dec
　　　1876
　　Library Table, 2:3, Jan
　　　1877
　　Nation, 23:372, 21 Dec
　　　1876
　　Overland, 2d S, 8:109,

　　Jul 1886
　　Picayune, 15 Oct 1876, [p.
　　　4]; 25 Apr 1886, p. 8
　Ramona
　　Athenaeum, 2982:802, 20
　　　Dec 1884
　　Atlantic, 55:127-30, Jan
　　　1885
　　Nation, 40:100-1, 29 Jan
　　　1885
　　North American Review,
　　　143:241-54, Sep 1886
　　Overland, 2d S, 5:330,
　　　Mar 1885
　　Saturday Review, 59:187,
　　　7 Feb 1885
　Saxe Holm's Stories
　　Nation, 27:199, 26 Sep 1878
　　Saturday Review, 37:128, 24
　　　Jan 1874; 38:130, 25 Jul
　　　1874
　　Sunday Afternoon, 2:288,
　　　Sep 1878
　Zeph
　　Athenaeum, 3050:485-6, 10
　　　Apr 1886
　　Overland, 2d S, 7:655, Jun
　　　1886
　　Saturday Review, 62:23-5,
　　　3 Jul 1886

Jackson, Margaret (Doyle)
　A Daughter of the Pit
　　Nation, 76:276, 2 Apr 1903
　　Saturday Review, 96:vii,
　　　Suppl., 21 Nov 1903

James, Henry
　The Ambassadors
　　Athenaeum, 3970:714, 28
　　　Nov 1903
　　Bookman (NY), 18:532-4,
　　　Jan 1904
　　Nation, 78:95, 4 Feb 1904
　　Outlook, 75:958, 19 Dec
　　　1903
　　Poet-Lore, 16:94, Winter
　　　1905
　　Quarterly Review, 198:358,
　　　Oct 1903
　　Saturday Review, 96:551,

James, Henry
  31 Oct 1903
    Times Literary Supple-
      ment, 16 Oct 1903, p.
      296
  The American
    Athenaeum, 2593:14-5,
      7 Jul 1877
    Atlantic, 40:108-9, Jul
      1877
    Library Table, 3:154,
      30 Aug 1877
    Nation, 24:325-6, 31 May
      1877
    North American Review,
      125:309-15, Sep 1877
    Picayune, 3 Jun 1877,
      [p. 12]
    Quarterly Review, 198:358,
      Oct 1903
    Saturday Review, 44:214-5,
      18 Aug 1877
  The American Scene
    Athenaeum, 4141:282-3,
      9 Mar 1907
    Bookman (London), 31:265-
      66, Mar 1907
    Bookman (NY), 25:188-90,
      Apr 1907
    North American Review,
      185:214-8, 17 May 1907
  The Aspern Papers
    Athenaeum, 3186:659-60,
      17 Nov 1888
    Epoch, 4:290, 23 Nov
      1888
    Nation, 48:353, 25 Apr
      1889
    Quarterly Review, 198:358,
      Oct 1903
    Saturday Review, 66:526-7,
      3 Nov 1888
  The Awkward Age
    Athenaeum, 3735:651-2,
      27 May 1899
    Bookman (London), 16:81,
      Jun 1899
    Bookman (NY), 9:472-3,
      Jul 1899
    Nation, 69:155, 24 Aug
      1899
    North American Review,
      176:125-37, Jan 1903
    Outlook, 62:314, 3 Jun 1899
    Quarterly Review, 198:358,
      Oct 1903
    Saturday Review, 87:598, 13
      May 1899
    Sewanee Review, 8:112-3,
      Jan 1900
  The Better Sort
    Athenaeum, 3941:591, 9 May
      1903
    Atlantic, 92:278, Aug 1903
    Bookman (London), 24:30,
      Apr 1903
    Nation, 76:460, 4 Jun 1903
    Quarterly Review, 198:358,
      Oct 1903
    Saturday Review, 95:396,
      28 Mar 1903
    Times Literary Supplement,
      6 Mar 1903, p. 72
  The Bostonians
    Athenaeum, 3045:323, 6 Mar
      1886
    Atlantic, 57:850-7, Jun 1886
    Nation, 42:407-8, 13 May
      1886
    Picayune, 11 Apr 1886, p. 14
    Saturday Review, 61:791-2,
      5 Jun 1886
    Sewanee Review, 11:360, Jul
      1903
  A Bundle of Letters
    Saturday Review, 51:372-3,
      19 Mar 1881
  Confidence
    Athenaeum, 2723:16, 3 Jan
      1880
    Atlantic, 46:125-6, Jul 1880;
      46:140-1, Jul 1880
    Harper's, 60:945-6, May
      1880
    Nation, 30:289-90, 25 Mar
      1880
    Saturday Review, 49:25-6, 3
      Jan 1880
  Daisy Miller
    Athenaeum, 2679:275-6, 1
      Mar 1879
    Atlantic, 71:124, Jan 1893

Continent, 3:508, 18
Apr 1883
Harper's, 58:310, Jan
1879
North American Review,
128:105-6, Jan 1879
Overland, 2d S, 2:554-6,
Nov 1883
Picayune, 24 Nov 1878,
[p. 5]; 7 Oct 1883,
[p. 7]
Quarterly Review, 198:358,
Oct 1903
Saturday Review, 47:561-2,
3 May 1879
Embarrassments
Athenaeum, 3588:158,
1 Aug 1896
Atlantic, 79:137, Jan
1897
Nation, 63:91, 30 Jul
1896
The Europeans
Athenaeum, 2658:431,
5 Oct 1878
Atlantic, 43:167-9, Feb
1879
Harper's, 58:309, Jan
1879
Library Table, 4:511-2,
7 Dec 1878
North American Review,
128:101-5, Jan 1879
Quarterly Review, 198:358,
Oct 1903
Sunday Afternoon, 2:574,
Dec 1878
The Finer Grain
Athenaeum, 4332:552,
5 Nov 1910
Bookman (London), 39:95-6,
Nov 1910
Nation, 91:522-3, 1 Dec
1910
Saturday Review, 110:553-
54, 29 Oct 1910
Times Literary Supple-
ment, 13 Oct 1910,
p. 377
The Golden Bowl
Athenaeum, 4038:332,

18 Mar 1905
Atlantic, 95:696, May 1905
Bookman (NY), 20:418-9,
Jan 1905
Times Literary Supplement,
10 Feb 1905, p. 47
In the Cage
Athenaeum, 3704:564-5, 22
Oct 1898
Bookman (London), 14:165-6,
Sep 1898
Nation, 67:432, 8 Dec 1898
Saturday Review, 86:319-20,
3 Sep 1898
The Lesson of the Master [and
Other Stories]
Athenaeum, 3360:369-70,
19 Mar 1892
Atlantic, 69:711, May 1892
Bookman (London), 2:27,
Apr 1892
Nation, 54:326, 28 Apr 1892
Picayune, 24 Apr 1892, p.
12
Saturday Review, 73:575,
14 May 1892
A London Life [and Other Sto-
ries]
Athenaeum, 3211:597-8, 11
May 1889
Epoch, 5:389, 19 Jul 1889
Harper's, 79:477, Aug 1889
Nation, 49:77, 25 Jul 1889
Saturday Review, 68:47-8,
13 Jul 1889
The Madonna of the Future,
and Other Tales
Athenaeum, 2715:593-4, 8
Nov 1879
The Novels and Tales
Bookman (NY), 30:138-43,
Oct 1909
Quarterly Review, 212:393-
408, Apr 1910
Sewanee Review, 18:486,
Oct 1910
The Other House
Athenaeum, 3601:597, 31
Oct 1896
Atlantic, 79:137, Jan 1897
Bookman (London), 11:49,

James, Henry
  Nov 1896
  Bookman (NY), 4:359-60,
    Dec 1896
  Nation, 64:71, 28 Jan
    1897
  Overland, 2d S, 29:106,
    Jan 1897
  Quarterly Review, 198:358,
    Oct 1903
  Saturday Review, 82:474-
    75, 31 Oct 1896
A Passionate Pilgrim, and
  Other Tales
  Atlantic, 35:490-5, Apr
    1875
  Nation, 20:425-7, 24
    Jun 1875
  Saturday Review, 39:550,
    24 Apr 1875
The Portrait of a Lady
  Athenaeum, 2822:699,
    26 Nov 1881
  Atlantic, 49:126-30, Jan
    1882
  Harper's, 64:474, Feb
    1882
  Quarterly Review, 198:358,
    Oct 1903
  Saturday Review, 52:703-
    704, 3 Dec 1881
The Princess Casamassima
  Athenaeum, 3080:596-7,
    6 Nov 1886
  Epoch, 1:19, 11 Feb
    1887
  Harper's, 74:829, Apr
    1887
  Nation, 44:123-4, 10
    Feb 1887
  Picayune, 28 Nov 1886,
    p. 7
  Saturday Review, 62:728-9,
    27 Nov 1886
The Private Life, Lord
  Beaupré, The Visits
  Athenaeum, 3428:60-1,
    8 Jul 1893
  Atlantic, 72:695-6, Nov
    1893
  Godey's, 127:620, Nov

    1893
  Nation, 57:416-7, 30 Nov
    1893
  Quarterly Review, 198:358,
    Oct 1903
  Saturday Review, 76:46-7,
    8 Jul 1893
The Real Thing, and Other
  Tales
  Athenaeum, 3420:601-2,
    13 May 1893
  Atlantic, 72:695-6, Nov
    1893
  Cottage Hearth, 19:245,
    May 1893
  Godey's, 126:771, Jun 1893
  Overland, 2d S, 21:660,
    Jun 1893
  Saturday Review, 75:603,
    3 Jun 1893
The Reverberator
  Athenaeum, 3164:759, 16
    Jun 1888
  Epoch, 4:55, 24 Aug 1888
  Harper's, 77:802, Oct 1888
  Nation, 47:273, 4 Oct 1888
  North American Review,
    147:599, Nov 1888
Roderick Hudson
  Athenaeum, 2697:12-3, 5
    Jul 1879
  Atlantic, 37:237-8, Feb
    1876
  Library Table, 1:16-7, Jan
    1876
  North American Review,
    122:420-5, Apr 1876
  Poet-Lore, 16:95-6, Winter
    1905
  Quarterly Review, 198:358,
    Oct 1903
The Sacred Fount
  Athenaeum, 3827:272, 2
    Mar 1901
  Bookman (NY), 13:442, Jul
    1901
  North American Review,
    176:125-37, Jan 1903
  Quarterly Review, 198:358,
    Oct 1903
  Saturday Review, 91:574,

James, Henry
Nation, 27:117-8, 22
Aug 1878
Sunday Afternoon, 2:384,
Oct 1878
What Maisie Knew
Athenaeum, 3654:629,
6 Nov 1897
Bookman (London), 13:22,
Oct 1897
Bookman (NY), 6:562,
Feb 1898
Nation, 66:135, 17 Feb
1898
Picayune, 17 Nov 1897,
p. 6
Quarterly Review, 198:358,
Oct 1903
Saturday Review, 84:537-
38, 20 Nov 1897
The Wheel of Time, Colla-
boration, Owen Wingrave
Atlantic, 73:568, Apr
1894
Nation, 57:416-7, 30
Nov 1893
The Wings of the Dove
Athenaeum, 3907:346,
13 Sep 1902
Bookman (London), 23:24-
25, Oct 1902
Bookman (NY), 16:259-60,
Nov 1902
Nation, 75:330-1, 23
Oct 1902
North American Review,
176:125-37, Jan 1903
Quarterly Review, 198:358,
Oct 1903
Saturday Review, 95:79-
80, 17 Jan 1903
See also The Whole Family.

[James, Samuel Humphreys]
A Prince of Good Fellows
Ed. N. Warrington Crab-
trie [pseud.].
America, 6:135, 30
Apr 1891

[Jamison, Cecilia Viets (Dakin)

Hamilton]
A Crown from the Spear
Picayune, 28 Apr 1872, [p.
15]
Lady Jane
Saturday Review, 78:719-20,
29 Dec 1894
My Bonnie Lass
Nation, 25:275, 1 Nov 1877
Picayune, 26 Aug 1877, [p.
9]
Seraph, the Little Violinist
Picayune, 10 Jan 1897, p.
11
The Story of an Enthusiast
Nation, 46:304, 12 Apr 1888
Picayune, 11 Dec 1887, p.
6
Toinette's Phillip
Picayune, 18 Nov 1894, p.
15
Woven of Many Threads
Picayune, 16 Jul 1876, [p.
7]

Janeway, J. B. H.
His Love for Helen
Picayune, 29 Oct 1893, p.
16

Janney, Lucy N.
Alton-Thorpe
Nation, 31:382, 25 Nov 1880
Picayune, 17 Oct 1880, [p.
2]

Janvier, Thomas Allibone
The Aztec Treasure-House
Epoch, 8:190, 24 Oct 1890
Nation, 51:486, 18 Dec 1890
Picayune, 16 Jul 1893, p.
19
Color Studies
Nation, 41:539, 24 Dec 1885
Overland, 2d S, 6:551, Nov
1885
Color Studies, and A Mexican
Campaign
America, 6:360, 25 Jun 1891
Epoch, 9:397-8, 24 Jul 1891
Nation, 53:v, 9 Jul 1891

In Great Waters
Nation, 74:232, 20 Mar
1902
In Old New York
Nation, 59:470, 20 Dec
1894
In the Sargasso Sea
Bookman (NY), 8:68-9,
Sep 1898
Nation, 67:299, 20 Oct
1898
Outlook, 59:789, 30 Jul
1898
Saturday Review, 86:353,
10 Sep 1898
Legends of the City of
Mexico
Nation, 90:539, 26 May
1910
The Passing of Thomas
[and Other Stories]
Picayune, 24 Jun 1900,
II, 12
Santa Fé's Partner
Nation, 85:306-7, 3 Oct
1907
Stories of Old New Spain
America, 6:248, 28
May 1891
Nation, 52:484, 11 Jun
1891
The Uncle of an Angel,
and Other Stories
Atlantic, 69:269, Feb
1892
Epoch, 10:370, 8 Jan
1892
Harper's, 84:478-9, Feb
1892
Nation, 53:264, 1 Oct
1891
Picayune, 6 Sep 1891,
p. 10

[Jarboe, Mary Halsey
(Thomas)]
Robert Atterbury
By Thomas H. Brainerd
[pseud.].
Picayune, 13 Apr 1896,
p. 10

Jarrold, Ernest
Micky Finn Idyls
Outlook, 63:512, 28 Oct 1899

Jarvis, Thomas S.
Geoffrey Hampstead
Godey's, 121:347, Oct 1890

Jay, W. L. M. [pseud.].
See Woodruff, Julia Louise
Matilda (Curtiss).

Jeffrey, Rosa (Griffith) Vertner
Johnson
Marah
Godey's, 108:301, Mar 1884

[Jeffreys, Mrs. Arnold]
Under Foot
By Alton Clyde [pseud.].
Overland, 4:487, May 1870
Picayune, 20 Mar 1870, [p.
11]

Jenness, Annie
See Miller, Annie (Jenness).

Jennings, Louis John
The Philadelphian
Picayune, 10 May 1891, p.
12

Jennings, Napoleon Augustus
A Texas Ranger
Picayune, 4 Jun 1899, II, 9

Jerome, Ferris
High-Water-Mark
Nation, 28:391, 5 Jun 1879
Picayune, 18 May 1879, [p.
11]

Jessop, George Henry
Gerald Ffrench's Friends
Athenaeum, 3241:777-8, 7
Dec 1889
Nation, 50:117, 6 Feb 1890
Saturday Review, 70:458,
18 Oct 1890
Judge Lynch
Athenaeum, 3254:302-3,

Jessop, George Henry
  8 Mar 1890
  Saturday Review, 68:167-
    68, 10 Aug 1889
  See also Matthews, Brander,
    and George H. Jessop.

Jewett, Mrs. S. W.
  From Fourteen to Fourscore
  Nation, 13:13, 6 Jul
    1871

Jewett, Sarah Orne
  Betty Leicester
    Cottage Hearth, 16:23,
      Jan 1890
    Overland, 2d S, 15:111,
      Jan 1890
  Country By-Ways
    Atlantic, 49:421, Mar
      1882
    Cottage Hearth, 7:369,
      Dec 1881
    Nation, 33:479, 15 Dec
      1881
    Picayune, 27 Nov 1881,
      [p. 2]
  A Country Doctor
    Athenaeum, 2966:272,
      30 Aug 1884
    Atlantic, 54:418-20, Sep
      1884
    Continent, 6:127, (No. 4)
      1884
    Cottage Hearth, 10:250,
      Aug 1884
    Nation, 39:96-7, 31 Jul
      1894
    Overland, 2d S, 4:222,
      Aug 1884
    Saturday Review, 58:283-
      84, 30 Aug 1884
  The Country of the Pointed
    Firs
    Athenaeum, 3619:311,
      6 Mar 1897
    Atlantic, 79:272-3, Feb
      1897
    Bookman (NY), 5:80-1,
      Mar 1897
    Nation, 64:288, 15 Apr

1897
    Overland, 2d S, 29:106, Jan
      1897
  Deephaven
    Athenaeum, 3459:178, 10
      Feb 1894
    Atlantic, 39:759, Jun 1877;
      73:130-3, Jan 1894
    Cottage Hearth, 4:146, Jun
      1877
    Saturday Review, 43:811,
      30 Jun 1877
  The King of Folly Island, and
    Other People
    Athenaeum, 3181:480-1, 13
      Oct 1888; 3950:59, 11 Jul
      1903
    Bookman (London), 24:186-7,
      Aug 1903
    Cottage Hearth, 14:262, Aug
      1888
    Epoch, 4:88, 7 Sep 1888
    Harper's, 77:801, Oct 1888
    Nation, 47:274, 4 Oct 1888
    Overland, 2d S, 12:216,
      Aug 1888
    Saturday Review, 66:222,
      18 Aug 1888; 96:117-8,
      25 Jul 1903
  The Life of Nancy
    Atlantic, 77:279, Feb 1896
    Nation, 62:181-2, 27 Feb
      1896
    Overland, 2d S, 27:350-1,
      Mar 1896
    Picayune, 22 Nov 1895, p.
      9
  A Marsh Island
    Atlantic, 56:560-1, Oct 1885
    Cottage Hearth, 11:224, Jul
      1885
    Harper's, 71:477-8, Aug
      1885
    Nation, 41:158-9, 20 Aug
      1885
    Overland, 2d S, 5:662-3,
      Jun 1885
    Picayune, 4 Oct 1885, [p.
      9]
  The Mate of the Delight, and
    Friends Ashore

Johnson, Harry M.
Edith
Picayune, 15 Sep 1895,
p. 12
Johnson, Helen Louise (Kendrick)
Roddy's Romance
Saturday Review, 39:296,
27 Feb 1875

Johnson, Owen
Arrows of the Almighty
Athenaeum, 3848:119,
27 Jul 1901
Outlook, 67:966, 27 Apr
1901
Saturday Review, 92:280,
31 Aug 1901
The Eternal Boy
Bookman (NY), 28:596-8,
Feb 1909
Nation, 88:226, 4 Mar
1909
In the Name of Liberty
Sewanee Review, 14:378-
79, Jul 1906
Max Fargus
Bookman (NY), 24:161-2,
Oct 1906
The Varmint
Bookman (NY), 31:632-3,
Aug 1910
Nation, 91:264-5, 22
Sep 1910

Johnson, Virginia Wales
The Calderwood Secret
Harper's, 51:906-7,
Nov 1875
An English "Daisy Miller"
Nation, 35:183, 31 Aug
1882
Picayune, 20 Aug 1882,
[p. 2]
The Fainalls of Tipton
Harper's, 69:968, Nov
1884
A Foreign Marriage
Atlantic, 46:419, Sep
1880
The House of the Musician

Cottage Hearth, 13:262,
Aug 1887
Godey's, 115:260, Sep 1887
Joseph the Jew
Harper's, 48:449-50, Feb
1874
Miss Nancy's Pilgrimage
Godey's, 95:85, Jul 1877
Harper's, 54:168, Mar 1877
Library Table, 3:58, 7 Jun
1877
The Neptune Vase
Harper's, 63:795, Oct 1881
Nation, 33:235, 22 Sep 1881
A Sack of Gold
Godey's, 90:93, Jan 1875
Harper's, 50:138-9, Dec
1874
Travels of an American Owl
Godey's, 72:96, Jan 1871
Picayune, 20 Nov 1870, [p.
7]
Saturday Review, 31:256,
25 Feb 1871
The Treasure Tower of Malta
Saturday Review, 69:475-6,
19 Apr 1890
Two Old Cats
Nation, 35:79, 27 Jul 1882

Johnson, William Henry
King or Knave, Which Wins?
Picayune, 7 May 1899, III,
10
The King's Henchman
Picayune, 22 May 1898, II,
2
Saturday Review, 86:447, 1
Oct 1898

Johnston, Alma (Calder)
Miriam's Heritage
Harper's, 57:629, Sep 1878

Johnston, Henry Phelps
Doctor Congalton's Legacy
Atlantic, 78:568, Oct 1896

Johnston, Margaret Avery
In Acadia
Picayune, 6 Aug 1893, p. 17

Jones, Charles Henry
Davault's Mills
  Atlantic, 37:751-2, Jun
    1876
  Godey's, 92:567, Jun
    1876

Jones, John Beauchamp
The Rival Belles
  Picayune, 12 May 1878,
    [p. 10]

Jones, Major Joseph [pseud.].
See Thompson, William
Tappan.

Jones, Randolph
The Buccaneers
  Picayune, 3 Mar 1878,
    [p. 11]

Jordan, Elizabeth Garver
Many Kingdoms
  Nation, 87:526, 26 Nov
    1908
Tales of the City Room
  Bookman (NY), 7:524,
    Aug 1898
  Nation, 67:264, 6 Oct
    1898
  Outlook, 58:883, 2 Apr
    1898
  Picayune, 10 Apr 1898,
    p. 25
Tales of the Cloister
  Bookman (NY), 14:434,
    Dec 1901

Jordan, Kate
The Other House
  Picayune, 16 Oct 1892,
    p. 15

Josiah Allen's Wife [pseud.].
See Holley, Marietta.

Judah, Mrs. Mary Jameson
Down Our Way
  Picayune, 19 Dec 1897,
    p. 28
  Saturday Review, 86:153,

  30 Jul 1898

Judd, Sylvester
Margaret
  Atlantic, 27:144, Jan 1871
  Harper's, 42:400, Feb 1871
  Picayune, 6 Nov 1870, [p.
    9]
  Saturday Review, 31:126,
    28 Jan 1871
Richard Edney and the Gover-
nor's Family
  Atlantic, 46:414, Sep 1880

Justice, Maibelle Heicks (Monroe)
Love Affairs of a Worldly Man
  Picayune, 30 Mar, 1896, p.
    8

Kane, James Johnson
Ilian
  Atlantic, 63:141, Jan 1889
  Picayune, 2 Dec 1888, p.
    15
Miriam vs. Milton
  Saturday Review, 78:606, 1
    Dec 1894

Kavanagh, Julia
Two Lilies
  Godey's, 95:85, Jul 1877

Keenan, Henry Francis
The Aliens
  Athenaeum, 3061:840-1, 26
    Jun 1886
  Godey's, 112:537, May 1886
  Nation, 42:408, 13 May 1886
The Iron Game
  America, 6:162, 7 May 1891
The Money-Makers
  Godey's, 110:463, Apr 1885
  Harper's, 70:976-7, May
    1885
  Overland, 2d S, 5:431-3,
    Apr 1885
  Saturday Review, 59:479-80,
    11 Apr 1885
Trajan
  Athenaeum, 2999:503, 18
    Apr 1885

Harper's, 71:155-6, Jun
1885
Nation, 40:424, 21 May
1885
Overland, 2d S, 5:661,
Jun 1885
Saturday Review, 59:862-
63, 27 Jun 1885

Keith, Alyn Yates [pseud.].
See Morris, Eugenia Laura
(Tuttle).

Keller, Miss M. C.
See Miller, Martha Caro-
lyne (Keller).

Kelley, Adelaide (Skeel), and
William H. Brearley
King Washington
Godey's, 136:216, Feb
1898
Nation, 66:16, 6 Jan
1898

Kelley, James Douglas Jerrold
A Desperate Chance
Nation, 43:14, 1 Jul
1886
Overland, 2d S, 7:653,
Jun 1886

Kellogg, Elijah
Elm Island Stories
Saturday Review, 30:280-
81, 27 Aug 1870
Our Good Old Times
Cottage Hearth, 5:70,
Feb 1878
The Unseen Hand
Godey's, 104:189, Feb
1882

Kellogg, Eugenia
Poccalitto
Overland, 2d S, 43:515,
Jun 1904

Kellogg, Margaret Augusta
Leo Dayne
Picayune, 22 Oct 1899,

II, 6

Kelly, Florence (Finch)
Rhoda of the Underground
Nation, 90:188, 24 Feb 1910
With Hoops of Steel
Athenaeum, 3888:558, 3 May
1902
Nation, 72:183, 28 Feb 1901
Picayune, 28 Oct 1900, II, 9
Saturday Review, 94:176, 9
Aug 1902

Kelly, Myra
The Golden Season
Bookman (NY), 30:266-7,
Nov 1909
Nation, 89:356, 14 Oct 1909
The Isle of Dreams
Nation, 84:389-90, 25 Apr
1907
Little Aliens
Nation, 90:377, 14 Apr 1910
Little Citizens
Atlantic, 95:691, May 1905
Nation, 80:379, 11 May 1905
Wards of Liberty
Nation, 85:545, 12 Dec 1907

Kemble, Edward Windsor
Coontown's 400
Picayune, 28 Jan 1900, II, 7

Kemble, Frances Anne
Far Away and Long Ago
Nation, 49:120, 8 Aug 1889
Saturday Review, 67:684, 1
Jun 1889

Kennedy, D. Edwards
Philip the Forester
Athenaeum, 4271:262, 4 Sep
1909

Kennedy, Sara Beaumont (Cannon)
The Wooing of Judith
Bookman (London), 25:53-4,
Oct 1903

Kennedy, Walker
In the Dwellings of Silence

Kennedy, Walker
    Bookman (London), 6:183,
        Sep 1894
    Nation, 58:179, 8 Mar
        1894
    Saturday Review, 78:217,
        25 Aug 1894

Kent, James
    Sibyl Spencer
        Atlantic, 43:172, Feb
            1879
        Harper's, 58:146, Dec
            1878
        Nation, 27:318, 21 Nov
            1878

Keplinger, Mrs. E. M.
    Bernice
        Picayune, 12 May 1878,
            [p. 10]

Kerr, Alvah Milton
    Trean
        Atlantic, 64:720, Nov
            1889

Kerr, Orpheus C. [pseud.].
    See Newell, Robert Henry.

Kester, Vaughan
    John o' Jamestown
        Bookman (NY), 26:409,
            Dec 1907
        Nation, 86:129, 6 Feb
            1908
    The Manager of the B & A
        Harper's, 103:826-7,
            Oct 1901
        Outlook, 68:886, 10
            Aug 1901

Keyser, Charles S.
    Minden Armais
        Picayune, 10 Apr 1892,
            p. 15

Keyser, Harriette
    On the Borderland
        Nation, 35:447, 23 Nov
            1882

Saturday Review, 58:379,
    20 Sep 1884
Thorns in Your Side
    Saturday Review, 58:158,
        2 Aug 1884

Kieffer, Harry Martyn
    The Recollections of a Drum-
        mer-Boy
        Saturday Review, 56:848,
            29 Dec 1883

[Kimball, Annie Lydia (McPhail)]
    At Daybreak
        By A. Stirling [pseud.].
        Continent, 6:126, (No. 4)
            1884
        Nation, 39:19, 3 Jul 1884
        Overland, 2d S, 4:108, Jul
            1884

Kimball, Richard Burleigh
    A Student's Romance
        Picayune, 3 Dec 1893, p.
            19
    Undercurrents
        Picayune, 11 Mar 1894, p.
            25

King, Anna (Eichberg)
    See Lane, Anna (Eichberg)
        King.

King, Basil
    In the Garden of Charity
        Nation, 76:233, 19 Mar
            1903
    Let Not Man Put Asunder
        Athenaeum, 3882:368, 22
            Mar 1902
        Canadian Magazine, 17:579,
            Apr 1902
        North American Review,
            173:885-8, Dec 1901

King, Charles
    An Army Wife
        Overland, 2d S, 28:610,
            Nov 1896
        Picayune, 12 Jul 1896, p.
            23

Between the Lines
Epoch, 5:373, 12 Jul
1889
Cadet Days
Atlantic, 74:417, Sep
1894
Godey's, 128:[741], Jun
1894
Campaigning with Crook,
and Stories of Army Life
Epoch, 8:320, 19 Dec
1890
Captain Blake
Atlantic, 69:138, Jan
1892
Picayune, 28 Jun 1891,
p. 12
Saturday Review, 72:124,
25 Jul 1891
Captain Close, and Sergeant
Croesus
Picayune, 28 Apr 1895,
p. 22
The Colonel's Christmas
Dinner
Godey's, 122:98, Jan
1891
Picayune, 7 Dec 1890,
p. 8
The Colonel's Daughter
Continent, 3:445, 4 Apr
1883
Cottage Hearth, 18:287,
Sep 1892
Nation, 36:152, 15 Feb
1883
Picayune, 28 Jan 1882,
[p. 12]
Saturday Review, 55:422,
31 Mar 1883
Comrades in Arms
Overland, 2d S, 44:637,
Dec 1904
The Deserter, and From
the Ranks
Godey's, 117:84, Jul
1888
Picayune, 20 May 1888,
p. 10
Dunraven Ranch
Saturday Review, 67:579,

11 May 1889
Foes in Ambush
Picayune, 23 Jul 1893, p.
22
Saturday Review, 77:127-8,
3 Feb 1894
From School to Battle Field
Picayune, 27 Nov 1898, p.
10
A Garrison Tangle
Godey's, 135:447, Oct 1897
Overland, 2d S, 31:95, Jan
1898
Picayune, 29 Nov 1896, p.
18
The General's Double
Godey's, 137:108, Jul 1898
Picayune, 13 Mar 1898, p.
.21
An Initial Experience, and
Other Stories
Picayune, 24 Jun 1894, p.
15
Kitty's Conquest
Godey's, 108:591-2, Jun 1884
Nation, 38:450, 22 May 1884
Picayune, 30 Mar 1884, [p.
12]
Laramie
Epoch, 5:373, 12 Jul 1889
Picayune, 7 Jul 1889, p. 11
Saturday Review, 68:105-6,
27 Jul 1889
Marion's Faith
Nation, 43:102, 29 Jul 1886
Picayune, 15 Aug 1886, p. 6
Ray's Recruit
Godey's, 137:108, Jul 1898
A Soldier's Secret, and An
Army Portia
Picayune, 8 Jan 1893, p. 10
Starlight Ranch, and Other Sto-
ries
Epoch, 7:77, 7 Mar 1890
Picayune, 2 Mar 1890, p.
10
The Story of Fort Frayne
Godey's, 131:[206]-7, Aug
1895
Overland, 2d S, 29:657, Jun
1897

King, Charles
Sunset Pass
Picayune, 5 Oct 1890,
p. 13; 19 Jul 1891,
p. 10; 7 Jun 1896,
p. 18
A Trooper Galahad
Outlook, 61:791, 1 Apr
1899
Picayune, 2 Apr 1899,
III, 3
Trooper Ross and Signal
Butte
Picayune, 23 Dec 1895,
p. 9
Trumpeter Fred
Overland, 2d S, 28:237,
Aug 1896
Picayune, 3 May 1896,
p. 7
Under Fire
Picayune, 16 Dec 1894,
p. 2
Saturday Review, 79:631,
11 May 1895
Waring's Peril
Picayune, 11 Mar 1894,
p. 25
A War-Time Wooing
Epoch, 4:174, 12 Oct
1888

King, Clarence
Mountaineering in the Sierra
Nevada
North American Review,
114:445-8, Apr 1872

King, Edward Smith
The Gentle Savage
Athenaeum, 2886:211-2,
17 Feb 1883
Nation, 36:406, 10 May
1883
Joseph Zalmonah
Athenaeum, 3437:352,
9 Sep 1893

King, Mrs. Frankie Faling
Mark Maynard's Wife
Godey's, 111:297, Sep
1885

King, Grace Elizabeth
Balcony Stories
Atlantic, 73:557, Apr 1884
Godey's, 128:107, Jan 1894
Nation, 57:452, 14 Dec 1893
Picayune, 22 Oct 1893, p.
14
Bienville
Godey's, 126:100, Jan 1893
Earthlings
Picayune, 21 Oct 1888, p. 4
Monsieur Motte
Epoch, 3:355, 8 Jun 1888
Nation, 47:95, 2 Aug 1888
Picayune, 13 May 1888, p. 7
Tales of a Time and Place
Harper's, 85:156, Jun 1892
Nation, 55:34, 14 Jul 1892

King, Katherine
See Burr, Katherine Douglas
(King).

King, Stanton Henry
Dog Watches at Sea
Nation, 72:321-2, 18 Apr
1901

King, Thorold [pseud.].
See Gatchell, Charles.

The King's Men
By Robert Grant, John Boyle
O'Reilly, J. S. of Dale
[pseud.], John T. Wheel-
wright.
Nation, 39:315, 9 Oct 1884

Kingsbury, John H.
Kingsbury Sketches
Picayune, 3 Oct 1875, [p.
10]

Kingsford, Jane [pseud.].
See Barnard, Charles.

Kingsley, Florence (Morse)
The Cross Triumphant
Saturday Review, 90:vii,

[Kirk, Ellen Warner (Olney)]
   Cottage Hearth, 7:209,
      Jul 1881
   Nation, 33:55, 21 Jul
      1881
A Midsummer Madness
   Continent, 5:831, (No.
      26) 1884
Queen Money
   Atlantic, 61:843-5, Jun
      1888
   Epoch, 3:37-8, 17 Feb
      1888
   Nation, 46:303-4, 12
      Apr 1888
   Saturday Review, 65:479-
      80, 21 Apr 1888
A Revolutionary Love Story
   Outlook, 59:386, 11 Jun
      1898
Sons and Daughters
   Epoch, 1:92, 4 Mar
      1887
   Harper's, 74:828, Apr
      1887
   Nation, 44:300, 7 Apr
      1887
   Overland, 2d S, 10:216-
      17, Aug 1887
The Story of Lawrence
Garthe
   Atlantic, 75:823-4, Jun
      1895
The Story of Margaret Kent
By Henry Hayes [pseud.].
   Harper's, 72:810-1,
      Apr 1886
   Overland, 2d S, 10:217,
      Aug 1887
   Saturday Review, 61:902,
      26 Jun 1886
Through Winding Ways
   Nation, 29:444, 25 Dec
      1879
Walford
   Atlantic, 67:277-8, Feb
      1891
   Cottage Hearth, 17:25,
      Jan 1891
   Epoch, 8:350, 2 Jan
      1891

Godey's, 122:98, Jan 1891
Nation, 52:244-5, 19 Mar
   1891
Overland, 2d S, 17:661,
   Jun 1891

Kirk, Hyland Clare
When Age Grows Young
   Overland, 2d S, 13:210,
      Feb 1889
   Picayune, 4 Nov 1888, p.
      10

Kirkland, Joseph
The McVeys
   Atlantic, 63:276-80, Feb
      1889
   Cottage Hearth, 14:364,
      Nov 1888
   Epoch, 4:309, 30 Nov 1888
   Harper's, 78:987, May 1889
   Overland, 2d S, 13:213-4,
      Feb 1889
Zury, the Meanest Man in
Spring County
   Cottage Hearth, 13:262, Aug
      1887
   Epoch, 2:97, 9 Sep 1887
   Harper's, 77:152-3, Jun
      1888
   Nation, 45:57, 21 Jul 1887
   Overland, 2d S, 10:214-5,
      Aug 1887
   Picayune, 8 May 1887, p. 7

Kirkman, Marshall Monroe
Alexandrian Romances
   Nation, 90:212, 3 Mar 1910
The Romance of Gilbert Holmes
   Picayune, 23 Sep 1900, II, 9

Kiser, Samuel Ellsworth
Georgie
   Picayune, 24 Jun 1900, II,
      12

Kitchel, Eva Paine
   See Wood, Frances Hartson,
   and Eva Paine Kitchel.

Kleber, John C.
The Master Spirit
Overland, 2d S, 55:537-
38, May 1910

Klette, C. H. B.
The Lost Mine of the Mono
Overland, 2d S, 55:338,
Mar 1910

Knapp, Adeline
One Thousand Dollars a Day
Picayune, 10 Mar 1895,
p. 14
The Well in the Desert
Nation, 87:236, 10
Sep 1908
Overland, 2d S, 52:581-
82, Dec 1908

Knapp, Mary Clay
Whose Soul Have I Now?
Picayune, 14 Jun 1896,
p. 19

Knight, George
Dust in the Balance
Picayune, 11 Apr 1897,
p. 25

Knox, Adeline (Trafton)
Dorothy's Experience
Atlantic, 67:278, Feb
1891
Godey's, 122:278, Mar
1891
His Inheritance
Harper's, 57:629, Sep
1878
Library Table, 4:401,
14 Sep 1878
Sunday Afternoon, 2:189-
90, Aug 1878
Katharine Earle
Atlantic, 35:107-8, Jan
1875
Godey's, 79:567, Dec
1874
Harper's, 50:140, Dec
1874
Nation, 19:223, 1 Oct

1874

Knox, John Armoy
See Sweet, Alexander Edwin,
and John Armoy Knox.

Knox, Thomas W.
The Lost Army
Picayune, 25 Nov 1894, p.
10
Underground
Athenaeum, 2389:168-9, 9
Aug 1873

Kobbé, Gustav
Miriam
Outlook, 60:638, 5 Nov 1898
Picayune, 24 Oct 1898, I, 8
Signora
Nation, 86:84, 23 Jan 1908

[Kouns, Nathan Chapman]
Arius, the Libyan
Harper's, 68:325, Jan 1884
Nation, 38:58, 17 Jan 1884
Dorcas
Nation, 40:100, 29 Jan 1885

[Krausé, Lyda Farrington]
Fortune's Boats
By Barbara Yechton [pseud.].
Bookman (NY), 12:524, Jan
1901
A Little Turning Aside
By Barbara Yechton [pseud.].
Bookman (NY), 9:282, May
1899
Young Mrs. Teddy
By Barbara Yechton [pseud.].
Bookman (NY), 14:433-4,
Dec 1901
Outlook, 69:750, 16 Nov 1901
A Young Savage
By Barbara Yechton [pseud.].
Bookman (NY), 10:281, Nov
1899

[Krout, Caroline Virginia]
Knights in Fustian
By Caroline Brown [pseud.].
Outlook, 64:925, 21 Apr 1900

Kyle, Ruby Beryl
Paul St. Paul
  Overland, 2d S, 26:342,
    Sep 1895
  Picayune, 23 Dec 1894,
    p. 12

Laflesche, Francis
The Middle Five
  Picayune, 14 Oct 1900,
    II, 8

Laing, Caroline H. (Butler)
The Heroes of the Seven
  Hills
  Nation, 19:13, 2 Jul
    1876

Lamb, Mrs. Martha J.
Spicy
  Godey's, 86:282, Mar
    1873

Lancaster, Albert Edmund
See Vincent, Frank, and
  Albert Edmund Lancaster.

Lancaster, F. Hewes
Marie of Arcady
  Nation, 90:140, 10 Feb
    1910

Lander, Meta [pseud.].
See Lawrence, Margaret
  Oliver (Woods).

Lane, Anna (Eichberg) King
According to Maria
  Bookman (London), 38:85-
    86, May 1910
  North American Review,
    192:135-6, Jul 1910
  Outlook, 95:36, 7 May
    1910
  Saturday Review, 109:437,
    2 Apr 1910
Kitwyk Stories
  Atlantic, 77:571, Apr
    1896
  Bookman (London), 23:112-
    13, Dec 1902

Lane, Elinor Macartney
Katrine
  Bookman (NY), 29:318-9,
    May 1909
  Nation, 88:515, 20 May 1909
  North American Review,
    189:921, Jun 1909
Nancy Stair
  Outlook, 77:430, 18 Jun 1904

Lane, Mrs. John
See Lane, Anna (Eichberg)
  King.

Lanza, Clara (Hammond)
Basil Morton's Transgression
  Picayune, 15 Dec 1889, p.
    11
Mr. Perkins's Daughter
  Athenaeum, 2803:76, 16 Jul
    1881
A Modern Marriage
  Picayune, 13 Jul 1890, p. 11
A Righteous Apostate
  Continent, 4:607, 7 Nov 1883
  Manhattan, 2:481, Nov 1883
  Saturday Review, 56:549,
    27 Oct 1883
Tit for Tat
  Atlantic, 46:836-7, Dec 1880
See also Hammond, William A.,
  and Clara (Hammond) Lanza.

Lathrop, Clarissa Caldwell
A Secret Institution
  Picayune, 31 Aug 1890, p.
    12

Lathrop, George Parsons
Afterglow
  Atlantic, 40:109-10, Jul 1877
  Godey's, 95:175, Aug 1877
  Library Table, 3:27, Sep
    1877
  Saturday Review, 44:250, 25
    Aug 1877
An Echo of Passion
  Atlantic, 50:113, Jul 1882
  Continent, 2:285, 6 Sep 1882
  Picayune, 8 Mar 1885, [p.
    8]

Nation, 34:505, 15 Jun
1882
Saturday Review, 59:120-
21, 24 Jan 1885
Gold of Pleasure
Godey's, 125:646, Dec
1892
In the Distance
Athenaeum, 2841:440-1,
8 Apr 1882
Atlantic, 50:113-5, Jul
1882
Nation, 34:386, 4 May
1882
Saturday Review, 53:399,
1 Apr 1882
Newport
Godey's, 108:492-3,
May 1884
Harper's, 68:975, May
1884
Manhattan, 3:397-8,
Apr 1884
Picayune, 16 Mar 1884,
[p. 12]
Saturday Review, 57:792-
93, 14 Jun 1884
Somebody Else
Harper's, 57:788, Oct
1878
Picayune, 25 Aug 1878,
[p. 9]
Rose-Belford's, 1:256,
Aug 1878
Sunday Afternoon, 2:288,
Sep 1878
True, and Other Stories
Nation, 40:266, 26 Mar
1885
Two Sides of a Story
Nation, 49:317, 17 Oct
1889
Would You Kill Him?
Epoch, 6:758, 27 Dec
1889
Harper's, 80:482-3, Feb
1890
Nation, 50:160, 20 Feb
1890
Saturday Review, 70:595-
96, 22 Nov 1890

[Latimer, Elizabeth (Wormeley)]
My Wife and My Wife's Sister
Nation, 34:172, 23 Feb 1882
The Princess Amélie
Continent, 4:220, 15 Aug
1883; 4:350, 12 Sep 1883
Nation, 37:121, 9 Aug 1883
Salvage
Atlantic, 46:837-8, Dec 1880
Harper's, 62:154, Dec 1880
Nation, 31:382, 25 Nov 1880
Picayune, 26 Sep 1880, [p.
12]

Laughlin, Clara Elizabeth
Felicity
Atlantic, 100:133, Jul 1907
Bookman (NY), 25:284, Apr
1907
Nation, 84:291, 28 Mar 1907
Just Folks
Nation, 91:606, 22 Dec 1910

[Lawrence, Elizabeth]
The Worm That Ceased to Turn
By Gorham Silva [pseud.].
Picayune, 11 Aug 1895, p.
10

[Lawrence, Margaret Oliver
(Woods)]
Marion Graham
By Meta Lander [pseud.].
Godey's, 120:433, May 1890;
121:172, Aug 1890

[Lawson, Mrs. J. W.]
Brockley Moor
Nation, 19:92, 6 Aug 1874

Lawson, Thomas William
Friday the Thirteenth
Athenaeum, 4146:436-7, 13
Apr 1907
Bookman (London), 32:69,
May 1907
Nation, 84:201, 28 Feb 1907

Lazarus, Emma
Alide
Saturday Review, 37:544,

Lazarus, Emma
25 Apr 1874

Lea, Homer
The Vermilion Pencil
Nation, 86:354, 16 Apr
1908

Leahy, William Augustine
The Incendiary
Picayune, 2 May 1897,
p. 15

[Leavitt, John M'Dowell]
The American Cardinal
Godey's, 73:186, Aug
1871
Harper's, 43:458-9,
Aug 1871

LeBaron, Marie [pseud.].
See Urie, Mrs. Mary Le-
Baron (Andrews).

Lee, Addie McGrath
Playing 'Possum, and Other
Pine Woods Stories
Picayune, 15 Dec 1895,
p. 15

Lee, Albert (1858-[?])
Baronet in Corduroy
Outlook, 76:235, 23 Jan
1904
The Key of the Holy House
Bookman (London), 15:88,
Dec 1898
King Stork of the Netherlands
Saturday Review, 93:403,
29 Mar 1902

Lee, Albert (1868-1946)
Four for a Fortune
Bookman (London), 15:120,
Jan 1899
Bookman (NY), 7:524-5,
Aug 1898
Outlook, 59:86, 7 May
1898
Saturday Review, 86:759,
10 Dec 1898

Lee, Franklyn Warner
Senator Lars Erikson
Picayune, 25 Oct 1891, p.
3
A Shred of Lace
America, 6:276, 4 Jun 1891
Picayune, 10 May 1891, p.
12
Two Men and a Girl
Picayune, 4 Dec 1892, p. 8

Lee, Jennette Barbour (Perry)
Happy Island
Nation, 91:219, 8 Sep 1910
Kate Wetherell
Nation, 71:55, 19 Jul 1900
Outlook, 64:838, 7 Apr 1900
Picayune, 6 May 1900, III,
8
A Pillar of Salt
Bookman (NY), 13:287, May
1901
Nation, 72:399, 16 May 1901
Simeon Tetlow's Shadow
Nation, 88:443, 29 Apr 1909
Outlook, 92:21, 1 May 1909
Overland, 2d S, 53:459,
May 1909
The Son of a Fiddler
Nation, 74:411-2, 22 May
1902

Lee, Margaret
A Brighton Night and a Brook-
lyn Bachelor
Picayune, 10 Jun 1894, p.
12
Divorce
Atlantic, 51:411-2, Mar
1883
Continent, 3:60, 10 Jan 1883
Nation, 36:301-2, 5 Apr
1883
Picayune, 7 Jan 1883, [p.
17]; 7 Apr 1889, p. 12;
10 Jun 1894, p. 12
Saturday Review, 67:203,
16 Feb 1889
Lorimer and Wife
Godey's, 103:284, Aug 1881
Picayune, 24 Jul 1881, [p.

2]
One Touch of Nature
Picayune, 10 Apr 1892,
p. 15

Lee, Mary Catherine (Jenkins)
In the Cheering-Up Business
Godey's, 122:373, Apr
1891
An Island Plant
Poet-Lore, 9:150, (No.
1) 1897
A Quaker Girl of Nantucket
Epoch, 6:518, 13 Sep
1889
Nation, 48:352-3, 25
Apr 1889
Overland, 2d S, 14:98-9,
Jul 1889
A Soulless Singer
Atlantic, 75:844, Jun
1895

Lee, Vernon
Countess of Albany
Godey's, 110:110, Jan
1885

Lefèvre, Edwin
Sampson Rock of Wall Street
Nation, 84:201, 28 Feb
1907
Wall Street Stories
Outlook, 69:660, 9 Nov
1901

Leggett, Mortimer Dormer
A Dream of a Modest
Prophet
Epoch, 9:14, 6 Feb 1891

Leland, Charles Godfrey
The Algonquin Legends of
New England
Athenaeum, 2988:146-7,
31 Jan 1885
The Egyptian Sketch-Book
Athenaeum, 2394:330-1,
13 Sep 1873
Flaxius
Athenaeum, 3906:317,

6 Sep 1902

Leland, Henry P.
The Grey-bay Mare, and Other
Humorous American Sketches
Saturday Review, 30:280,
27 Aug 1870

Leland, Samuel Phelps
Peculiar People
Atlantic, 70:281, Aug 1892

Lemore, Clara
See Roberts, Clara (Lemore).

Lenore [pseud.].
See Rowland, K. Alice.

[Leppere, Adam Hamilton]
The Rainbow Creed
Nation, 20:299, 29 Apr 1875
Picayune, 2 May 1875, [p.
2]
Saturday Review, 40:281,
28 Aug 1875

Lessing, Bruno [pseud.].
See Block, Rudolph.

Lewis, Alfred Henry
An American Patrician
Nation, 86:492-3, 28 May
1908
The Boss, and How He Came
to Rule New York
Bookman (NY), 18:486-94,
Jan 1904
Overland, 2d S, 42:461,
Nov 1903
Poet-Lore, 15:143-4, Win-
ter 1904
The President
Atlantic, 95:693, May 1905
Poet-Lore, 15:143, Winter
1904
Sandburrs
Picayune, 13 May 1900, III,
3
The Sunset Trail
Saturday Review, 101:761,
16 Jun 1906

Lewis, Alfred Henry
The Throwback
    Athenaeum, 4169:330,
      21 Sep 1907
Wolfville
    Bookman (London), 13:50,
      Nov 1897
    Bookman (NY), 6:162-3,
      Oct 1897
    Overland, 2d S, 31:90-1,
      Jan 1898
    Saturday Review, 95:753,
      13 Jun 1903
Wolfville Days
    Bookman (London), 24:31,
      Apr 1903
    Saturday Review, 95:753,
      13 Jun 1903
    Times Literary Supple-
      ment, 27 Mar 1903,
      p. 97
Wolfville Folks
    Nation, 86:516, 4 Jun
      1908

[Lewis, Estelle Anna Blanche
(Robinson)]
Minna Monté
    By Stella [pseud.].
    Nation, 14:410, 20 Jun
      1872

Lewis, Harriet Newell
(O'Brien)
Beatrix Rohan
    Picayune, 4 Sep 1892,
      p. 7
Guy Tresillian's Fate
    Picayune, 6 Aug 1893,
      p. 17
Tresillian Court
    Picayune, 16 Jul 1893,
      p. 19

Lewis, Julius A.
A Prince of the Blood
    Outlook, 60:1021, 24
      Dec 1898

Lewis, S. L.
See Hazel, Harry, and S. L.
Lewis.

Libbey, Laura Jean
Florabell's Lover
    Picayune, 10 Apr 1892, p.
      15

Libby, Laura Jean
The Heiress of Cameron Hall
    Picayune, 28 Oct 1888, p.
      7
Miss Middleton's Lover
    Picayune, 29 Jul 1888, p.
      7
That Pretty Young Girl
    Picayune, 29 Sep 1889, p.
      14
We Parted at the Altar
    Picayune, 21 Feb 1892, p.
      10

Lighton, William Rheem
The Shadow of a Great Rock
    Athenaeum, 4163:150, 10
      Aug 1907
    Canadian Magazine, 29:579,
      Oct 1907
The Ultimate Moment
    Nation, 77:389, 12 Nov 1903

Liljencrantz, Ottilie Adaline
The Thrall of Leif the Lucky
    Bookman (London), 27:7,
      Christmas Suppl., Dec
      1904

Lillibridge, William Otis
Ben Blake
    Bookman (NY), 22:634-5,
      Feb 1906
The Dissolving Circle
    Bookman (NY), 27:306-7,
      May 1908
The Quest Eternal
    Bookman (NY), 28:381-2,
      Dec 1908
Where the Trail Divides
    Bookman (NY), 25:285-6,
      Apr 1907

Lillie, Lucy Cecil (White)
Glen Holly
Epoch (NY), 4:251, 9
Nov 1888
Jo's Opportunity
Picayune, 29 Aug 1886,
p. 6
Prudence
Nation, 34:385-6, 4
May 1882
Roslyn's Trust
Athenaeum, 3239:704-5,
23 Nov 1889
Saturday Review, 68:744,
28 Dec 1889

Lin, Frank [pseud.].
See Atherton, Gertrude
Franklin.

Lincoln, Jeanie Thomas
(Gould)
Her Washington Season
Continent, 5:735, (No.
23) 1884
Cottage Hearth, 10:154,
Apr 1884
Godey's, 108:591, Jun
1884
Saturday Review, 57:682-
84, 24 May 1884
A Pretty Tory
Picayune, 17 Dec 1899,
III, 8

Lincoln, Joseph Crosby
Cap'n Eri
Atlantic, 93:852, Jun
1904
Bookman (NY), 19:511-2,
Jul 1904
Cy Whittaker's Place
Nation, 87:525-6, 26
Nov 1908
The Old Home House
Nation, 85:235, 12 Sep
1907
Partners of the Tide
Nation, 81:123, 10 Aug
1905

Linden, Annie
Gold
Picayune, 16 Nov 1896, p.
6

Linden, Paul
Mr. and Mrs. Beever
Picayune, 14 Aug 1892, p.
17

Lindsay, Mayne
The Whirligig
Outlook, 68:888, 10 Aug
1901

Lindsey, William
Cinder-Path Tales
Bookman (NY), 4:162, Oct
1896
The Severed Mantle
Nation, 89:573, 9 Dec 1909
Saturday Review, 110:306,
3 Sep 1910

Linn, Beth
One Little Mustard Seed
Epoch, 7:110, 21 Mar 1890

Linn, James Weber
The Chameleon
Bookman (NY), 17:188-9,
Apr 1903
The Second Generation
Athenaeum, 3898:57, 12 Jul
1902
Atlantic, 89:707, May 1902
Bookman (NY), 15:198-9,
Apr 1902
Nation, 74:213-4, 13 Mar
1902

Litchfield, Grace Denio
Criss-Cross
Nation, 41:539, 24 Dec 1885
Overland, 2d S, 6:553, Nov
1885
Saturday Review, 61:60, 9
Jan 1886
A Hard-Won Victory
Athenaeum, 3195:81-2, 19
Jan 1889

Litchfield, Grace Denio
Nation, 47:274, 4 Oct
1888
Overland, 2d S, 12:435,
Oct 1888
Saturday Review, 66:562,
10 Nov 1888
In the Crucible
Bookman (London), 12:129,
Aug 1897
Bookman (NY), 5:522,
Aug 1897
Picayune, 18 Apr 1897,
p. 17
Saturday Review, 84:299,
11 Sep 1897
The Knight of the Black
Forest
Nation, 41:18, 2 Jul
1885
Overland, 2d S, 5:661,
Jun 1885
Little Venice, and Other
Stories
Athenaeum, 3294:814,
13 Dec 1890
Overland, 2d S, 17:662,
Jun 1891
Only an Incident
Nation, 38:301, 3 Apr
1884
Overland, 2d S, 3:556,
May 1884
Picayune, 24 Feb 1884,
[p. 10]
Saturday Review, 57:423,
29 Mar 1884
The Supreme Gift
Nation, 86:402, 30 Apr
1908

Little, Frances [pseud.].
See Macaulay, Fannie
(Caldwell).

Livingston, Margaret Vere
(Farrington)
Fra Lippo Lippi
Saturday Review, 70:629,
29 Nov 1890

Lloyd, John Uri
The Captain's Wife
Nation, 86:536, 11 Jun 1908
Etidorpha
Canadian Magazine, 17:488,
Sep 1901
Saturday Review, 82:271-2,
5 Sep 1896
Stringtown on the Pike
Bookman (NY), 12:352-3,
Dec 1900
Canadian Magazine, 16:188,
Dec 1900
Nation, 72:361, 2 May 1901
Picayune, 18 Nov 1900, III,
4
Saturday Review, 91:344,
16 Mar 1901

Lloyd, Nelson McAllister
The Chronic Loafer
Outlook, 65:133, 12 May
1900
Picayune, 20 May 1900, III,
7
A Drone and a Dreamer
Athenaeum, 3866:731, 30
Nov 1901
Overland, 2d S, 38:319,
Nov 1901
Mrs. Radigan
Bookman (NY), 23:108, Mar
1906
The Soldier of the Valley
Athenaeum, 4024:802, 10
Dec 1904
Saturday Review, 99:54, 14
Jan 1905

Locke, David Ross
The Demagogue
Cottage Hearth, 16:385, Dec
1890
Godey's, 122:96, Jan 1891
Overland, 2d S, 18:440, Oct
1891
Hannah Jane
By Petroleum V. Nasby
[pseud.].
Godey's, 103:572, Dec 1881
A Paper City

Library Table, 5:27,
18 Jan 1879
Nation, 28:106, 6 Feb
1879

Lockwood, George Roe
Just One Day
Nation, 29:30, 10 Jul
1879

Lockwood, Ingersoll
Travels and Adventures of
Little Baron Trump . . .
Godey's, 120:94, Jan
1890

[Lockwood, Melancthon Clarence]
The New Minister
By Kenneth Paul [pseud.].
Picayune, 31 Dec 1893,
p. 22

[Lodge, Mrs. James]
A Week Away from Time
Nation, 45:58, 21 Jul
1887

Logan, Celia
See Connelley, Celia (Logan)
Kellogg.

Logan, Olive [pseud.].
See Mrs. Wirt Sikes.

London, Jack
Before Adam
Athenaeum, 4204:633-4,
23 May 1908
Atlantic, 100:125, Jul
1907
Bookman (London), 35:57,
Oct 1908
Bookman (NY), 25:115-6,
Apr 1907; 25:183-4,
Apr 1907
Canadian Magazine,
28:614-5, Apr 1907
Outlook, 85:718, 23 Mar
1907
Overland, 2d S, 49:xxvi,

May 1907
Saturday Review, 105:793-4,
20 Jun 1908
Burning Daylight
Bookman (NY), 32:157-8,
Oct 1910
Nation, 91:443-4, 10 Nov
1910
The Call of the Wild
Athenaeum, 3957:279, 29
Aug 1903
Bookman (London), 24:220,
Sep 1903
Bookman (NY), 18:159-60,
Oct 1903
Nation, 77:287, 8 Oct 1903
Outlook, 74:762, 25 Jul 1903
Overland, 2d S, 42:272, Sep
1903
Saturday Review, 96:678, 28
Nov 1903
Children of the Frost
Athenaeum, 3925:77, 17
Jan 1903
Bookman (NY), 17:83-4,
Mar 1903
Overland, 2d S, 41:79, Jan
1903
The Cruise of the Dazzler
Athenaeum, 4121:477, 20
Oct 1906
A Daughter of the Snows
Athenaeum, 4005:140, 30
Jul 1904
Bookman (London), 26:177,
Aug 1904
Overland, 2d S, 40:553,
Dec 1902
Saturday Review, 98:145,
30 Jul 1904
Times Literary Supplement,
22 Jul 1904, p. 229
The Faith of Men
Athenaeum, 3998:748, 11
Jun 1904
Nation, 78:500, 23 Jun 1904
Saturday Review, 97:822,
25 Jun 1904
The Game
Athenaeum, 4057:138, 29
Jul 1905

1906
Overland, 2d S, 48: [503
misnumbered 493],
Dec 1906
Times Literary Supple-
ment, 8 Feb 1907,
p. 46
See also The Spinners'
Book of Fiction.

Long, John Luther
Felice
Nation, 88:67, 21 Jan
1909
The Fox-Woman
Outlook, 63:841, 2 Dec
1899
Heimweh
Saturday Review, 100:vi,
Suppl., 9 Dec 1905
Madame Butterfly
Picayune, 24 Oct 1898,
p. 8
Miss Cherry-Blossom of
Tokyo
Saturday Review, 82:684,
26 Dec 1896
Sixty Jane, and Other Sto-
ries
Nation, 77:508, 24 Dec
1903
Overland, 2d S, 42:554,
Dec 1903

Long, Lily Augusta
Apprentices to Destiny
Picayune, 11 Mar 1894,
p. 25
The Hemlock Avenue
Mystery
By Roman Doubleday
[pseud.].
Nation, 86:219, 5 Mar
1908
Overland, 2d S, 51:[391],
Apr 1908
A Squire of Low Degree
Godey's, 122:98, Jan
1891

Long, William Joseph

Northern Trails
Bookman (NY), 23:89-90,
Mar 1906

Longstreet, Augustus B.
Master William Mitten
Atlantic, 69:279, Feb 1892
Georgia Scenes
Bookman (NY), 6:67-8, Sep
1897

Longstreet, Rachel Abigail
(Buchanan)
A Debutante in New York
Society
Epoch, 3:416, 29 Jun 1888
Godey's, 117:168, Aug 1888
Nation, 47:96, 2 Aug 1888

Loomis, Charles Battell
Cheerful Americans
Nation, 77:287, 8 Oct 1903
Poet-Lore, 14:136, Winter
1903
Four-Masted Cat-Boat, and
Other Truthful Tales
Outlook, 63:933, 16 Dec 1899
Picayune, 17 Dec 1899, III,
8
Minerva's Maneuvers
Bookman (NY), 23:340-1,
May 1906
More Cheerful Americans
Nation, 79:441, 1 Dec 1904

"Lord Comissioner" [pseud.].
See McCoy, John.

Lorimer, George Horace
Jack Spurlock, Prodigal
Athenaeum, 4216:177, 15
Aug 1908
Canadian Magazine, 31:378,
Aug 1908
Saturday Review, 106:274,
29 Aug 1908
Times Literary Supplement,
3 Sep 1908, p. 285
Old Gorgon Graham
Atlantic, 95:694, May 1905
Bookman (NY), 20:157-9,

Lorimer, George Horace
    Oct 1904
    Poet-Lore, 15:142, Winter 1904

Loring, Frederic Wadsworth
  Two College Friends
    Nation, 13:359, 30 Nov 1871
  See also Six of One, by Half a Dozen of Another.

Loth, Moritz
  The Forgiving Kiss
    Godey's, 79:281, Sep 1874

[Lothrop, Harriet Mulford (Stone)]
  An Adirondack Cabin
    By Margaret Sidney [pseud.].
    Epoch, 8:351, 2 Jan 1891
  A Little Maid of Concord Town
    By Margaret Sidney [pseud.].
    Picayune, 24 Oct 1898, 8
  Our Town
    By Margaret Sidney [pseud.].
    Cottage Hearth, 15:344, Oct 1889
  The Pettibone Name
    By Margaret Sidney [pseud.].
    Picayune, 13 Dec 1885, p. 8
  The Stories Polly Pepper Told
    By Margaret Sidney [pseud.].
    Outlook, 62:670, 22 Jul 1899

Loughead, Flora (Haines) Apponyi
  The Black Curtain
    Athenaeum, 3724:302, 11 Mar 1899
    Bookman (London), 15:187, Mar 1899

    Outlook, 60:638, 5 Nov 1898
  A Crown of Thorns
    Picayune, 31 Jan 1892, p. 3
  The Man Who Was Guilty
    Nation, 43:101, 29 Jul 1886
    Overland, 2d S, 8:107, Jul 1886
  Santos's Brother
    Picayune, 6 Mar 1892, p. 18

"Louisiana" [pseud.].
  Blue and Gray
    Picayune, 27 Dec 1885, p. 8

Lowell, Prudence
  A Millionaire's Wife
    Cottage Hearth, 16:161, May 1890
    Godey's, 120:433, May 1890

Lowell, Robert Traill Spence
  Anthony Brade
    Atlantic, 34:749-50, Dec 1874
    Nation, 19:304, 5 Nov 1874
  A Story or Two from an Old Dutch Town
    Harper's, 58:309, Jan 1879
    Library Table, 4:529, 21 Dec 1878
    Nation, 27:319, 21 Nov 1878
    Rose-Belford's, 1:635-6, Nov 1878
    Saturday Review, 46:703, 30 Nov 1878
    Sunday Afternoon, 3:95, Jan 1879

Ludlow, James Meeker
  The Captain of the Janizaries
    Epoch, 1:520-1, 8 Jul 1887; 7:317, 20 Jun 1890
    Overland, 2d S, 10:328, Sep 1887
    Picayune, 26 Jun 1887, p. 8; 6 Jul 1890, p. 12; 10 Dec 1893, p. 16
  Jesse ben David
    Nation, 86:15, 2 Jan 1908

A King of Tyre
  Epoch, 10:387, 15 Jan
    1892
"A Man's a Man for A'
  That"
  Athenaeum, 2711:461-2,
    11 Oct 1879
  Harper's, 59:955, Nov
    1879
  Nation, 29:444, 25 Dec
    1879
That Angelic Woman
  Atlantic, 70:419, Sep
    1892

Ludlum, Jean Kate
  Lida Campbell
  Picayune, 10 Apr 1892,
    p. 15

Lummis, Charles Fletcher
  The Enchanted Burro
  Bookman (NY), 7:166,
    Apr 1898
  Nation, 66:135-6, 17 Feb
    1898
  Picayune, 19 Dec 1897,
    p. 28
The Gold Fish of Gran
  Chimú
  Nation, 62:399, 21 May
    1896
The King of the Broncos,
  and Other Stories of New
  Mexico
  Nation, 66:135-6, 17
    Feb 1898
  Picayune, 7 Nov 1897,
    p. 6
The Land of Poco Tiempo
  Nation, 58:127-8, 15
    Feb 1894
  Picayune, 12 Nov 1893,
    p. 14
The Man Who Married the
  Moon
  Picayune, 18 Nov 1894,
    p. 15
A New Mexico David, and
  Other Stories and Sketches
  . . .

Picayune, 25 Oct 1891, p. 3

Lush, Charles Keeler
  The Autocrats
  Athenaeum, 3880:304, 8 Mar
    1902
  Bookman (NY), 14:95, Sep
    1901
  Times Literary Supplement,
    18 Apr 1902, p. 109
The Federal Judge
  Bookman (NY), 6:150-1, Oct
    1897
  Nation, 66:407, 26 May 1898
  Picayune, 17 Oct 1897, p.
    10

Luska, Sidney [pseud.].
  See Harland, Henry.

Luther, Mark Lee
  The Crucible
  Bookman (NY), 26:554-5,
    Jan 1908
The Favor of Princes
  Bookman (London), 17:154,
    Feb 1900
  Outlook, 63:841, 2 Dec 1899
  Picayune, 17 Dec 1899, III,
    8
  Saturday Review, 89:147, 3
    Feb 1900
  Sewanee Review, 8:128, Jan
    1900
The Henchman
  Athenaeum, 3936:430-1, 4
    Apr 1903
  Bookman (NY), 16:483-4,
    Jan 1903
The Mastery
  Outlook, 78:388, 8 Oct 1904

Lydston, George Frank
  Poker Jim, Gentleman
  Overland, 2d S, 49:xiv, Apr
    1907

Lyle, Eugene P., Jr.
  The Missourian
  Athenaeum, 4074:718, 25
    Nov 1905

Lyle, Eugene P. , Jr.
  Bookman (London),
    29:225, Feb 1906
  Bookman (NY), 22:135,
    Oct 1905

[Lynch, Harriet Louise (Hus-
ted)]
  Patricia
  By Marie St. Felix [pseud.].
    Picayune, 10 Nov 1895,
    p. 10

Lynch, Lawrence L. [pseud.].
  See Van Deventer, Emma
  Murdock.

Lynde, Francis
  Empire Builders
    Bookman (NY), 26:164,
      Oct 1907
    Outlook, 87:45, 7 Sep
      1907
  The Grafters
    Bookman (NY), 19:392-3,
      Jun 1904
    Nation, 78:500, 23 Jun
      1904
    Outlook, 76:1044, 30
      Apr 1904
  The Helpers
    Outlook, 63:464, 21 Oct
      1899
  A Private Chivalry
    Picayune, 14 Oct 1900,
      II, 8
  The Quickening
    Outlook, 82:571, 10
      Mar 1906
  A Romance in Transit
    Picayune, 26 Dec 1897,
      p. 9
  The Taming of Red Butte
  Western
    Nation, 90:630, 23 Jun
      1910

Lyon, Annie Bozeman
  No Saint
    Picayune, 28 Jun 1891,
      p. 12

Lyndon [pseud.].
  See Hughes, Mrs. Reginald.

Lyon, Harris Merton
  Sardonics
    Bookman (NY), 29:79, Mar
      1909

Lyon, Sidney
  For a Mess of Pottage
    Godey's, 121:85, Jul 1890
    Picayune, 25 May 1890, p.
      14

Lysaght, Sidney Royse
  The Marplot
    Godey's, 126:770, Jun 1893

Mabie, Hamilton Wright
  Parables of Life
    Overland, 2d S, 39:984-5,
      Jun 1902

McAlilly, Alice
  The Larkin's Wedding
    Overland, 2d S, 46:590, Dec
      1905

McAnally, David Rice, Jr.
  Irish Wonders
    Atlantic, 61:846-7, Jun 1888

[Macaulay, Fannie (Caldwell)]
  The Lady of the Decoration
  By Frances Little [pseud.].
    Athenaeum, 4096:510, 28
      Apr 1906
    Bookman (London), 30:37,
      Apr 1906
    Nation, 82:434, 24 May
      1906
    Saturday Review, 101:625,
      19 May 1906
  Little Sister Snow
    Athenaeum, 4278:489, 23
      Oct 1909
    Overland, 2d S, 54:534,
      Nov 1909

McCabe, Gillie (Cary)
  Uncle Jerry's Platform

Picayune, 16 Feb 1896,
p. 16

M'Caleb, Thomas
Anthony Melgrave
Atlantic, 71:561, Apr
1893
Picayune, 17 Jul 1892,
p. 13; 14 Aug 1892,
p. 17

McCall, Sidney [pseud.].
See Fenollosa, Mary (Mc-
Neil).

MacCarthy, Emma W.
Congressman John and His
Wife's Satisfaction
Picayune, 1 Mar 1891,
p. 10

McChesney, Dora Greenwell
Beatrix Infelix
Saturday Review, 85:664,
14 May 1898
Cornet Strong of Ireton's
Horse
Bookman (London), 24:30-
31, Apr 1903
Saturday Review, 95:428,
4 Apr 1903
London Roses
Saturday Review, 96:241,
22 Aug 1903
Miriam Cromwell
Saturday Review, 83:278,
13 Mar 1897
Rupert, by the Grace of
God--
Bookman (London), 16:113,
Jul 1899
Nation, 69:413, 30 Nov
1899
Outlook, 62:624, 15 Jul
1899
Saturday Review, 88:53,
8 Jul 1899
The Wounds of a Friend
Times Literary Supple-
ment, 3 Dec 1908,
p. 446

Yesterday's To-morrow
Saturday Review, 99:462, 8
Apr 1905

[Macchetta, Blanche Roosevelt
(Tucker)]
The Copper Queen
By Blanche Roosevelt [pseud.].
Athenaeum, 3084:741, 4 Dec
1886
Saturday Review, 62:854-5,
25 Dec 1886
Hazel Fane
By Blanche Roosevelt [pseud.].
Athenaeum, 3341:613-5, 7
Nov 1891
Saturday Review, 72:532-3,
7 Nov 1891
Stage-Struck
By Blanche Roosevelt [pseud.].
Continent, 6:126, (No. 4)
1884
Cottage Hearth, 10:250, Aug
1884
Nation, 39:116, 7 Aug 1894
Overland, 2d S, 4:223, Aug
1884
Saturday Review, 58:56-7,
12 Jul 1884

McClellan, Mrs. George
See McClellan, Harriet (Hare).

McClellan, Harriet (Hare)
Broken Chords Crossed by the
Echo of a False Note
Picayune, 8 Jan 1893, p. 10
A Carpet Knight
By Harford Flemming [pseud.].
Atlantic, 55:848, Jun 1885
Godey's, 110:571, May 1885
Nation, 40:423, 21 May 1885
Overland, 2d S, 5:659, Jun
1885
Cupid and the Sphinx
By Harford Flemming [pseud.].
Athenaeum, 2674:119-20, 25
Jan 1879
Harper's, 58:309, Jan 1879

McClelland, Mary Greenway
  Broadoaks
    Picayune, 4 Jun 1893,
      p. 18
  Burkett's Lock
    Picayune, 31 Mar 1889,
      p. 7
  Madame Silva
    Picayune, 29 Jul 1888,
      p. 7
    Nation, 47:503, 20 Dec
      1888
  Manitou Island
    Atlantic, 70:852, Dec
      1892
    Godey's, 125:522, Nov
      1892
    Sewanee Review, 1:254-
      55, Feb 1893
  A Nameless Novel
    Picayune, 12 Jul 1891,
      p. 10
  Oblivion
    Atlantic, 57:269-70, Feb
      1886
    Nation, 42:39, 14 Jan
      1886
  The Old Post-Road
    Picayune, 19 Aug 1894,
      p. 12
  Princess
    Nation, 43:376, 4 Nov
      1886
  St. John's Wooing
    Atlantic, 76:278, Aug
      1895

McClintock, Walter
  The Old North Trail
    Bookman (London),
      39:72-3, Christmas
      Suppl., Dec 1910

McCook, Henry Christopher
  The Latimers
    Godey's, 136:216-7, Feb
      1898

[McCowan, Archibald]
  Christ the Socialist
    Picayune, 25 Nov 1894,

    p. 10

[McCoy, John]
  A Prophetic Romance
    By "Lord Commissioner"
    [pseud.].
    Picayune, 4 Oct 1896, p. 16

McCrackin, Josephine (Woempner)
  Clifford
  Another Juanita, and Other Sto-
  ries
    Overland, 2d S, 23:217, Feb
      1894
    Picayune, 24 Jun 1877, [p.
      9]

McCray, Florine Thayer
  Environment
    Epoch, 2:75, 2 Sep 1887
    Overland, 2d S, 10:216-7,
      Aug 1887
    Picayune, 5 Jun 1887, p. 6
    Saturday Review, 65:23-4,
      7 Jan 1888

McCutcheon, George Barr
  Beverly of Graustark
    Bookman (London), 28:31,
      Apr 1905
  Castle Craneycrow
    Athenaeum, 3971:750, 5
      Dec 1903
    Bookman (NY), 16:276-7,
      Nov 1902
    Outlook, 71:1033, 23 Aug
      1902
  The Daughter of Anderson
  Crow
    Athenaeum, 4177:613, 16
      Nov 1907
    Saturday Review, 104:582,
      9 Nov 1907
  Graustark
    Athenaeum, 3887:525, 26
      Apr 1902
  The Husbands of Edith
    Nation, 87:56, 16 Jul 1908
  Jane Cable
    Athenaeum, 4158:11, 6 Jul
      1907

Bookman (London),
32:142, Jul 1907
Bookman (NY), 24:248-9,
Nov 1906; 24:280,
Nov 1906
Saturday Review, 104:369,
21 Sep 1907
Nedra
Athenaeum, 4125:614,
17 Nov 1906
Overland, 2d S, 46:592,
Dec 1905
The Rose in the Ring
Bookman (NY), 32:294,
Nov 1910

Macdonald, George
Salted with Fire
Godey's, 135:667, Dec
1897

McDonald, Robert
A Princess and a Woman
Picayune, 5 Jul 1897,
p. 9

Macdonald, Ronald
A Human Trinity
Saturday Review, 103:756,
15 Jun 1907
The Sword of the King
Outlook, 65:746, 21 Jul
1900

MacDonough, Glen
See Chapin, Anna Alice,
and Glen MacDonough.

[McDowell, Katherine Sher-
wood (Bonner)]
Dialect Tales
By Sherwood Bonner
[pseud.].
Godey's, 107:94, Jul
1883
Harper's, 66:964, May
1883
Manhattan, 1:507, Jun
1883
Like unto Like
By Sherwood Bonner

[pseud.].
Cottage Hearth, 5:394, Nov
1878
Harper's, 58:146, Dec 1878
Library Table, 4:504, 7 Dec
1878
Suwanee River Tales
By Sherwood Bonner [pseud.].
Godey's, 109:652, Dec 1884

McElroy, John
The Red Acorn
Overland, 2d S, 1:653, Jun
1883

McElroy, Lucy (Cleaver)
Juletty
Sewanee Review, 9:498, Oct
1901; 11:112, Jan 1903;
11:357, Jul 1903

MacFarlane, Margaret Russell
The Magic of a Voice
Nation, 43:357, 23 Oct 1886
Saturday Review, 62:625-6,
6 Nov 1886
Odds Against Her
Picayune, 22 Jul 1888, p. 9

McGlasson, Eva Wilder
See Brodhead, Eva Wilder
(McGlasson).

McGovern, John
Burritt Durand
Picayune, 6 Jul 1890, p. 12
Daniel Trentworthy
Picayune, 5 Jul 1891, p. 12

Mac Gowan, Alice
The Last Word
Athenaeum, 3962:448, 3 Oct
1903
Overland, 2d S, 40:482-3,
Nov 1902
The Sword in the Mountains
Bookman (London), 39:9,
Christmas Suppl. , Dec
1910
The Wiving of Lance Cleaver-
age

MacGowan, Alice
    Nation, 89:600, 16 Dec
        1909
    See also Cooke, Grace Mac-
        Gowan, and Alice Mac-
        Gowan.

MacGrath, Harold
    Arms and the Woman
        Bookman (NY), 10:282-
        83, Nov 1899
    The Best Man
        Outlook, 87:451, 26 Oct
        1907
    Enchantment
        Overland, 2d S, 46:375,
        Oct 1905
    The Grey Cloak
        Bookman (London), 29:43,
        Oct 1905
    Half a Rogue
        Overland, 2d S, 49:184-5,
        Feb 1907
    The Lure of the Mask
        Athenaeum, 4254:556,
        8 May 1909
    The Princess Elopes
        Overland, 2d S, 45:565,
        Jun 1905
    The Puppet Crown
        Bookman (NY), 13:250-1,
        May 1901
        Canadian Magazine,
        17:580, Oct 1901
        Saturday Review, 94:370,
        20 Sep 1902

MacGregor, Annie Lyndsay
    The Professor's Wife
        Nation, 10:262, 21 Apr
        1870
        Saturday Review, 29:426,
        26 Mar 1870

Machar, Agnes Maule
    Roland Graeme, Knight
        Godey's, 126:100, Jan
        1893

MacHarg, William
    See Balmer, Edwin, and

William MacHarg.

McIntyre, John T.
    In the Dead of Night
        Nation, 86:558, 18 Jun 1908

McKean, Thomas
    The Punishment
        Athenaeum, 4272:293, 11
        Sep 1909

McKeen, Phebe F.
    Theodora
        Saturday Review, 41:154,
        29 Jan 1876
    Thornton Hall
        Harper's, 47:131, Jun 1873

McKeever, Harriet B.
    Maude and Miriam
        Picayune, 10 Sep 1871, [p.
        5]
    Westbrook Parsonage
        Picayune, 9 Jan 1870, [p.
        11]

McKenzie, Christine [pseud.].
    See Duffell, Annie.

Mackie, John
    The Devil's Playground
        Bookman (NY), 1:116, Mar
        1895
    No Man's Land
        Godey's, 130:544, May 1895

Mackie, Pauline Bradford
    See Hopkins, Pauline Bradford
        (Mackie).

McKinney, Annie Booth
    See Cooke, Grace (MacGowan),
        and Annie Booth McKinney.

McKnight, Charles
    Old Fort Ququesne
        Nation, 18:336, 21 May 1874

Mackubin, Ellen
    The King of the Town
        Outlook, 58:639, 5 May 1898

Picayune, 10 Apr 1898,
p. 25

[McLain, Mary Webster]
Lifting the Veil
Harper's, 41:623, Sep
1870
Overland, 5:199, Aug
1870
Saturday Review, 30:122,
23 Jul 1870
The Story of Mary MacLane
Bookman (London), 23:95,
Dec 1902

McLaws, Emily Lafayette
When the Land Was Young
Bookman (London), 21:69,
Nov 1901

Maclay, Arthur Collins
Mito Yashiki
Overland, 2d S, 15:438,
Apr 1890

McLean, Clara Victoria
(Dargan)
Light o' Love
Picayune, 22 Nov 1891,
p. 12

McLean, Sarah Pratt
See Greene, Sarah Pratt
(McLean).

McLeod, Clara Nevada
Then, and Not 'Til Then
Overland, 2d S, 31:95,
Jan 1898

McManus, Blanche
See Mansfield, Blanche
(McManus).

McNamara, Mrs. M. H.
Prince Coastwind's Vic-
tory
Picayune, 1 Jan 1888,
p. 15

McNeill, Orange

A Jesuit of To-Day
Overland, 2d S, 27:468, Apr
1896

[Macnie, John]
The Diothas
By Ismar Thiusen [pseud.].
Manhattan, 2:480, Nov 1883
Nation, 37:419, 15 Nov 1883
Picayune, 7 Oct 1883, [p.
7]

McNutt, Cyrus F.
Broken Lives
Overland, 2d S, 14:100-1,
Jul 1889

Macquoid, Catherine S.
Appledore Farm
Godey's, 125:407, Oct 1892

McVickar, Henry Goelet, and
Price Collier
A Parish of Two
Bookman (NY), 18:167, Oct
1903

Madame Bigot [pseud.].
See Healy, Mary.

Madison, Lucy (Foster)
A Maid of the First Century
Outlook, 64:130, 13 Jan 1900

Magee, Knox
With Ring of Shield
Outlook, 66:857, 1 Dec 1900

Magill, Mary Tucker
The Holcombs
Godey's, 73:89, Jul 1871
Saturday Review, 31:818,
24 Jun 1871
Women
Canadian Monthly, 1:91-2,
Jan 1872
Picayune, 31 Dec 1871, [p.
5]
Saturday Review, 33:258,
24 Feb 1872

Magruder, Julia
Across the Chasm
Harper's, 72:322-3, Jan
1886
Nation, 41:18, 2 Jul
1885
Overland, 2d S, 5:659,
Jun 1885
Saturday Review, 59:835-
36, 20 Jun 1885
Dead Selves
Athenaeum, 3693:189,
6 Aug 1898
Bookman (London),
14:138-9, Aug 1898
Picayune, 5 Dec 1897,
p. 26
Saturday Review, 86:447,
1 Oct 1898
A Magnificent Plebian
Epoch, 3:76-7, 2 Mar
1888
A Manifest Destiny
Picayune, 25 Mar 1900,
III, 5
Miss Ayr of Virginia, &
Other Stories
Bookman (NY), 5:168,
Apr 1897
Picayune, 31 Jan 1897,
p. 17
Poet-Lore, 9:439,
Summer 1897
A Realized Ideal
Outlook, 59:86, 7 May
1898
Picayune, 8 May 1898,
p. 7
Struan
Outlook, 60:731, 19
Nov 1898
Picayune, 7 Nov 1898,
p. 8
Saturday Review, 88:82,
15 Jul 1899
The Violet
Nation, 64:71, 28 Jan
1897
Picayune, 11 Oct 1896,
p. 11

Maitland, Christal V.
A Woman's Web
Picayune, 4 Sep 1892, p. 7

Major, Charles
The Bears of Blue River
Saturday Review, 94:147, 2
Aug 1902
Dorothy Vernon of Haddon Hall
Athenaeum, 3895:778, 21
Jun 1902
Bookman (NY), 15:371-3,
Jun 1902
A Forest Hearth
Bookman (NY), 18:419-20,
Dec 1903
Saturday Review, 97:210,
13 Feb 1904
A Gentle Knight of Old Bran-
denburg
Nation, 90:13, 6 Jan 1910
Saturday Review, 109:408,
26 Mar 1910
When Knighthood Was in Flow-
er
By Edwin Caskoden [pseud.].
Bookman (London), 16:139,
Aug 1899
Bookman (NY), 8:374-5, Dec
1898
Outlook, 60:920, 10 Dec 1898
Picayune, 22 Oct 1899, II,
6
Yolanda
Bookman (London), 29:255,
Mar 1906

Malcolm, David
Fifty Thousand Dollars Ransom
Overland, 2d S, 27:579,
May 1896

Malone, Walter
The Coming of the King
Picayune, 4 Apr 1897, p.
17

Manley, R. M.
The Queen of Ecuador
Picayune, 29 Jul 1894, p.
12

Mann, Mary E.
  The Cedar Star
    Picayune, 12 Dec 1897,
      p. 25
  Gran'ma's Jane
    Times Literary Supple-
      ment, 13 Nov 1903,
      p. 328
  Susannah
    Atlantic, 79:136, Jan
      1897

Mann, Mary Tyler (Peabody)
  Juanita
    Nation, 45:57, 21 Jul
      1887

Manning, Marie
  See Gasch, Marie (Manning).

Mansfield, Blanche (McManus)
  Our Little French Cousin
    Overland, 2d S, 46:590,
      Dec 1905

Manton, Kate
  Man's Wrongs
    Godey's, 81:184-5, Aug
      1870
    Nation, 10:426, 30 Jun
      1870

Mapes, Victor
  Partner's Three
    Nation, 89:101, 29 Jul
      1909

Marabell, William
  The Wattersons
    Overland, 2d S, 51:486-
      87, May 1908

Marbourg, Dolores [pseud.].
  See Bacon, Mary Schell
  (Hoke).

Marcy, Randolph B.
  Border Reminiscences
    Saturday Review, 33:130,
      27 Jan 1872

Marr, Kate Thyson
  Confessions of a Grass Widow
    Overland, 2d S, 46:84, Jul
      1905

Marriott, Charles
  Genevra
    Overland, 2d S, 44:639,
      Dec 1904

Marsh, Charles Leonard
  A Gentleman Juror
    Picayune, 29 Oct 1899, II,
      12

Marshall, Edward, and Charles
Dazey
  The Old Flute-Player
    Nation, 91:606, 22 Dec 1910

Martin, Amarala (Arter)
  Our Uncle and Aunt
    Nation, 48:331, 18 Apr 1889
    Picayune, 7 Oct 1888, p. 10
    Saturday Review, 66:598,
      17 Nov 1888

Martin, Caroline
  The Blue Ridge Mystery
    Picayune, 30 Jan 1898, p.
      17

Martin, Edward Sandford
  The Courtship of a Careful
  Man
    Bookman (NY), 21:545, Jul
      1905
    Nation, 80:379-80, 11 May
      1905
    Outlook, 79:1058, 29 Apr
      1905

Martin, Elizabeth Gilbert (Davis)
  Whom God Hath Joined
    Nation, 42:494, 10 Jun 1886

Martin, Mrs. George Madden
  Emmy Lou
    Bookman (London), 25:103,
      Nov 1903
    Sewanee Review, 11:357,

Martin, Mrs. George Madden
 Jul 1903
 The House of Fulfillment
  Athenaeum, 4028:11,
   7 Jan 1905
  Atlantic, 95:691, May
   1905

Martin, Helen (Reimensnyder)
 The Crossways
  Nation, 90:263, 17 Mar
   1910
 His Courtship
  Bookman (NY), 26:80-1,
   Sep 1907
  Nation, 85:37, 11 Jul
   1907
 The Revolt of Anne Royle
  Bookman (NY), 29:543-4,
   Jul 1909
  Overland, 2d S, 52:581,
   Dec 1908
 Sabina
  Outlook, 81:336, 30 Sep
   1905
 Unchaperoned
  Picayune, 3 Aug 1896,
   p. 8
 Warren Hyde
  Outlook, 58:437, 12 Feb
   1898

Martin, James M.
 Which Way, Sirs, the Better?
  Picayune, 10 Nov 1895,
   p. 10

Mason, Caroline (Atwater)
 Holt of Heathfield
  Saturday Review, 97:86,
   16 Jan 1904
 A Lily of France
  Overland, 2d S, 39:919,
   May 1902
 A Minister of the World
  Outlook, 58:979, 16
   Apr 1898
 A Titled Maiden
  Saturday Review, 69:709,
   7 Jun 1890
 A Woman of Yesterday

Bookman (London), 20:194,
 Sep 1901
Bookman (NY), 12:513, Jan
 1901
Nation, 71:410, 22 Nov 1900
Outlook, 66:621, 3 Nov 1900

Mason, Charles Welsh
 Rape of the Gamp
  Overland, 15:205, Aug 1875

Mason, E. H.
 The Real Agatha
  Bookman (NY), 27:104-5,
   Mar 1908

[Mason, Fanny Witherspoon]
 Daddy Dave
  By Mary Frances [pseud.].
  Nation, 45:403, 17 Nov 1887
  Picayune, 12 Sep 1886, p.
   12

[Mason, James Frederick]
 Cupid's Game with Hearts
  Overland, 2d S, 31:478,
   May 1898

Mason, Mary Murdock
 Mae Madden
  Nation, 22:83, 3 Feb 1876

Masson, Thomas Lansing
 A Bachelor's Baby
  Nation, 85:423, 7 Nov 1907

Mathew, Amanda
 Hieroglyphics of Love
  Overland, 2d S, 49:187, Feb
   1907

[Mathews, Frances Aymar]
 His Way and Her Will
  By A. X. [pseud.].
  Picayune, 27 May 1888, p.
   14
  Saturday Review, 66:723,
   15 Dec 1888
 A Married Man
  Bookman (NY), 11:95, Mar
   1900

Picayune, 1 Oct 1899,
II, 4

Mathews, Joanna H.
Edith Murray
Picayune, 16 Feb 1879,
[p. 11]
Maggie Bradford's School-
mates
Epoch, 8:366, 9 Jan
1891

Mathews, Julia A.
Bessie Harrington's Ven-
ture
Picayune, 17 Feb 1878,
[p. 10]

Matthews, Brander
The Action and the Word
Nation, 71:156-7, 23
Aug 1900
Outlook, 65:86, 5 May
1900
Picayune, 27 May 1900,
III, 7
A Confident To-Morrow
Bookman (NY), 10:325-8,
Dec 1899
Nation, 70:16-7, 4 Jan
1900
Sewanee Review, 8:121-
22, Jan 1900
A Family Tree, and Other
Stories
Atlantic, 65:576, Apr
1890
Epoch, 6:758-9, 27
Dec 1889
Nation, 50:57, 16 Jan
1890
Saturday Review, 68:684,
14 Dec 1889
His Father's Son
Athenaeum, 3564:216,
15 Feb 1896
Bookman (NY), 2:418-20,
Jan 1896
Nation, 62:182, 27 Feb
1896
Saturday Review, 82:453-

54, 24 Oct 1896
In the Vestibule Limited
Nation, 54:326-7, 28 Apr 1892
The Last Meeting
Athenaeum, 3035:837-8, 26
Dec 1885
Atlantic, 57:261-3, Feb 1886
Godey's, 112:103, Jan 1886
Nation, 41:470, 3 Dec 1885
Saturday Review, 60:750-1,
5 Dec 1885
Outlines in Local Color
Bookman (NY), 6:362-3, Dec
1897
Nation, 66:136, 17 Feb 1898
Sewanee Review, 6:106-9,
Jan 1898
The Royal Marine
Atlantic, 75:423, Mar 1895
A Secret of the Sea
Athenaeum, 3073:367, 18
Sep 1886
Nation, 43:357, 28 Oct 1886
Saturday Review, 62:466-7,
2 Oct 1886
The Story of a Story, and Oth-
er Stories
Atlantic, 72:850, Dec 1893
Nation, 57:32, 13 Jul 1893
Tales of Fantasy and Fact
Atlantic, 79:423, Mar 1897
Godey's, 133:432, Oct 1896
Vignettes of Manhattan
Atlantic, 74:848, Dec 1894
Nation, 59:311-2, 25 Oct 1894
Sewanee Review, 11:355,
Jul 1903
With My Friends
Atlantic, 69:269, Feb 1892
Nation, 53:471, 17 Dec 1891
Saturday Review, 72:504-5,
31 Oct 1891

_____, and George H. Jessop
Check and Counter-Check
Saturday Review, 66:557-8,
10 Nov 1888

_____, and H. C. Bunner
In Partnership
Godey's, 109:652, Dec 1884

Matthews, Brander, and H.
C. Bunner
    Nation, 39:463-4, 27
        Nov 1884
    Saturday Review, 58:760-
        61, 13 Dec 1884

Matthews, Sue Froman
Sic Vita Est
    Picayune, 20 Dec 1896,
        p. 20

Maxwell, Ellen Blackmar
The Bishop's Conversion
    Godey's, 126:106, Jan
        1893

Maxwell, William Babington
Vivien
    Outlook, 81:684, 18
        Nov 1905

May, Ansley [pseud.].
    See Dickinson, Edith May.

May, Florence Land
The Broken Wheel
    Overland, 2d S, 56:[337],
        Sep 1910

May, Mattie [pseud.].
    See Brown, Mrs. C. K.

May, Sophie [pseud.].
    See Clarke, Rebecca Sophia.

[May, Thomas P.]
The Earl of Mayfield
    Godey's, 99:469, Nov
        1879
    Nation, 29:277-8, 23
        Oct 1879
    Picayune, 29 May 1881,
        [p. 2]
A Prince of Breffny
    Nation, 33:338, 27 Oct
        1881
    Picayune, 30 Oct 1881,
        [p. 3]

Mayo, William Starbuck

Kaloolah
    Nation, 16:41, 16 Jan
        1873
    Picayune, 30 Oct 1887, p.
        14
    Saturday Review, 64:775, 3
        Dec 1887
Never Again
    Atlantic, 31:750-1, Jun 1873
    Harper's, 46:776, Apr 1873
    Nation, 16:220, 27 Mar 1873
    Saturday Review, 35:253-4,
        22 Feb 1873

Mead, Leon
The Bow-Legged Ghost, and
Other Stories
    Outlook, 63:604, 4 Nov 1899
In Thralldom
    Overland, 2d S, 11:435, Apr
        1888

Mead, Lucia True (Ames)
The Memoirs of a Millionaire
    Cottage Hearth, 15:416, Dec
        1889
    Epoch, 6:708, 6 Dec 1889
    Nation, 50:160, 20 Feb 1890
    Overland, 2d S, 15:437-8,
        Apr 1890

Meade, L. T. [pseud.].
    See Smith, Elizabeth Thomas
    (Meade).

Mears, Mary Martha
The Breath of the Runners
    Nation, 83:417-8, 15 Nov
        1906

Meekins, Lynn Roby
Adam Rush
    Outlook, 72:699, 22 Nov
        1902
The Robb's Island Wreck, and
Other Stories
    Nation, 58:473, 21 Jun 1894
Some of Our Own People
    Outlook, 59:587, 2 Jul 1898
    Picayune, 19 Jun 1898, II,
        12

[Meissner, Sophie (Radford)
de]
   The Terrace of Mon Désir
      Nation, 43:460, 2 Dec
      1886

Meline, Mary M.
   Charteris
      Picayune, 27 Sep 1874,
      [p. 6]

Mercier, Alfred
   Johnelle
      Picayune, 12 Jul 1891,
      p. 10
   Lidia
      Picayune, 4 Dec 1887,
      p. 16

Meredith, William Tuckey
   Not of Her Father's Race
      Picayune, 19 Oct 1890,
      p. 3

Meriwether, Elizabeth (Avery)
   Black and White
      Picayune, 4 Mar 1883,
      [p. 8]
   The Master of Red Leaf
      Picayune, 28 Mar 1880,
      [p. 10]
      Saturday Review, 47:811-
      12, 28 Jun 1879

Merran, Eleanor
   As the Wind Blows
      Picayune, 14 Oct 1895,
      p. 9; 23 Aug 1896,
      p. 15

Merrick, George Byron
   Old Times on the Upper
      Mississippi
      Athenaeum, 4252:495,
      24 Apr 1909

Merriman, Effie (Woodward)
   Pards
      Godey's, 122:97, Jan
      1891
   A Queer Family

Cottage Hearth, 17:182, Jun
      1891

[Merwin, Samuel]
   Calumet "K"
      By Merwin-Webster [pseud.].
      Times Literary Supplement,
      7 Feb 1902, p. 28
   His Little World
      Poet-Lore, 14:135-6, Winter
      1903
   The Merry Anne
      Athenaeum, 3995:649, 21
      May 1904
      Nation, 78:500, 23 Jun 1904
   The Road Builders
      Atlantic, 97:45, Jan 1906
   The Short Line War
      By Merwin-Webster [pseud.].
      Bookman (London), 16:170-1,
      Sep 1899
      Outlook, 62:171, 20 May
      1899
   The Whip Hand
      Nation, 77:508, 24 Dec 1903

Merwin-Webster [pseud.].
   See Merwin, Samuel.

[Meyer, Annie (Nathan)]
   Helen Brent, M. D.
      Atlantic, 70:707, Nov 1892
      Godey's, 125:644-5, Dec
      1892
      Saturday Review, 76:27, 1
      Jul 1893
   Robert Annys, Poor Priest
      Athenaeum, 3843:784, 22
      Jun 1901
      Bookman (NY), 13:576-8,
      Aug 1901

Meyers, Robert Cornelius V.
   Miss Margery's Roses
      Godey's, 99:279, Sep 1879
      Harper's, 59:632, Sep 1879

Meynardie, Florella
   Amy Oakley
      Picayune, 28 Mar 1880, [p.
      10]

Michelson, Miriam
Anthony Overman
Bookman (NY), 24:179,
Oct 1906
Nation, 83:188-9, 30
Aug 1906
The Awakening of Zojas
Bookman (London), 38:222-
23, Aug 1910
Nation, 90:539, 26 May
1910
In the Bishop's Carriage
Bookman (NY), 19:303-5,
May 1904
The Madigans
Overland, 2d S, 44:635-
36, Dec 1904
Michael Thwaites's Wife
Bookman (NY), 30:63-4,
Sep 1909
Nation, 89:142, 12 Aug
1909
A Yellow Journalist
Atlantic, 97:47, Jan
1906
Bookman (NY), 22:373-4,
Dec 1905
See also The Spinners' Book
of Fiction.

Mighels, Mrs. Philip Verrill
The Full Glory of Diantha
Nation, 89:238-9, 9
Sep 1909

Mighels, [Mrs. (?)] Philip
Verrill
The Inevitable
Overland, 2d S, 41:317,
Apr 1903
Nella
Picayune, 25 Nov 1900,
II, 7
The Ultimate Passion
Atlantic, 97:45, Jan
1906
Bookman (NY), 21:602,
Aug 1905

Miles, Austin
About My Father's Business

Picayune, 6 May 1900, III,
8

Millard, Bailey
A Pretty Bandit
Nation, 66:74, 27 Jan 1898
See also The Spinners' Book
of Fiction.

Millard, Frank Bailey
See Millard, Bailey.

Miller, Alice Duer
The Blue Arch
Nation, 91:606-7, 22 Dec
1910
Less Than Kin
Nation, 89:186-7, 26 Aug
1909
The Modern Obstacle
Atlantic, 92:278, Aug 1903

Miller, Annie (Jenness)
Barbara Thayer
Cottage Hearth, 10:218, Jul
1884
Nation, 39:19, 3 Jul 1884
Overland, 2d S, 4:106, Jul
1884
Picayune, 29 Jun 1884, [p.
9]
The Philosopher of Driftwood
Picayune, 3 Oct 1897, p. 15
'Twixt Love and Law
Picayune, 17 Feb 1889, p. 7

Miller, Elizabeth
Saul of Tarsus
Overland, 2d S, 48:[503 mis-
numbered 493], Dec 1906

Miller, Joaquin
The Building of the City Beau-
tiful
Atlantic, 74:134, Jul 1894
Overland, 2d S, 47:386, Apr
1906
Picayune, 17 Dec 1893, p.
26
The Destruction of Gotham
Nation, 43:102, 29 Jul 1886

Overland, 2d S, 8:107,
Jul 1886
Picayune, 13 Jun 1886,
p. 5
ʻ49
Nation, 39:464, 27 Nov
1884
Picayune, 12 Oct 1884,
[p. 2]
Saturday Review, 59:151,
31 Jan 1885
Life Among the Modocs
Athenaeum, 2389:168,
9 Aug 1873
Memorie and Rime
Athenaeum, 2968:331-2,
13 Sep 1884
The One Fair Woman
Athenaeum, 2526:421-2,
25 Mar 1876

Miller, John Henderson
Where the Rainbow Touches
the Ground
Overland, 2d S, 49:184,
Feb 1907

Miller, Martha Charlyne
(Keller)
The Fair Enchantress
Godey's, 107:583, Dec
1883
Picayune, 28 Oct 1883,
[p. 6]
Love and Rebellion
Picayune, 7 Jun 1891,
p. 10
Severed at Gettysburg
Picayune, 5 Aug 1888,
p. 7

Millet, Francis Davis
A Capillary Crime, and
Other Stories
Atlantic, 70:280, Aug
1892
Nation, 54:402, 26 May
1892

Mills, Weymer Jay
The Van Rensselaers of

Old Manhattan
Nation, 86:84, 23 Jan 1908

Miln, Louise (Jordan)
A Woman and Her Talent
Athenaeum, 4051:746-7, 17
Jun 1905
Bookman (London), 28:173,
Aug 1905
Saturday Review, 99:812-3,
17 Jun 1905

Minor, R. D.
See Not Pretty, but Precious.

[Minor, Thomas Chalmers]
Her Ladyship
Atlantic, 46:122, Jul 1880
.Nation, 31:17, 1 Jul 1880

Minton, Maurice M.
Country Lane and City Pave-
ments
Picayune, 29 Apr 1894, p.
23

Mitchell, Donald G.
Bound Together
Picayune, 6 Apr 1884, [p.
12]
The Reveries of a Bachelor
Athenaeum, 2964:201-2,
16 Aug 1884
Continent, 4:640, 14 Nov
1883
Seven Stories, with Basement
and Attic
Godey's, 107:583, Dec 1883
Picayune, 30 Sep 1883, [p.
6]

Mitchell, John Ames
Amos Judd
Atlantic, 78:137, Jul 1896
Bookman (NY), 3:68-9, Mar
1896
Nation, 62:182, 27 Feb 1896
Gloria Victis
Bookman (NY), 7:167, Apr
1898
Nation, 66:407-8, 26 May

Oct 1897
Nation, 66:16, 6 Jan
1898
Overland, 2d S, 30:568,
Dec 1897
Picayune, 10 Oct 1897,
p. 12
Sewanee Review, 11:356,
Jul 1903
In War Time
Atlantic, 55:123, Jan
1885
Godey's, 133:[652]-4,
Dec 1896
Harper's, 72:323, Jan
1886
Nation, 40:265, 26 Mar
1885
Overland, 2d S, 5:214-5,
Feb 1885
Saturday Review, 59:317-
19; 7 Mar 1885, 59:727-
28, 30 May 1885
Little Stories
Overland, 2d S, 43:84,
Jan 1904
New Samaria, and The
Summer of St. Martin
Saturday Review, 100:26,
1 Jul 1905
Philip Vernon
Picayune, 26 May 1895,
p. 16
The Red City
Athenaeum, 4233:756,
12 Dec 1908
Bookman (NY), 28:475,
Jan 1909
Canadian Magazine,
32:386, Feb 1909
Overland, 2d S, 52:580,
Dec 1908
Sewanee Review, 18:431,
Oct 1910
Roland Blake
Athenaeum, 3087:858,
25 Dec 1886
Godey's, 133:[652]-4,
Dec 1896
Nation, 44:17-8, 6 Jan
1887

Overland, 2d S, 9:322-3,
Mar 1887
Saturday Review, 63:231-2,
12 Feb 1887
A Venture in 1777
Nation, 87:606, 17 Dec 1908
When All the Woods Are Green
Godey's, 133:[652]-4, Dec
1896
Picayune, 18 Nov 1894, p.
15

Mitchell, Walter
Bryan Maurice
Picayune, 24 Feb 1889, p.
12

Moffett, Cleveland Langston
The Battle
Nation, 89:122, 5 Aug 1909
A King in Rags
Athenaeum, 4192:253, 29
Feb 1908
Nation, 86:84, 23 Jan 1908

Montague, Charles Howard
The Romance of the Lilies
Godey's, 113:191, Aug 1886
Picayune, 13 Jun 1886, p. 5
Two Strokes of the Bell
Godey's, 112:427, Apr 1886

_____, and Clement Milton
Hammond
The Doctor's Mistake
Godey's, 117:170, Aug 1888

[Monti, Luigi]
Adventures of a Consul Abroad
By Samuel Sampleton [pseud.].
Harper's, 57:468, Aug 1878
Leone
Athenaeum, 2864:366, 16
Sep 1882
Continent, 2:285, 6 Sep 1882
Nation, 35:183, 31 Aug 1882

Moodey, Martha Livingston
Alan Thorne
Picayune, 28 Apr 1889, p.
10

Moodey, Martha Livingston
  The Tragedy of Brinkwater
    Picayune, 12 Sep 1888,
      p. 7

Moore, David Albert
  How She Won Him
    Atlantic, 46:122, Jul
      1880

Moore, F. Frankfort
  Castle Omeragh
    Times Literary Supple-
      ment, 1 May 1903,
      p. 137
  The Conscience of Coralie
    Picayune, 23 Dec 1900,
      II, 12
  The Fatal Gift
    Outlook, 60:537, 29 Oct
      1898
  The Impudent Comedian
    Picayune, 11 Apr 1897,
      p. 25
  The Jessamy Bride
    Picayune, 25 Apr 1897,
      p. 23
  The Millionaires
    Picayune, 31 Jul 1898,
      II, 6
  One Fair Daughter
    Picayune, 28 Apr 1895,
      p. 22; 2 Mar 1896,
      p. 6

Moore, Mrs. Bloomfield H.
  See Bloomfield-Moore,
  Clara Sophia (Jessup).

Moore, Susan Teackle
  Ryle's Open Gate
    Atlantic, 69:280, Feb
      1892
    Epoch, 9:414-5, 31 Jul
      1891
    Picayune, 14 Jun 1891,
      p. 15
    Saturday Review, 72:278-
      79, 5 Sep 1891

Moos, Herman M.

Hannah
  Harper's, 44:300, Jan 1872

[Morford, Henry]
  The Spur of Monmouth
    By an Ex-Pension Agent.
      Atlantic, 38:751-2, Dec 1876
      Nation, 24:61, 25 Jul 1877
      Picayune, 19 Nov 1876, [p.
        10]
      Saturday Review, 42:552,
        28 Oct 1876

[Morgan, Carrie A.]
  Mistaken Paths
    By Herbert G. Dick [pseud.].
      Epoch, 1:559, 22 Jul 1887
      Godey's, 115:180, Aug 1887
  Sounding Brass
    By Herbert G. Dick [pseud.].
      Picayune, 25 Aug 1889, p.
        11

Morgan, Emily Malbone
  Madonnas of the Smoke
    Cottage Hearth, 19:497, Oct
      1893
  A Poppy Garden
    Cottage Hearth, 19:497, Oct
      1893

Morgan, Sallie B.
  Tahoe
    Picayune, 5 Mar 1882, [p.
      14]

Morris, Charles
  Historical Tales
    Picayune, 20 Nov 1898, III,
      3

Morris, Clara
  A Pasteboard Crown
    Bookman (London), 23:215,
      Feb 1903
    Nation, 75:134, 14 Aug 1902
    Overland, 2d S, 40:198-9,
      Aug 1902
  A Silent Singer
    Bookman (NY), 10:90, Sep
      1899

Nation, 70:17-8, 4 Jan
1900
The Trouble Woman
Overland, 2d S, 43:426,
May 1904

Morris, Eugenia Laura (Tuttle)
A Hilltop Summer
By Alyn Yates Keith
[pseud.].
Atlantic, 77:423, Mar
1896
Overland, 2d S, 25:107,
Jan 1895
A Spinster's Leaflets
By Alyn Yates Keith
[pseud.].
Nation, 58:234, 29 Mar
1894

Morris, Gouverneur
Aladdin O'Brien
Nation, 75:468, 11 Dec
1902
The Footprint, and Other
Stories
Bookman (NY), 27:283-4,
May 1908; 27:307-8,
May 1908
Nation, 86:219, 5 Mar
1908
Putting on the Screws
Nation, 90:13, 6 Jan
1910
The Spread Eagle
Bookman (NY), 32:433-4,
Dec 1910
Tom Beauling
Nation, 73:458-9, 12 Dec
1901
The Voice in the Rice
Bookman (NY), 31:297,
May 1910
Nation, 90:458, 5 May
1910

Morris, Ramsey
Crucify Her!
Picayune, 9 Sep 1888,
p. 10

Morrison, Arthur
Tales of Mean Streets
Godey's, 131:[430]-2, Oct
1895

Morrison, Mary Gray
The Sea-Farers
Nation, 71:157, 23 Aug 1900
Outlook, 65:228, 26 May
1900
Overland, 2d S, 36:189-90,
Aug 1900

Morrow, William Chambers
The Ape, the Idiot, and Other
People
Athenaeum, 3684:721-2, 4
Jun 1898
Bookman (London), 14:140,
Aug 1898
Picayune, 11 Apr 1897, p.
25
Saturday Review, 85:785,
11 Jun 1898
Blood-Money
Overland, 2d S, 1:202, Feb
1883
Bohemian Paris of To-Day
Picayune, 26 Nov 1899, II,
8
A Man, His Mark
Bookman (London), 18:157,
Aug 1900
Saturday Review, 90:89, 21
Jul 1900
See also The Spinners' Book
of Fiction.

Morse, Clara Frances
Blush Roses
Atlantic, 43:170-2, Feb 1879
Harper's, 57:941, Nov 1878
Library Table, 4:483, 23
Nov 1878

Morse, Lucy (Gibbons)
Rachel Stanwood
Atlantic, 73:569, Apr 1894
Godey's, 128:233, Feb 1894
Nation, 58:180, 8 Mar 1894

Morton, Frank
Self-Accused
Picayune, 12 Feb 1893,
p. 16

Morton, Martha
Helen Buderoff
Picayune, 23 Feb 1890,
p. 14

Morton, S. S.
A Little Comedy of Errors
Picayune, 14 Feb 1892,
p. 14

Moss, Mary
The Poet and the Parish
Nation, 83:417, 15 Nov
1906

[Motley, Mrs. Francis E.]
Olive Varcoe
By Francis Derrick
[pseud.].
Nation, 15:222, 3 Oct
1872

Mott, Edward Harold
The Black Homer of Jim-
town
Picayune, 24 Jun 1900,
II, 12
Pike County Folks
Saturday Review, 61:60,
9 Jan 1886

Mott, Lawrence
Jules of the Great Heart
Athenaeum, 4079:889,
30 Dec 1905
Nation, 81:448, 30 Nov
1905
The White Darkness
Bookman (NY), 25:183,
Apr 1907
Nation, 84:201, 28 Feb
1907

Moulton, Louise (Chandler)
Miss Eyse from Boston,
and Others

Cottage Hearth, 15:272, Aug
1889
Nation, 49:317, 17 Oct 1889
Saturday Review, 68:45-6,
13 Jul 1889
Some Women's Hearts
Godey's, 79:190, Aug 1874
Harper's, 49:444, Aug 1874
Nation, 19:10, 2 Jul 1874
Stories Told at Twilight
Nation, 53:107, 6 Aug 1891

Mowbray, J. P. [pseud.].
See Carpenter, Wheeler Andrew.

Muir, John
Stickeen
Nation, 89:37, 8 Jul 1909

Muir, Olive Beatrice
With Malice Toward None
Picayune, 21 Oct 1900, II, 9

Mulford, Clarence E.
Bar-20
Nation, 85:168, 22 Aug 1907
Hopalong Cassidy
Nation, 90:349, 7 Apr 1910

[Munday, John William]
The Lost Canyon of the Toltecs
By Charles Sumner Seeley
[pseud.].
Picayune, 11 Mar 1894, p.
25
The Spanish Galleon
By Charles Sumner Seeley
[pseud.].
Atlantic, 69:567, Apr 1892
Nation, 54:154, 25 Feb 1892

Munn, Charles Clark
Uncle Terry
Canadian Magazine, 17:200,
Jun 1901

Munroe, Kirk
At War with Pontiac
Saturday Review, 80:844, 21
Dec 1895

Cab and Caboose
  Saturday Review, 74:779,
    13 Dec 1892
Derrick Sterling
  Epoch, 3:337, 1 Jun
    1888
The Flamingo Feather
  Epoch, 1:360, 20 May
    1887
Forward, March!
  Saturday Review, 88:viii,
    Suppl. , 9 Dec 1899
The Fur Seal's Tooth
  Saturday Review, 80:712,
    30 Nov 1895
The Golden Days of '49
  Athenaeum, 3245:13-4,
    4 Jan 1890
  Nation, 50:117, 6 Feb
    1890
  Saturday Review, 68:720,
    21 Dec 1889
Shine Terrill
  Outlook, 62:669, 22 Jul
    1899
Through Swamp and Glade
  Picayune, 20 Dec 1896,
    p. 20
Under the Great Bear
  Saturday Review, 92:xi,
    Suppl. , 7 Dec 1901
The White Conquerors
  Godey's, 127:762, Dec
    1893
  Picayune, 25 Oct 1893,
    p. 16

[Murfree, Mary Noailles]
  The Amulet
    By Charles Egbert Crad-
      dock [pseud.].
    Nation, 83:463-4, 29
      Nov 1906
    Sewanee Review, 15:248,
      Apr 1907
  The Bushwhackers, and
  Other Stories
    By Charles Egbert Crad-
      dock [pseud.].
    Outlook, 62:265, 30 Sep
      1899

The Champion
  By Charles Egbert Craddock
    [pseud.].
  Nation, 75:331, 23 Oct 1902
The Despot of Broomsedge
Cove
  By Charles Egbert Craddock
    [pseud.].
  Atlantic, 64:122-5, Jul 1889
  Cottage Hearth, 15:56, Feb
    1889
  Epoch, 5:35-6, 15 Feb 1889
  Harper's, 78:985, May 1889
  Nation, 48:351-2, 25 Apr
    1889
  Overland, 2d S, 13:214-5,
    Feb 1889
  Saturday Review, 68:192-3,
    17 Aug 1889
Down the Ravine
  By Charles Egbert Craddock
    [pseud.].
  Cottage Hearth, 11:224, Jul
    1885
  Harper's, 71:805, Oct 1885
  Overland, 2d S, 6:327, Sep
    1885
  Saturday Review, 62:405, 18
    Sep 1886
The Fair Mississippian
  By Charles Egbert Craddock
    [pseud.].
  Nation, 88:42, 14 Jan 1909
The Frontiersmen
  By Charles Egbert Craddock
    [pseud.].
  Atlantic, 94:707, Nov 1904
His Vanished Star
  By Charles Egbert Craddock
    [pseud.].
  Athenaeum, 3499:672, 17
    Nov 1894
  Bookman (London), 7:55,
    Nov 1894
  Nation, 59:67, 26 Jul 1894
  Picayune, 24 Jun 1894, p.
    15
In the Clouds
  By Charles Egbert Craddock
    [pseud.].
  Epoch, 1:19, 11 Feb 1887

By Charles Egbert Craddock [pseud.].
 Athenaeum, 3029:634, 14 Nov 1885
 Atlantic, 55:123-5, Jan 1885
 Harper's, 70:493, Feb 1885
 Nation, 39:314, 9 Oct 1894
 Saturday Review, 59:61-2, 10 Jan 1885; 60:258-9, 22 Aug 1885
The Windfall
 By Charles Egbert Craddock [pseud.].
 Athenaeum, 4177:614, 16 Nov 1907
 Nation, 84:479, 23 May 1907
The Young Mountaineers
 By Charles Egbert Craddock [pseud.].
 Nation, 66:135, 17 Feb 1898
 Picayune, 24 Oct 1897, p. 9

Murfree, Fanny N. D.
 Felicia
 Epoch, 9:414-5, 31 Jul 1891
 Harper's, 83:642, Sep 1891
 Overland, 2d S, 19:331, Mar 1892
 Picayune, 14 Jun 1891, p. 15
 A Singer's Wife
 Saturday Review, 73:18, 2 Jan 1892

Murray, Charles Theodore
 Mlle. Fouchette
 Bookman (London), 23:95, Dec 1902
 Outlook, 70:783, 29 Mar 1902

Murray, David Christie
 Cynic Fortune

Nation, 43:397, 11 Nov 1886

Murray, Tom Fisher
 Father Tom and the Pope
 Picayune, 13 Apr 1879, [p. 12]

Murray, William Henry Harrison
 Adirondack Tales
 Harper's, 55:307, Jul 1877
 Saturday Review, 43:811, 30 Jun 1877; 45:250-1, 23 Feb 1878
 How Deacon Tubman and Parson Whitney Kept New Year's, and Other Stories
 Nation, 47:14, 5 Jul 1888
 Picayune, 15 Jan 1888, p. 10

Musick, John Roy
 Braddock
 Godey's, 127:495, Oct 1893
 Brother Against Brother
 Overland, 2d S, 11:435, Apr 1888
 Calamity Row
 Picayune, 4 Dec 1887, p. 16
 A Century Too Soon
 Godey's, 126:776, Jun 1893
 Columbia
 Epoch, 9:414-5, 31 Jul 1891
 Overland, 2d S, 27:239, Feb 1896
 Picayune, 5 Jul 1891, p. 12
 Esteven
 Godey's, 125:408, Oct 1892
 Overland, 2d S, 27:350, Mar 1896
 Independence
 Godey's, 127:622, Nov 1893
 Saint Augustine
 Overland, 2d S, 27:579, May 1896
 The Witch of Salem
 Godey's, 127:236, Aug 1893

Myers, George L.
 Aboard "The American Duchess"
 Picayune, 11 Feb 1900, II, 8

Myrick, Herbert
  Cache la Poudre
    Athenaeum, 4084:132,
      3 Feb 1906

Nasby, Petroleum V. [pseud.].
  See Locke, David Ross.

Nason, Frank Lewis
  The Blue Goose
    Athenaeum, 3941:590,
      9 May 1903
    Nation, 76:275, 2 Apr
      1903
  To the End of the Trail
    Athenaeum, 3907:348,
      13 Sep 1902
  The Vision of Elijah Berl
    Bookman (NY), 21:367,
      Jun 1905
    Overland, 2d S, 46:81,
      Jul 1905

Nauman, Mary Dommet
  See Robinson, Mary Dommet
    (Nauman).

Naylor, James Ball
  Ralph Marlowe
    Athenaeum, 3853:280,
      31 Aug 1901
  The Sign of the Prophet
    Athenaeum, 3907:347-8,
      13 Sep 1902
    Saturday Review, 93:372,
      22 Mar 1902

Nelson, Alice Ruth (Moore)
Dunbar
  The Goodness of Saint Roc-
    que, and Other Stories
    Nation, 71:157, 23 Aug
      1900

Nesbit, Wilbur Dick
  The Gentleman Ragman
    Nation, 83:308-9, 11
      Oct 1906
    North American Review,
      184:308-11, 1 Feb 1907

Neville, Constance Maude
  Behind the Arras
    Nation, 26:204, 21 Mar 1878

New, Clarence Herpert
  Franc Elliott
    Picayune, 18 Aug 1895, p.
      23

Newberry, Fannie E.
  By Strange Paths
    Athenaeum, 3702:489, 8 Oct
      1898
    Saturday Review, 86:480, 8
      Oct 1898

Newcomb, Simon
  His Wisdom the Defender
    Nation, 71:452, 6 Dec 1900
    Picayune, 18 Nov 1900, III,
      4

Newell, Charles Martin
  Kalani of Oahu
    Cottage Hearth, 7:337, Nov
      1881
  Kaméhaméha, the Conquering
  King
    Nation, 40:526, 25 Jun 1883
    North American Review,
      145:219-20, Aug 1887
    Overland, 2d S, 6:323, 326-7,
      Sep 1885
    Picayune, 21 Jun 1885, [p.
      7]

[Newell, Robert Henry]
  The Cloven Foot
    By Orpheus C. Kerr [pseud.].
    Godey's, 72:193, Feb 1871
    Picayune, 18 Dec 1870, [p.
      13]
  There Was Once a Man
    By Orpheus C. Kerr [pseud.].
    Continent, 5:832, (No. 26)
      1884
    Godey's, 109:312-3, Sep 1884
    Picayune, 27 Jul 1884, [p. 8]
  The Walking Doll
    By Orpheus C. Kerr [pseud.].
    Harper's, 44:780, Apr 1872

[Newhall, Mrs. Laura Eugenia]
  Hazel Verne
    By Ada L. Halstead
    [pseud.].
    Picayune, 21 Sep 1890,
      p. 12

Newport, W. [pseud.].
  See Dow, Joy Wheeler.

[Newton, William Wilberforce]
  The Priest and the Man
    Nation, 36:553, 28 Jun
      1883

Nicholas, Anna
  The Idyl of the Wabash,
  and Other Stories
    Picayune, 7 Nov 1898,
      p. 8

Nicholl, Edith M.
  See Bowyer, Edith M.
    (Nicholl).

[Nicholls, Charles Wilber de
  Lyon]
  The Greek Madonna
    By Shelton Chauncey
    [pseud.].
    Picayune, 4 Feb 1894,
      p. 16

Nichols, Mary S. (Gore)
  Jerry
    Saturday Review, 33:411-
      12, 30 Mar 1872

Nicholson, Meredith
  The House of a Thousand
  Candles
    Athenaeum, 4130:797,
      22 Dec 1906
    Bookman (London), 31:29,
      Christmas Suppl.,
      Dec 1906
    Bookman (NY), 22:495,
      Jan 1906
    Overland, 2d S, 46:594,
      Dec 1905

The Lords of High Decision
  Bookman (London), 38:51,
    Spring Suppl., Apr 1910
  Bookman (NY), 30:523-4,
    Jan 1910
The Main Chance
  Bookman (NY), 17:617-8,
    Aug 1903
  Nation, 76:460-1, 4 Jun 1903
The Port of Missing Men
  Bookman (NY), 25:85-6, Mar
    1907
  Canadian Magazine, 29:290,
    Jul 1907
  Nation, 84:246, 14 Mar 1907
Rosalind at Red Gate
  Bookman (NY), 26:665-6,
    Feb 1908
  Nation, 86:62, 16 Jan 1908
The Seige of the Seven Suitors
  Bookman (NY), 32:431-2,
    Dec 1910
  Nation, 91:445, 10 Nov 1910
Zelda Dameron
  Overland, 2d S, 44:637, Dec
    1904

Nicolls, William Jasper
  Brunhilda of Orr's Island
    Nation, 87:289, 24 Sep 1908

Niles, Willys [pseud.].
  See Hume, John Ferguson.

Niswonger, Charles Elliot
  The Isle of Feminine
    Picayune, 14 Jan 1894, p.
      23

[Nitsch, Helen Alice (Matthews)]
  Molly Bishop's Family
    By Catherine Owen [pseud.].
    Cottage Hearth, 14:364, Nov
      1888

Noble, Annette Lucille
  A Crazy Angel
    Athenaeum, 3880:304, 8
      Mar 1902
  Eunice Lathrop, Spinster
    Nation, 34:279, 30 Mar 1882

Nation, 88:607, 17 Jun
1909
Saturday Review, 108:264,
28 Aug 1909
Sewanee Review, 17:501,
Oct 1909
See also The Spinners' Book
of Fiction.

Norris, Mary Harriott
Lakewood
Saturday Review, 81:359,
4 Apr 1896
The Story of Christina
Nation, 86:84, 23 Jan
1908

Norton, Frances Marie
(Guiteau)
Cast Thou the First Stone
Picayune, 17 Jul 1898,
II, 6
The Stalwarts
Picayune, 24 Mar 1889,
p. 7
Saturday Review, 68:18-
19, 6 Jul 1889

Norton, Frank Henry
The Malachite Cross
Picayune, 26 Jul 1897,
p. 8

Not Pretty, but Precious,
and Other Short Stories
By Margaret Field, Mar-
garet Hosmer, Clara F.
Guernsey, John Hay,
Chauncey Hickox, Lucy
Hamilton Hooper, J. W.
De Forest, J. R. Hader-
mann, Harriet Prescott
Spofford, and R. D.
Minor
Godey's, 85:466, Nov
1872

Nye, Bill [pseud.].
See Nye, Edgar William.

Nye, Edgar William

Bill Nye's History of England
Godey's, 134:[428]-30, Apr
1897
Bill Nye's History of the
United States
Godey's, 134:[428]-30, Apr
1897
Saturday Review, 78:366,
29 Sep 1894
Bill Nye's Sparks
Godey's, 134:[428]-30, Apr
1897
Bill Nye's Thinks
Saturday Review, 68:305-6,
14 Sep 1889
A Guest at the Ludlow, and
Other Stories
By Bill Nye [pseud.].
Bookman (NY), 4:473, Jan
1897
Godey's, 134:[428]-30, Apr
1897
Overland, 2d S, 29:336,
Mar 1897
See also His Fleeting Ideal.

_____, and James Whitcomb
Riley
Nye and Riley's Railway Guide
Saturday Review, 68:305-6,
14 Sep 1889

[Obenchain, Eliza Caroline (Cal-
vert)]
Aunt Jane of Kentucky
By Eliza Calvert Hall
[pseud.].
Bookman, 37:54-5, Oct 1909
Overland, 2d S, 49:xiv, Jun
1907
Saturday Review, 108:539-
40, 30 Oct 1909
The Land of Long Ago
Overland, 2d S, 55:225,
Feb 1910

Ober, Fred A.
Under the Cuban Flag
Saturday Review, 86:679, 19
Nov 1898

Oberholtzer, Ellis Paxson
The New Man
Picayune, 24 Oct 1897,
p. 9
Saturday Review, 85:435,
26 Mar 1898

Oberholtzer, Mrs. S. L.
See Oberholtzer, Sara
Louise (Vickers).

Oberholtzer, Sara Louise
(Vickers).
Hope's Heart Bells
Godey's, 108:199, Feb
1884
Manhattan, 3:398, Apr
1884

O'Brien, Fitz-James
The Diamond Lens, with
Other Stories
Saturday Review, 59:835,
20 Jun 1885; 64:867-
68, 24 Dec 1887

O'Connor, William Douglas
Three Tales
Atlantic, 69:269, Feb
1892
Nation, 53:471, 17 Dec
1891

Ogden, G. W.
Tennessee Todd
Nation, 78:134, 18 Feb
1904

Ogden, Ruth [pseud.].
See Ide, Francis Otis
(Ogden).

O'Higgins, Harvey J.
Don-a-Dreams
Nation, 83:333, 18 Oct
1906
A Grand Army Man
Bookman (NY), 28:589,
Feb 1909
Old Clinkers
Nation, 90:211, 3 Mar

1910

Olcott, Henry Steel
People from the Other World
Athenaeum, 2499:366-7, 18
Sep 1875

Oldboy, Oliver [pseud.].
George Bailey
Atlantic, 46:837, Dec 1880

Oldham, Henry
The Man from Texas
Saturday Review, 58:760-1,
13 Dec 1884

Oliphant, Margaret Oliphant (Wilson)
See Aldrich, Thomas Bailey,
and M. O. W. Oliphant.

Olney, Ellen W.
See Kirk, Ellen Warner (Olney).

On a Western Campus
By the Class of '98, Iowa
College, Grinnell, Iowa
Nation, 66:53, 20 Jan 1898

O'Neill, Rose Cecil
The Lady in the White Veil
Bookman (NY), 29:641, Aug
1909

Oppenheim, James
Doctor Rast
Bookman (NY), 30:393-4,
Dec 1909
Nation, 89:461, 11 Nov 1909
Wild Oats
Nation, 91:189, 1 Sep 1910

Optic, Oliver [pseud.].
See Adams, William Taylor.

Orcutt, Harriet E.
A Modern Love Story
Picayune, 11 Mar 1894, p.
25

Orcutt, William Dana
The Spell
Bookman (NY), 29:410-2,
Jun 1909
Nation, 88:337, 1 Apr
1909
North American Review,
189:921, Jun 1909

O'Reilly, John Boyle
Moondyne
Harper's, 59:631-2, Sep
1879
Nation, 29:115, 14 Aug
1879
Saturday Review, 48:125,
26 Jul 1879; 67:327,
16 Mar 1889
See also The King's Men.

"Orleanian" [pseud.].
See Wharton, Edward Clifton.

Orpen, Adela E.
The Chronicles of Sid
Godey's, 127:766-7,
Dec 1893
The Jay-Hawkers
Nation, 71:118, 9 Aug
1900

Osborne, Duffield
The Lion's Brood
Bookman (London), 20:192,
Sep 1901
The Secret of the Crater
Bookman (London), 19:27,
Oct 1900
Outlook, 65:598, 7 Jun
1900
The Spell of Ashtaroth
Epoch, 3:278, 11 May
1888
North American Review,
147:116, Jul 1888
Picayune, 20 May 1888,
p. 10
Saturday Review, 66:752,
22 Dec 1888

Osborne, William Hamilton
The Red Mouse
Bookman (NY), 28:598-9,
Feb 1909
Nation, 88:256, 11 Mar 1909

Osbourne, Lloyd
The Adventurer
Bookman (London), 35:58,
Oct 1908
Nation, 85:518-9, 5 Dec
1907
Baby Bullet
Bookman (London), 29:225,
Feb 1906
Saturday Review, 100:689,
25 Nov 1905
Harm's Way
Saturday Review, 108:233,
21 Aug 1909
Infatuation
Bookman (NY), 29:406-8,
Jun 1909
Love, the Fiddler
Bookman (London), 25:262-
63, Mar 1904
Saturday Review, 97:306,
5 Mar 1904
The Queen versus Billy, and
Other Stories
Nation, 72:182, 28 Feb 1901
Saturday Review, 91:377,
23 Mar 1901
The Tin Diskers
Overland, 2d S, 48:501,
Dec 1906
Wild Justice
Bookman (London), 30:75-6,
May 1906
Saturday Review, 101:625,
19 May 1906

_____, and Stevenson, R. L.
The Ebb Tide
Bookman (London), 7:19-
20, Oct 1894

Osgood, Irene (DeBellot)
My Wickedness
Overland, 2d S, 23:217,
Feb 1894

Osgood, Irene (DeBellot)
  The Shadow of Desire
    Overland, 2d S, 23:217,
      Feb 1894
    Picayune, 4 Jun 1893,
      p. 18
    Saturday Review, 76:47,
      8 Jul 1893

Otis, James
  An American Fireman
    Outlook, 59:985, 20
      Aug 1898
  Christmas at Deacon Hac-
    kett's
    Outlook, 63:510, 28 Oct
      1899

Ottolengui, Rodrigues
  An Artist in Crime
    Overland, 2d S, 21:660-
      61, Jun 1893
    Saturday Review, 75:612,
      3 Jun 1893
  A Conflict of Evidence
    Saturday Review, 76:369,
      23 Sep 1893

Overton Gwendolen
  Anne Carmel
    Bookman (NY), 18:160-1,
      Oct 1903
  The Captain's Daughter
    Athenaeum, 3982:237,
      20 Feb 1904
    Saturday Review, 97:306,
      5 Mar 1904
  Captains of the World
    Bookman (London), 28:68,
      May 1905
    Saturday Review, 99:213,
      18 Feb 1905
  The Heritage of Unrest
    Athenaeum, 3833:461,
      13 Apr 1901
    Bookman (London), 20:124,
      Jul 1901
    Bookman (NY), 14:97,
      Sep 1901
    Nation, 72:399, 16 May
      1901

Outlook, 67:644, 16 Mar
  1901
Saturday Review, 91:777-8,
  15 Jun 1901

Owanda [pseud.].
  See Robinson, Edgar William.

Owen, Catherine [pseud.].
  See Nitsch, Helen Alice
    (Matthews).

Owen, Mary Alicia
  Voodoo Tales
    Atlantic, 72:280, Aug 1893
    Godey's, 126:776, Jun 1893

Owen, Robert Dale
  Beyond the Breakers
    Godey's, 80:574, Jun 1870
    Picayune, 12 Oct 1873, [p.
      5]
  Village Life in the West
    Picayune, 12 Oct 1873, [p.
      5]

Paddock, Mrs. A. G.
  See Paddock, Mrs. Cornelia.

Paddock, Mrs. Cornelia
  The Fate of Madame La Tour
    Nation, 33:138, 18 Aug 1881
    Saturday Review, 53:378, 25
      Mar 1882
  In the Toils
    Nation, 29:115, 14 Aug 1879

Page, Abraham [pseud.].
  See Holt, John Saunders.

Page, Thomas Nelson
  Bred in the Bone
    South Atlantic Quarterly,
      4:97, Jan 1905
  The Burial of the Guns
    Atlantic, 76:566, Oct 1895
    Bookman (London), 7:121,
      Jan 1895
    Nation, 59:483, 27 Dec 1894
    Picayune, 9 Dec 1894, p.
      10

Palmer, Mary Towle
  The Doctor of Deane
    Cottage Hearth, 14:226,
      Jul 1888
    Nation, 46:266, 29 Mar
      1888

Pangborn, Georgia (Wood)
  Roman Biznet
    Athenaeum, 3923:11,
      3 Jan 1903
    Nation, 74:449, 5 Jun
      1902

Pansy [pseud.].
  See Alden, Isabella (Mac-
    donald).

Parker, Bessie
  See Parker, Elizabeth Low-
    ber (Chandler).

Parker, Clara
  An Eventful Night
    Outlook, 64:837, 7 Apr
      1900

Parker, Elizabeth Lowber
  (Chandler)
  Miss Lomax, Millionaire
    By Bessie Parker
    Bookman (London), 29:41,
      Oct 1905
    Saturday Review, 100:x,
      Suppl. , 14 Oct 1905

Parker, Gay [pseud.].
  See Green, Miss M. P.

Parker, Gilbert
  See Tales of Our Coast.

Parker, Jane Marsh
  The Midnight Cry
    Nation, 42:533, 24 Jun
      1886

Parker, Lottie Blair
  Homespun
    Nation, 89:212, 2 Sep
      1909

Parker, William Hardwar
  Recollections of a Naval Officer
    Picayune, 30 Sep 1883, [p.
      6]

Parkman, Francis
  The Oregon Trail
    Atlantic, 30:489, Oct 1872

Parmele, Mary (Platt)
  Answered in the Negative, and
    Ariel
    Atlantic, 70:564, Oct 1892

Parrish, Randall
  Beth Norvell
    Athenaeum, 4176:580, 9 Nov
      1907
    Bookman (NY), 26:270, Nov
      1907
  Bob Hampton of Placer
    Bookman (NY), 25:90, Mar
      1907
  The Last Voyage of the Donna
    Isabel
    Nation, 87:236, 10 Sep 1908
  My Lady of the North
    Athenaeum, 4039:365, 25
      Mar 1905
  Prisoners of Chance
    Athenaeum, 4207:724, 13
      Jun 1908
    Nation, 86:448, 14 May 1908
  A Sword of the Old Frontier
    Athenaeum, 4086:194, 17
      Feb 1906
    Bookman (London), 29:255,
      Mar 1906
  When Wilderness Was King
    Athenaeum, 4014:442, 1 Oct
      1904
    Saturday Review, 99:389, 25
      Mar 1905

Patch, Kate (Whiting)
  Middleway
    Picayune, 19 Dec 1897, p.
      28

Paton, William Agnew
  Down the Islands

Paton, William Agnew
Athenaeum, 3162:690-1,
2 Jun 1888

Pattee, Frederick Lewis
The House of the Black
Ring
Bookman (NY), 21:600,
Aug 1905
Mary Garvin
Nation, 74:412, 22 May
1902

Patterson, Joseph Medill
A Little Brother of the
Rich
Overland, 2d S, 52:581,
Dec 1908

Paul, Kenneth [pseud.].
See Lockwood, Melancthon
Clarence.

Payne, Will
Jerry, the Dreamer
Saturday Review, 82:427-
28, 17 Oct 1896
The Losing Game
Nation, 90:377, 14 Apr
1910
Mr. Salt
Nation, 78:134, 18 Feb
1904
Outlook, 75:661, 14
Nov 1903
The Money Captain
Atlantic, 83:285, Feb
1899
Outlook, 60:676, 12
Nov 1898
On Fortune's Road
Athenaeum, 3912:519,
18 Oct 1902
Nation, 75:368, 6 Nov
1902
The Story of Eva
Athenaeum, 3852:247,
24 Aug 1901
Bookman (London), 20:190,
Sep 1901
Bookman (NY), 13:247-9,

May 1901
Outlook, 67:970, 27 Apr
1901
Saturday Review, 92:341,
14 Sep 1901
When Love Speaks
Nation, 83:441, 22 Nov 1906

Paynter, Mary Moncure
Caleb, the Irrepressible
Continent, 4:319, 5 Sep 1883

Payson, William Farquhar
Barry Gordon
Nation, 87:553, 3 Dec 1908
The Copy-Maker
Picayune, 16 Jan 1898, p.
11
John Vytal
Canadian Magazine, 17:88,
May 1901
Outlook, 67:692, 23 Mar
1901
Periwinkle
Bookman (NY), 32:304-5,
Nov 1910
The Title-Mongers
Bookman (NY), 8:255, Dec
1898
Outlook, 60:538, 29 Oct 1898

Peake, Elmore Elliott
The Darlingtons
Athenaeum, 3855:340, 14
Sep 1901
Bookman (NY), 12:622-3,
Feb 1901
Nation, 72:361-2, 2 May
1901
Outlook, 66:759, 24 Nov 1900
Picayune, 11 Nov 1900, II, 4
Sewanee Review, 9:499, Oct
1901
The House of Hawley
Bookman (NY), 21:181-2,
Apr 1905
Outlook, 79:503, 25 Feb
1905

Peale, Margaret
In the Time of the Cherry

Viewing
Nation, 50:17, 2 Jan
1890
Overland, 2d S, 15:322,
Mar 1890

Pearson, Henry Clemens
His Opportunity
Cottage Hearth, 12:128,
Apr 1886

Pease, Verne Seth
In the Wake of War
Picayune, 24 Jun 1900,
II, 12

Peattie, Elia (Wilkinson)
The Edge of Things
Bookman (NY), 18:312-3,
Nov 1903
A Mountain Woman
Atlantic, 78:849, Dec
1896
Nation, 63:201, 10 Sep
1896
Saturday Review, 82:684,
26 Dec 1896
The Shape of Fear, and
Other Ghostly Tales
Atlantic, 83:287-8, Feb
1899

[Peck, Ellen]
Ecce Femina
By Cuyler Pine [pseud.].
Godey's, 91:93, Jul
1875
Harper's, 51:602, Sep
1875

[Peck, George Wilbur]
Peck's Bad Boy
South Atlantic Quarterly,
5:223, Jul 1906

Peck, Samuel Minturn
Alabama Sketches
Nation, 74:293-4, 10
Apr 1902
Outlook, 70:781, 29
Mar 1902

[Peebles, Mary Louise (Parme-
lee)]
Where Honor Leads
By Lynde Palmer [pseud.].
Picayune, 9 Dec 1894, p. 10

Pemberton, Jeannette
Buffeting
Picayune, 11 Dec 1892, p.
2

Pendleton, Edmund
A Complication in Hearts
Overland, 2d S, 23:218,
Feb 1894
A Conventional Bohemian
Godey's, 112:536, May 1886
Nation, 42:240-1, 18 Mar
1886
Overland, 2d S, 7:653, Jun
1886
Saturday Review, 62:457-8,
2 Oct 1886
One Woman's Way
America, 6:738, 17 Sep
1891
Athenaeum, 3389:479-80,
8 Oct 1892
A Virginia Inheritance
Godey's, 117:338, Oct 1888
Nation, 47:273, 4 Oct 1888
North American Review,
147:598, Nov 1888
Saturday Review, 66:269-
70, 1 Sep 1888

Pendleton, Louis Beauregard
Bewitched
Epoch, 4:54, 24 Aug 1888
Picayune, 29 Jul 1888, p. 7
Carita
Outlook, 58:782, 26 Mar
1898
Corona of the Nantahalas
Picayune, 12 May 1895, p.
7
Saturday Review, 80:54-5,
13 Jul 1895
In the Wire-Grass
Godey's, 119:176, Aug 1889
Nation, 50:17, 2 Jan 1890

Pendleton, Louis Beauregard
   Saturday Review, 68:274-
      75, 7 Sep 1889
   King Tom and the Runaways
      Saturday Review, 70:689,
      13 Dec 1890
   The Sons of Ham
      Athenaeum, 3564:216,
      15 Feb 1896
   The Wedding Garment
      Atlantic, 74:565, Oct
      1894
      Saturday Review, 78:279,
      8 Sep 1894

Penn, Rachel [pseud.].
   See Willard, Caroline Mc-
   Coy (White).

Pennell, Joseph, and Eliza-
   beth Robins
   An Italian Pilgrimage
      Athenaeum, 3091:123,
      22 Jan 1887
   Our Sentimental Journey
      Athenaeum, 3149:274,
      3 Mar 1888

Pennot, Rev. Peter [pseud.].
   See Round, William Marshall Fitts.

Peple, Edward Henry
   The Prince Chap
      Athenaeum, 4026:870,
      24 Dec 1904
   Semiramis
      Bookman (NY), 26:269-
      70, Nov 1907
   The Spitfire
      Athenaeum, 4262:9, 3
      Jul 1909

Perkins, Frederic Beecher
   My Three Conversations
   with Miss Chester
      Nation, 25:274, 1 Nov
      1877
   Scrope
      Nation, 19:206-7, 24
      Sep 1874

Picayune, 2 Aug 1874, [p.
   2]
See also Six of One, by Half
a Dozen of Another.

[Perrin, Raymond St. James]
   The Student's Dream
      Saturday Review, 51:702,
      28 May 1881

Perry, Alice
   Esther Pennefather
      Harper's, 57:468, Aug 1878
      Library Table, 4:321, 6 Jul
      1878
   The Schoolmaster's Trial
      Picayune, 27 Feb 1881, [p.
      11]

Perry, Bliss
   The Broughton House
      America, 4:187, 15 May
      1890
      Atlantic, 66:857, Dec 1890
      Epoch, 7:238, 16 May 1890
      Nation, 51:254, 25 Sep 1890
      Picayune, 25 May 1890, p.
      14
   The Plated City
      Atlantic, 76:558, Oct 1895
      Nation, 61:278, 17 Oct 1895
   The Powers at Play
      Bookman (NY), 10:502, Jan
      1900
      Nation, 70:17, 4 Jan 1900
      Outlook, 62:265, 30 Sep 1899
   Salem Kittredge, and Other Sto-
   ries
      Atlantic, 74:564, Oct 1894
      Nation, 59:68, 26 Jul 1894
      Picayune, 3 Jun 1894, p. 10
      Sewanee Review, 3:83-4, Nov
      1894

Perry, Nora
   A Book of Love Stories
      Nation, 33:99, 4 Aug 1881
   A Flock of Girls
      Saturday Review, 64:802, 10
      Dec 1887
   For a Woman

Nation, 41:539, 24 Dec
1885
Overland, 2d S, 6:551,
Nov 1885
Saturday Review, 60:719-
20, 28 Nov 1885
The Tragedy of the Unex-
pected, and Other Stories
Saturday Review, 50:124,
24 Jul 1880

Perryman, E. G.
Our New Minister
Saturday Review, 41:283,
26 Feb 1876

[Peters, William Andrew]
Human Natur'
By Joel Sloper [pseud.].
Godey's, 111:403, Oct
1885

Peterson, Belle
Rose Sherwood
Picayune, 6 Nov 1881,
[p. 2]

[Peterson, Charles Jacob]
The Heiress of Sweetwater
By J. Thornton Randolph
[pseud.].
Godey's, 87:379, Oct
1873
Picayune, 3 Aug 1873,
[?]

Peterson, Henry
Bessie's Six Lovers
Godey's, 115:260, Sep
1887
Dulcibel
Nation, 84:591, 27 Jun
1907
Pemberton
Atlantic, 32:747-8, Dec
1873
Godey's, 86:377, Apr
1873
Harper's, 47:131, Jun
1873
Nation, 16:220, 27 Mar

1873
Picayune, 26 Jan 1873, [p.
10]; 11 Dec 1898, II, 11

Phelps, Charles Edward Davis
The Accolade
Outlook, 80:137, 13 May
1905

_____, and Leigh North
[pseud. of Elizabeth Stewart
(Natt) Phelps]
The Bailiff of Tewkesbury
Atlantic, 73:705, May 1894

Phelps, Elizabeth Stuart
See Ward, Elizabeth Stuart
(Phelps).

Philips, Melville
The Devil's Hat
Overland, 2d S, 10:329,
Sep 1887

Phillips, Barnett
Burning Their Ships
Harper's, 60:152, Dec 1879
A Struggle
Harper's, 57:629, Sep 1878
Picayune, 7 Jul 1878, [p. 3]

Phillips, David Graham
The Cost
Athenaeum, 4064:366, 16
Sep 1905
Nation, 79:121, 11 Aug 1904
Times Literary Supplement,
1 Sep 1905, p. 280
The Deluge
Bookman (NY), 22:372-3,
Dec 1905
Outlook, 81:887, 9 Dec 1905
Overland, 2d S, 46:591-2,
Dec 1905
The Fashionable Adventures of
Joshua Craig
Bookman (NY), 29:95-6,
Mar 1909
Nation, 88:225-6, 4 Mar
1909
Outlook, 91:533, 6 Mar 1909

Phillips, David Graham
  The Fortune Seeker
    Bookman (NY), 24:179,
      Oct 1906
  The Hungry Heart
    Nation, 89:186, 26 Aug
      1909
  The Husband's Story
    Bookman (NY), 32:292-3,
      Nov 1910
    Nation, 91:339, 13 Oct
      1910
  The Master Rogue
    Athenaeum, 3984:301,
      5 Mar 1904
    Saturday Review, 97:400,
      26 Mar 1904
  Old Wives for New
    Bookman (NY), 27:495-6,
      Jul 1908
    Nation, 86:264, 19 Mar
      1908
  The Plum Tree
    Atlantic, 97:44, Jan
      1906
    Overland, 2d S, 46:[79]-
      80, Jul 1905
  The Second Generation
    Nation, 84:85, 24 Jan
      1907
  The Social Secretary
    Overland, 2d S, 46:588,
      Dec 1905
  White Magic
    Nation, 90:607, 16 Jun
      1910
  A Woman Ventures
    Outlook, 72:562, 1 Nov
      1902

Phillips, Henry Wallace
  Mr. Scraggs
    Bookman (NY), 23:197-8,
      Apr 1906
  Red Saunders
    Athenaeum, 2957:283,
      29 Aug 1903
  Red Saunders' Pets, and
  Other Critters
    Atlantic, 99:126, Jan
      1907

    Bookman (London), 32:110,
      Jun 1907

Phillips, Walter Shelley
  Totem Tales
    Picayune, 6 Dec 1896, p. 15
    Nation, 64:35-6, 14 Jan 1897

Picard, George Henry
  A Matter of Taste
    Nation, 40:59, 15 Jan 1885
  A Mission Flower
    Atlantic, 57:265-6, Feb 1886
    Harper's, 72:323-4, Jan
      1886
    Nation, 41:469, 3 Dec 1885
    Saturday Review, 61:195, 6
      Feb 1886

[Picton, Nina]
  At the Threshold
    By Laura Dearborn [pseud.].
    Picayune, 5 Mar 1893, p.
      16

Pidgin, Charles Felton
  Quincy Adams Sawyer and
  Mason's Corner Folks
    Athenaeum, 3870:870, 28
      Dec 1901
    Picayune, 25 Nov 1900, II,
      7

Pier, Arthur Stanwood
  The Ancient Grudge
    Atlantic, 97:51, Jan 1906
    Bookman (NY), 22:495, Jan
      1906
  The Pedagogues
    Bookman (NY), 9:558-9, Aug
      1899
    Picayune, 9 Jul 1899, III, 3
  The Sentimentalists
    Athenaeum, 3853:280, 31
      Aug 1901
    Bookman (NY), 13:249-50,
      May 1901
    Harper's, 103:825, Oct 1901
    Outlook, 67:646, 16 Mar
      1901
  The Triumph

Bookman (NY), 17:517-8,
Jul 1903

Pierce, Gilbert Ashville
Zachariah, the Congress-
man
Atlantic, 46:121-2, Jul
1880

Pierce, Squier Littell
Stolen Steps
Picayune, 19 Jun 1892,
p. 18

Pierson, Ernest De Lancey
A Bargain in Souls
Picayune, 28 Feb 1892,
p. 11
The Black Ball
Picayune, 26 May 1889,
p. 12
A Vagabond's Honor
Picayune, 23 Feb 1890,
p. 14

[Pike, Frances West (Atherton)]
Every Day
Harper's, 42:461, Feb
1871

Pine, Cuyler [pseud.].
See Peck, Ellen.

Piner, Howell Lane
Ruth
Picayune, 24 Jan 1896,
p. 9

Pinkerton, Allan
Bucholz and the Detectives
Saturday Review, 50:410,
25 Sep 1880
Claude Melnotte, As a De-
tective, and Other Stories
Saturday Review, 40:567-
68, 30 Oct 1875
A Double Life and the De-
tectives
Picayune, 1 May 1892,
p. 12

The Expressman and the Detec-
tive
Saturday Review, 60:567-8,
30 Oct 1875
The Gypsies and the Detectives
Saturday Review, 48:806, 27
Dec 1879
Professional Thieves and the
Detective
Saturday Review, 51:286, 26
Feb 1881
The Spiritualists and the Detec-
tives
Picayune, 17 Jul 1892, p. 13
Strikers and Communists
Picayune, 4 Sep 1892, p. 7

Pinkham, Edwin George
Fate's a Fiddler
Nation, 87:265, 17 Sep 1908

Pinson, William Washington
In White and Black
Nation, 72:438, 30 May 1901

Pitkin, Helen
An Angel by Brevet
Outlook, 78:789, 26 Nov 1904
South Atlantic Quarterly,
4:97-8, Jan 1905

Pollard, Joseph Percival
Lingo Dan
Overland, 2d S, 42:462, Nov
1903

Pollock, Guy C.
See Pollock, Walter Herries,
and Guy C. Pollock.

Pollock, Walter Herries
King Zub, and Other Stories
Bookman (London), 3:60,
Nov 1892
Saturday Review, 74:418,
8 Oct 1892
A Nine Men's Morrice
Nation, 48:331, 18 Apr 1889

_____, and Guy C. Pollock
Hay Fever

Pollock, Walter Herries, and
Guy C. Pollock
  Saturday Review, 99:674,
    20 May 1905

Pool, Maria Louise
Dally
    Atlantic, 68:710, Nov
      1891
    Cottage Hearth, 19:ad-
      vert. 15, Dec 1893
    Epoch, 10:198, 30 Oct
      1891
    Nation, 53:125, 13 Aug
      1891
    Picayune, 20 Aug 1893,
      p. 18
    Saturday Review, 72:598,
      21 Nov 1891
Friendship and Folly
    Athenaeum, 3816:790,
      15 Dec 1900
    Picayune, 7 Nov 1898,
      p. 8
A Golden Sorrow
    Atlantic, 83:285, Feb
      1899
In a Dike Shanty
    Atlantic, 78:426, Sep
      1896
    Nation, 63:91, 30 Jul
      1892
    Picayune, 14 Jun 1896,
      p. 19
In Buncombe County
    Atlantic, 79:423-4, Mar
      1897
    Nation, 63:479-80, 24
      Dec 1896
    Picayune, 22 Nov 1896,
      p. 10
    Poet-Lore, 9:149-50,
      (No. 1) 1897
In the First Person
    Atlantic, 79:424, Mar
      1897
    Nation, 64:400, 27 May
      1897
Katharine North
    Atlantic, 74:848, Dec
      1894

Nation, 56:297, 20 Apr 1893
The Meloon Farm
    Outlook, 65:698, 21 Jul 1900
    Picayune, 5 Aug 1900, III, 3
Mrs. Keats Bradford
    Atlantic, 70:851, Dec 1892
The Red-Bridge Neighborhood
    Nation, 67:265, 6 Oct 1898
    Outlook, 58:638, 5 Mar 1898
Roweny in Boston
    Atlantic, 70:851, Dec 1892
    Nation, 54:362, 12 May 1892
Sand 'n' Bushes
    Nation, 69:95, 3 Aug 1899
    Outlook, 62:171, 20 May
      1899
Tenting at Stony Beach
    Epoch, 3:337, 1 Jun 1888
    Overland, 2d S, 12:434,
      Oct 1888
The Two Salomes
    Atlantic, 74:279, Aug 1894
    Nation, 57:292, 19 Oct 1893
A Widower & Some Spinsters
    Outlook, 63:696, 18 Nov
      1899

Poole, Mary Belle
What the Years Brought
    Picayune, 21 Jan 1894, p.
      24

Poor, Agnes Blake
Boston Neighbors in Town and
Out
    Bookman (London), 14:109,
      Jul 1898
    Outlook, 58:731, 19 Mar
      1898
Brothers and Strangers
    Godey's, 128:236, Feb 1894
    Nation, 58:277, 12 Apr 1894

Pope, Gustavus W.
Journey to Mars
    Picayune, 4 Mar 1894, p.
      25

Pope, Marion (Manville)
Up the Matterhorn in a Boat
    Picayune, 24 Oct 1897, p. 9

Porch, Hester Edwards
  An Ideal Fanatic
    Continent, 4:735, 5
      Dec 1883
    Picayune, 30 Dec 1883,
      [p. 9]

Porter, Mrs. A. E.
  See Porter, Lydia Ann
    (Emerson).

Porter, David Dixon
  Allen Dare and Robert le
    Diable
    Harper's, 70:816-7, Apr
      1885
    Overland, 2d S, 5:433-4,
      Apr 1885

Porter, Gene Stratton
  Freckles
    Saturday Review, 99:353,
      18 Mar 1905
    Times Literary Supple-
      ment, 27 Jan 1905,
      p. 31
  A Girl of the Limberlost
    Bookman (NY), 31:77-8,
      Mar 1910

[Porter, Linn Boyd]
  A Black Adonis
    By Albert Ross [pseud.].
    Picayune, 4 Aug 1895,
      p. 12
  Her Husband's Friend
    By Albert Ross [pseud.].
    Picayune, 8 Feb 1891,
      p. 9
  His Private Character
    By Albert Ross [pseud.].
    Picayune, 18 Aug 1889,
      p. 11
  In Stella's Shadow
    By Albert Ross [pseud.].
    Picayune, 3 Aug 1890,
      p. 10
  Love at Seventy
    By Albert Ross [pseud.].
    Picayune, 8 Jul 1894,
      p. 7

Moulding a Maiden
    By Albert Ross [pseud.].
    Picayune, 28 Jun 1891, p.
      12
  An Original Sinner
    By Albert Ross [pseud.].
    Picayune, 2 Jul 1893, p. 17
  Speaking of Ellen
    By Albert Ross [pseud.].
    Picayune, 2 Mar 1890, p.
      10
  Thy Neighbor's Wife
    By Albert Ross [pseud.].
    Picayune, 12 Feb 1893, p.
      16
  Why I'm Single
    By Albert Ross [pseud.].
    Picayune, 17 Jul 1892, p.
      13
  Young Fawcett's Mabel
    By Albert Ross [pseud.].
    Picayune, 8 Mar 1896, p.
      25
  Young Miss Giddy
    By Albert Ross [pseud.].
    Picayune, 4 Feb 1894, p.
      16

Porter, Lydia Ann (Emerson)
  Cousin Polly's Gold Mine
    Harper's, 58:146-7, Dec
      1878
    Library Table, 4:505, 7
      Dec 1878
  Married for Both Worlds
    Harper's, 43:459, Aug 1871
    Picayune, 18 Jun 1871, [p.
      9]

Porter, Mary W.
  Poor Papa
    Nation, 29:115, 14 Aug 1879

Porter, Mrs. Mel-Inda Jennie
  Frankincense
    Picayune, 26 Jun 1887, p. 8

Porter, Rose
  Fire
    Harper's, 41:622-3, Sep
      1870

247

Porter, Rose
Foundations
Harper's, 43:301, Jun
1871
Picayune, 11 Jun 1871,
[p. 10]
My Son's Wife
Picayune, 27 May 1877,
[p. 5]
Saturday Review, 82:596,
5 Dec 1896

[Porter, William Sydney]
Cabbages and Kings
By O. Henry [pseud.].
Bookman (NY), 20:561-
62, Feb 1905; 31:136-
37, Apr 1910
The Four Million
By O. Henry [pseud.].
Atlantic, 99:126-7, Jan
1907
North American Review,
187:781-3, May 1908
Outlook, 83:42, 5 May
1906
The Gentle Grafter
By O. Henry [pseud.].
Nation, 88:42, 14 Jan
1909
Overland, 2d S, 53:57,
Jan 1909
The Heart of the West
By O. Henry [pseud.].
Nation, 85:496-7, 28
Nov 1907
North American Review,
187:781-3, May 1908
Options
By O. Henry [pseud.].
Nation, 89:540, 2 Dec
1909
Roads of Destiny
By O. Henry [pseud.].
Nation, 89:56, 15 Jul
1909
Strictly Business
By O. Henry [pseud.].
Nation, 90:348-9, 7
Apr 1910
The Trimmed Lamp, and

Other Stories of the Four
Million
By O. Henry [pseud.].
Atlantic, 100:134, Jul
1907
Bookman (NY), 26:79-80,
Sep 1907
Nation, 85:16, 4 Jul 1907
North American Review,
187:781-3, May 1908
The Voice of the City
By O. Henry [pseud.].
Nation, 87:12, 2 Jul 1908
Overland, 2d S, 53:53, Jan
1909
Whirligigs
By O. Henry [pseud.].
Nation, 91:417-8, 3 Nov
1910

Post, Melville Davisson
The Corrector of Destinies
Nation, 87:498, 19 Nov 1908
Dwellers in the Hills
Athenaeum, 3966:578, 31
Oct 1903
Bookman (NY), 13:501, Jul
1901
The Strange Schemes of Ran-
dolph Mason
Overland, 2d S, 30:96, Jul
1897

Post, Waldron Kintzing
Harvard Stories
Bookman (London), 12:100,
Jul 1897
Godey's, 131:[546]-8, Nov
1895
Nation, 61:69, 25 Jul 1895

Potter, Margaret Horton
See Black, Margaret Horton
(Potter).

Pottle, Emery
Handicapped
Nation, 87:13, 2 Jul 1908

Powell, Ella Mary
Clio, a Child of Fate

Picayune, 15 Jun 1890,
p. 14
Winona
Atlantic, 70:564, Oct
1892

Pratt, Cornelia Atwood
See Comer, Cornelia At-
wood (Pratt).

Pratt, Ella (Farman)
A White Hand
Harper's, 51:298, Jul
1875

Prentiss, Elizabeth (Payson)
The Home at Greylock
Harper's, 54:619, Mar
1877
Library Table, 2:3,
Jan 1877
Nation, 24:62, 25 Jan
1877
Saturday Review, 43:121-
22, 27 Jan 1877
Nidworth
Harper's, 40:299, Jan
1870
Pemaquid
Harper's, 56:629, Mar
1878
Library Table, 3:40,
24 Nov 1877
Nation, 26:66, 24 Jan
1878
Stepping Heavenward
Harper's, 40:299-300,
Jan 1870
The Story Lizzie Told
Harper's, 42:780, Apr
1871

Preston, Harriet Waters
Aspendale
Godey's, 72:293, Mar
1871
Picayune, 8 Jan 1871,
[p. 13]
Saturday Review, 31:256,
25 Feb 1871
The Guardians

Cottage Hearth, 14:364, Nov
1888
Is That All?
Atlantic, 39:500-1, Apr 1877
Godey's, 94:190, Feb 1877
Harper's, 54:618, Mar 1877
Library Table, 3:59, 7 Jun
1877
Nation, 24:181, 22 Mar 1877
Saturday Review, 43:122, 27
Jan 1877
Love in the Nineteenth Century
Atlantic, 32:375-6, Sep 1873
Godey's, 87:568, Dec 1873
Harper's, 47:777, Oct 1873
Nation, 17:73-4, 31 Jul 1873
Saturday Review, 36:291, 30
Aug 1873
A Year in Eden
Harper's, 74:828, Apr 1887
Nation, 44:300, 7 Apr 1887
Overland, 2d S, 9:325-7,
Mar 1887
Saturday Review, 63:103,
15 Jan 1887
See also Dodge, Louise Pres-
ton, and H. W. Preston.

Price, Ella Brown
The Major's Love
Cottage Hearth, 14:160,
May 1888

Prime, William Cowper
I Go a-Fishing
Saturday Review, 36:351-2,
13 Sep 1873

Prince, Helen Choate (Pratt)
At the Sign of the Silver Cres-
cent
Athenaeum, 3693:189, 6 Aug
1898
Outlook, 58:929, 9 Apr 1898
Picayune, 17 Apr 1898, p.
16
The Story of Christine Roche-
fort
Atlantic, 75:844, Jun 1895
Nation, 61:243, 3 Oct 1895
Saturday Review, 80:119,

Prince, Helen Choate (Pratt)
27 Jul 1895
A Transatlantic Chatelaine
Athenaeum, 3675:434,
2 Apr 1898
Nation, 66:74, 27 Jan
1898
Picayune, 25 Apr 1897,
p. 23

Pugh, Eliza Lofton (Phillips)
In a Crucible
Picayune, 31 Dec 1871,
[p. 5]; 25 Feb 1872,
[p. 12]

Pullen, Elisabeth (Jones) Ca-
vazza
Don Finimondone
Overland, 2d S, 20:444,
Oct 1892

Putnam, Eleanor [pseud.].
See Bates, Harriet Leo-
nora (Vose).

Putnam, George Israel
In Blue Uniform
Atlantic, 72:849, Dec
1893
Nation, 57:105, 10
Aug 1893
Picayune, 18 Jun 1893,
p. 19
On the Offensive
Atlantic, 74:417, Sep
1894
Nation, 58:413, 31 May
1894

Pyle, Howard
The Garden Behind the
Moon
Bookman (London), 9:101,
Dec 1895
A Modern Aladdin
Nation, 54:154, 25 Feb
1892
Otto of the Silver Hand
Epoch, 4:391, 28 Dec
1888

The Rose of Paradise
Picayune, 11 Mar 1894, p.
25
Twilight Land
Bookman (London), 9:4,
Suppl., Dec 1895
Within the Capes
Atlantic, 57:264-5, Feb 1886
Nation, 41:140, 13 Aug 1885
Overland, 2d S, 5:662, Jun
1885
Picayune, 24 May 1885, [p.
3]
Saturday Review, 60:94, 18
Jul 1885
The Wonder-Clock
Epoch, 2:315, 25 Nov 1887

"Q"
See Tales of Our Coast.

Quin, Dan [pseud.].
See Lewis, Alfred Henry.

Quincy, Edmund
Wensley, and Other Stories
Saturday Review, 60:128-9,
25 Jul 1885

Quincy, Josiah Phillips
The Peckster Professorship
Athenaeum, 3204:371-2, 23
Mar 1889
Nation, 48:273, 28 Mar 1889
Overland, 2d S, 13:210, Feb
1889

Quondam [pseud.].
See Stevens, Charles Mc-
Clellan.

R., F. W.
See Rankin, Fannie W.

Raffensperger, Mrs. Anna Fran-
ces
Led in Unknown Paths
Picayune, 4 Oct 1891, p. 10
Patience Preston, M. D.
Picayune, 4 Mar 1888, p.
7

Ragozin, Mme. Zénaïde
Alexeïevna
  Beowulf, the Hero of the
  Anglo-Saxons
    Outlook, 60:638, 5
    Nov 1898
  Siegfried, the Hero of the
  North
    Outlook, 60:638, 5
    Nov 1898

Ragsdale, Lulah
  The Crime of Philip Guth-
  rie
    Picayune, 14 Aug 1892,
    p. 17
  A Shadow's Shadow
    Godey's, 125:646, Dec
    1892
    Picayune, 20 Nov 1892,
    p. 18

Raimond, C. E. [pseud.].
  See Robins, Elizabeth.

Ralph, Julian
  An Angel in a Web
    Atlantic, 83:285, Feb
    1899
    Nation, 68:358, 11 May
    1899
    Outlook, 60:1021, 24
    Dec 1898
  The Millionairess
    Outlook, 72:613, 8 Nov
    1902
  A Prince of Georgia, and
  Other Tales
    Outlook, 62:83, 2 Sep
    1899

Ramsay, Allan
  See Adler, Cyrus, and
  Allan Ramsay.

Ramsey, Milton Worth
  Six Thousand Years Hence
    America, 6:482, 23 Jul
    1891

Rand, Edward Augustus

Up North in a Whaler
  Saturday Review, 70:658, 6
  Dec 1890

Randle, Fred A.
  Nil
    Picayune, 9 Jan 1898, p. 20

Randolph, George
  Aunt Abigail Dykes
    Athenaeum, 3285:476-7, 11
    Oct 1890

Randolph, J. Thornton [pseud.].
  See Peterson, Charles Jacob.

[Rankin, Fannie W.]
  True to Him Ever
  By F. W. R.
    Godey's, 79:190, Aug 1874

Rathborne, St. George Henry
  The Cartaret Affairs
    Picayune, 1 Mar 1891, p. 10
  The Colonel by Brevet
    Picayune, 31 Jul 1892, p. 10
  The Fair Maid of Fez
    Picayune, 12 May 1895, p.
    7
  Her Rescue from the Turks
    Picayune, 20 Dec 1896, p.
    20
  Major Matterson of Kentucky
    Picayune, 30 Apr 1893, p.
    21
  The Man from Wall Street
    Picayune, 12 Feb 1893, p.
    16
  Marked in Mystery
    Picayune, 7 Feb 1897, p. 12
  Mynheer Joe
    Picayune, 6 Aug 1893, p. 17
  The Nabob of Singapore
    Picayune, 10 Nov 1895, p.
    10

Ravenswood [pseud.].
  See Beebe, Charles Washington.

Rawson, Abel M.
  The Junior Partners

251

Rawson, Abel M.
Picayune, 13 Dec 1891,
p. 12

Ray, Anna Chapin
Half a Dozen Girls
Picayune, 20 Sep 1891,
p. 10
Janet
Saturday Review, 104:vii,
Suppl., 7 Dec 1907
Over the Quicksands
Nation, 90:377, 14 Apr
1910
Quickened
Nation, 86:469, 21 May
1908
Teddy: Her Book
Saturday Review, 104:vii,
Suppl., 7 Dec 1907

Raymond, Evelyn (Hunt)
Among the Lindens
Picayune, 31 Oct 1898,
p. 7
Mixed Pickles
Picayune, 25 Sep 1892,
p. 13
My Lady Barefoot
Outlook, 64:88, 6 Jan
1900
The Sun Maid
Athenaeum, 3826:239,
23 Feb 1901

[Raymond, George Lansing]
Modern Fishers of Men
Rose-Belford's, 2:384,
Mar 1879

Raymond, Walter Marion
Good Souls of Ciderland
Bookman (London), 20:194,
Sep 1901
Tryphena in Love
Atlantic, 76:279, Aug
1895
Two Men and Some Women
Sewanee Review, 9:106,
Jan 1901
Two Men o' Mendip

Nation, 69:96, 3 Aug 1899
Outlook, 61:647, 18 Mar
1899

Rayner, Emma
Free to Serve
Athenaeum, 3823:139-40,
2 Feb 1901
Bookman (London), 19:131,
Jan 1901
Bookman (NY), 6:356-7,
Dec 1897
Godey's, 136:217, Feb 1898
Picayune, 17 Nov 1897, p.
6
Handicapped Among the Free
Athenaeum, 3963:478, 10
Oct 1903
Bookman (London), 25:52,
Oct 1903
Nation, 76:359, 30 Apr 1903
In Castle and Colony
Bookman (NY), 10:186-7,
Oct 1899
Outlook, 62:265, 30 Sep
1899
Visiting the Sin
Nation, 72:98, 31 Jan 1901
Picayune, 18 Nov 1900, III,
4
Saturday Review, 93:211,
15 Feb 1902
Sewanee Review, 9:103-4,
Jan 1901

Read, Emily
Aytown
Harper's, 45:624, Sep 1872
Nation, 15:172, 12 Sep 1872
Saturday Review, 34:260, 24
Aug 1872
See also Reeves, Marian C.
L., and Emily Read.

Read, Opie
An Arkansas Planter
Godey's, 135:[443]-5, Oct
1897
Bolanyo
Bookman (NY), 6:164-5,
Oct 1897

Rhodes, Harrison
The Adventures of Charles
Edward
Bookman (NY), 27:414-5,
Jun 1908; 27:501-2,
Jul 1908
Overland, 2d S, 52:[191]-
2, Aug 1908
The Flight to Eden
Nation, 85:545, 12 Dec
1907
Sewanee Review, 16:381,
Jul 1908

Rhone, Mrs. D. L.
See Rhone, Rosamond (Dod-
son).

Rhone, Rosamond (Dodson)
Among the Dunes
Outlook, 58:679, 12
Mar 1898

Rice, Alice Caldwell (Hegan)
Captain June
Athenaeum, 4171:399-400,
5 Oct 1907
Lovey Mary
Overland, 2d S, 41:316-7,
Apr 1903
Saturday Review, 96:212,
15 Aug 1903
Sewanee Review, 11:357,
Jul 1903
Mr. Opp
Athenaeum, 4256:612,
22 May 1909
Bookman (London), 36:94,
May 1909
Bookman (NY), 29:412-3,
Jun 1909
Nation, 89:16-7, 1 Jul
1909
Mrs. Wiggs of the Cabbage
Patch
Atlantic, 90:418, Sep
1902
Bookman (London), 23:94-
95, Dec 1902; 35:37-
38, Christmas Suppl.,
Dec 1908

Sewanee Review, 11:357, Jul
1903
Sandy
Athenaeum, 4049:684-5, 3
Jun 1905
Bookman (London), 28:65-6,
May 1905
Overland, 2d S, 46:84, Jul
1905
Saturday Review, 99:601, 6
May 1905

Richards, Laura Elizabeth (Howe)
Grandmother
Outlook, 87:745, 30 Nov
1907
Love and Rocks
Outlook, 58:1078, 30 Apr
1898
Mrs. Tree's Will
Overland, 2d S, 46:586, Dec
1905
Quicksilver Sue
Outlook, 63:513, 28 Oct 1899
Rita
Overland, 2d S, 37:656, Jan
1901
Rosin the Beau
Outlook, 58:1078, 30 Apr
1898
The Wooing of Calvin Parks
Nation, 87:340-1, 8 Oct
1908

Richards, M. E.
Zandrie
Bookman (NY), 30:281-2,
Nov 1909

[Richardson, George Tilton]
My Lady Laughter
By Dwight Tilton [pseud.].
Bookman (London), 28:172,
Aug 1905

Richardson, Norval
The Lead of Honour
Nation, 91:392, 27 Oct 1910

Richardson, Warren
Dr. Zell and the Princess

Richardson, Warren
  Charlotte
    Picayune, 21 Feb 1892,
      p. 20

Rickert, Edith
  The Beggar in the Heart
    Athenaeum, 4278:489,
      23 Oct 1909
    Bookman (NY), 30:394-5,
      Dec 1909
    Nation, 89:651, 30 Dec
      1909
    Saturday Review, 109:24,
      1 Jan 1910
  Folly
    Bookman (NY), 23:191,
      Apr 1906
    Saturday Review, 101:465-
      66, 14 Apr 1906
  The Golden Hawk
    Atlantic, 100:134, Jul
      1907
    Bookman (NY), 25:392,
      Jun 1907
    Nation, 84:435, 9 May
      1907
    Times Literary Supple-
      ment, 1 Mar 1907,
      p. 70
  Out of the Cypress Swamp
    Saturday Review, 93:404,
      29 Mar 1902
    Times Literary Supple-
      ment, 21 Mar 1902,
      p. 77
  The Reaper
    Bookman (London), 27:179,
      Jan 1905
    Nation, 79:420-1, 24
      Nov 1904
    Times Literary Supple-
      ment, 14 Oct 1904,
      p. 312

Riddle, Albert Gallatin
  Alice Brand
    Godey's, 90:477, May
      1875
    Nation, 20:299, 29 Apr
      1875

    Saturday Review, 39:670, 22
      May 1875
  Ansel's Cave
    Nation, 57:104, 10 Aug 1893
  The House of Ross, and Other
  Tales
    Godey's, 102:573, Jun 1881
  The Tory's Daughter
    Overland, 2d S, 13:216-7,
      Feb 1889
    Picayune, 23 Dec 1888, p.
      14

Rideing, William Henry
  How Tyson Came Home
    Athenaeum, 4003:75, 16 Jul
      1904

Rideout, Henry Milner
  Admiral's Light
    Nation, 86:39, 9 Jan 1908
  Beached Keels
    Bookman (NY), 24:591, Feb
      1907
  Dragon's Blood
    Nation, 89:141-2, 12 Aug
      1909
  The Siamese Cat
    Nation, 84:544-5, 13 Jun
      1907
  The Twisted Foot
    Athenaeum, 4316:64, 16 Jul
      1910
    Nation, 91:145, 18 Aug 1910
  See also The Spinners' Book of
    Fiction.

Ridgeway, Algernon [pseud.].
  See Wood, Anna (Cogswell).

Riemensnyder, Helen
  See Martin, Helen (Reimensnyder).

Riis, Jacob August
  Children of the Tenements
    Bookman (London), 26:30,
      Apr 1904
    Times Literary Supplement,
      8 Jan 1904, p. 7
  Out of Mulberry Street

Picayune, 11 Dec 1898,
II, 11
Quarterly Review, 196:413,
Oct 1902

Riley, Henry Hiram
The Puddleford Papers
Continent, 2:381, 27
Sep 1882
Cottage Hearth, 8:327,
Oct 1882
Godey's, 90:190, Feb
1875

Riley, James Whitcomb
Pipes o' Pan at Zekesbury
Outlook, 58:639, 5
Mar 1898

Rinehart, Mary (Roberts)
The Man in Lower Ten
Athenaeum, 4287:786,
25 Dec 1909
The Window at the White
Cat
Nation, 91:340, 13 Oct
1910

Rion, Hanna
See VerBeck, Hanna (Rion).

Risley, Richard Voorhees
Men's Tragedies
Bookman (NY), 9:471,
Jul 1899
Nation, 68:422, 1 Jun
1899
Outlook, 62:171, 20
May 1899
Picayune, 9 Jul 1899,
III, 3
Saturday Review, 88:273,
26 Aug 1899
The Sledge
Bookman (NY), 12:521-2,
Jan 1901

Rivers, George Robert Russell
The Count's Snuff-Box
Picayune, 31 Oct 1898,
p. 7

A Fancy Sketch
Saturday Review, 79:196, 9
Feb 1895
The Governor's Garden
Nation, 63:145, 20 Aug 1896

Rives, Amélie
See Troubetzkoy, Amélie
(Rives) Chanler.

Rives, Hallie Erminie
The Castaway
Athenaeum, 4196:381, 28
Mar 1908
Nation, 79:122, 11 Aug 1904
Outlook, 77:567, 2 Jul 1904
A Fool in Spots
Picayune, 3 Mar 1895, p.
14
A Furnace of Earth
Bookman (NY), 12:193, Oct
1900
Nation, 71:409, 22 Nov 1900
Picayune, 14 Oct 1900, II, 8
Smoking Flax
Godey's, 136:331, Mar 1898
Overland, 2d S, 31:476, May
1898
Picayune, 12 Dec 1897, p.
25

Robbins, Charles Henry
The Gam
Nation, 69:194, 7 Sep 1899
Picayune, 27 Aug 1899, II,
12
"Down the O-hi-o"
America, 5:734-5, 26 Mar
1891
Atlantic, 69:567, Apr 1892
Epoch, 9:302, 12 Jun 1891
Nation, 52:384-5, 7 May
1891
Overland, 2d S, 18:440, Oct
1891

Roberts, Clara (Lemore)
A Covenant with the Dead
Bookman (London), 2:60,
May 1892

[Roe, William James]
1886

Rogers, Robert Cameron
Old Dorset
Nation, 64:186, 11 Mar
1897
Picayune, 7 Feb 1897,
p. 12
Saturday Review, 83:453,
24 Apr 1897
Will o' the Wasp
Nation, 63:145, 20 Aug
1896

Rohlfs, Anna Katharine
(Green)
Agatha Webb
Athenaeum, 3797:148,
4 Aug 1900
Bookman (NY), 10:90-1,
Sep 1899
Outlook, 62:669, 22 Jul
1899
Picayune, 30 Jul 1899,
II, 8
The Amethyst Box
Saturday Review, 100:600,
4 Nov 1905
Behind Closed Doors
Epoch, 4:391, 28 Dec
1888
Nation, 48:142, 14 Feb
1889
Overland, 2d S, 13:210,
Feb 1889
Picayune, 4 Nov 1888,
p. 10
The Circular Study
Bookman (London),
22:178-9, Aug 1902
Nation, 82:390, 10 May
1906
Cynthia Wakeham's Money
Athenaeum, 3392:585-6,
29 Oct 1892
Picayune, 7 Aug 1892,
p. 11
Saturday Review, 74:687,
10 Dec 1892
A Difficult Problem . . .

and Other Stories
Picayune, 22 May 1900, III,
7
The Doctor, His Wife and the
Clock
Atlantic, 75:567-8, Apr 1895
Bookman (NY), 1:196, Apr
1895
Godey's, 130:655-6, Jun 1895
Saturday Review, 80:418-9,
28 Sep 1895
Doctor Izard
Atlantic, 76:421, Sep 1895
The Filagree Ball
Saturday Review, 97:400, 26
Mar 1904
The Forsaken Inn
Saturday Review, 69:201-2,
15 Feb 1890
Hand and Ring
Nation, 38:58, 17 Jan 1884
Overland, 2d S, 3:220, Feb
1884
Picayune, 16 Dec 1883, [p.
14]
Saturday Review, 58:635, 15
Nov 1884
The House in the Mist
Overland, 2d S, 45:565, Jun
1905
The House of the Whispering
Pines
Nation, 90:238, 10 Mar 1910
The Leavenworth Case
Athenaeum, 2677:213, 15 Feb
1879
Bookman (London), 37:169,
Jan 1910
Harper's, 58:467, Feb 1879
Nation, 29:214, 25 Sep 1879
Picayune, 19 Jan 1879, [p.
11]
Saturday Review, 47:126, 25
Jan 1879; 57:792-3, 14
Jun 1884
Lost Man's Lane
Godey's, 137:108, Jul 1898
Outlook, 58:979, 16 Apr 1898
Marked "Personal"
Atlantic, 73:568, Apr 1894
Godey's, 127:235, Aug 1893

Nation, 57:104, 10 Aug
1893
Picayune, 11 Jun 1893,
p. 16
A Matter of Millions
Athenaeum, 3281:351,
13 Sep 1890
Epoch, 8:253, 21 Nov
1890
Picayune, 2 Nov 1890,
p. 14; 24 May 1891,
p. 12
Saturday Review, 70:376-
77, 27 Sep 1890
The Mill Mystery
Nation, 42:409, 13 May
1886
Overland, 2d S, 7:652,
Jun 1886
Picayune, 18 Apr 1886,
p. 8
Saturday Review, 61:686,
15 May 1886
The Millionaire Baby
Athenaeum, 4050:714,
10 Jun 1905
Overland, 2d S, 45:342,
Apr 1905
Miss Hurd, an Enigma
Atlantic, 75:133, Jun
1895
Picayune, 30 Sep 1894,
p. 22
Saturday Review, 79:164-
65, 2 Feb 1895
The Old Stone House, and
Other Sketches
Picayune, 17 Jan 1892,
p. 2
7 to 12
Nation, 45:57, 21 Jul
1887
A Strange Disappearance
Harper's, 60:632, Mar
1880
Nation, 30:141, 19 Feb
1880
Picayune, 18 Jan 1880,
[?]
Saturday Review, 58:635-
36, 15 Nov 1884

The Sword of Damocles
Athenaeum, 2804:109-10, 23
Jul 1881
Saturday Review, 51:829, 25
Jun 1881
That Affair Next Door
Bookman, 12:43, May 1897
Godey's, 135:109, Jul 1897
Overland, 2d S, 30:191, Aug
1897
Picayune, 31 Jan 1897, p.
17
X Y Z
Saturday Review, 56:848, 29
Dec 1883

Rohlfs, Mrs. Charles
See Rohlfs, Anna Katharine
(Green).

Roker, A. B. [pseud.].
See Barton, Samuel.

Roland, Mrs. Alice Kate
Rosalind Morton
Picayune, 28 Aug 1898, II, 4

Rollins, Alice Marland (Welling-
ton)
The Story of a Ranch
Picayune, 20 Dec 1885, p.
14
Uncle Tom's Tenement
Epoch, 3:516, 3 Aug 1888
Harper's, 77:801-2, Oct 1888
Nation, 47:481, 13 Dec 1888
Picayune, 5 Aug 1888, p. 7
Saturday Review, 66:307, 8
Sep 1888

Rollins, Clara Harriot (Sherwood)
A Burne-Jones Head, and Other
Sketches
Picayune, 8 Jul 1894, p. 7

Rollins, Frank West
The Lady of the Violets
Outlook, 58:82, 1 Jan 1898

Rood, Henry Edward
The Company Doctor

Rood, Henry Edward
  Picayune, 5 May 1895,
    p. 7; 16 Jun 1895,
    p. 28

Roosevelt, Blanche [pseud.].
  See Macchetta, Blanche
  Roosevelt (Tucker).

Roosevelt, Robert Barnwell
  Love and Luck
    Nation, 43:272, 30 Sep
    1886
    Picayune, 29 Aug 1886,
    p. 6
  Progressive Petticoats
    Nation, 20:137, 25 Feb
    1875

Root, Frederick Stanley
  Tousled Hair
    Outlook, 62:83, 2 Sep
    1899

Roseboro', Viola
  The Joyous Heart
    Atlantic, 92:279, Aug
    1903
  Players and Vagabonds
    Saturday Review, 99:118,
    28 Jan 1905

Rosen, Lew [pseud.].
  See Rosenthal, Lewis.

[Rosenthal, Lewis]
  Grisette
    By Lew Rosen [pseud.].
    Picayune, 9 Jun 1889,
    p. 13
    Saturday Review, 68:496-
    97, 2 Nov 1889

Ross, Albert [pseud.].
  See Porter, Linn Boyd.

Ross, Clinton
  The Adventures of Three
  Worthies
    Atlantic, 69:269, Feb
    1892

  Picayune, 2 Aug 1891, p.
    13
Chalmette
  Bookman (NY), 6:475, Jan
    1898
  Godey's, 136:328, Mar 1898
  Picayune, 22 Apr 1900, III,
    4
The Countess Bettina
  Atlantic, 76:421, Sep 1895
  Saturday Review, 81:436,
    25 Apr 1896
The Gallery of a Random Col-
lector
  Atlantic, 63:140, Jan 1889
Improbable Tales
  Atlantic, 70:420, Sep 1892
The Meddling Hussy
  Nation, 66:54, 20 Jan 1898
The Puppet
  Picayune, 10 Jan 1897, p.
    11
The Scarlet Coat
  Bookman (NY), 5:81, Mar
    1897
  Picayune, 10 Jan 1897, p.
    11
The Silent Workman
  Nation, 44:148, 17 Feb 1887
The Speculator
  Epoch, 9:237, 15 May 1891
  Overland, 2d S, 19:332, Mar
    1892
  Picayune, 26 Apr 1891, p.
    15
Zuleka
  Picayune, 17 Dec 1899, III,
    8

Rouse, Adelaide Louise
  Under My Own Roof
    Overland, 2d S, 39:918, May
    1902

[Round, William Marshall Fitts]
  Achsah
    By Rev. Peter Pennot [pseud.].
    Atlantic, 38:244-5, Aug 1876
    Cottage Hearth, 3:174, Jul
    1876
    Harper's, 53:629, Sep 1876

Library Table, 1:78-80,
Jun 1876
Nation, 22:369, 8 Jun
1876
Child Marian Abroad
Cottage Hearth, 5:34,
Jan 1878
Hal
Atlantic, 46:124, Jul
1880
Nation, 30:240, 25 Mar
1880
Rosecroft
Cottage Hearth, 7:241,
Aug 1881
Nation, 33:99, 4 Aug
1881

Rowland, Henry Cottrell
The Countess Diane
Bookman (NY), 28:476,
Jan 1909
Germaine
Bookman (NY), 30:652,
Feb 1910
In the Service of the Princess
Bookman (NY), 31:298,
May 1910
In the Shadow
Bookman (NY), 23:414-5,
Jun 1906
The Mountain of Fears
Bookman (NY), 22:492-3,
Jan 1906
Nation, 81:449, 30 Nov
1905
Sea Scamps
Bookman (NY), 18:270,
Nov 1903
Nation, 77:326, 22 Oct
1903
To Windward
Nation, 78:356, 5 May
1904

[Rowland, K. Alice]
Fickle Fate
By Lenore [pseud.].
Picayune, 5 Feb 1893,
p. 18

Royce, Josiah
The Feud of Oakfield Creek
Nation, 44:453, 26 May 1887
Overland, 2d S, 10:102-3,
Jul 1887
Saturday Review, 63:917, 25
Jun 1887

Royle, Edwin Milton
The Silent Call
Nation, 91:36, 14 Jul 1910

Ruddy, Ella Augusta (Giles)
Bachelor Ben
Saturday Review, 40:409, 25
Sep 1875

Ruffin, M. E.
See Ruffin, Margaret Ellen
(Henry).

Ruffin, Margaret Ellen (Henry)
The North Star
Sewanee Review, 13:122-3,
Jan 1905

Runkle, Bertha
The Helmet of Navarre
Athenaeum, 3842:754, 15
Jun 1901
Bookman (NY), 13:340-1,
Jun 1901
Nation, 72:513, 27 Jun 1901
The Truth About Tolna
Bookman (NY), 23:285, May
1906

Russell, Charles Wells
The Fall of Damascus
Godey's, 97:171, Aug 1878

Russell, Ernest E.
The Reason Why
Saturday Review, 82:505, 7
Nov 1896

Russell, W. Clark
Jack's Courtship
Nation, 40:59, 15 Jan 1885
Picayune, 23 Nov 1884, [p.
7]

Russell, W. Clark
The Lady Maud, Schooner
Yacht
Nation, 35:181, 31 Aug
1882
Marooned
Picayune, 8 Sep 1889,
p. 12
A Marriage at Sea
Picayune, 26 Oct 1890,
p. 10
My Danish Sweetheart
Picayune, 12 Jul 1891,
p. 10
My Shipmate Louise
Picayune, 2 Nov 1890,
p. 14
My Watch Below
Nation, 35:289-90, 5
Oct 1882
An Ocean Free Lance
Harper's, 63:635, Sep
1881
Nation, 33:99, 4 Aug
1881
An Ocean Tragedy
Picayune, 15 Dec 1889,
p. 11
On the Fo'k'sle Head
Nation, 41:139-40, 13
Aug 1885
Round the Galley Fire
Nation, 38:58, 17 Jan
1884
A Sailor's Sweetheart
Harper's, 62:153, Dec
1880
Nation, 32:17, 6 Jan
1881
A Sea Queen
Harper's, 67:317, Jul
1883
Overland, 2d S, 2:211,
Aug 1883
Picayune, 27 May 1883,
[p. 13]
See also Tales of Our
Coast.

Russell, Fox
The Honourable Bill

Saturday Review, 98:116,
23 Jul 1904

Rutherford, Mildred
Mannie Brown and Edward
Kennedy
Picayune, 7 Feb 1897, p.
12

Ryals, John Vincent
Yankee Doodle Dixie
Picayune, 1 Mar 1891, p.
10

Ryan, Marah Ellis (Martin)
The Bondwoman
Picayune, 12 Nov 1899, II,
3
A Chance Child . . .
Picayune, 4 Apr 1897, p.
17
A Flower of France
Godey's, 129:114, Jul 1894
For the Soul of Rafael
Athenaeum, 4165:204, 24
Aug 1907
Bookman (NY), 24:52, Sep
1906
Squaw Élouise
Godey's, 125:646, Dec 1892
Picayune, 23 Oct 1892, p.
18
Told in the Hills
America, 5:561, 5 Mar 1891

S., D. T. [pseud.].
See Balch, Elizabeth.

S., M. E. W.
See Sherwood, Mary Elizabeth
(Wilson).

Safford, Mary J.
Lorelei, and Other Stories
Picayune, 16 Oct 1892, p.
15

[Sage, Robert F.]
Charette
Picayune, 31 Oct 1875, [p.
10]

Sage, William
The Claybornes
  Outlook, 71:185, 17
    May 1902
The District Attorney
  Bookman (NY), 24:52-3,
    Sep 1906
  Nation, 83:39, 12 Jul
    1906
Robert Tournay
  Outlook, 65:88, 5 May
    1900
  Picayune, 20 May 1900,
    III, 7

St. Felix, Marie [pseud.].
See Lynch, Harriet Louise
  (Husted).

Saltus, Edgar Everston
Daughters of the Rich
  Nation, 89:16, 1 Jul
    1909
Eden
  Picayune, 5 Aug 1888,
    p. 7
  Saturday Review, 66:723-
    24, 15 Dec 1888
Enthralled
  Picayune, 15 Apr 1894,
    p. 14
Madame Sapphira
  Picayune, 19 Mar 1893,
    p. 10
Mary Magdalene
  Picayune, 17 May 1891,
    p. 15; 16 Feb 1896,
    p. 16
Mr. Incoul's Misadventure
  Athenaeum, 3958:310,
    5 Sep 1903
  Epoch, 2:35, 19 Aug
    1887
  Nation, 45:402-3, 17
    Nov 1887
  Overland, 2d S, 10:327-
    28, Sep 1887
The Pace That Kills
  Atlantic, 64:720, Nov
    1889
A Transaction in Hearts

  Atlantic, 63:859, Jun 1889
  Picayune, 31 Mar 1889, p.
    7
The Truth About Tristrem
Varick
  Epoch, 3:517, 3 Aug 1888
  Picayune, 11 Mar 1888, p.
    12
  Saturday Review, 66:269-70,
    1 Sep 1888
Vanity Square
  Athenaeum, 4105:792, 30
    Jun 1906

Sampleton, Samuel [pseud.].
See Monti, Luigi.

Sanborn, Alvan Francis
Meg McIntyre's Raffle, and
  Other Stories
  Atlantic, 79:423, Mar 1897
  Picayune, 17 Jun 1897, p.
    10
Moody's Lodging House, and
  Other Tenement Sketches
  Atlantic, 77:280, Feb 1896

Sanborn, Mary Farley (Sanborn)
It Came to Pass
  Atlantic, 70:706, Nov 1892
Paula Ferris
  Cottage Hearth, 19:447, Sep
    1893
Sweet and Twenty
  America, 6:361, 25 Jun 1891
  Epoch, 10:79, 4 Sep 1891

Sanderson, James Gardner
Cornell Stories
  Bookman (NY), 8:166, Oct
    1898

"Sandette" [pseud.].
See Walsh, Marie A.

Sandys, Edwyn William
Trapper Jim
  Saturday Review, 96:146, 1
    Aug 1903

Sanford, Frederick R.
The Bursting of a Boom
Epoch, 6:791, 10 Jan
1890
Nation, 50:118, 6 Feb
1890

Sargent, Epes
Peculiar
Picayune, 27 Mar 1892,
p. 13

Satterthwait, Mrs. Elisabeth
Carpenter
A Son of the Carolinas
Picayune, 20 Nov 1898,
III, 3

Saunders, John
The Sherlocks
Harper's, 59:148, Jun
1879

Saunders, Ripley D.
John Kenadie
Nation, 75:134, 14 Aug
1902

Sauzade, John S.
Mark Gildersleeve
Picayune, 20 Apr 1873,
[p. 4]

Savage, Minot Judson
Bluffton
Cottage Hearth, 5:250,
Jul 1878
Godey's, 97:171, Aug
1878
Library Table, 4:322,
6 Jul 1878
Nation, 27:117, 22 Aug
1878
Sunday Afternoon, 2:188,
Aug 1878

Savage, Richard Henry
The Anarchist
Saturday Review, 77:695,
30 Jun 1894
Captain Landon

Picayune, 28 Jan 1900, II,
7
Checked Through
Picayune, 3 Aug 1896, p. 8
Delilah of Harlem
Picayune, 20 Aug 1893, p.
18
For a Young Queen's Bright
Eyes
Athenaeum, 3913:548, 25
Oct 1902
For Her Life
Picayune, 3 Oct 1897, p. 15
Her Cuban Sweetheart
Picayune, 9 Feb 1896, p. 11
In the House of His Friends
Saturday Review (London),
93:53, 11 Jan 1902
In the Old Chateau
Saturday Review, 79:798, 15
Jun 1895
The King's Secret
Saturday Review, 92:307, 7
Sep 1901
The Little Lady of Lagunitas
Picayune, 19 Jun 1892, p.
18
Saturday Review, 74:150, 30
Jul 1892
The Masked Venus
Overland, 2d S, 21:661, Jun
1893
Saturday Review, 75:389, 8
Apr 1893
The Midnight Passenger
Athenaeum, 3833:461, 13
Apr 1901
Miss Devereux of the Mariquita
Picayune, 14 Oct 1895, p. 9;
22 Aug 1897, p. 24
Saturday Review, 82:22, 4
Jul 1896
A Modern Corsair
Picayune, 16 May 1897, p.
21
My Official Wife
Picayune, 12 Jul 1891, p. 10
Saturday Review, 72:85-6,
18 Jul 1891
The Mystery of a Shipyard
Saturday Review, 93:606, 10

May 1902
Prince Shamyl's Wooing
  Overland, 2d S, 20:662,
    Dec 1892
  Picayune, 2 Oct 1892,
    p. 11
  Saturday Review, 74:538,
    5 Nov 1892
The Princess of Alaska
  Saturday Review, 78:224,
    25 Aug 1894
The Spider of Truxillo
  Picayune, 22 Mar 1896,
    p. 10
The White Lady of Khamin-
avatka
  Picayune, 30 Jan 1899,
    p. 10

[Savidge, Eugene Coleman]
  Wallingford
    Epoch, 1:540, 15 Jul
      1887

[Savile, Frank Mackenzie]
  John Ship, Mariner
    By Knarf Elivas [pseud.].
    Outlook, 59:789, 30
      Jul 1898

Sawtelle, Mrs. Mary P.
  The Heroine of '49
    Overland, 2d S, 19:333,
      Mar 1892

Sawyer, Edith Augusta
  Mary Cameron
    Outlook, 62:670, 22 Jul
      1899

Sawyer, Walter Leon
  A Local Habitation
    Picayune, 26 Nov 1899,
      II, 8

Schallenberger, V. [pseud.].
  See Simmons, Vesta S.

Schayer, Julia (Thompson)
von Stosch
  Tiger Lily, and Other

Stories
  Continent, 4:189, 8 Aug 1883
  Nation, 37:120, 9 Aug 1883

[Schoeffel, Florence Blackburn
(White)]
  Clarice
    By Wenona Gilman [pseud.].
    Picayune, 15 Dec 1889, p.
      11
  Miss Davis of Brooklyn
    By Wenona Gilman [pseud.].
    Saturday Review, 68:333-4,
      21 Sep 1889

Scholl, Anna McClure
  The Law of Life
    Bookman (NY), 18:300-2,
      Dec 1903

Scollard, Clinton
  The Cloistering of Ursula
    Bookman (NY), 15:176, Apr
      1902
    Saturday Review, 95:iii,
      Suppl., 10 Jan 1903
  Count Falcon of the Eyrie
    Poet-Lore, 14:138, Winter
      1903
  A Man-at-Arms
    Bookman (NY), 7:353-4, Jun
      1898
    Outlook, 59:235, 28 May
      1898
  The Vicar of the Marshes
    Nation, 91:606, 22 Dec 1910

Scott, John Reed
  Beatrix of Clare
    Saturday Review, 105:698,
      30 May 1908
  The Princess Dehra
    Saturday Review, 106:798,
      800, 26 Dec 1908
  The Woman in Question
    Atlantic, 104:680, Nov 1909

Scott, Leroy
  To Him That Hath
    Bookman (NY), 26:164-5,
      Oct 1907

269

Scott, Leroy
  The Walking Delegate
    Bookman (London), 28:172,
      Aug 1905
    Bookman (NY), 22:86-7,
      Sep 1905
    Saturday Review, 100:90,
      15 Jul 1905

Scott, Mary E.
  Keith
    Picayune, 27 Mar 1881,
      [p. 6]

[Scrimshaw, F. C.]
  The Dogs and the Fleas
    By One of the Dogs
    Picayune, 28 Jan 1894,
      p. 16

Scudder, Horace Elisha
  The Dwellers in Five-
  Sisters Court
    Harper's, 53:629, Sep
      1876
    Library Table, 1:106,
      Aug 1870
    Nation, 23:303, 16 Nov
      1876
  Stories and Romances
    Atlantic, 47:281-3, Feb
      1881
    Nation, 31:346-7, 11
      Nov 1880
    Saturday Review, 50:687,
      27 Nov 1880

[Scudder, Moses Lewis]
  Brief Honors
    Harper's, 55:789, Oct
      1877
    Nation, 25:184, 20 Sep
      1877
    Saturday Review, 44:250,
      25 Aug 1877

Scudder, Vida Dutton
  The Disciple of a Saint
    Nation, 84:567, 20 Jun
      1907
  A Listener in Babel

Poet-Lore, 15:148, Spring
  1904

[Seaman, Elizabeth Cockrane]
  The Mystery of Central Park
    By Nellie Bly [pseud.].
    Overland, 2d S, 15:434, Apr
      1890

Searing, Anne Eliza (Pidgeon)
  A Social Experiment
    Overland, 2d S, 6:550, Nov
      1885
    Saturday Review, 61:124, 23
      Jan 1886

Sears, Hamblen
  See Sears, Joseph Hamblen.

Sears, Joseph Hamblen
  None but the Brave
    Bookman (NY), 15:260, May
      1902

Seawell, Molly Elliot
  The Berkeley's and Their
  Neighbors
    Godey's, 126:232, Feb 1893
    Nation, 50:17, 2 Jan 1890
  Children of Destiny
    Cottage Hearth, 19:245, May
      1893
    Godey's, 126:771, Jun 1893
    Nation, 57:31, 13 Jul 1893
  The Fortunes of Fifi
    Athenaeum, 4165:204, 24
      Aug 1907
    Bookman (NY), 18:166-7,
      Oct 1903
  Francezka
    Bookman (NY), 16:377-8,
      Dec 1902
  The History of Lady Betty
  Stair
    Athenaeum, 3680:597, 7 May
      1898
    Bookman (NY), 6:257, Dec
      1897
    Overland, 2d S, 30:473, Nov
      1897
  The Last Duchess of Belgarde

Nation, 87:36, 9 Jul
1908
Little Jarvis
Epoch, 8:350, 2 Jan
1891
Godey's, 122:98, Jan
1891
The Loves of the Lady
Arabella
Bookman (London),
15:155, Feb 1899
Bookman (NY), 8:493,
Jan 1899
Outlook, 60:394, 8 Oct
1898
Overland, 2d S, 33:93,
Jan 1899
Saturday Review, 86:583,
29 Oct 1898
The Rock of the Lion
Outlook, 58:82, 1 Jan
1898
The Secret of Toni
Bookman (NY), 25:90,
Mar 1907
The Sprightly Romance
of Marsac
Atlantic, 79:273, Feb
1897
Picayune, 8 Nov 1896,
p. 6
A Strange, Sad Company
Bookman (NY), 4:74,
Sep 1896
Picayune, 31 May 1896,
p. 27
Throckmorton
Godey's, 121:262, Sep
1890
Nation, 51:135, 14 Aug
1890
A Virginia Cavalier
Bookman (NY), 5:261,
May 1897

Sedgwick, Anne Douglas
Amabel Channice
Nation, 87:466-7, 12
Nov 1908
North American Review,
189:784, May 1909

Times Literary Supplement,
5 Nov 1905, p. 390
The Confounding of Camelia
Bookman (London), 16:57,
May 1899
Outlook, 61:884, 15 Apr
1899
Picayune, 16 Apr 1899, II,
12
Saturday Review, 87:407-8,
1 Apr 1899
The Dull Miss Archinard
Outlook, 59:86, 7 May 1898
Picayune, 29 May 1898, II,
2
Saturday Review, 85:855, 25
Jun 1898
A Fountain Sealed
Nation, 85:446-7, 14 Nov
1907
Franklin Kane
Athenaeum, 4298:303, 12
Mar 1910
Nation, 91:315, 6 Oct 1910
Saturday Review, 109:437, 2
Apr 1910
Paths of Judgment
Atlantic, 95:693, May 1905
Times Literary Supplement,
11 Nov 1904, p. 348
The Rescue
Atlantic, 90:280, Aug 1902
The Shadow of Life
Atlantic, 99:124, Jan 1907
Bookman (London), 30:225-
26, Sep 1906
North American Review,
182:929, Jun 1906
Times Literary Supplement,
23 Mar 1906, p. 105
Valerie Upton
Bookman (London), 33:148,
Dec 1907
Saturday Review, 105:21, 4
Jan 1908
Times Literary Supplement,
7 Nov 1907, p. 341

Seeley, Charles Sumner [pseud.].
See Munday, John William.

Seely, Howard
  A Border Leander
    Cottage Hearth, 19:447,
      Sep 1893
    Nation, 57:200, 14 Sep
      1893
  The Jonah of Lucky Valley,
    and Other Stories
    Cottage Hearth, 18:255,
      Aug 1892
    Picayune, 17 Apr 1892,
      p. 22
  A Lone Star Bo-Peep, and
    Other Tales of Texas
    Ranch Life
    Overland, 2d S, 6:551,
      Nov 1885
  A Nymph of the West
    Godey's, 117:168, Aug
      1888
    Nation, 47:95-6, 2 Aug
      1888
    North American Review,
      147:357, Sep 1888
  A Ranchman's Stories
    Nation, 43:201, 2 Sep
      1886

Seemüller, Anne Moncure
  (Crane)
  Reginald Archer
    Nation, 12:325, 11 May
      1871
    Picayune, 31 Dec 1871,
      [p. 5]

Seibert, Mary Frances
  "Zulma"
    Picayune, 5 Sep 1897,
      p. 21

Seiver, Mrs. Julia A. B.
  Birkwood
    Picayune, 4 Oct 1896,
      p. 16

[Sellers, Elizabeth Jaudon]
  From 18 to 20
    Epoch, 4:103, 14 Sep
      1888

Seton, Ernest Thompson
  Animal Heroes
    Bookman (NY), 23:90-1,
      Mar 1906

Severance, Mark Sibley
  Hammersmith
    Harper's, 57:628-9, Sep
      1878
    Saturday Review, 46:126,
      27 Jul 1878
    Sunday Afternoon, 2:288,
      Sep 1878

Severn, Lawrence [pseud.].
  See Trotter, Ada M.

Shackleton, Robert
  The Great Adventurer
    Atlantic, 93:852, Jun 1904
  Toomey and Others
    Outlook, 65:137, 12 May
      1900

Shafer, Sara (Andrew)
  The Day Before Yesterday
    Atlantic, 93:852, Jun 1904
    Saturday Review, 98:276,
      27 Aug 1904

Sharkey, Mrs. Tallula K.
  Mate to Mate
    Picayune, 2 Nov 1879, [p.
      12]

Sharp, William
  Children of To-Morrow
    Picayune, 9 Mar 1890, p. 7
  The Gypsy Christ, and Other
    Tales
    Nation, 62:182, 27 Feb 1896
  See also Teuffel, Blanche
    Willis (Howard) von, and
    William Sharp.

Shaw, Adele Marie
  A Romance of the Adventurous
    Times of the First Self-Made
    American
    Overland, 2d S, 41:235,
      Mar 1903

Shaw, Adele Marie, and
Carmelita Beckwith
The Lady of the Dynamos
Bookman (NY), 29:403,
Jun 1909
Nation, 88:539, 27 May
1909

Sheldon, Charles Monroe
Edward Blake, College
Student
Saturday Review, 91:608-
609, 11 May 1901
The Heart of the World
Canadian Magazine,
25:376, Aug 1905
Malcolm Kirk
Outlook, 58:1030, 23
Apr 1898
The Reformer
Outlook, 73:224, 24
Jan 1903

Sheldon, Mrs. Georgie
[pseud.].
See Downs, Sarah Eliza-
beth (Forbush).

Sheldon, Louise (Vescelius)
An L D. B. in South
Africa
Saturday Review, 68:45-
46, 13 Jul 1889

Shelton, William Henry
A Man Without a Memory,
and Other Stories
Picayune, 21 Apr 1895,
p. 20

[Shepherd, Elizabeth Lee
(Kirkland)]
Boss
By Odette Tyler [pseud.].
Nation, 62:458, 11 Jun
1896

Sheppard, Francis Henry
Love Afloat
Picayune, 13 Jun 1875,
[p. 6]

Saturday Review, 40:281, 28
Aug 1875

Sherlock, Charles Reginald
The Red Anvil
Nation, 75:134, 14 Aug 1902

[Sherman, Charles Pomeroy]
A Bachelor's Wedding Trip
By Himself . . .
Epoch, 5:214, 3 May 1889
Picayune, 7 Apr 1889, p.
12

Sherwood, John D.
The Comic History of the
United States
Athenaeum, 2202:57, 8 Jan
1870

Sherwood, Margaret Pollock
The Coming of the Tide
Athenaeum, 4082:72, 20 Jan
1906
An Experiment in Altruism
By Elizabeth Hastings [pseud.].
Atlantic, 76:419, Sep 1895
Picayune, 26 May 1895, p.
16
Poet-Lore, 8:42, (No. 1)
1896
Henry Worthington, Idealist
Bookman (London), 17:90,
Dec 1899
Saturday Review, 89:534,
28 Apr 1900
The Princess Pourquoi
Nation, 85:474, 21 Nov 1907
A Puritan Bohemia
Atlantic, 79:137-8, Jan 1897
Bookman (NY), 4:569-70,
Feb 1897

[Sherwood, Mary Elizabeth (Wil-
son)]
The Sarcasm of Destiny
By M. E. W. S.
Godey's, 96:260, Mar 1878
Library Table, 4:160, 2
Mar 1878
Nation, 26:264, 18 Apr 1878

273

[Sherwood, Mary Elizabeth
(Wilson)]
The Transplanted Rose
Harper's, 65:967-8,
Nov 1882
Nation, 36:405, 10 May
1883
Overland, 2d S, 1:202,
Feb 1883
Picayune, 10 Jul 1892,
p. 20

Sherwood, Mary Neal
Barberine
Picayune, 22 Feb 1891,
p. 13

Shevitch, S.
See Ventura, Luigi Donato,
and S. Shevitch.

Shillaber, Benjamin Penhallow
Partingtonian Patchwork
Picayune, 27 Apr 1873,
[p. 3]

Shinn, Charles Howard
The Story of the Mine
Overland, 2d S, 29:656,
Jun 1897

Shipman, Louis Evan
Urban Dialogues
Picayune, 11 Apr 1897,
p. 25

Shippen, Edward
A Christmas at Sea
Nation, 34:59-60, 19 Jan
1882

Shirley, Penn [pseud.].
See Clarke, Sarah J.

Shirley, Philip [pseud.].
See Townsend, Mrs. Anne
Lake.

Shores, Herman
The Keys of Fate
Picayune, 16 Jun 1895,

p. 28

Shorthouse, J. Henry
Blanche, Lady Falaise
Nation, 53:472, 17 Dec 1891
The Countess Eve
Nation, 48:166, 21 Feb 1889
Sir Percival
Nation, 44:124, 10 Feb 1887
A Teacher of the Violin, and
Other Tales
Nation, 47:96, 2 Aug 1888

Shortz, Robert Packer
A Passing Emperor
Athenaeum, 3741:62, 8 Jul
1899

Shuman, Andrew
The Loves of a Lawyer
Nation, 22:84, 3 Feb 1876

Sibley, Edwin Day
Stillman Gott
Nation, 75:369, 6 Nov 1902

Sibley, Louise (Lyndon)
A Lighthouse Village
Nation, 74:117, 6 Feb 1902

Sidney, Margaret [pseud.].
See Lothrop, Harriet Mulford
(Stone).

[Sikes, Mrs. Wirt]
They Met by Chance
By Olive Logan [pseud.].
Godey's, 87:379, Oct 1873
Picayune, 3 Aug 1873, [?]

Silva, Gorham [pseud.].
See Lawrence, Elizabeth.

Simmons, Vesta S.
Green Tea
Bookman (London), 2:28,
Apr 1892
Men and Women
Saturday Review, 76:47, 8
Jul 1893
A Village Drama

By V. Schallenberger
[pseud.].
Saturday Review, 82:96,
25 Jul 1896

Sinclair, Ellery
Christie's Choice
Nation, 42:409, 13 May
1886

Sinclair, Upton
The Journal of Arthur Stir-
ling
Athenaeum, 3947:778-9,
20 Jun 1903
Bookman (NY), 17:84-5,
Mar 1903; 20:178,
Nov 1904
The Jungle
Athenaeum, 4094:446,
14 Apr 1906
Atlantic, 99:122, Jan
1907
Bookman (London), 30:75,
May 1906
Bookman (NY), 23:195-7,
Apr 1906
North American Review,
182:925-6, Jun 1906
Saturday Review, 101:661-
62, 26 May 1906
Times Literary Supple-
ment, 1 Jun 1906,
p. 201
King Midas
Overland, 2d S, 39:576,
Jan 1902
Saturday Review, 103:22,
5 Jan 1907
Manassas
Nation, 79:441, 1 Dec
1904
Saturday Review, 99:149-
50, 4 Feb 1905
The Metropolis
Athenaeum, 4197:413,
4 Apr 1908
Bookman (NY), 27:121-3,
Apr 1908
Nation, 86:263-4, 19
Mar 1908

Outlook, 88:838, 11 Apr 1908
Saturday Review, 105:409,
28 Mar 1908
Times Literary Supplement,
12 Mar 1908, p. 85
The Moneychangers
Bookman (NY), 28:111-5,
Oct 1908
Nation, 87:389, 22 Oct 1908
Saturday Review, 106:581-2,
7 Nov 1908
Prince Hagen
Athenaeum, 4148:502, 27
Apr 1907
Saturday Review, 96:464,
466, 10 Oct 1903
Samuel the Seeker
Athenaeum, 4317:93-4, 23
Jul 1910
Bookman (London), 38:268,
Sep 1910
Nation, 90:629, 23 Jun 1910
Saturday Review, 110:365,
17 Sep 1910
Times Literary Supplement,
7 Jul 1910, p. 242

Six of One, by Half a Dozen of
Another
By Harriet Beecher Stowe, Ade-
line D. T. Whitney, Lucretia
P. Hale, Frederic W. Loring,
Frederic B. Perkins, Ed-
ward E. Hale
Athenaeum, 2342:332-3, 14
Sep 1872
Godey's, 85:467, Nov 1872
Harper's, 45:624, Sep 1872
Saturday Review, 34:260, 24
Aug 1872

Skeel, Adelaide
See Kelley, Adelaide (Skell),
and William H. Brearley.

Skene, Alexander Johnson Chal-
mers
True to Themselves
Picayune, 12 Sep 1897, p.
20

Picayune, 17 Jan 1892,
p. 2

Smith, Edgar Maurice
A Daughter of Humanity
Picayune, 26 Jan 1896,
p. 16

[Smith, Elizabeth Thomas
(Meade)]
Bel Marjory
By L. T. Meade [pseud.].
Harper's, 59:148, Jun
1879
A Girl of the People
By L. T. Meade [pseud.].
Picayune, 18 May 1890,
p. 2
A Handful of Silver
By L. T. Meade [pseud.].
Outlook, 59:386, 11
Jun 1898
The Honorable Miss
By L. T. Meade [pseud.].
Picayune, 14 Dec 1890,
p. 12
Jill
By L. T. Meade [pseud.].
Picayune, 23 Aug 1896,
p. 15
A Life for a Love
By L. T. Meade [pseud.].
Picayune, 31 May 1891,
p. 12

[Smith, Fannie N.]
Shiftless Folks
By Christabel Goldsmith
[pseud.].
Godey's, 91:190, Aug
1875

Smith, Francis Hopkinson
At Close Range
Athenaeum, 4054:44,
8 Jul 1905
Nation, 80:379, 11 May
1905
Outlook, 79:912, 8 Apr
1905
Saturday Review, 100:186,

5 Aug 1905
Caleb West, Master Diver
Athenaeum, 3706:641, 5
Nov 1898
Atlantic, 83:282-3, Feb 1899
Bookman (London), 15:25,
Oct 1898
Bookman (NY), 7:346-7, Jun
1898
Nation, 67:265, 6 Oct 1898
Outlook, 58:1077, 30 Apr
1898
Saturday Review, 86:418, 17
Sep 1898
Colonel Carter of Cartersville
Atlantic, 69:139, Jan 1892
Cosmopolitan, 11:384, Jul
1891
Epoch, 9:302, 12 Jun 1891
Nation, 52:483, 11 Jun 1891
Overland, 2d S, 18:440, Oct
1891
Picayune, 31 May 1891, p.
12
Saturday Review, 72:113-4,
25 Jul 1891
Colonel Carter's Christmas
Overland, 2d S, 42:554, Dec
1903
A Day at Laguerre's, and Other
Days
Athenaeum, 3376:58-9, 9 Jul
1892
Nation, 54:451, 16 Jun 1892
Saturday Review, 73:755, 25
Jun 1892
The Fortunes of Oliver Horn
Athenaeum, 3914:581-2, 1
Nov 1902
Bookman (London), 23:94,
Dec 1902
Bookman (NY), 16:275-6,
Nov 1902
Nation, 75:369, 6 Nov 1902
Saturday Review, 95:206, 14
Feb 1903
Forty Minutes Late
Nation, 89:461, 11 Nov 1909
A Gentleman Vagabond, and
Some Others
Atlantic, 77:266-7, Feb 1896

Smith, Francis Hopkinson
 Bookman (London),
  10:174, Sep 1896
 Bookman (NY), 2:531,
  Feb 1896
 Picayune, 1 Dec 1895,
  p. 17
The Novels, Stories, and
 Sketches of . . . [Bea-
 con Edition]
 Nation, 78:235, 24 Mar
  1904
The Other Fellow
 Nation, 69:396, 23 Nov
  1899
 Overland, 2d S, 35:91,
  Jan 1900
 Picayune, 4 Dec 1899,
  p. 10
Peter
 Bookman (NY), 28:153,
  Oct 1908
The Romance of an Old-
 Fashioned Gentleman
 Nation, 85:446, 14 Nov
  1907
The Tides of Barnegat
 Athenaeum, 4124:578,
  10 Nov 1906
 Bookman (London), 31:96,
  Nov 1906
 Bookman (NY), 24:55-6,
  Sep 1906
 Nation, 83:188, 30 Aug
  1906
Tom Grogan
 Athenaeum, 3582:804,
  20 Jun 1896
 Bookman (London),
  10:175, Sep 1896
 Bookman (NY), 3:264-6,
  May 1896
 Godey's, 133:[94]-5,
  Jul 1896
 Nation, 63:180, 3 Sep
  1896
 Overland, 2d S, 28:235,
  Aug 1896
 Picayune, 3 May 1896,
  p. 7
 Saturday Review, 82:200,

  22 Aug 1896
The Underdog
 Atlantic, 92:282, Aug 1903
 Nation, 77:77, 23 Jul 1903
The Veiled Lady, and Other
 Men and Women
 Nation, 84:501, 30 May
  1907
The Wood Fire in No. 3
 Athenaeum, 4123:545, 3
  Nov 1906
 Overland, 2d S, 46:592,
  Dec 1905

Smith, Gertrude
The Boys of Marmiton Prairie
 Outlook, 63:604, 4 Nov 1899
Dedora Heywood
 Picayune, 30 Mar 1896, p. 8
The Rousing of Mrs. Potter,
 and Other Stories
 By Jane Nelson [pseud.].
 Atlantic, 75:423-4, Mar
  1895
 Bookman (London), 5:190-1,
  Mar 1894
 Cottage Hearth, 20:250, May
  1894
 Nation, 58:413, 31 May 1894

Smith, Harry James
Amédée's Son
 Nation, 87:341, 8 Oct 1908
Enchanted Ground
 Athenaeum, 4330:484, 22
  Oct 1910
 Bookman (London), 39:105,
  Nov 1910
 Bookman (NY), 32:174, Oct
  1910

[Smith, Helen Butler]
A Modern Jacob
 By Hester Stuart [pseud.].
 Cottage Hearth, 14:262, Aug
  1888
 Picayune, 2 Sep 1888, p. 7

Smith, Mrs. J. Gregory
 See Smith, Ann Eliza (Brainerd).

Smith, Jabez Burritt
"High Joe"
Outlook, 65:411, 16
Jun 1900

Smith, Johnston [pseud.].
See Crane, Stephen.

Smith, Joseph Emerson
Oakridge
Saturday Review, 39:837,
26 Jun 1875

[Smith, Mrs. Julie P.]
Chris and Otho
Godey's, 81:559, Dec
1870
Overland, 5:486-7,
Nov 1870
The Married Belle
Godey's, 85:544, Dec
1872
Picayune, 1 May 1892,
p. 12
An Ugly Heroine
By Christine Faber [pseud.]
Picayune, 12 May 1883,
[p. 15]
Widow Goldsmith's Daughter
Godey's, 80:291, Mar
1870
Nation, 10:325, 19 May
1870
The Widower
Picayune, 25 Oct 1891,
p. 3

[Smith, Mary Prudence
(Wells)]
Jolly Good Times
By P. Thorne [pseud.].
Saturday Review, 40:821,
25 Dec 1875
The Young Puritans in
Captivity
Picayune, 12 Nov 1899,
II, 3

Smith, Mary Stuart (Harrison)
Lang Syne
Picayune, 5 May 1889,

p. 10

Smith, Minna Caroline
Mary Paget
Outlook, 64:417, 17 Feb 1900

Smith, Nora Archibald
Under the Cactus Flag
Picayune, 22 Oct 1899, II, 6

Smith, Saqui
Back from the Dead
Picayune, 21 Feb 1892, p.
10
The Serpent Tempted Her
Saturday Review, 68:21-2,
6 Jun 1889

Smith, William Hawley
The Promoters
Overland, 2d S, 44:480-1,
Oct 1904

Snow, Chauncey Edgar
Sister Gratia
Picayune, 16 Jun 1895, p.
28

Sola [pseud.].
See Anderson, Olive Santa
Louise.

Sommers, Lillian E.
Jerome Leaster, of Roderick,
Leaster & Co.
Atlantic, 67:710-1, May 1891

Southgate, Horatio
The Cross Above the Crescent
Saturday Review, 44:787, 22
Dec 1877

Southwick, Albert Plympton
The Catherwood Mystery
Cottage Hearth, 18:255, Aug
1892
Godey's, 125:520, Nov 1892
Picayune, 17 Jul 1892, p. 13
13

Southworth, Emma Dorothy
Eliza (Nevitte)
A Beautiful Fiend
  Godey's, 78:285, Mar
    1874
The Bride's Fate
  Picayune, 8 Mar 1885,
    [p. 8]; 18 Aug 1889,
    p. 11
Cruel as the Grave
  Picayune, 2 Apr 1871,
    [p. 9]
The Curse of Clifton
  Cottage Hearth, 12:298,
    Sep 1886
  Godey's, 113:293, Sep
    1886
  Picayune, 15 Aug 1886,
    p. 6
The Discarded Daughter
  Picayune, 23 Dec 1888,
    p. 14
"Em"
  Godey's, 126:364, Mar
    1893
Em's Husband
  Picayune, 15 Jan 1893,
    p. 20
The Family Doom
  Picayune, 5 Aug 1888,
    p. 7
The Fatal Marriage
  Picayune, 19 Mar 1882,
    [p. 16]
The Fatal Secret
  Picayune, 8 Jul 1894,
    p. 7
The Fortune Seeker
  Godey's, 90:477, May
    1875
A Gipsey's Prophecy
  Cottage Hearth, 12:368,
    Nov 1886
  Godey's, 113:391, Oct
    1886
  Picayune, 19 Sep 1886,
    p. 5
Ishmael
  Godey's, 108:493, May
    1884
  Picayune, 6 Jan 1884,

  [p. 11]
  Saturday Review, 46:540-1,
    26 Oct 1878
The Last Heir of Linlithgow
  Godey's, 84:480, May 1872
The Last Heiress
  Overland, 2d S, 21:662, Jun
    1893
Miriam
  Cottage Hearth, 16:161, May
    1890
  Godey's, 90:92, Jan 1875
The Missing Bride
  Cottage Hearth, 12:298, Sep
    1886
  Godey's, 113:293, Sep 1886;
    120:353, Apr 1890
  Picayune, 1 Aug 1886, p.
    15; 23 Feb 1890, p. 14
The Mother-in-Law
  Godey's, 95:525, Dec 1877
  Library Table, 3:8, 27 Oct
    1877
  Picayune, 21 Oct 1877, [p.
    9]
The Mystery of Dark Hollow
  Godey's, 91:284, Sep 1875
  Picayune, 27 Jun 1875, [p.
    9]
A Noble Lord
  Picayune, 12 May 1872, [p.
    10]
The Phantom Wedding
  Picayune, 17 Mar 1878, [p.
    11]
The Red Hill Tragedy
  Godey's, 96:259, Mar 1878
  Picayune, 13 Jan 1878, [p.
    12]
Retribution
  Picayune, 17 Nov 1889, p.
    11; 8 Dec 1889, p. 14
Self-Raised
  Picayune, 28 Sep 1884, [p.
    10]
  Saturday Review, 42:276, 26
    Aug 1876
Sybil Brotherton
  Picayune, 13 Apr 1879, [p.
    12]
Tried for Her Life

Godey's, 73:89, Jul
1871
Picayune, 21 May 1871,
[p. 11]; 23 Sep 1888,
p. 7
Victor's Triumph
Godey's, 78:565, Jun
1874
The Wife's Victory
Picayune, 3 Jun 1894,
p. 10

Spangler, Helen King
The Physician's Wife
Atlantic, 36:630, Nov
1875

Sparhawk, Frances Campbell
A Chronicle of Conquest
Cottage Hearth, 16:161,
May 1890
Overland, 2d S, 16:440,
Oct 1890
A Lazy Man's Work
Atlantic, 47:861, Jun
1881
Cottage Hearth, 8:133,
Apr 1882
Nation, 32:302, 28 Apr
1881
Onoqua
Cottage Hearth, 18:255,
Aug 1892
Godey's, 125:90, Jul
1892
Picayune, 29 May 1892,
p. 13

Spearman, Frank Hamilton
The Close of the Day
Outlook, 76:429, 13
Feb 1904
The Daughter of a Magnate
Nation, 77:389, 12 Nov
1903
Doctor Bryson
Nation, 75:448, 4 Dec
1902
The Nerve of Foley
Outlook, 64:597, 10
Mar 1900

Picayune, 18 Mar 1900, II,
5
Whispering Smith
Bookman (NY), 24:160-1,
· Oct 1906

Spears, John Randolph
The Fugitive
Outlook, 62:216, 23 Sep 1899
The Port of the Missing Ships
and Other Stories
Godey's, 135:[331], Sep 1897
Overland, 2d S, 30:95, Jul
1897
Picayune, 30 May 1897, p.
16

Specht, Emma E. H.
Alfrieda
Picayune, 23 Nov 1890, p.
10

Spencer, Mrs. George E. [pseud.].
See Spencer, William Loring
(Nuñez).

[Spencer, William Loring (Nuñez)]
Calamity Jane
By Mrs. George E. Spencer
[pseud.].
Picayune, 7 Aug 1887, p. 6
Dennis Day, Carpet-Bagger
By Mrs. George E. Spencer
[pseud.].
Picayune, 10 Jul 1887, p. 5
A Plucky One
By Mrs. George E. Spencer
[pseud.].
Picayune, 21 Nov 1886, p.
11
Salt-Lake Fruit
"By an American."
Picayune, 21 Jun 1891, p.
12

Spenser, Mary Clare
The Benefit of the Doubt
Overland, 2d S, 1:202, Feb
1883
Brinka
Epoch, 3:457, 13 Jul 1888

The Spinners' Book of Fiction
  By Gertrude Atherton, Mary
  Austin, Geraldine Bonner,
  Mary Halleck Foote, Eleanor
  Gates, James Hopper, Jack
  London, Bailey Millard,
  Miriam Michelson, W.
  C. Morrow, Frank Norris,
  Henry Milner Rideout,
  Charles Warren Stoddard,
  Isabel Strong, Richard
  Walton Tully, and Her-
  man Whitaker
    Nation, 86:107, 30 Jan
      1908

Spofford, Harriet Elizabeth
(Prescott)
  Hester Stanley at St. Mark's
    Nation, 36:41, 11 Jan
      1883
  An Inheritance
    Picayune, 9 May 1897,
      p. 17
  A Lost Jewel
    Overland, 2d S, 17:662,
      Jun 1891
  The Maid He Married
    Bookman (NY), 10:90,
      Sep 1899
  The Marquis of Carabas
    Continent, 2:285, 6
      Sep 1882
  A Master Spirit
    Atlantic, 78:138, Jul
      1896
  New England Legends
    Harper's, 43:937, Nov
      1871
  Priscilla's Love-Story
    Outlook, 59:86, 7 May
      1898
  The Thief in the Night
    Athenaeum, 2329:748,
      15 Jun 1872
    Atlantic, 29:626, May
      1872
    Godey's, 84:482, May
      1872
    Harper's, 45:139, Jun
      1872

Nation, 14:310, 9 May 1872
Picayune, 31 Mar 1872, [p.
  16]
See also Not Pretty, but Precious.

[Sprague, Mary Aplin]
  An Earnest Trifler
    Good Company, 4:381-2,
      (No. 4) 1879
    Nation, 30:64-5, 22 Jan 1880

Springer, Rebecca (Ruter)
  Beechwood
    Nation, 16:221, 27 Mar 1873
    Picayune, 26 Jan 1873, [p.
      10]
  Self
    Nation, 32:227, 31 Mar 1881
    Picayune, 9 Jan 1881, [p.
      10]

Spurr, George Graham
  The Land of Gold
    Saturday Review, 52:839, 31
      Dec 1881

"Staats" [pseud.].
  See Staats, William.

[Staats, William]
  A Tight Squeeze
    By "Staats" [pseud.].
      Continent, 2:413, 4 Oct 1882
      Cottage Hearth, 8:327, Oct
        1882
      Nation, 35:290, 5 Oct 1882

[Stabler, Mrs. Jennie Latham]
  Edith's Mistake
    By Jennie Woodville [pseud.].
      Picayune, 3 Dec 1871, [?]
      Saturday Review, 39:296, 27
        Feb 1875
  Left to Herself
    By Jennie Woodville [pseud.].
      Godey's, 84:287, Mar 1872

Stanley, Hiram Alonzo
  The Backwoodsman
    Nation, 74:195, 6 Mar 1902

Outlook, 69:138, 14
Sep 1901

Stark, Harriet
The Bacillus of Beauty
Outlook, 66:369, 6 Oct
1900

Stearns, Winfrid Alden
Wrecked on Labrador
Picayune, 9 Dec 1888,
p. 10

[Stebbins, Sarah (Bridges)]
He and I
Godey's, 96:83, Jan
1878

Stedman, S. O.
Allen Bay
Nation, 23:139, 31 Jul
1876
Picayune, 13 Aug 1876,
[p. 4]

Steele, James William
Cuban Sketches
Picayune, 29 Nov 1885,
p. 10
Fur, Feathers and Fuzz
Picayune, 23 Feb 1890,
p. 14

Steell, Willis
Isidra
Cottage Hearth, 14:226,
Jul 1888
Epoch, 3:257, 4 May
1888
Nation, 47:13, 5 Jul
1888
Overland, 2d S, 12:215-
16, Aug 1888
Mortal Lips
Godey's, 121:84, Jul
1890

Steffens, Josephine Bontecou
Letitia Berkeley, A. M.
Bookman (NY), 10:91,
Sep 1899

Stein, Gertrude
Three Lives
Nation, 90:65, 20 Jan 1910

Stella [pseud.].
See Lewis, Estelle Anna
Blanche (Robinson).

Stephens, Mrs. Ann S.
See Stephens, Ann Sophia
(Winterbotham).

Stephens, Ann Sophia (Winter-
botham)
Bellehood and Bondage
Godey's, 87:567, Dec 1873
Picayune, 12 Oct 1873, [p.
5]
Bertha's Engagement
Godey's, 91:189, Aug 1875
The Curse of Gold
Picayune, 8 Jul 1894, p. 7
Lord Hope's Choice
Picayune, 27 Apr 1873, [p.
3]
Married in Haste
Godey's, 81:376, Oct 1870
Picayune, 26 Aug 1894, p.
16
Saturday Review, 31:126, 28
Jan 1871
A Noble Woman
Godey's, 84:287, Mar 1872
Picayune, 31 Dec 1871, [p.
5]
Norston's Rest
Godey's, 95:261, Sep 1877
Picayune, 17 Jun 1877, [p.
11]
The Old Countess
Godey's, 87:188, Aug 1873
Picayune, 1 Jun 1873, [p.
2]
Palaces and Prisons
Godey's, 73:570, Dec 1871
Picayune, 8 Oct 1871, [p. 3]
Phemie Frost's Experiences
Godey's, 78:565, Jun 1874
The Reigning Belle
Godey's, 85:370, Oct 1872
Picayune, 29 Mar 1885, [p. 5]

Stephens, Robert Neilson
The Bright Face of Danger
Saturday Review, 98:338,
10 Sep 1904
Captain Ravenshaw
Athenaeum, 3885:463,
12 Apr 1902
Canadian Magazine,
17:580, Oct 1901
Overland, 2d S, 39:734,
Mar 1902
The Continental Dragoon
Athenaeum, 3853:280,
31 Aug 1901
Picayune, 22 May 1898,
II, 2
An Enemy to the King
Bookman (London), 15:25,
Oct 1898
Picayune, 26 Dec 1897,
p. 9
A Gentleman Player
Picayune, 9 Jul 1899,
III, 3
Saturday Review, 88:495,
14 Oct 1899
Philip Winwood
Athenaeum, 3827:272,
2 Mar 1901
Bookman (London), 19:61,
Nov 1900
Picayune, 3 Jun 1900,
III, 7
Saturday Review, 90:592,
10 Nov 1900

_____, and G. H. West-
ley
Clementina's Highwayman
Saturday Review,
105:730, 6 Jun 1908

Stephenson, Henry Thew
Patroon Van Volkenberg
Canadian Magazine,
16:293, Jan 1901
Picayune, 25 Nov 1900,
II, 7

Stephenson, Nathaniel Wright
The Beautiful Mrs. Moulton

Bookman (NY), 16:484-5,
Jan 1903
Saturday Review, 95:i,
Suppl. , 10 Jan 1903
Sewanee Review, 11:113,
Jan 1903
Eleanor Dayton
Bookman (NY), 18:165-6,
Oct 1903
Outlook, 75:232, 26 Sep
1903
Saturday Review, 96:678,
28 Nov 1903
Sewanee Review, 11:503-4,
Oct 1903
They That Took the Sword
Athenaeum, 3850:183, 10
Aug 1901
Sewanee Review, 9:494-6,
Oct 1901; 11:357, Jul
1903

Sterne, Stuart [pseud.].
See Bloede, Gertrude.

Stetson, Charlotte (Perkins)
See Gilman, Charlotte (Perkins) Stetson.

Stetson, Grace Ellery (Channing)
Sea Drift
Outlook, 62:720, 29 Jul 1899
The Sister of a Saint, and Oth-
er Stories
Nation, 62:458, 11 Jun 1896

[Stevens, Charles McClellan]
The Adventures of Uncle Jere-
miah and Family at the Great
Fair
By "Quondam" [pseud.].
Picayune, 9 Jul 1893, p. 24

Stevens, Mary Fletcher
By Subtle Fragrance Held
Atlantic, 71:849, Jun 1893

Stevenson, Burton Egbert
Affairs of State
Saturday Review, 104:306,
7 Sep 1907

The Heritage
  Outlook, 72:656, 15
    Nov 1902
The Holladay Case
  Nation, 77:508, 24 Dec
    1903
The Marathon Mystery
  Bookman (NY), 20:560-
    61, Feb 1905

Stevenson, Edward Irenaeus
Prime
  Janus
    Atlantic, 64:129, Jul
      1889

Stewart, Charles D.
  The Fugitive Blacksmith
    Bookman (London),
      28:68-9, May 1905
    Bookman (NY), 21:544-
      45, Jul 1905
  Partners of Providence
    Athenaeum, 4174:514,
      26 Oct 1907
    Bookman (NY), 25:299-
      300, Apr 1907
    Outlook, 86:475, 29
      Jun 1907

Stewart, Mary
  Unspotted from the World
    Outlook, 58:731, 19
      Mar 1898

Stickney, Mary Etta (Smith)
  Brown of Lost River
    Nation, 71:117, 9 Aug
      1900
    Picayune, 12 Aug 1900,
      II, 8

[Stimson, Frederic Jesup]
  The Crime of Henry Vane
    By J. S. of Dale [pseud.].
    Atlantic, 54:417-8, Sep
      1884
    Continent, 6:127, (No.
      4) 1884
    Godey's, 109:211, Aug
      1884

Nation, 39:95-6, 31 Jul 1884
Saturday Review, 58:283-4,
  30 Aug 1884; 58:443, 4
    Oct 1884
First Harvests
  Nation, 48:165, 21 Feb 1889
  Picayune, 16 Dec 1888, p.
    14
Guerndale
  By J. S. of Dale [pseud.].
  Continent, 2:27, 12 Jul 1882
  Nation, 35:79, 27 Jul 1882
  Saturday Review, 54:422, 23
    Sep 1882
In Cure of Her Soul
  Nation, 83:59-60, 19 Jul
    1906
In the Three Zones
  Picayune, 5 Mar 1893, p.
    16
Jethro Bacon, and the Weaker
Sex
  Nation, 75:486, 18 Dec 1902
King Noanett
  By J. S. of Dale [pseud.].
  Bookman (NY), 4:54-6, Sep
    1896
  Godey's, 134:204, Feb 1897
  Nation, 64:400, 27 May 1897
Mrs. Knollys, and Other Sto-
ries
  Athenaeum, 3745:189, 5 Aug
    1899
  Nation, 66:447, 9 Jun 1898
Pirate Gold
  Nation, 63:180, 3 Sep 1896
The Residuary Legatee
  Epoch, 4:71-2, 31 Aug 1888
  Godey's, 117:169, Aug 1888
  Nation, 47:274, 4 Oct 1888
  North American Review,
    147:238, Aug 1888
The Sentimental Calendar
  By J. S. of Dale [pseud.].
  Nation, 44:300, 7 Apr 1887
See also The King's Men.

Stimpson, Herbert Baird
  The Regeneration
    Picayune, 4 Oct 1896, p. 16
  The Tory Maid

Stimpson, Herbert Baird
  Bookman (NY), 10:283,
    Nov 1899
  Overland, 2d S, 34:476,
    Nov 1899

[Stimtz, Stephen Conrad]
  Mrs. Jim and Mrs. Jimmie
  By Stephen Conrad [pseud.].
    Bookman (London), 29:38,
      Oct 1905
    Overland, 2d S, 46:591,
      Dec 1905

Stirling, A. [pseud.].
  See Kimball, Annie Lydia
    (McPhail).

Stockton, Frank Richard
  The Adventures of Captain
  Horn
    Atlantic, 76:554-5, Oct
      1895
    Bookman (London), 8:117,
      Jul 1895
    Bookman (NY), 1:410-1,
      Jul 1895
    Nation, 61:244, 3 Oct
      1895
    Overland, 2d S, 26:677,
      Dec 1895
    Saturday Review, 80:54,
      13 Jul 1895; 87:696,
      3 Jun 1899
  Afield and Afloat
    Athenaeum, 3838:626,
      18 May 1901
    Bookman (London), 20:59,
      May 1901
    Outlook, 66:278, 29 Sep
      1900
    Picayune, 14 Oct 1900,
      II, 8
    Saturday Review, 91:676-
      77, 25 May 1901
  Amos Kilbright . . . with
  Other Stories
    Athenaeum, 3196:113-4,
      26 Jan 1889
    Atlantic, 63:141, Jan
      1889

    Epoch, 4:215, 26 Oct 1888
    Nation, 47:482, 13 Dec 1888
    Picayune, 9 Jun 1889, p. 13
    Saturday Review, 67:353, 23
      Mar 1889
  Ardis Claverden
    Athenaeum, 3294:814, 13
      Dec 1890
    Atlantic, 74:416, Sep 1894
    Outlook, 64:415, 17 Feb 1900
    Picayune, 2 Nov 1890, p. 14
    Saturday Review, 70:563-4,
      15 Nov 1890
  The Associate Hermits
    Athenaeum, 3745:188-9, 5
      Aug 1899
    Saturday Review, 86:890-1,
      31 Dec 1898
  The Bee-Man of Orn, and Oth-
  er Fanciful Tales
    Athenaeum, 3195:81-2, 19
      Jan 1889
    Nation, 45:484-5, 15 Dec
      1887
    Overland, 2d S, 11:436, Apr
      1888
    Picayune, 30 Oct 1887, p.
      14
    Saturday Review, 66:713-4,
      15 Dec 1888
  A Bicycle of Cathay
    Athenaeum, 3831:399, 30
      Mar 1901
    Bookman (London), 20:59,
      May 1901
    Picayune, 2 Dec 1900, II, 9
  A Borrowed Month
    Saturday Review, 64:296,
      27 Aug 1887
  Buccaneers and Pirates of Our
  Coasts
    Athenaeum, 3745:188-9, 5
      Aug 1899
    Picayune, 20 Nov 1898, III,
      3
  Captain Chap
    Godey's, 134:94, Jan 1897
    Picayune, 22 Nov 1896, p.
      10
  The Captain's Toll-Gate
    Athenaeum, 3966:577-8,

31 Oct 1903

Nation, 77:77-8, 23 Jul
1903

Saturday Review, 96:x,
Suppl., 17 Oct 1903

Times Literary Supple-
ment, 9 Oct 1903,
p. 288

The Casting Away of Mrs.
Lecks and Mrs. Aleshine

Nation, 43:547-8, 30
Dec 1886

Picayune, 31 Oct 1886,
p. 9

Sewanee Review, 11:476,
Oct 1903

A Chosen Few Short Sto-
ries

Atlantic, 77:131, Jan
1896

The Clocks of Rondaine,
and Other Stories

Saturday Review, 74:779,
31 Dec 1892

The Dusantes

Nation, 46:304, 12 Apr
1888

North American Review,
147:479, Oct 1888

Picayune, 26 Feb 1888,
p. 14

Saturday Review, 65:425,
7 Apr 1888

Sewanee Review, 11:476,
Oct 1903

The Floating Prince, and
Other Fairy Tales

Athenaeum, 3254:304,
8 Mar 1890

Saturday Review, 69:355,
22 Mar 1890

The Girl at Cobhurst

Athenaeum, 3689:63,
9 Jul 1898

Outlook, 59:134, 14
May 1898

Picayune, 15 May 1898,
III, 2

Saturday Review, 85:664,
14 May 1898

The Great Stone of Sardis

Saturday Review, 86:119,
23 Jul 1898

The Great War Syndicate

Saturday Review, 67:191-2,
16 Feb 1889

The House of Martha

Athenaeum, 3355:210-1, 13
Feb 1892

Epoch, 11:78, 4 Mar 1892

Nation, 54:114, 11 Feb 1892

Saturday Review, 72:533-4,
7 Nov 1891

The Hundredth Man

Athenaeum, 3143:83, 21 Jan
1888

Epoch, 2:457, 13 Jan 1888

Nation, 45:485, 15 Dec 1887

Picayune, 15 Jan 1888, p.
10

Saturday Review, 65:19-20,
7 Jan 1888

Sewanee Review, 11:476,
Oct 1903

John Gayther's Garden, and the
Stories Told Therein

Nation, 75:486, 18 Dec 1902

Saturday Review, 95:492-3,
18 Apr 1903

Kate Bonnet

Athenaeum, 3883:396, 29
Mar 1902

Bookman (London), 22:31,
Apr 1902

Bookman (NY), 14:256-7,
May 1902

Nation, 74:258, 27 Mar 1902

Overland, 2d S, 39:917, May
1902

Saturday Review, 93:563-4,
3 May 1902

Times Literary Supplement,
21 Mar 1902, p. 77

The Lady or the Tiger? and
Other Stories

Athenaeum, 2975:560, 1
Nov 1884

Godey's, 109:315, Sep 1884

Manhattan, 4:121-2, Jul
1884

Picayune, 22 Jun 1884, [p.
9]

22
The Vizier of the Two-
horned Alexander
    Athenaeum, 3765:862,
        23 Dec 1899
    Overland, 2d S, 35:91,
        Jan 1900
    Picayune, 24 Dec 1899,
        II, 7
    Saturday Review, 88:ix-
        x, Suppl. , 9 Dec 1899
The Watchmaker's Wife,
    and Other Stories
    Atlantic, 73:569, Apr
        1894
    Godey's, 128:234, Feb
        1894
    Nation, 58:277, 12 Apr
        1894
What Might Have Been Ex-
    pected
    Saturday Review, 38:840,
        26 Dec 1874; 68:721,
        21 Dec 1889
The Young Master of Hyson
    Hall
    Athenaeum, 3765:862,
        23 Dec 1899
    Picayune, 26 Nov 1899,
        II, 8
    Saturday Review, 88:x,
        Suppl. , 9 Dec 1899

Stockton, John P. , Jr.
Zaphra
    Picayune, 31 Mar 1895,
        p. 10

[Stockton, Louise]
Dorothea
    Continent, 2:91, 26 Jul
        1882
    Nation, 34:505, 15 Jun
        1882

Stoddard, Charles Warren
The Island of Tranquil
    Delights
    Overland, 2d S, 44:638,
        Dec 1904
The Pleasures of His

Company
    Overland, 2d S, 42:364-6,
        Oct 1903
South Sea Idylls
    Godey's, 125:645, Dec 1892
    Nation, 17:411, 18 Dec 1873
    Saturday Review, 36:712, 29
        Nov 1873
See also The Spinners' Book of
    Fiction.

Stoddard, Elizabeth Drew (Bar-
stow).
The Morgesons
    Atlantic, 88:848-50, Dec
        1901
    Epoch, 6:628-9, 1 Nov 1889
    Harper's, 78:987, May 1889
    Picayune, 1 Sep 1889, p. 7
Temple House
    Atlantic, 64:126-9, Jul 1889;
        88:848-50, Dec 1901
    Bookman (NY), 16:260-3,
        Nov 1902
    Epoch, 4:290, 23 Nov 1888
    Harper's, 78:987, May 1889
    Nation, 48:272-3, 28 Mar
        1889
Two Men
    Atlantic, 88:848-50, Dec 1901
    Epoch, 4:173-4, 12 Oct 1888
    Harper's, 78:987, May 1889
    Nation, 47:118, 9 Aug 1888
    Picayune, 1 Jul 1888, p. 3

Stoddard, William Osborn
Among the Lakes
    Picayune, 16 Sep 1883, [p.
        5]
Chumley's Post
    Athenaeum, 3611:46, 9 Jan
        1897
Esau Hardery
    Saturday Review, 53:378, 25
        Mar 1882
Guert Ten Eyck
    Godey's, 128:106, Jan 1894
The Heart of It
    Atlantic, 46:122-3, Jul 1880
    Nation, 30:313, 22 Apr 1880
    Picayune, 31 Oct 1897, p. 11

Stoddard, William Osborn
The Noank's Log
    Picayune, 22 Jul 1900,
        II, 8
On the Old Frontier
    Bookman (London), 7:11,
        Suppl., Dec 1894
    Saturday Review, 78:690,
        22 Dec 1894
Red Beauty
    Picayune, 28 Nov 1886,
        p. 7
Ulric the Jarl
    Outlook, 63:742, 25
        Nov 1899
    Picayune, 12 Nov 1899,
        II, 3
Winter Fun
    Athenaeum, 3035:837-8,
        26 Dec 1885

Stone, Mary E.
    See Bassett, Mary E.
    (Stone).

Stone, Mrs. C. H.
One of "Berrian's" Novels
    America, 5:50, 9 Oct
        1890
    Epoch, 8:335-6, 26
        Dec 1890
    Overland, 2d S, 17:659,
        Jun 1891

Stories of the South
    By Thomas Nelson Page,
    Harrison Robertson, Joel
    C. Harris, and Re-
    becca Harding Davis
    Picayune, 16 Jul 1893,
        p. 19

Story, James P.
Choisy
    Harper's, 45:624-5,
        Sep 1872
    Nation, 14:424, 27 Jun
        1872

Story, William Wetmore
Fiammetta

    Overland, 2d S, 7:323, Mar
        1886

Stowe, Harriet Elizabeth
(Beecher)
Betty's Bright Idea
    Picayune, 26 Mar 1876, [p.
        6]
Deacon Pitkin's Farm
    Picayune, 26 Mar 1876, [p.
        6]
The First Christmas of New
England
    Picayune, 26 Mar 1876, [p.
        6]
My Wife and I
    Atlantic, 29:110-1, Jan 1872
    Godey's, 84:98, Jan 1872
    Harper's, 44:462-3, Feb
        1872
    Nation, 13:324-5, 16 Nov
        1871
    Saturday Review, 32:860,
        30 Dec 1871
Oldtown Fireside Stories
    Atlantic, 29:363, 365-6,
        Mar 1872
Palmetto Leaves
    Athenaeum, 2381:759, 14
        Jun 1873
    Overland, 10:583, Jun 1873
    Saturday Review, 35:697, 24
        May 1873
Pink and White Tyranny
    Atlantic, 28:377-8, Sep 1871
    Overland, 7:288-9, Sep 1871
    Nation, 13:94, 10 Aug 1871
    Saturday Review, 32:24-5,
        1 Jul 1871
Poganuc People
    Athenaeum, 2654:303-4, 7
        Sep 1878
    Harper's, 57:467, Aug 1878
    Library Table, 4:283, 8 Jun
        1878
    Nation, 27:118, 22 Aug 1878
    Picayune, 8 Sep 1878, [p.
        4]
    Rose-Belford's, 1:122-3,
        Jul 1878
    Sunday Afternoon, 2:189-90,

Aug 1878
Uncle Tom's Cabin
  Atlantic, 43:407-8,
    Mar 1879
  Cosmopolitan, 12:637-8,
    Mar 1891
  Cottage Hearth, 11:360,
    Nov 1885
  Harper's, 58:467, Feb
    1879
  Rose-Belford's, 2:123-
    25, Jan 1879
We and Our Neighbors
  Athenaeum, 2477:519-20,
    17 Apr 1875
  Atlantic, 36:248, Aug
    1875
  Harper's, 51:298, Jul
    1875
  Overland, 15:301, Sep
    1875
  Picayune, 9 May 1875,
    [p. 11]
See also Six of One, by
Half a Dozen of Another.

Stratemeyer, Edward
  To Alaska for Gold
    Outlook, 63:463, 21
      Oct 1899

Stringer, Arthur John Ar-
buthnot
  Phantom Wires
    Nation, 84:362-3, 18
      Apr 1907
  The Silver Poppy
    Bookman (NY), 18:164,
      Oct 1903
  The Under Groove
    Nation, 86:557, 18 Jun
      1908

Strobridge, Idah (Meacham)
  In Miner's Mirage Land
    Overland, 2d S, 44:633,
      Dec 1904
  The Loom of the Desert
    Overland, 2d S, 51:488,
      May 1908; 51:583,
      Jun 1908

Strong, Isabel
  See The Spinner's Book of Fic-
    tion.

Strong, Latham Cornell
  Poke o' Moonshine
    Library Table, 4:243, 11
      May 1878

Stuart, Eleanor [pseud.].
  See Childs, Eleanor Stuart
    (Patterson).

Stuart, Henry Longan
  Weeping Cross
    Saturday Review, 106:488,
      17 Oct 1908

Stuart, Hester [pseud.].
  See Smith, Helen Butler.

Stuart, Ruth McEnery
  Aunt Amity's Silver Wedding,
    and Other Stories
    Nation, 89:600, 16 Dec 1909
  Carlotta's Intended, and Other
    Tales
    Atlantic, 74:706, Nov 1894
  A Golden Wedding, and Other
    Tales
    Atlantic, 72:126, Jul 1893
  Holly and Pizen, and Other
    Stories
    Nation, 70:77, 25 Jan 1900
  In Simpkinsville
    Bookman (NY), 6:164, Oct
      1897
    Saturday Review, 85:216, 12
      Feb 1898
  Moriah's Mourning, and Other
    Half-Hour Sketches
    Outlook, 59:690, 16 Jul 1898
  Napoleon Jackson
    Saturday Review, 95:207, 14
      Feb 1903
  The Second Wooing of Selina
    Sue
    Bookman (NY), 22:182-3,
      Oct 1905
  Sonny
    Picayune, 29 Nov 1896, p. 18

Stuart, Ruth McEnery
  The Story of Babette
    Nation, 62:61, 16 Jan
      1896
  The Unlived Life of Little
    Mary Ellen
    Nation, 91:580, 15 Dec
      1910
  The Woman's Exchange
    of Simpkinsville
    Nation, 85:423, 7 Nov
      1907

Sullivan, James William
  Tenement Tales of New
    York
    Atlantic, 77:131, Jan
      1896
    Bookman (NY), 1:414,
      Jul 1895
    Godey's, 131:[430]-2,
      Oct 1895

Sullivan, John L.
  See His Fleeting Ideal.

Sullivan, Thomas Russell
  Ars et Vita, and Other
    Stories
    Outlook, 59:183, 21
      May 1898
  Day and Night Stories
    Nation, 51:292-3, 9
      Oct 1890
    Picayune, 25 May 1890,
      p. 14
  Day and Night Stories,
    Second Series
    Nation, 56:476, 29 Jun
      1893
  Roses of Shadow
    Atlantic, 57:263-4, Feb
      1886
    Godey's, 112:103, Jan
      1886
    Nation, 42:365, 29 Apr
      1886
    Picayune, 1 Nov 1885,
      p. 11
    Saturday Review, 61:547-
      48, 17 Apr 1886

Tom Sylvester
  Atlantic, 73:568, Apr 1894
  Picayune, 12 Nov 1893, p.
    14

Surghnor, Mrs. M. F.
  Uncle Tom of the Old South
    Picayune, 8 May 1898, p. 7

Sutphen, Van Tassel
  See Sutphen, William Gilbert
    Van Tassel.

Sutphen, William Gilbert Van
  Tassel
  The Doomsmen
    Bookman (NY), 23:643, Aug
      1906
  The Gates of Chance
    Nation, 79:121, 11 Aug 1904
  The Golficide, and Other Tales
    of the Fair Green
    Bookman (NY), 7:526, Aug
      1898
    Outlook, 59:87, 7 May 1898

Sweet, Alexander Edwin, and John
  Armoy Knox
  On a Mexican Mustang Through
    Texas
    Continent, 4:319, 5 Sep 1883

Sweetser, Moses Foster
  Allston
    Library Table, 4:529, 21
      Dec 1878

Swift, Augustus M.
  Cupid, M. D.
    Nation, 36:42, 11 Jan 1883

Swift, John Franklin
  Robert Greathouse
    Atlantic, 26:384, Sep 1870
    Overland, 5:387, Oct 1870

Sydney, Joseph
  The American "L'Assommoir"
    Godey's, 100:565, Jan 1880

T. , M. A.
  See Tincker, Mary Agnes.

Taber, Harry P.
  See Wells, Carolyn, and
  Harry P. Taber.

[Talbot, Hannah Lincoln]
  Not in the Prospectus
    By Parke Danforth [pseud.].
    Nation, 43:272, 30 Sep
      1886
    Overland, 2d S, 8:327,
      Sep 1886

Talcott, Hannah Elizabeth
  (Bradbury) Goodwin
  One Among Many
    Cottage Hearth, 10:218,
      Jul 1884

Tales of Our Coast
  By S. R. Crockett, Gilbert
  Parker, Harold Frederic,
  W. Clark Russell, and
  "Q."
    Godey's, 134:[203],
      Feb 1897

Tarbell, Ida Minerva
  He Knew Lincoln
    Atlantic, 100:135, Jul
      1907

Tarkington, Booth
  The Arena
    Athenaeum, 4046:589,
      13 May 1905
  The Beautiful Lady
    Bookman (NY), 21:615,
      Aug 1905
    Times Literary Supple-
      ment, 29 Sep 1905,
      p. 319
  Cherry
    Athenaeum, 4008:234,
      20 Aug 1904
    Bookman (NY), 18:656,
      Feb 1904
  The Conquest of Canaan
    Athenaeum, 4077:829,

    16 Dec 1905
    Bookman (NY), 22:517-8,
      Jan 1906
    Canadian Magazine, 26:297-
      98, Jan 1905
    North American Review,
      182:926-7, Jun 1906
  The Gentleman from Indiana
    Athenaeum, 3779:395, 31
      Mar 1900
    Bookman (London), 18:98,
      Jun 1900
    Bookman (NY), 10:381, Dec
      1899; 11:415, Jul 1900
    Overland, 2d S, 35:188, Feb
      1900
    Saturday Review, 89:816, 30
      Jun 1900; 91:342, 16 Mar
      1901; 95:206-7, 14 Feb
      1903
  The Guest of Quesnay
    Athenaeum, 4233:757, 12
      Dec 1908
    Bookman (NY), 28:278-9,
      Nov 1908
  His Own People
    Bookman (NY), 26:279-80,
      Nov 1907
    Nation, 85:400, 31 Oct 1907
    Saturday Review, 105:21, 4
      Jan 1908
  In the Arena
    Bookman (London), 28:136,
      Jul 1905
    Bookman (NY), 21:188-9,
      Apr 1905
    Saturday Review, 99:709,
      27 May 1905
  Monsieur Beaucaire
    Athenaeum, 3839:656, 25
      May 1901
    Bookman (London), 20:94,
      Jun 1901
    Outlook, 65:413, 16 Jun 1900
    Saturday Review, 95:206-7,
      14 Feb 1903
  The Two Vanrevels
    Athenaeum, 3920:791, 13
      Dec 1902
    Bookman (London), 23:169,
      Jan 1903

Teller, Charlotte
The Cage
Bookman (NY), 25:184,
Apr 1907
Nation, 84:267, 21
Mar 1907

Templeton, Faith [pseud.].
See Barber, Harriet
Boomer.

Tenney, Edward Payson
Agamenticus
Cottage Hearth, 5:250,
Jul 1878
Library Table, 4:402,
14 Sep 1878
Nation, 27:243-4, 17
Oct 1878
Sunday Afternoon, 2:383-
84, Oct 1878
Agatha and the Shadow
North American Review,
145:470, Oct 1887
Overland, 2d S, 9:324-5,
Mar 1887
Constance of Acadia
Harper's, 73:478, Aug
1886
Nation, 43:200-1, 2
Sep 1886
Overland, 2d S, 8:328,
Sep 1886
Coronation
Harper's, 55:789, Oct
1877
Nation, 25:123, 23 Aug
1877

Terhune, Albert Payson
Caleb Conover, Railroader
Athenaeum, 4175:547,
2 Nov 1907
See also Terhune, Mary
Virginia (Hawes), and
Albert Payson Terhune.

[Terhune, Mary Virginia
(Hawes)]
At Last
By Marion Harland

[pseud.].
Godey's, 72:193, Feb 1871
Picayune, 27 Nov 1870, [p.
11]; 24 May 1891, p. 12
The Empty Heart
By Marion Harland [pseud.].
Godey's, 72:574, Jun 1871
Picayune, 9 Apr 1871, [p.
7]
Eve's Daughters
By Marion Harland [pseud.].
Continent, 2:25-6, 12 Jul
1882
Godey's, 110:356, Mar 1885
A Gallant Fight
By Marion Harland [pseud.].
Epoch, 5:70, 1 Mar 1889
His Great Self
By Marion Harland [pseud.].
Athenaeum, 3366:562-3, 30
Apr 1892
Bookman (London), 2:28,
Apr 1892
Godey's, 125:522, Nov 1892
Picayune, 20 Mar 1892, p.
10
Saturday Review, 73:718, 18
Jun 1892
Husbands and Homes
By Marion Harland [pseud.].
Picayune, 7 Aug 1892, p.
11
In Our County
By Marion Harland [pseud.].
Overland, 2d S, 39:668,
Feb 1902
Jessamine
By Marion Harland [pseud.].
Godey's, 78:91, Jan 1874
Harper's, 48:449, Feb 1874
Nation, 18:79, 29 Jan 1874
Picayune, 16 Nov 1873, [p.
5]; 11 Jun 1893, p. 16
Judith
By Marion Harland [pseud.].
Continent, 3:764, 13 Jun
1883; 4:799, 19 Dec 1883
Cottage Hearth, 10:25, Jan
1884
Godey's, 108:97, Jan 1884
Nation, 38:58, 17 Jan 1884

[Terhune, Mary Virginia
(Hawes)]
Overland, 2d S, 3:220,
Feb 1884
Picayune, 2 Dec 1883,
[p. 3]
Mr. Wayt's Wife's Sister
By Marion Harland
[pseud.].
Picayune, 18 Feb 1894,
p. 23
My Little Love
By Marion Harland
[pseud.].
Harper's, 54:618, Mar
1877
Picayune, 29 Oct 1893,
p. 16
Saturday Review, 42:827,
30 Dec 1876
An Old Field School Girl
By Marion Harland
[pseud.].
Picayune, 31 Oct 1897,
p. 11
Phemie's Temptation
By Marion Harland
[pseud.].
Godey's, 80:194-5, Feb
1870
Picayune, 3 Jun 1894,
p. 10
True as Steel
By Marion Harland
[pseud.].
Godey's, 84:577, Jun
1872
Overland, 9:196, Aug
1872
Picayune, 21 Apr 1872,
[p. 13]
With the Best Intentions
By Marion Harland
[pseud.].
Epoch, 8:108-9, 19 Sep
1890
Nation, 52:385, 7 May
1891
Picayune, 10 Aug 1890,
p. 10

_____, and Albert Payson
Terhune
Dr. Dale
Nation, 72:362, 2 May 1901
Picayune, 18 Nov 1900, III,
4

Teuffel, Blanche Willis (Howard)
von
Aulnay Tower
Atlantic, 56:558-60, Oct
1885
Cottage Hearth, 14:328, Oct
1888
Godey's, 111:516, Nov 1885
Overland, 2d S, 6:323-4,
Sep 1885
Saturday Review, 61:340, 6
Mar 1886
Aunt Serena
Nation, 33:436, 1 Dec 1881
Overland, 2d S, 11:437, Apr
1888
Dionysius the Weaver's Heart's
Dearest
Picayune, 12 Nov 1899, II,
3
The Garden of Eden
Picayune, 3 Jun 1900, III, 7
Guenn
Continent, 5:410-1, (No. 13)
1884
Cottage Hearth, 10:62, Feb
1884
Godey's, 108:199, Feb 1884
Manhattan, 3:92, Jan 1884
Overland, 2d S, 3:218-9,
Feb 1884; 10:217, Aug
1887
Picayune, 16 Dec 1883, [p.
14]
Saturday Review, 57:582, 3
May 1884
One Summer
Saturday Review, 40:281, 28
Aug 1875
The Open Door
America, 2:151, 2 May 1889
Atlantic, 63:858-9, Jun 1889
Cottage Hearth, 15:201, Jun
1889

Epoch, 5:326, 21 Jun
    1889
Nation, 49:76, 25 Jul
    1889
Overland, 2d S, 14:206,
    Aug 1889
Saturday Review, 68:137,
    3 Aug 1889
Seven on the Highway
    Picayune, 17 Nov 1897,
    p. 6
Tony, the Maid
    Epoch, 2:295-6, 18
    Nov 1887
Saturday Review, 66:269-
    70, 1 Sep 1888

_____, and William
Sharp
    A Fellowe and His Wife
    Atlantic, 69:847, Jun
        1892
    Nation, 55:34, 14 Jul
        1892
    Picayune, 17 Sep 1893,
        p. 23
    Saturday Review, 73:575-
        76, 14 May 1892

Thanet, Octave [pseud.].
    See French, Alice.

Thaxter, Celia (Laighton)
    Among the Isles of Shoals
    Atlantic, 32:106, Jul
        1873
    Overland, 11:196, Aug
        1873
    Picayune, 8 Jun 1873,
        [p. 2]

Thickstun, Frederick [pseud.].
    See Clark, Frederick Thick-
    stun.

Thiusen, Ismar [pseud.].
    See Macnie, John.

Thomas, Chauncey
    The Crystal Button
    Epoch, 9:142, 3 Apr

1891
Overland, 2d S, 18:439,
    Oct 1891

Thomas, Henry Wilton
    The Last Lady of Mulberry
    Nation, 70:402-3, 24 May
        1900
    Picayune, 27 May 1900, III,
        7

Thomas, Katherine Elwes
    Not All the King's Horses
    Picayune, 22 Nov 1896, p.
        10

Thomas, Mary Von Erden
    Winning the Battle
    Picayune, 12 Mar 1882, [p.
        4]

Thompson, Adele Eugenia
    Beck's Fortune
    Outlook, 63:510, 28 Oct
        1899

Thompson, Annie E.
    A Moral Dilemma
    Bookman (London), 3:162,
        Feb 1893

Thompson, Charles Miner
    The Calico Cat
    Nation, 88:118, 4 Feb 1909

Thompson, Ernest Seton
    The Biography of a Grizzly
    Bookman (NY), 11:397, Jun
        1900

Thompson, Helen Stuart
    Windy Creek
    Nation, 69:300, 19 Oct 1899
    Outlook, 62:351, 10 Jun 1899

Thompson, Mrs. M. Agnes
    Metairie, and Other Old Aunt
    Tilda of New Orleans Sketches
    Picayune, 23 Oct 1892, p.
        18

Thompson, Maurice
Alice of Old Vincennes
Bookman (NY), 12:348-9,
Dec 1900
Picayune, 14 Oct 1900,
II, 8
Saturday Review, 91:344,
16 Mar 1901; 92:501-
502, 19 Oct 1901
Sewanee Review, 11:356,
Jul 1903
At Love's Extremes
Nation, 41:157-8, 20
Aug 1885
Picayune, 14 Jun 1885,
[p. 5]
A Banker of Bankersville
Picayune, 19 Dec 1886,
p. 11
A Fortnight of Folly
Epoch, 4:215, 26 Oct
1888
His Second Campaign
Athenaeum, 2915:302-3,
8 Sep 1883
Continent, 4:319, 5 Sep
1883
Godey's, 107:300, Sep
1883
Harper's, 67:641, Sep
1883
Manhattan, 2:189-90,
Aug 1883
Saturday Review, 56:257,
25 Aug 1883
Hoosier Mosaics
Saturday Review, 40:568,
30 Oct 1875
The King of Honey Island
Godey's, 126:645, May
1893
Picayune, 12 Mar 1893,
p. 21
Saturday Review, 76:313,
9 Sep 1893
Stories of the Cherokee
Hills
Atlantic, 83:287, Feb
1899
Outlook, 60:536, 29
Oct 1898

Picayune, 16 Oct 1898, II,
2
Sweetheart Manette
Athenaeum, 3890:620, 17
May 1902
A Tallahassee Girl
Nation, 34:386, 4 May 1882
Overland, 2d S, 11:437, Apr
1888
Saturday Review, 53:679, 27
May 1882

Thompson, William Tappa
Rancy Cottem's Courtship
By Major Joseph Jones
[pseud.].
Picayune, 5 Oct 1879, [p.
10]

Thorne, P. [pseud.].
See Smith, Mary Prudence
(Wells).

Thornet, Teresa A. [pseud.].
See Holloway, Mrs. Anna.

Thornton, M. Jacqueline
Di Cary
Nation, 29:444, 25 Dec 1879
Picayune, 30 Nov 1879, [p.
13]
Rose-Belford's, 4:104, Jan
1880

Thorpe, Kamba [pseud.].
See Bellamy, Elizabeth Whitfield (Croom).

Thruston, Lucy Meacham (Kidd)
Called to the Field
Nation, 82:390, 10 May 1906

Thurber, Alwyn M.
The Hidden Faith
Picayune, 8 Dec 1895, p. 4
Quaint Crippen, Commercial
Traveler
Bookman (NY), 3:551-2, Aug
1896

Thurston, Ida (Treadwell)
  The Big Brother of Sabin
  Street
    Nation, 89:541, 2 Dec
    1909
  The Captain of the Cadets
    Outlook, 63:468, 21 Oct
    1899

Thwing, Eugene
  The Red-Keggers
    Athenaeum, 3996:685-6,
    28 May 1904

Ticknor, Caroline
  A Hypocritical Romance,
  and Other Stories
    Atlantic, 78:568, Oct
    1896

[Tiernan, Frances Christine
  (Fisher)]
  After Many Days
    By Christian Reid [pseud.].
    Library Table, 4:159,
    2 Mar 1878
    Picayune, 3 Jun 1877,
    [p. 12]
  Armine
    By Christian Reid [pseud.].
    Nation, 39:18-9, 3 Jul
    1884
  Bonnie Kate
    Harper's, 57:629, Sep
    1878
    Library Table, 4:337,
    20 Jul 1878
    Picayune, 7 Jul 1878,
    [p. 3]
  Carmeri's Inheritance
    By Christian Reid [pseud.].
    Picayune, 2 Nov 1873,
    [p. 7]
  A Chase of an Heiress
    By Christian Reid [pseud.].
    Outlook, 59:889, 6
    Aug 1898
  A Daughter of Bohemia
    By Christian Reid [pseud.].
    Atlantic, 34:493, Oct
    1874

    Godey's, 78:565, Jun 1874
    Nation, 19:10, 2 Jul 1874
  Ebb-Tide, and Other Stories
    By Christian Reid [pseud.].
    Godey's, 85:543, Dec 1872
    Nation, 15:222, 3 Oct 1872
  Heart of Steel
    By Christian Reid [pseud.].
    Continent, 3:348, 14 Mar
    1883
    Godey's, 106:189, Feb 1883
    Nation, 36:152, 15 Feb 1883
    Picayune, 28 Jan 1882, [p.
    12]
  Hearts and Hands
    By Christian Reid [pseud.].
    Atlantic, 35:623, May 1875
    Godey's, 90:477, May 1875
    Nation, 21:10, Jul 1875
  "The Land of the Sky"
    By Christian Reid [pseud.].
    Godey's, 93:188, Aug 1876
    Library Table, 1:93, Jul
    1876
    Nation, 23:45, 20 Jul 1876
  The Land of the Sun
    By Christian Reid [pseud.].
    Godey's, 130:431, Apr 1895
  Mabel Lee
    By Christian Reid [pseud.].
    Godey's, 84:577, Jun 1872
    Picayune, 7 Apr 1872, [p.
    10]
  Miss Churchill
    By Christian Reid [pseud.].
    Godey's, 114:507, May 1887
    Nation, 44:431, 19 May 1887
  Morton House
    By Christian Reid [pseud.].
    Picayune, 5 Nov 1871, [p.
    12]
  Nina's Atonement, and Other
  Stories
    By Christian Reid [pseud.].
    Picayune, 12 Oct 1873, [p.
    5]
    Nation, 17:372-3, 4 Dec
    1873
  Princess Nadine
    By Christian Reid [pseud.].
    Nation, 86:379, 23 Apr 1908

[Tiernan, Frances Christine
(Fisher)]
 A Question of Honor
  By Christian Reid [pseud.].
  Godey's, 91:478, Nov
   1875
  Nation, 21:106, 12 Aug
   1875
  Picayune, 15 Aug 1875,
   [p. 9]
 Roslyn's Fortune
  By Christian Reid [pseud.].
  Godey's, 110:463, Apr
   1885
  Overland, 2d S, 5:659,
   Jun 1885
 A Summer Idyl
  By Christian Reid [pseud.].
  Godey's, 97:435, Nov
   1878
  Harper's, 57:941, Nov
   1878
  Library Table, 4:401,
   14 Sep 1878
  Nation, 27:244, 17 Oct
   1878
 Valerie Aylmer
  By Christian Reid [pseud.].
  Atlantic, 26:761-3, Dec
   1870
  Godey's, 72:96-7, Jan
   1871
  Harper's, 42:400, Feb
   1871
  Picayune, 30 Oct 1870,
   [p. 9]
 Weighed in the Balance
  By Christian Reid [pseud.].
  Outlook, 65:746, 28 Jul
   1900
 Works
  Sewanee Review, 18:223-
   32, Apr 1910

Tiernan, Mary Spear (Nicho-
las)
 Homoselle
  Harper's, 63:954-5,
   Nov 1881
  Nation, 33:258, 29 Sep
   1881

Saturday Review, 52:839, 31
   Dec 1881
 Jack Horner
  Atlantic, 66:429, Sep 1890
  Godey's, 121:84, Jul 1890
  Nation, 51:135-6, 14 Aug
   1890
  Overland, 2d S, 16:440-1,
   Oct 1890
 Suzette
  Atlantic, 57:268-9, Feb 1886
  Nation, 42:39-40, 14 Jan
   1886

Tilton, Dwight [pseud.].
 See Richardson, George Tilton.

Tilton, Theodore
 Swabian Stories
  Saturday Review, 54:872, 30
   Dec 1882
 Tempest Tossed
  Nation, 19:9, 2 Jul 1874
  Picayune, 4 Mar 1883, [p.
   8]

Timsol, Robert [pseud.].
 See Bird, Frederic Mayer.

Tincker, Mary Agnes
 Aurora
  Godey's, 120:353, Apr 1890
  Saturday Review, 61:820, 12
   Jun 1886
 By the Tiber
  Athenaeum, 3817:525-6, 22
   Oct 1881
  Atlantic, 47:860-1, Jun 1881
  Harper's, 63:154, Jun 1881
  Saturday Review, 52:800-1,
   24 Dec 1881
 The House of Yorke
  Nation, 15:173, 13 Sep 1872
  Picayune, 26 May 1872, [p.
   9]
 The Jewel in the Lotos
  Nation, 38:59, 17 Jan 1884
  Saturday Review, 57:388-9,
   22 Mar 1884
 San Salvador
  Nation, 54:402, 26 May 1892

Signor Monaldini's Niece
Athenaeum, 2748:815-6,
26 Jun 1880
Harper's, 58:785-6, Apr
1879
Nation, 28:187, 13 Mar
1879
Picayune, 2 Mar 1879,
[p. 10]
Rose-Belford's, 2:382,
Mar 1879
Saturday Review, 50:122-
23, 24 Jul 1880
Sunday Afternoon, 3:575,
Jun 1879
Two Coronets
Overland, 2d S, 15:320,
Mar 1890
Picayune, 29 Sep 1889,
p. 14

Todd, Mary Van Lennup (Ives)
Deborah
Picayune, 11 Oct 1896,
p. 11
The New Adam and Eve
Picayune, 13 Jul 1890,
p. 11
Violina
Overland, 2d S, 44:482,
Oct 1904

Todkill, Anas [pseud.].
See Cooke, John Esten.

Tomlinson, Everett Titsworth
Elder Boise
Outlook, 68:598, 6 Jul
1901
The Red Chief
Outlook, 81:579, 4 Nov
1905

Tompkins, Elizabeth Knight
The Broken Ring
Godey's, 133:655, Dec
1896
The Things That Count
Outlook, 65:364, 9 Jun
1900
An Unlessoned Girl

Overland, 2d S, 26:456, Oct
1895

Tompkins, Juliet W.
Dr. Ellen
Bookman (NY), 26:672, Feb
1908

Tourgee, Albion Winegar
An Appeal to Caesar
Godey's, 109:652, Dec 1884
Black Ice
Epoch, 3:157, 30 Mar 1888
Nation, 46:529-30, 28 Jun
1888
Bricks Without Straw
Atlantic, 47:119-21, Jan 1881
Harper's, 62:153-4, Dec
1880
Nation, 31:347, 11 Nov 1880
Rose-Belford's, 5:665-6,
Dec 1880
Saturday Review, 50:817, 25
Dec 1880
Button's Inn
Epoch, 2:157, 30 Sep 1887
Nation, 45:403, 17 Nov 1887
Overland, 2d S, 11:438-9,
Apr 1888
"89"
By Edgar Henry [pseud.].
Picayune, 20 May 1888, p.
10
Figs and Thistles
Atlantic, 45:682-4, May 1880
Nation, 29:278, 23 Oct 1879
A Fool's Errand
By One of the Fools.
Athenaeum, 2728:181-2, 7
Feb 1880
Atlantic, 46:422-4, Sep 1880
Bookman (NY), 21:458-9, Jul
1905
Bystander, 1:303-4, Jun 1880
Good Company, 4:478-9,
(No. 5) 1880
Harper's, 60:472, Feb 1880
Nation, 29:444, 25 Dec 1879
Picayune, 25 Apr 1880, [p.
4]
Saturday Review, 50:817,

Bookman (NY), 13:458-
59, Jul 1901
Fort Birkett
Bookman (NY), 17:615-
16, Aug 1903
Lees and Leaven
Nation, 76:276, 2 Apr
1903
Overland, 2d S, 42:174-
75, Aug 1903
A Summer in New York
Bookman (NY), 17:615,
Aug 1903

Townsend, George Alfred
Bohemian Days
Nation, 32:226, 31 Mar
1881
Picayune, 19 Dec 1880,
[p. 4]
The Entailed Hat
Harper's, 69:317-8, Jul
1884
Nation, 38:450, 22 May
1884
Picayune, 25 May 1884,
[p. 4]; 7 Sep 1890,
p. 13
Katy of Catoctin
Godey's, 121:261, Sep
1890
Nation, 44:17, 6 Jan
1887
Picayune, 7 Mar 1880,
[p. 6]
Tales of the Chesapeake
Saturday Review, 49:549,
24 Apr 1880

Townsend, Virginia Frances
A Boston Girl's Adventures
Cottage Hearth, 12:400,
Dec 1886
Godey's, 113:592, Dec
1886
But a Philistine
Cottage Hearth, 10:250,
Aug 1884
Nation, 39:19, 3 Jul
1884
Picayune, 29 Jun 1884,

[p. 9]
The Deerings of Medbury
Cottage Hearth, 12:400,
Dec 1886
Godey's, 84:193, Feb 1872
Lenox Dare
Cottage Hearth, 7:85, Mar
1881
Godey's, 102:381, Apr 1881
Harper's, 62:956, May 1881
Margery Keith
Saturday Review, 41:283, 26
Feb 1876
The Mills of Tuxbury
Godey's, 73:91, Jul 1871
Harper's, 43:459, Aug 1871
Mostly Marjorie Daw
Epoch, 11:13, 5 Feb 1892
One Woman's Two Lovers
Picayune, 27 Dec 1874, [p.
6]
Sirs, Only Seventeen
Overland, 2d S, 25:104, Jan
1895
Six in All
Picayune, 16 Feb 1873, [p.
6]
That Queer Girl
Picayune, 21 Feb 1875, [p.
2]
A Woman's Word and How She
Kept It
Harper's, 58:309-10, Jan
1879
Sunday Afternoon, 3:96, Jan
1879

Townshend, Dorothea
See Townshend, Richard Baxter, and Dorothea.

Townshend, Richard Baxter
Lone Pine
Bookman (London), 16:24,
Apr 1899
Outlook, 61:833, 8 Apr 1899;
65:936, 18 Aug 1900
Saturday Review, 87:664,
27 May 1899

Townshend, Richard Baxter,
and Dorothea
   The Bride of a Day
      Nation, 82:182, 1 Mar
      1906
      Saturday Review, 101:56,
      13 Jan 1906

Trafton, Adeline
   See Knox, Adeline (Trafton).

Trail, Florence
   Under the Second Renais-
   sance
      Picayune, 17 Jun 1894,
      p. 15

Train, Arthur Cheney
   "McAllister and His Double"
      Overland, 2d S, 46:589,
      Dec 1905
   Mortmain
      Nation, 85:474, 21 Nov
      1907

Train, Elizabeth Phipps
   The Autobiography of a
   Professional Beauty
      Picayune, 6 Apr 1896,
      p. 11
   A Deserter from Philistia
      Bookman (London),
      13:133, Jan 1897
   Doctor Lamar
      Picayune, 13 Sep 1891,
      p. 12
   Madam of the Ivies
      Picayune, 17 Apr 1898,
      p. 10
   A Marital Liability
      Bookman (London),
      16:110, Jul 1899
      Picayune, 11 Apr 1897,
      p. 25
   A Queen of Hearts
      Godey's, 136:105-6, Jan
      1898
   A Social Highwayman
      Athenaeum, 3702:489,
      8 Oct 1898
      Bookman (London), 15:25,

Oct 1898

Trammell, William Dugas
   Ça Ira
      Nation, 19:10, 2 Jul 1874

Trask, Kate (Nichols)
   Free Not Bound
      Poet-Lore, 14:136, Winter
      1903
   John Leighton, Jr.
      Bookman (NY), 6:557-8,
      Feb 1898
   Lessons in Love
      Outlook, 67:84, 5 Jan 1901

Traver, Graham
   Mona Maclean
      Godey's, 127:233, Aug 1893

Travis, Elma (Allen)
   The Cobbler
      Nation, 87:76, 23 Jul 1908
      Overland, 2d S, 52:[191],
      Aug 1908

Trebor [pseud.].
   See Davis, Robert S.

Trimmer, Frederick Mortimer
   The Golden Crocodile
      Overland, 2d S, 31:95, Jan
      1898
      Saturday Review, 84:299,
      11 Sep 1897

[Tripp, George Henry]
   Student-Life at Harvard
      Atlantic, 39:373-4, Mar
      1877
      Picayune, 14 Oct 1877,
      [p. 11]
      Saturday Review, 43:245,
      24 Feb 1877

Trotter, Ada M.
   Bledisloe
      Nation, 46:219, 15 Mar 1888
      North American Review,
      145:701-2, Dec 1887
   Heaven's Gate

By Lawrence Severn
[pseud.].
Saturday Review, 62:428-
29, 25 Sep 1886

Troubetzkay, Amélie (Rives)
Chanler
According to St. John
Athenaeum, 3346:797-8,
12 Dec 1891
Nation, 53:471, 17 Dec
1891
Picayune, 18 Oct 1891,
p. 16
Saturday Review, 72:589,
21 Nov 1891
Athelwold
Godey's, 126:770, Jun
1893
Barbara Dering
Athenaeum, 3396:736-7,
26 Nov 1892
Atlantic, 72:125, Jul
1893
Godey's, 126:104, Jan
1893
Picayune, 27 Nov 1892,
p. 22
A Brother to Dragons, and
Other Old-Time Tales
Athenaeum, 3214:693-4,
1 Jun 1889
Epoch, 3:217, 20 Apr
1888
Godey's, 136:104, Jan
1898
The Golden Rose
Bookman (NY), 27:413-4,
Jun 1908
Nation, 86:493, 28 May
1908
Meriel
Athenaeum, 3687:816,
25 Jun 1898
Pan's Mountain
Athenaeum, 4334:621,
19 Nov 1910
Nation, 91:550, 8 Dec
1910
The Quick or the Dead?
Athenaeum, 3203:341,

16 Mar 1889
Saturday Review, 67:393, 30
Mar 1889
Tanis, the Sang-Digger
Athenaeum, 3449:767, 2 Dec
1893
Atlantic, 73:137, Jan 1894
Trix and Over-the-Moon
Nation, 90:112, 3 Feb 1910
Virginia of Virginia
Athenaeum, 3214:693-4, 1
Jun 1889
Nation, 47:274, 4 Oct 1888
The Witness of the Sun
America, 2:24, 4 Apr 1889
Athenaeum, 3214:693-4, 1
Jun 1889
Epoch, 5:180, 19 Apr 1889
Nation, 48:530, 27 Jun 1889

[Trowbridge, John]
The Great Match, and Other
Matches
Godey's, 94:463, May 1877

Trowbridge, William Rutherford
Hayes
Dazzling Reprobate
Bookman (London), 31:192,
Jan 1907
An Inarticulate Genius
Saturday Review, 97:464, 9
Apr 1904
The Situations of Lady Patricia
Bookman (London), 25:53,
Oct 1903
Saturday Review, 96:740,
12 Dec 1903

Trumbull, Annie Eliot
A Cape Cod Week
Picayune, 10 Jul 1898, II, 6
A Christmas Accident, and
Other Stories
Nation, 67:264, 6 Oct 1898
Outlook, 58:679, 12 Mar
1898
Picayune, 24 Apr 1898, p.
25
Life's Common Way
Atlantic, 92:280, Aug 1903

Trumbull, Annie Eliot
Mistress Content Craddock
Nation, 69:96, 3 Aug
1899
Picayune, 18 Jun 1899,
III, 1
Rod's Salvation
Outlook, 59:484, 18 Jun
1898
White Birches
By Annie Eliot [pseud.].
Atlantic, 72:696-7, Nov
1893
Cottage Hearth, 19:345,
Jul 1893

Tucker, George Fox
A Quaker Home
Atlantic, 67:711, May
1891

Tucker, St. George
The Devoted Bride
Picayune, 3 Mar 1878,
[p. 11]

Tufts, William Whittemore
A Market for an Impulse
Picayune, 16 Jun 1895,
p. 28
Saturday Review, 82:636,
12 Dec 1896

Tully, Walton
See The Spinners' Book of
Fiction.

Tupper, Mrs. Edith Sessions
By Whose Hand?
Overland, 2d S, 15:434,
Apr 1890
Picayune, 22 Dec 1889,
p. 17

Turnbull, Charlotte
The Lawrences: a Twenty
Years' History
Saturday Review, 35:431,
29 Mar 1873

Turnbull, Francese Hubbard

(Litchfield)
The Catholic Man
Nation, 50:226-7, 13 Mar
1890
Val-Maria
Atlantic, 42:704, Nov 1893

Turnbull, Mrs. Lawrence
See Turnbull, Francese Hubbard (Litchfield).

Turner, Bessie
A Woman in the Case
Picayune, 26 Dec 1875, [p.
4]

Twells, Mrs. J. H.
See Twells, Julia Helen
(Watts).

Twells, Julia Helen (Watts)
Mignon
Nation, 26:204, 21 Mar 1878
The Mills of the Gods
Athenaeum, 2487:851-2, 26
Jun 1875
Godey's, 91:92, Jul 1875
Souci
Athenaeum, 2635:539, 27
Apr 1878
Saturday Review, 45:542,
27 Apr 1878
A Triumph of Destiny
Picayune, 7 Feb 1897, p. 12

Twombly, Alexander Stevenson
Kelea, the Surf-Rider
Picayune, 21 Oct 1900, II,
9

Tyler, Odette [pseud.].
See Shepherd, Elizabeth Lee
(Kirkland).

Tyler, Randall Irving
The Blind Goddess
Picayune, 14 May 1899, II,
12
"Four Months After Date"
Picayune, 11 Sep 1898, II,
3

Tyner, Paul
  Through the Invisible
  Picayune, 17 Nov 1897,
    p. 6

[Ulmann, Albert]
  Chaperoned
  Picayune, 8 Jul 1894,
    p. 7
  Frederick Struther's Ro-
    mance
  Epoch, 5:212, 3 May
    1889
  Picayune, 5 May 1889,
    p. 10

Underwood, Francis Henry
  Doctor Gray's Quest
  Bookman (NY), 2:56,
    Sep 1895
  Nation, 62:458, 11 Jun
    1896
  Overland, 2d S, 26:458,
    Oct 1895
  Saturday Review, 79:703,
    25 May 1895
  Lord of Himself
  Athenaeum, 2446:346-7,
    12 Sep 1874
  Atlantic, 34:362-3, Sep
    1874
  Godey's, 79:281, Sep
    1874
  Nation, 19:92, 6 Aug
    1874
  Picayune, 4 Oct 1874,
    [p. 6]
  Saturday Review, 38:417,
    26 Sep 1874
  Man Proposes
  Godey's, 102:183, Feb
    1881
  Quabbin
  Godey's, 126:232-3,
    Feb 1893

Underwood, Mary Lanman
  An American Mother, and
  Other Stories
  Nation, 66:408, 26 May
    1898

Up de Graff, Thad S.
  Bodines
  Saturday Review, 48:250,
    23 Aug 1879

[Urie, Mary Le Baron (Andrews)]
  The Villa Bohemia
  By Marie Le Baron [pseud.].
    Cottage Hearth, 8:231, Jul
    1882

Vachell, Horace Annesley
  Brothers
  Athenaeum, 4000:811, 25
    Jun 1904
  Bookman (London), 26:139-
    40, Jul 1904
  Overland, 2d S, 46:374, Oct
    1905
  Saturday Review, 97:822, 25
    Jun 1904
  A Drama in Sunshine
  Athenaeum, 3702:489, 8 Oct
    1898
  Bookman (London), 15:121,
    Jan 1899; 31:94, Nov 1906
  Outlook, 62:265, 30 Sep 1899
  Saturday Review, 86:744, 3
    Dec 1898; 102:617, 17
    Nov 1906
  The Face of Clay
  Athenaeum, 4097:541, 5 May
    1906
  Bookman (London), 30:118-
    19, Jun 1906
  Bookman (NY), 25:83-4, Mar
    1907
  Nation, 83:308, 11 Oct 1906
  Saturday Review, 101:698, 2
    Jun 1906
  Her Son
  Athenaeum, 4148:501-2, 27
    Apr 1907
  Bookman (London), 32:179,
    Aug 1907
  Bookman (NY), 26:278, Nov
    1907
  The Hill
  Athenaeum, 4047:619, 20
    May 1905
  Bookman (London), 29:238-

Vachell, Horace Annesley
40, Mar 1906
Bookman (NY), 23:298-
99, May 1906
Saturday Review, 99:744-
45, 3 Jun 1905
An Impending Sword
Saturday Review, 107:v,
Suppl. , 22 May 1909
John Charity
Bookman (London), 29:91,
Dec 1900
Bookman (NY), 13:188,
Apr 1901
Outlook, 67:692, 23 Mar
1901
Overland, 2d S, 37:1143,
Jun 1901
The Model of Christian
Gay
Athenaeum, 3516:342,
16 Mar 1895
Overland, 2d S, 25:548-
49, May 1895
The Other Side
Athenaeum, 4316:65,
16 Jul 1910
Nation, 91:418, 3 Nov
1910
Saturday Review, 110:86,
16 Jul 1910
Times Literary Supple-
ment, 30 Jun 1910,
p. 234
The Paladin
Athenaeum, 4276:422,
9 Oct 1909
Bookman (London), 37:161,
Dec 1909
Bookman (NY), 30:394,
Dec 1909
Nation, 89:573-4, 9 Dec
1909
The Pinch of Prosperity
Bookman (London),
24:149, Jul 1903
Saturday Review, 96:145,
1 Aug 1903
The Procession of Life
Athenaeum, 3724:302-3,
11 Mar 1899

Bookman (London), 16:81-2,
Jun 1899
Bookman (NY), 9:283, May
1899
Saturday Review, 87:344, 18
Mar 1899
Picayune, 2 Apr 1899, III,
3
The Quicksands of Pactolus
Athenaeum, 3590:220, 15
Aug 1896
Atlantic, 78:849, Dec 1896
Bookman (NY), 4:166-7,
Oct 1896
The Romance of Judge Ketcham
Bookman (London), 9:163,
Feb 1896
Overland, 2d S, 25:686-7,
Jun 1895
The Shadowy Third
Athenaeum, 3896:812, 28
Jun 1902
Bookman (London), 22:110-
11, Jun 1902
Saturday Review, 94:51, 12
Jul 1902
The Waters of Jordan
Athenaeum, 4229:602-3, 14
Nov 1908
Saturday Review, 106:676,
28 Nov 1908

Vaile, Charlotte Marion (White)
The M. M. C.
Outlook, 59:184, 21 May
1898
Wheat and Huckleberries
Outlook, 63:652, 11 Nov
1899

Valentine, Edward U.
Hecla Sandwith
Saturday Review, 100:186,
5 Aug 1905

Valerio, Katherine [pseud.].
See Washburn, Mrs. Katharine
(Sedgwick).

Vanamee, Lida (Ostrom)
An Adirondack Idyl

Picayune, 29 Oct 1893,
p. 16

Vance, J. Wilson
Big John Baldwin
Nation, 89:628, 23 Dec
1909
Saturday Review, 109:729,
4 Jun 1910
God's War
Picayune, 7 May 1899,
III, 10
Little Amy's Christmas
Picayune, 19 Dec 1880,
[p. 4]
Princes' Favors
Atlantic, 47:714-5, May
1881
Picayune, 7 Nov 1880,
[p. 8]

Vance, Louis Joseph
The Black Bag
Athenaeum, 4211:39,
11 Jul 1908
Nation, 86:237, 12 Mar
1908
The Brass Bowl
Athenaeum, 4180:723,
7 Dec 1907
Bookman (London),
33:216, Feb 1908
Saturday Review, 104:768-
69, 21 Dec 1907
The Fortune Hunter
Nation, 90:238-9, 10
Mar 1910
The Pool of Flame
Bookman (London),
38:224, Aug 1910
Nation, 90:37, 13 Jan
1910
Saturday Review, 110:365-
66, 17 Sep 1910
The Private War
Outlook, 83:141, 19
May 1906
Saturday Review, 102:492,
20 Oct 1906

Vance, Susa S.

Lois Carrol
Nation, 19:10, 2 Jul 1874
Saturday Review, 37:826,
27 Jun 1874

Van der Naillen, Albert
In the Sanctuary
Picayune, 29 Dec 1895, p.
15

Vanderpoole, Lew
The Magnet of Death
Epoch, 8:190, 24 Oct 1890

Van Deventer, Emma Murdoch
Against Odds
Picayune, 24 Jun 1894, p.
15
A Dead Man's Step
By Lawrence L. Lynch
[pseud.].
Picayune, 25 Mar 1894, p.
16
The Last Stroke
By Lawrence L. Lynch
[pseud.].
Bookman (London), 12:157,
Sep 1897
Madeline Payne
By Lawrence L. Lynch
[pseud.].
Picayune, 9 Mar 1884, [p.
9]
Moina
By Lawrence L. Lynch
[pseud.].
Picayune, 28 Jun 1891, p.
12
Under Fate's Wheel
By Lawrence L. Lynch
[pseud.].
Athenaeum, 3801:276, 1 Sep
1900
Saturday Review, 90:304, 8
Sep 1900
The Unseen Hand
By Lawrence L. Lynch
[pseud.].
Athenaeum, 3762:757, 2
Dec 1899

Van Dyke, Henry
  The Blue Flower
    Nation, 76:233, 19 Mar
      1903
    Overland, 2d S, 41:78-9,
      Jan 1903
    Saturday Review, 95:206,
      14 Feb 1903
  The Music Lover
    Bookman (London), 22:68,
      May 1902
  The Ruling Passion
    Bookman (London), 22:68,
      May 1902
    Nation, 73:418, 28 Nov
      1901
    North American Review,
      173:875-6, Dec 1901
    Saturday Review, 93:405,
      29 Mar 1902

Van Dyke, Theodore Strong
  Flirtation Camp
    Saturday Review, 51:573,
      30 Apr 1881

Van Hoessen, Antoinette
  See Wakeman, Antoinette
    Prudence (Van Hoessen).

Van Loon, Mrs. Elizabeth
  A Heart Twice Won
    Godey's, 119:258, Sep
      1889
  The Mystery of Allanwold
    Atlantic, 46:828-9, Dec
      1880
    Godey's, 101:294, Sep
      1880
    Picayune, 1 Aug 1880,
      [p. 10]
  The Shadow of Hampton
    Mead
    Picayune, 9 Feb 1879,
      [p. 11]
  Under the Willows
    Nation, 29:115, 14 Aug
      1879

Van Rensselaer, Mariana
  (Griswold)

One Man Who Was Content
    Bookman (NY), 5:351, Jun
      1897
    Overland, 2d S, 29:655, Jun
      1897

Van Rensselaer, Mrs. John
  See Van Rensselaer, May
    (King).

Van Rensselaer, May (King)
  The Goede Vrouw of Mana-ha-
    ta
    Bookman (NY), 8:256, Nov
      1898

Van Rensselaer, Mrs. Schuyler
  See Van Rensselaer, Mariana
    (Griswold).

Van Vorst, Bessie (McGinnis)
  The Issues of Life
    Nation, 78:355-6, 5 May
      1904
  Letters to Women in Love
    Nation, 83:375, 1 Nov 1906

_____, and Marie Van Vorst
  Bagsby's Daughter
    Nation, 73:476, 19 Dec 1901
  The Woman Who Toils
    Bookman (NY), 17:187-8,
      Apr 1903
    Overland, 2d S, 41:397-8,
      May 1903

Van Vorst, Frederick B.
  Without a Compass
    The Nation, 41:469, 3 Dec
      1885

Van Vorst, Mrs. John
  See Van Vorst, Bessie (Mc-
    Ginnis).

Van Vorst, Marie
  Amanda of the Mill
    Athenaeum, 4040:395, 1 Apr
      1905
    Atlantic, 97:51, Jan 1906
    Bookman (London), 28:168-9,

Ver Beck, Hanna (Rion)
  The Smiling Road
    Nation, 91:580, 15 Dec
      1910

Verdendorp, Basil [pseud.].
  The Verdendorps
    Athenaeum, 2761:399-
      400, 25 Sep 1880
    Nation, 31:17, 1 Jul
      1880
    Picayune, 9 May 1880,
      [p. 7]
    Saturday Review, 50:560,
      30 Oct 1880

Victor, Metta Victoria (Fuller)
  Passing the Portal
    Saturday Review, 42:429,
      30 Sep 1876

Vielé, Herman Knickerbocker
  Heartbreak Hill
    Bookman (London),
      36:191-2, Jul 1909
    Bookman (NY), 28:476-
      77, Jan 1909
    Nation, 87:318, 1 Oct
      1908
  The Inn of the Silver Moon
    Bookman (NY), 12:613,
      Feb 1901
    Nation, 72:280, 4 Apr
      1901
  Myra of the Pines
    Athenaeum, 3986:366,
      19 Mar 1904
    Bookman (NY), 15:567-
      69, Aug 1902
    Nation, 75:134, 14 Aug
      1902
  On the Lightship
    Nation, 89:628, 23 Dec
      1909

"Vieux Moustache" [pseud.].
  See Gordon, Clarence.

Vincent, Frank, and Albert
  Edmund Lancaster
  The Lady of Cawnpore

Saturday Review, 73:155, 6
  Feb 1892

Vivian, Thomas Jondrie
  Luther Strong
    Picayune, 24 Dec 1899, II,
      27

Vorse, Albert White
  Laughter of the Sphinx
    Picayune, 22 Jul 1900, II,
      8

Vorse, Mary Heaton
  The Breaking in of a Yacht-
    man's Wife
    Nation, 86:515-6, 4 Jun
      1908

Vynne, Harold Richard
  Love Letters
    Picayune, 27 Feb 1898, p.
      17; 12 Aug 1900, II, 8

W., C. H.
  See Chaplin, Heman White.

Wade, Decius Spear
  Clare Lincoln
    Nation, 23:303, 16 Nov 1876

Wadleigh, Frances Ellen
  'Twixt Wave and Sky
    Godey's, 99:279, Sep 1879

Wagnalls, Mabel
  Miserere
    Picayune, 31 Jan 1892, p.
      3
  The Palace of Danger
    Bookman (London), 37:162,
      Dec 1909
    Overland, 2d S, 53:53, Jan
      1909

Walt, Frona Eunice [pseud.].
  See Colburn, Frona Eunice
    Wait (Smith).

Waite, Carlton
  A Silver Baron

Picayune, 14 Sep 1896,
p. 9

Wakeman, Antoinette Prudence
(Van Hoessen)
Questions of Conscience
Picayune, 29 Apr 1900,
III, 5

Walcott, Earle Ashley
The Apple of Discord
Overland, 2d S, 51:[vxi],
Feb 1908
Blindfolded
Overland, 2d S, 48:502,
Dec 1906

Waldstein, Charles
The Surface of Things
Picayune, 17 Dec 1899,
III, 8

Wallace, Mrs. E. D.
Strife
Picayune, 25 Jun 1871,
[p. 5]

Wallace, Lewis
Ben-Hur
Atlantic, 47:710-1, May
1881
Harper's, 62:152-3,
Dec 1880
Sewanee Review, 2:240,
Feb 1894
The Fair God
Nation, 17:372, 4 Dec
1873
Overland, 11:479, Nov
1873; 2d S, 34:476,
Nov 1899
Picayune, 21 Sep 1873,
[p. 6]
Saturday Review, 36:712,
29 Nov 1873; 63:916-
17, 25 Jun 1887
The Prince of India
Athenaeum, 3452:878,
23 Dec 1893
Atlantic, 74:847, Dec
1894

Canadian Magazine, 1:704,
Oct 1893
Harper's, 88:314, Jan 1894
Picayune, 22 Oct 1893, p.
14
Saturday Review, 76:388, 30
Sep 1893
Sewanee Review, 2:244, Feb
1894

Wallace, Susan E.
The Storied Sea
Continent, 4:702, 28 Nov
1883
Saturday Review, 56:550,
27 Oct 1883

Waller, Mary Ella
Flamsted Quarries
Bookman (NY), 32:185, Oct
1910
Nation, 91:365, 20 Oct 1910
Overland, 2d S, 56:436, Oct
1910
Mary, the Queen of the House
of David and Mother of Jesus
Saturday Review, 65:362-3,
24 Mar 1888
Sanna
Outlook, 80:143, 13 May
1905
The Wood-Carver of 'Lympus
Athenaeum, 4274:358, 25
Sep 1909
Bookman (London), 37:58,
Oct 1909
A Year Out of Life
Bookman (London), 37:285,
Mar 1910
Bookman (NY), 29:404-5,
Jun 1909
Nation, 88:632, 24 Jun 1909

Walsh, James
The White Baby
Overland, 2d S, 27:351,
Mar 1896

Walsh, Marie
Saints and Sinners
Picayune, 1 Sep 1889, p. 7

[Walsh, Marie A.]
My Queen
By "Sandette" [pseud.].
Nation, 29:213, 25 Sep
1879

Walsingham, Charlotte
Annette
Godey's, 90:476, May
1875
Picayune, 14 Feb 1875,
[p. 10]
Saturday Review, 39:670,
22 May 1875
O'er Moor and Fen
Godey's, 92:284, Mar
1876

Walter, Carrie (Stevens)
An Idyl of Santa Barbara
Overland, 2d S, 9:219,
Feb 1887

Walton, Francis
See Willard, Josiah Flynt,
and Francis Walton [pseud.
of Alfred Hodder].

Waltz, Elizabeth Cherry
The Ancient Landmark
Athenaeum, 4086:194,
17 Feb 1906
Nation, 81:368, 2 Nov
1905
Saturday Review, 101:178,
10 Feb 1906
Pa Gladden
Athenaeum, 3992:561,
30 Apr 1904
Bookman (London), 26:25-
26, Apr 1904
Nation, 77:389, 12 Nov
1903

Walworth, Jeannette Ritchie
(Hadermann)
Against the World
Picayune, 13 Apr 1873,
[p. 10]
Saturday Review, 36:291,
30 Aug 1873

The Bar Sinister
Nation, 41:326-7, 15 Oct
1885
Overland, 2d S, 6:553, Nov
1885
Dead Men's Shoes
Canadian Monthly and Na-
tional Review, 2:94-5,
Jul 1872
Picayune, 3 Mar 1872, [p.
13]
Saturday Review, 33:548,
27 Apr 1872
Forgiven at Last
Godey's, 81:474, Nov 1870
Picayune, 28 Aug 1870, [p.
13]; 30 Oct 1870, [p. 9]
Saturday Review, 30:540, 22
Oct 1870
A Little Radical
Nation, 51:136, 14 Aug 1890
Picayune, 23 Feb 1890, p.
14
The New Man at Rossmere
Picayune, 29 Aug 1886, p.
6
Saturday Review, 63:139, 22
Jan 1887
On the Winning Side
Outlook, 58:489, 19 Feb
1898
Picayune, 27 Feb 1898, p.
17
Scruples
Picayune, 6 Jun 1886, p. 14
Southern Silhouettes
Epoch, 2:337, 2 Dec 1887
Harper's, 75:321, Jan 1888
Picayune, 30 Oct 1887, p.
14
A Splendid Egotist
Atlantic, 64:143, Jul 1889
Saturday Review, 68:496,
2 Nov 1889
A Strange Pilgrimage
Picayune, 9 Dec 1888, p. 10
That Girl from Texas
Picayune, 21 Oct 1888, p.
11
True to Herself
Picayune, 5 Aug 1888, p. 7

Without Blemish
  Nation, 44:533, 23 Jun
    1887
  Overland, 2d S, 7:652,
    Jun 1886
  Picayune, 14 Feb 1886,
    p. 14
  See also Not Pretty, but
  Precious.

Walworth, Mansfield Tracy
  Beverly
    Picayune, 12 May 1872,
      [p. 10]
  Delaplaine
    Harper's, 43:784, Oct
      1871
  Stormcliff
    Picayune, 11 Jan 1891,
      p. 10

Ward, A. B. [pseud.].
  See Bailey, Alice (Ward).

Ward, Elizabeth Stuart (Phelps)
  Avery
    Athenaeum, 3941:590,
      9 May 1903
    Saturday Review, 96:464,
      10 Oct 1903
  Beyond the Gates
    Atlantic, 53:138-43, Jan
      1884
    Continent, 5:158, (No. 5)
      1884
    Cottage Hearth, 10:25,
      Jan 1884
    Godey's, 109:210, Aug
      1884
    Manhattan, 3:187-8, Feb
      1884
    Overland, 2d S, 3:109,
      Jan 1884
  Burglars in Paradise
    Nation, 42:533, 24 Jun
      1886
    Overland, 2d S, 8:107,
      Jul 1886
    Picayune, 23 May 1886,
      p. 14
    Saturday Review, 63:70,

  8 Jan 1887
Doctor Zay
  Cottage Hearth, 8:401, Dec
    1882
  Overland, 2d S, 1:102, Jan
    1883
  Picayune, 12 Nov 1882, [p.
    13]
Donald Marcy
  Cottage Hearth, 19:295, Jun
    1893
  Godey's, 127:105, Jul 1893
  Overland, 2d S, 21:660, Jun
    1893
  Saturday Review, 76:159, 5
    Aug 1893
Fourteen to One
  Athenaeum, 3339:546, 24
    Oct 1891
  Atlantic, 68:710-1, Nov 1891;
    69:268, Feb 1892
  Epoch, 9:302, 12 Jun 1891
  Nation, 52:484, 11 Jun 1891
  Overland, 2d S, 18:442, Oct
    1891
  Saturday Review, 72:504-5,
    31 Oct 1891
Friends
  Athenaeum, 2808:236, 20
    Aug 1881
  Atlantic, 48:566-8, Oct 1881
  Cottage Hearth, 7:241, Aug
    1881
  Nation, 33:258, 29 Sep 1881
  Saturday Review, 52:282, 27
    Aug 1881
The Gates Ajar
  Godey's, 108:95, Jan 1884
The Gates Between
  Epoch, 2:176-7, 7 Oct 1887
  Godey's, 115:429, Nov 1887
  Nation, 45:335, 27 Oct 1887
  Overland, 2d S, 11:439-40,
    Apr 1888
  Picayune, 30 Oct 1887, p.
    14
Gypsy Breynton
  Picayune, 25 Nov 1894, p.
    10
Hedged In
  Athenaeum, 2217:547, 23

Ward, Elizabeth Stuart (Phelps)
Apr 1870
Atlantic, 25:756-7, Jun
1870
Harper's, 40:925, May
1870
Nation, 10:244, 14 Apr
1870
Overland, 4:484, May
1870
Picayune, 27 Mar 1870,
[p. 11]
Jack the Fisherman
Epoch, 2:217, 21 Oct
1887
Godey's, 115:516, Dec
1887
Nation, 45:485, 15 Dec
1887
Overland, 2d S, 11:111,
Jan 1888
Picayune, 30 Oct 1887,
p. 14
Jonathan and David
Nation, 89:487-8, 18
Nov 1909
North American Review,
190:843, Dec 1909
The Madonna of the Tubs
Cottage Hearth, 12:400,
Dec 1886
Saturday Review, 63:451,
26 Mar 1887
The Man in the Case
Athenaeum, 4130:797,
22 Dec 1906
Nation, 83:287, 4 Oct
1906
Saturday Review, 103:56,
12 Jan 1907
The Oath of Allegiance,
and Other Stories
Nation, 89:487-8, 18
Nov 1909
Saturday Review, 109:144,
29 Jan 1910
Old Maids, and Burglars
in Paradise
Cottage Hearth, 13:396,
Dec 1887
Epoch, 2:497, 27 Jan

1888
Overland, 2d S, 11:437, Apr
1888
An Old Maid's Paradise
Godey's, 111:403, Oct 1885
Overland, 2d S, 6:327, Sep
1885
Saturday Review, 60:819, 19
Dec 1885
Sealed Orders
Good Company, 4:382, (No.
4) 1879
Harper's, 60:314, Jan 1880
Nation, 30:65-6, 22 Jan
1880
The Silent Partner
Athenaeum, 2266:398, 1 Apr
1871
Harper's, 43:300-1, Jun
1871
Overland, 6:577, Jun 1871
Picayune, 9 Apr 1871, [p.
7]
Saturday Review, 31:573-4,
6 May 1871
A Singular Life
Bookman (NY), 3:261-3,
May 1896
The Story of Avis
Cottage Hearth, 5:34, Jan
1878; 5:142-3, Apr 1878
Harper's, 56:310, Jan 1878
Library Table, 3:79-80, 22
Dec 1877
Nation, 26:202, 21 Mar 1878
Picayune, 25 Nov 1877, [p.
14]
Sunday Afternoon, 1:92-3,
Jan 1878
The Successors of Mary the
First
Overland, 2d S, 38:234-5,
Sep 1901
Though Life Us Do Part
Nation, 87:415-6, 29 Oct
1908
Outlook, 90:502, 31 Oct
1908
Overland, 2d S, 53:56, Jan
1909
Walled In

Nation, 85:590-1, 26
Dec 1907
See also The Whole Family.

_____, and Herbert D.
Ward
Come Forth!
Athenaeum, 3284:441,
4 Oct 1890
Atlantic, 66:699-700,
Nov 1890
Cottage Hearth, 16:359,
Nov 1890
Epoch, 8:267-8, 28 Nov
1890
Overland, 2d S, 17:658-
59, Jun 1891
The Master of the Magi-
cians
Athenaeum, 3267:733-4,
7 Jun 1890
Atlantic, 66:131-3, Jul
1890
Cottage Hearth, 16:225,
Jul 1890
Epoch, 7:335, 27 Jun
1890
Godey's, 12:84, Jul
1890
Nation, 51:252, 25 Sep
1890
Overland, 2d S, 16:442-
43, Oct 1890
Saturday Review, 70:18-
19, 5 Jul 1890

Ward, Herbert Dickinson
The Burglar Who Moved
Paradise
Nation, 66:74, 27 Jan
1898
Picayune, 6 Jun 1897,
p. 17
The Light of the World
Outlook, 67:739, 30
Mar 1901
The White Crown, and
Other Stories
Atlantic, 74:705, Nov
1894

Ward, Herbert D.
See also Ward, Elizabeth Stu-
art (Phelps), and Herbert D.
Ward.

Warddel, Nora Helen
The Romance of a Quiet Water-
ing Place
North American Review,
147:238-9, Aug 1888

Warfield, Mrs. C. A.
See Warfield, Catherine Ann
(Ware).

Warfield, Catherine Ann (Ware)
The Cardinal's Daughter
Godey's, 94:550, Jun 1877
Picayune, 6 May 1877, [p.
5]
A Double Wedding
Godey's, 91:380, Oct 1875
Picayune, 1 Aug 1875, [p.
10]; 8 May 1892, p. 10
Saturday Review, 40:694,
27 Nov 1875
Ferne Fleming
Picayune, 1 Apr 1877, [p.
7]
Hester Howard's Temptation
Godey's, 91:569, Dec 1875
Picayune, 10 Oct 1875, [p.
10]
Saturday Review, 61:154, 29
Jan 1876
The Household of Bouverie
Godey's, 91:380, Oct 1875
Lady Ernestine
Godey's, 93:568, Dec 1876
Picayune, 29 Oct 1876, [p.
11]
Saturday Review, 42:827,
30 Dec 1876
Miriam Monfort
Nation, 17:277, 23 Oct 1873
Picayune, 5 Oct 1873, [p.
5]
Miriam's Memories
Picayune, 12 Mar 1876, [p.
6]
Monfort Hall

Warfield, Catherine Ann
(Ware)
    Godey's, 92:476-7, May
      1876
    Picayune, 12 Mar 1876,
      [p. 6]

Waring, George Edward
  Horse Stories
    Saturday Review, 56:848,
      29 Dec 1883

Warman, Cy
  The Express Messenger,
   and Other Tales of the
   Rail
    Nation, 66:74, 27 Jan
      1898
    Picayune, 31 Oct 1897,
      p. 11
  Frontier Stories
    Outlook, 60:732, 19
      Nov 1898
    Picayune, 27 Nov 1898,
      p. 10
  Short Rails
    Outlook, 66:669, 10
      Nov 1900
  Snow on the Headlight
    Outlook, 62:902, 19
      Aug 1899
    Picayune, 20 Aug 1899,
      II, 12
  Tales of an Engineer
    Bookman (NY), 2:330-1,
      Dec 1895
  The White Mail
    Nation, 69:300, 19 Oct
      1899
    Outlook, 62:216, 23
      Sep 1899
    Picayune, 1 Oct 1899,
      II, 4

Warner, Anna
  See also Warner, Susan Bogert,
  and Anna Warner.

Warner, Anna Bartlett
  Cross Corners
    Cottage Hearth, 13:396,

    Dec 1887
  My Brother's Keeper
    Godey's, 85:543, Dec
      1872
  Patience
    Atlantic, 67:567, Apr 1891
    Epoch, 9:29, 13 Feb 1891
    Picayune, 11 Jan 1891, p.
      10

Warner, Anne
  See French, Anne (Warner).

Warner, Charles Dudley
  The Golden House
    Atlantic, 75:820-1, Jun 1895
    Nation, 60:205-6, 14 Mar
      1895
    Poet-Lore, 6:527, (No. 10)
      1894
    Saturday Review, 79:518-9,
      20 Apr 1895
  In the Wilderness
    Library Table, 4:368, 17
      Aug 1878
    Picayune, 8 Sep 1878, [p.
      4]
    Rose-Belford's, 1:382, Sep
      1878
    Sunday Afternoon, 2:286,
      Sep 1878
  A Little Journey in the World
    Athenaeum, 3250:176, 8 Feb
      1890
    Atlantic, 65:567-9, Apr 1890
    Harper's, 80:483-4, Feb
      1890
    Nation, 50:226, 13 Mar 1890
    Picayune, 20 May 1894, p.
      9
    Saturday Review, 69:244, 22
      Feb 1890; 79:488, 13 Apr
      1895
  On Horseback
    Harper's, 78:492, Feb 1889
  That Fortune
    Athenaeum, 3782:484, 21
      Apr 1900
    Bookman (London), 16:169,
      Sep 1899
    Outlook, 62:623, 15 Jul 1899

Picayune, 20 Aug 1899,
II, 12
Saturday Review, 88:306,
2 Sep 1899
Their Pilgrimage
Godey's, 114:617, Jun
1887
See also [Clemens, Samuel],
and Charles Dudley Warner.

[Warner, Susan Bogert]
Bread and Oranges
Saturday Review, 40:821,
25 Dec 1875
Daisy Plains
Saturday Review, 60:816,
19 Dec 1885
Diana
Library Table, 3:22,
10 Nov 1877
Sunday Afternoon, 1:288,
Mar 1878
The End of a Coil
Harper's, 62:313, Jan
1881
The Letter of Credit
Nation, 33:338, 27 Oct
1881
Nobody
Nation, 35:447, 23 Nov
1882; 35:448, 23 Nov
1882
Opportunities
Harper's, 42:931, May
1871
Queechy
By Elizabeth Wetherell
[pseud.].
Picayune, 18 Mar 1894,
p. 27
The Wide, Wide World
By Elizabeth Wetherell
[pseud.].
Atlantic, 70:852, Dec
1892
Picayune, 7 Aug 1892,
p. 11

_____, and Anna Warner
The Gold of Chickaree
Atlantic, 39:370-1, Mar

1877
Nation, 24:282, 10 May 1877
Picayune, 17 Dec 1876, [p.
11]
Wych Hazel
Atlantic, 38:368, Sep 1876
Nation, 22:370, 8 Jun 1876

Warren, Charles
The Girl and the Governor
Bookman (NY), 12:505-6,
Jan 1901
Nation, 71:410, 22 Nov 1900
Picayune, 4 Nov 1900, II, 9

Warren, Cornelia
Miss Wilton
Saturday Review, 74:664, 3
Dec 1892

Warren, Frances
The Woman's Side
Picayune, 14 Sep 1890, p.
14

Warren, Maude Lavinia (Radford)
The Land of the Living
Athenaeum, 4220:297, 12
Sep 1908
Nation, 87:289, 24 Sep 1908
Peter-Peter
Saturday Review, 108:viii,
Suppl., 16 Oct 1909

Warren, Thomas Robinson
Juliette Irving and the Jesuit
Picayune, 2 Jun 1895, p. 16

[Warriner, Edward Augustus]
Victor la Tourette
By a Broad Churchman
Harper's, 51:298, Jul 1875

Washburn, Katharine (Sedgwick)
Ina
By Katherine Valerio [pseud.].
Atlantic, 28:254-5, Aug 1871
Perfect Love Casteth Out Fear
Picayune, 20 Jun 1875, [p.
6]
Saturday Review, 39:837,

Washburn, Katharine (Sedgwick)
    26 Jun 1875

[Washburn, William Tucker]
    Fair Harvard
        Overland, 4:197, Feb
            1870
        Picayune, 29 May 1870,
            [p. 6]
        Saturday Review, 29:128-
            29, 22 Jan 1870
    The Unknown City
        Saturday Review, 51:413,
            26 Mar 1881

Wasson, George S.
    Cap'n Simeon's Store
        Atlantic, 92:282, Aug
            1903
        Nation, 76:421, 21 May
            1903
    Home from Sea
        Nation, 86:492, 28 May
            1908

Watauna, Onoto [pseud.].
    See Badcock, Winnifred
    (Eaton).

Waterloo, Stanley
    Armageddon
        Picayune, 7 Nov 1898,
            p. 8
    The Cassowary
        Overland, 2d S, 49:186,
            Feb 1907
    The Launching of a Man
        Picayune, 18 Jun 1899,
            III, 1
    A Man and a Woman
        Athenaeum, 3569:378,
            21 Mar 1896
        Atlantic, 70:706-7, Nov
            1892
        Picayune, 9 Jan 1898,
            p. 20
        Saturday Review, 82:46,
            11 Jul 1896
    An Odd Situation
        Godey's, 126:646, May
            1893

Nation, 63:200-1, 10 Sep
    1896
Picayune, 5 Mar 1893, p.
    16
Saturday Review, 82:271,
    5 Sep 1896
The Seekers
    Outlook, 64:597, 10 Mar
        1900
    Picayune, 25 Mar 1900, III,
        5
The Story of Ab
    Picayune, 17 Nov 1897, p.
        6
    Saturday Review, 85:56-7,
        8 Jan 1898
The Wolf's Long Howl
    Outlook, 62:400, 17 Jun
        1899

Waters, Clara (Erskine) Clement
    Eleanor Maitland
        Nation, 33:437, 1 Dec 1881

Waters, Gay
    Alma
        Picayune, 3 Mar 1889, p.
            14

[Watrous, Charles]
    Told at Tuxedo
        By A. M. Emory [pseud.].
        Nation, 45:58, 21 Jul 1887
        Overland, 2d S, 10:330, Sep
            1887
        Picayune, 10 Jul 1887, p. 5

Watson, Augusta (Campbell)
    Dorothy the Puritan
        Godey's, 127:237, Aug 1893
    The Old Harbor Town
        Picayune, 1 May 1892, p.
            12

Watson, Lewis H.
    Not to the Swift
        America, 6:190, 14 May
            1891
    A Strange Infatuation
        By Lewis Harrison [pseud.].
        America, 4:187, 15 May

Wells, Carolyn
Nation, 85:568, 19 Dec
1907
Patty in the City
Overland, 2d S, 46:591,
Dec 1905
The Story of Betty
Outlook, 63:510, 28
Oct 1899

_____, and Harry P.
Taber
The Matrimonial Bureau
Nation, 80:379, 11 May
1905

Wells, Catherine Boott
(Gannett)
Miss Curtis
Nation, 46:121, 9 Feb
1888
North American Review,
146:235-6, Feb 1888
Two Modern Women
Epoch, 8:109, 19 Sep
1890
Picayune, 7 Sep 1890,
p. 13

Wells, David Dwight
Her Ladyship's Elephant
Nation, 67:54, 21 Jul
1898
Saturday Review, 85:854-
55, 25 Jun 1898
His Lordship's Leopard
Athenaeum, 3786:618,
19 May 1900
Bookman (London), 18:98,
Jun 1900
Nation, 71:156, 23 Aug
1900
Outlook, 65:183, 19
May 1900
Saturday Review, 89:592,
12 May 1900
Parlous Times
Athenaeum, 3841:722,
8 Jun 1901
Nation, 72:182, 28 Feb
1901

Picayune, 2 Dec 1900, II, 9

[Wells, Eleanor P. Bell]
Madame Lucas
Cottage Hearth, 8:133, Apr
1882

Wells, Henry Parkhurst
City Boys in the Woods
Saturday Review, 70:655-6,
6 Dec 1890

Wells, Kate Gannett [pseud.].
See Wells, Catherine Boott
(Gannett).

Welsh, James
A White Baby
Saturday Review, 80:56, 13
Jul 1895

Wendell, Barrett
The Duchess Emilia
Atlantic, 55:849-51, Jun
1885
Overland, 2d S, 10:217-8,
Aug 1887
Saturday Review, 60:22-3,
4 Jul 1885
Rankell's Remains
Nation, 44:124, 10 Feb 1887
Saturday Review, 63:304, 26
Feb 1887

Wernberny, John, and Another
Love & Company, Limited
Nation, 65:282, 7 Oct 1897

Wescott, Blanche
Jean
Nation, 28:106, 6 Feb 1879

West, Mary
A Born Player
Atlantic, 71:708, May 1893

Westcott, Edward Noyes
David Harum
Athenaeum, 3768:45, 13 Jan
1900
Bookman (NY), 8:491, Jan

1899
Nation, 67:491, 29 Dec
1898
Picayune, 7 Nov 1898,
p. 8
Saturday Review, 87:473,
15 Apr 1899
Sewanee Review, 11:356,
Jul 1903
South Atlantic Quarterly,
5:219, Jul 1906
The Teller
    Overland, 2d S, 38:506,
    Dec 1901

Westcott, Margaret Jane Cook
Bessie Wilmerton
    Godey's, 78:382, Apr
    1874

Westley, G. H.
See Stephens, Robert Neilson, and G. H. Westley.

Westmoreland, Maria Elizabeth (Jourdan)
Clifford Troup
    Picayune, 16 Mar 1873,
    [p. 3]

Wetherell, Elizabeth [pseud.].
See Warner, Susan Bogert.

Wetherill, Julie K.
See Baker, Julie Keim
(Wetherill).

Wetmore, Claude Hazeltine
Sweepers of the Sea
    Picayune, 8 Jul 1900,
    II, 8
Incaland
    Outlook, 72:657, 15
    Nov 1902

Wharton, Anne Hollingworth
Through Colonial Doorways
    Picayune, 23 Apr 1893,
    p. 21

Wharton, Edith Newbold (Jones)

Crucial Instances
    Athenaeum, 3850:186, 10
    Aug 1901
    Bookman (London), 20:192-
    93, Sep 1901
    Bookman (NY), 13:441-2,
    Jul 1901
    Harper's, 103:823, Oct 1901
    Outlook, 67:921, 20 Apr
    1901
    Saturday Review, 92:280,
    31 Aug 1901
The Descent of Man, and Other
Stories
    Athenaeum, 4001:13-4, 2
    Jul 1904
    Atlantic, 94:708, Nov 1904
    Bookman (London), 26:140-
    41, Jul 1904
    Bookman (NY), 19:512-3,
    Jul 1904
    Times Literary Supplement,
    10 Jun 1904, p. 180
The Fruit of the Tree
    Athenaeum, 4181:762, 14
    Dec 1907   —
    Bookman (NY), 26:273-4,
    Nov 1907
    Canadian Magazine, 30:293-
    94, Jan 1908
    Nation, 85:352-3, 17 Oct
    1907
    Sewanee Review, 16:381-2,
    Jul 1908
    Times Literary Supplement,
    5 Dec 1907, p. 373
A Gift from the Grave
    Athenaeum, 3799:210, 18
    Aug 1900
    Bookman (London), 18:189,
    Sep 1900
    Times Literary Supplement,
    18 Mar 1904, p. 83
The Greater Inclination
    Athenaeum, 3745:189, 5 Aug
    1899
    Bookman (NY), 9:344-6, Jun
    1899; 16:11-2, Sep 1902
    Outlook, 61:832, 8 Apr 1899
    Picayune, 16 Apr 1899, II,
    12

Wharton, Edith Newbold (Jones)
    Saturday Review, 88:82,
      15 Jul 1899
    Times Literary Supple-
      ment, 18 Mar 1904,
      p. 83
The Hermit and the Wild
   Woman
    Athenaeum, 4230:644,
      21 Nov 1908
    Nation, 87:525, 26 Nov
      1908
    Athenaeum, 4074:718,
      25 Nov 1905
The House of Mirth
    Atlantic, 97:52, Jan
      1906
    Atlantic, 98:217-28,
      Aug 1906
    Bookman (London), 29:130-
      31, Dec 1905
    Bookman (NY), 22:364-
      66, Dec 1905
    Nation, 81:447-8, 30
      Nov 1905
    North American Review,
      182:922-4, Jun 1906
    Saturday Review, 101:209-
      10, 17 Feb 1906
    South Atlantic Quarterly,
      5:220, Jul 1906;
      5:260-3, Jul 1906
Italian Backgrounds
    Bookman (NY), 21:609-
      10, Aug 1905
Madame de Treymes
    Athenaeum, 4149:535,
      4 May 1907
    Atlantic, 100:131, Jul
      1907
    Bookman (NY), 25:303-
      304, Apr 1907
    Canadian Magazine,
      29:195-6, Jun 1907
    Nation, 84:313, 4 Apr
      1907
    North American Review,
      185:218-21, 17 May
      1907
Sanctuary
    Athenaeum, 3971:750,

      5 Dec 1903
    Atlantic, 98:217-28, Aug
      1906
    Bookman (London), 25:150,
      Dec 1903
    Bookman (NY), 18:410-1,
      Dec 1903
    Nation, 77:508, 24 Dec 1903
    Saturday Review, 98:276, 27
      Aug 1904
    Times Literary Supplement,.
      30 Oct 1903, p. 312
Tales of Men and Ghosts
    Athenaeum, 4336:700, 3 Dec
      1910
    Nation, 91:496, 24 Nov 1910
    Times Literary Supplement,
      3 Nov 1910, p. 424
The Touchstone
    Atlantic, 86:418-9, Sep 1900;
      98:217-28, Aug 1906
    Bookman (NY), 11:319-23,
      Jun 1900
    Outlook, 65:137, 12 May
      1900
    Picayune, 13 May 1900, III,
      3
    Times Literary Supplement,
      18 Mar 1904, p. 83
The Valley of Decision
    Athenaeum, 3894:748-9, 14
      Jun 1902
    Atlantic, 89:710, May 1902;
      98:217-28, Aug 1906
    Bookman (NY), 15:173-5, Apr
      1902
    Saturday Review, 93:405, 29
      Mar 1902; 93:673, 24 May
      1902
    Times Literary Supplement,
      25 Apr 1902, pp. 116-7;
      18 Mar 1904, p. 83

[Wharton, Edward Clifton]
The War of the Bachelors
   By "Orleanian" [pseud.].
    Continent, 4:319, 5 Sep 1883
    Manhattan, 2:481, Nov 1883
    Picayune, 10 Sep 1882, [p.
      2]

Wharton, Thomas Isaac
"Bobbo" and Other Fancies
Bookman (NY), 6:165,
Oct 1897
Nation, 66:54, 20 Jan
1898
Hannibal of New York
Nation, 43:356-7, 28
Oct 1886

Wheaton, Campbell [pseud.].
See Campbell, Helen (Stuart).

[Wheeler, Andrew Carpenter]
The Toltec Cup
By Nym Crinkle [pseud.].
Epoch, 8:77, 5 Sep
1890
Overland, 2d S, 16:442,
Oct 1890
Picayune, 3 Aug 1890,
p. 10

Wheeler, Esther Gracie
[Lawrence]
Stray Leaves from Newport
Epoch, 4:71, 31 Aug
1888
Godey's, 116:564, Jun
1888

Wheeler, William W.
Life
Picayune, 23 Nov 1890,
p. 10; 24 Feb 1895,
p. 23
Rest
Picayune, 24 Feb 1895,
p. 23

Wheelwright, John Tyler
A Bad Penny
Bookman (NY), 3:551,
Aug 1896
Nation, 63:145, 20 Aug
1896
A Child of the Century
Epoch, 1:335, 13 May
1887
Nation, 44:453, 26 May

1887
Overland, 2d S, 10:216, Aug
1887
See also The King's Men.

Whitaker, Herman
The Planter
Nation, 88:631, 24 Jun 1909
Outlook, 91:814, 10 Apr 1909
The Probationer, and Other
Stories
Nation, 80:442, 1 Jun 1905
The Settler
Outlook, 87:828, 14 Dec
1907
See also The Spinner's Book
of Fiction.

Whitaker, Robert
The Man Who Might Have Been
Outlook, 63:464, 21 Oct 1899

White, Alfred Ludlow
Doctor Hildreth
Nation, 30:66, 22 Jan 1880

White, Caroline (Earle)
Love in the Tropics
Godey's, 120:517, Jun 1890
Picayune, 27 Apr 1890, p.
10
A Modern Agrippa and Patience
Barker
Picayune, 28 May 1895, p.
24

White, Eliza Orne
The Coming of Theodora
Atlantic, 77:265-6, Feb 1896
Bookman (London), 9:65,
Nov 1895
Bookman (NY), 2:230, Nov
1895
Nation, 62:62, 16 Jan 1896
Overland, 2d S, 26:676, Dec
1895
Saturday Review, 80:640, 16
Nov 1895
Lesley Chilton
Nation, 78:55, 21 Jan 1904
A Lover of Truth

White, Eliza Orne
Athenaeum, 3706:641,
5 Nov 1898
Atlantic, 83:520-1, Apr
1899
Bookman (NY), 8:492,
Jan 1899
Miss Brooks
Atlantic, 66:720, Nov
1890
Harper's, 81:804, Oct
1890
Picayune, 1 Mar 1891,
p. 10
The Wares of Edgefield
Nation, 89:434, 4 Nov
1909
Winterborough
Atlantic, 71:278, Feb
1893
Godey's, 126:497, Apr
1893

White, Grace Miller
Tess of the Storm Country
Overland, 2d S, 55:537,
May 1910

White, Hervey
Differences
Bookman (NY), 10:383-4,
Dec 1899
Outlook, 63:605, 4 Nov
1899
Sewanee Review, 8:119,
Jan 1900
Quicksand
Bookman (NY), 12:511-2,
Jan 1901
Outlook, 66:899, 8 Dec
1900
Picayune, 25 Nov 1900,
II, 7
Sewanee Review, 9:105-
106, Jan 1901

White, Matthew
A Born Aristocrat
Bookman (NY), 7:255,
May 1898
Picayune, 8 May 1898,

p. 7
One of the Profession
Picayune, 6 Aug 1893, p. 17

White, Richard Grant
The Fate of Mansfield Humph-
reys
Nation, 39:96, 31 Jul 1884
Overland, 2d S, 4:219-22,
Aug 1884
Saturday Review, 58:127, 26
Jul 1884

White, Stewart Edward
Arizona Nights
Bookman (NY), 26:524-6,
Jan 1908
Blazed Trail Stories
Athenaeum, 3893:717-8, 7
Jun 1902; 4101:666, 2 Jun
1906
Bookman (London), 30:116,
Jun 1906
Bookman (NY), 20:219-20,
Nov 1904
Nation, 79:420, 24 Nov 1904
Outlook, 70:879, 29 Mar 1902
Overland, 2d S, 44:632, Dec
1904
Saturday Review, 94:176, 9
Aug 1902; 98:276, 27 Aug
1904; 101:761, 16 Jun
1906
The Claim Jumpers
Athenaeum, 4073:682, 18
Nov 1905
Conjuror's House
Athenaeum, 3992:557, 30
Apr 1904
Bookman (London), 25:52-3,
Oct 1903
Bookman (NY), 17:257-8,
May 1903
Outlook, 73:834, 4 Apr 1903
The Forest
Saturday Review, 98:276, 27
Aug 1904
The Mountains
Bookman (London), 27:253,
Mar 1905
The Pass

Bookman (London), 32:69,
May 1907
The Riverman
Athenaeum, 4234:784,
19 Dec 1908
Bookman (NY), 28:150-
51, Oct 1908
Nation, 87:340, 8 Oct
1908
Overland, 2d S, 53:57,
Jan 1909
The Silent Places
Athenaeum, 4026:870,
24 Dec 1904
Bookman (London), 27:81-
82, Nov 1904; 27:46,
Christmas Suppl.,
Dec 1904
Bookman (NY), 19:305-
307, May 1904
Nation, 78:499-500, 23
Jun 1904
Overland, 2d S, 44:383,
Sep 1904
Saturday Review, 98:276,
27 Aug 1904
The Westerners
Nation, 73:476, 19 Dec
1901
Saturday Review, 93:405,
29 Mar 1902

_____, and Samuel Hop-
kins Adams
The Mystery
Bookman (NY), 25:84-5,
Mar 1907
Nation, 84:61, 17 Jan
1907

White, William Allen
A Certain Rich Man
Athenaeum, 4276:424,
9 Oct 1909
Atlantic, 104:682, Nov
1909
Bookman (London), 37:9,
Oct 1909
Bookman (NY), 30:60-1,
Sep 1909
Canadian Magazine, 34:88,

Nov 1909
Nation, 89:163, 19 Aug 1909
North American Review,
190:565, Oct 1909
The Real Issue
Bookman (NY), 5:78-9, Mar
1897
Nation, 64:185-6, 11 Mar
1897
Stratagems and Spoils
North American Review,
173:876-8, Dec 1901
Times Literary Supplement,
4 Jul 1902, p. 196

Whitehead, Charles Edward
The Camp-Fires of the Ever-
glades
Athenaeum, 3349:7-8, 2 Jan
1892

Whiteley, Isabel (Nixon)
The Falcon of Langéac
Picayune, 18 Apr 1897, p.
17
Poet-Lore, 9:438, Summer
1897

Whitelock, Louise (Clarkson)
How Hindsight Met Provinci-
alatis
Picayune, 9 Apr 1899, II, 4
Bookman (NY), 2:228-9, Nov
1895
The Shadow of John Wallace
By L. Clarkson.
Nation, 39:508, 11 Dec 1884

Whitlock, Brand
The Gold Brick
Bookman (NY), 32:293, Nov
1910
The Happy Average
Bookman (NY), 20:365, Dec
1904
Overland, 2d S, 44:636-7,
Dec 1904
The 13th District
Bookman (NY), 15:463-5, Jul
1902
Nation, 74:470, 12 Jun 1902

Whittlesey, Sarah Johnson
Cogswell
Bertha, the Beauty
Picayune, 31 Dec 1871,
[p. 5]

The Whole Family: A Novel
by Twelve Authors [includ-
ing John Kendrick Bangs,
Mary E. (Wilkins) Free-
man, William D. Howells,
Henry James, Elizabeth
Stuart Phelps, and ot-
hers.]
Nation, 87:552-3, 3
Dec 1908
North American Review,
188:128, Dec 1908

Wickersham, James Alexander
Enoch Willoughby
Picayune, 29 Apr 1900,
III, 5
Nation, 70:304, 19 Apr
1900

Wiggin, Kate Douglas (Smith)
The Affair at the Inn
Bookman (London), 27:14,
Christmas Suppl. ,
Dec 1904
Bookman (NY), 20:374,
Dec 1904
Times Literary Supple-
ment, 21 Oct 1904,
p. 323
A Cathedral Courtship
Athenaeum, 3432:188-9,
5 Aug 1893
Atlantic, 72:279-80,
Aug 1893
Bookman (London), 4:154,
Aug 1893
Nation, 56:475, 29 Jun
1893
Picayune, 28 May 1893,
p. 24
Saturday Review, 76:167,
5 Aug 1893
The Diary of a Goose Girl
Athenaeum, 3897:31,

5 Jul 1902
Atlantic, 90:277, Aug 1902
Marm Lisa
Atlantic, 79:273, Feb 1897
Bookman (NY), 4:570-1,
Feb 1897
Overland, 2d S, 29:343,
Mar 1887
Picayune, 10 Jan 1897, p.
11
New Chronicles of Rebecca
Athenaeum, 4164:179-80,
17 Aug 1907
Atlantic, 100:133, Jul 1907
Bookman (NY), 25:304-5,
Apr 1907
Nation, 84:362, 18 Apr 1907
Saturday Review, 104:86, 20
·Jul 1907
Penelope's Experiences in Scot-
land
Athenaeum, 3688:32, 2 Jul
1898
Bookman (London), 14:109,
Jul 1898
Saturday Review, 86:513, 15
Oct 1898
Penelope's Irish Experience
Overland, 2d S, 37:1142,
Jun 1901
Picayune, 29 May 1898, II,
3
Polly Oliver's Problem
Atlantic, 73:569, Apr 1894
Bookman (London), 5:160,
Feb 1894
Cottage Hearth, 20:100, Feb
1894
Rebecca
Bookman (London), 25:186,
Jan 1904
Rebecca of Sunnybrook Farm
Bookman (London), 33:36,
Christmas Suppl. , Dec
1907; 37:165-6, Jan 1910
Bookman (NY), 18:652-3,
Feb 1904
Nation, 78:55, 21 Jan 1904
Saturday Review, 97:22, 2
Jan 1904
Rose o' the River

Wildman, Rounsevelle
Tales of the Malayan Coast
Outlook, 62:84, 6 May
1899

Wildrick, Mrs. Marion White
Lord Strahan
Picayune, 13 Apr 1879,
[p. 12]
A Zealot in Tulle
Epoch, 1:143-4, 18 Mar
1887
Nation, 44:454, 26 May
1887

Wilkins, Mary E.
See Freeman, Mary E.
(Wilkins).

Wilkins, William A.
The Cleverdale Mystery
Picayune, 22 Oct 1882,
[p. 3]
Saturday Review, 57:294,
1 Mar 1884

Wilkinson, Florence
See Evans, Florence (Wil-
kinson).

[Willard, Caroline McCoy
(White)]
A Son of Israel
By Rachel Penn [pseud.].
Outlook, 58:782, 26
Mar 1898
Saturday Review, 85:471,
2 Apr 1898

Willard, Mrs. Clara A.
Fifty Years Ago
Harper's, 45:139, Jun
1872

[Willard, Josiah Flynt]
Notes of an Itinerant Po-
liceman
By Josiah Flynt [pseud.].
Bookman (NY), 13:182-
84, Apr 1901
The Rise of Ruderick Clowd

By Josiah Flynt [pseud.].
Athenaeum, 3982:237, 20
Feb 1904
Saturday Review, 97:464-5,
9 Apr 1904
Tramping with Tramps
By Josiah Flynt [pseud.].
Bookman (NY), 10:279-80,
Nov 1899

_____, and Francis Walton
[pseud. of Alfred Hodder]
Powers That Prey
Bookman (NY), 12:506, Jan
1901

Williams, Anna Vernon (Dorsey)
Betty
Picayune, 22 Jun 1890, p.
10

Williams, Egerton Ryerson
Ridolfo
Nation, 83:353, 25 Oct 1906

Williams, Eustace Leroy
The Mutineers
Outlook, 74:1053, 29 Aug
1903

Williams, Francis Churchill
J. Devlin-Boss
Bookman (NY), 14:193-4,
Oct 1902

Williams, Francis Howard
Atman
Picayune, 15 Mar 1891, p.
14

Williams, Frank Purdy
A True Son of Liberty
Picayune, 17 Sep 1893, p.
23

[Williams, Harold]
Silken Threads
By George Afterem [pseud.].
Nation, 41:326, 15 Oct 1885

Williams, Jesse Lynch
The Adventures of a Fresh-
man
Picayune, 14 Jan 1900,
II, 7
The Day Dreamer
North American Review,
182:927, Jun 1906
The Girl and The Game
and Other College Stories
Nation, 87:56, 16 Jul
1908
My Lost Duchess
Nation, 87:12, 2 Jul
1908
Princeton Stories
Atlantic, 76:421, Sep
1895
Godey's, 131:[546]-8,
Nov 1895
Nation, 61:69, 25 Jul
1895
The Stolen Story, and Ot-
her Newspaper Stories
Athenaeum, 3743:125,
22 Jul 1899
Nation, 68:421-2, 1 Jun
1899
Outlook, 61:979, 29 Apr
1899
Picayune, 21 May 1899,
II, 12

Williams, Mrs. M. C.
Won on the Homestretch
Picayune, 8 Dec 1889,
p. 14

[Williams, Nathan Winslow]
A Master Hand
By Richard Dallas [pseud.].
Athenaeum, 3986:366-7,
19 Mar 1904
Nation, 77:390, 12 Nov
1903

Williams, Thad W.
In Quest of Life
Picayune, 16 Jul 1899,
III, 3

[Willis, Charles W.]
A Yankee in Halifax
By Allan Eric [pseud.].
Canadian Magazine, 4:401,
Mar 1895

Willis, Julia A.
What a Boy!
Godey's, 96:83, Jan 1878
Nation, 26:264-5, 18 Apr
1878
Saturday Review, 39:425,
27 Mar 1875

Wilson, Augusta Jane (Evans)
At the Mercy of Tiberius
Epoch, 2:354, 9 Dec 1887
Picayune, 30 Oct 1887, p.
14
Devota
Nation, 85:188, 29 Aug 1907
Infelice
Nation, 22:84, 3 Feb 1876
St. Elmo
Bookman (NY), 16:12-3, Sep
1902; 31:35-42, Mar 1910
A Speckled Bird
Bookman (NY), 16:178-80,
Oct 1902
Vashti
Godey's, 80:195, Feb 1870

Wilson, Harry Leon
The Boss of Little Arcady
Bookman (NY), 22:134, Oct
1905
Ewing's Lady
Bookman (NY), 26:415-7,
Dec 1907
Nation, 85:545, 12 Dec 1907
The Seeker
Athenaeum, 4042:459, 15
Apr 1905
Bookman (London), 28:68,
May 1905
Bookman (NY), 20:48-9, Sep
1904
Outlook, 78:148, 10 Sep 1904
Times Literary Supplement,
17 Mar 1905, p. 91
The Spenders

Bookman (NY), 16:52-3,
Sep 1902
Overland, 2d S, 40:337-
38, Sep 1902

Wilson, Henry R.
The Russian Refugee
Epoch, 1:541, 15 Jul
1887
Overland, 2d S, 23:217-
18, Feb 1894

[Wilson, James Grant]
The Desire of the Eyes
By Allen Grant [pseud.].
Picayune, 10 Jan 1897,
p. 11

Wilson, Marian Calvert
Manuelita
Picayune, 4 Sep 1892,
p. 7
Rénée
Epoch, 4:154, 28 Sep
1888
Picayune, 9 Sep 1888,
p. 10

[Wilson, Richard Henry]
The Venus of Cadiz
By Richard Fisguill
[pseud.].
Atlantic, 97:50, Jan
1906
Nation, 81:123, 10 Aug
1905
Sewanee Review, 14:106,
Jan 1906

Wilson, Robert Burns
Until the Day Break
Outlook, 66:232, 22
Sep 1900

Wilson, William Huntington
Rafnaland
Outlook, 66:619, 3
Nov 1900
Picayune, 25 Nov 1900,
II, 7

Wilson, William Robert Anthony
Good-for Nuthin'
Picayune, 22 Nov 1895, p.
9
A Knot of Blue
Overland, 2d S, 46:80, Jul
1905
A Rose of Normandy
Outlook, 74:199, 16 May
1903

Winchester, Carroll [pseud.].
See Curtis, Caroline Gardiner
(Cary).

Wingate, Charles E. L.
An Impossible Possibility
Picayune, 17 Feb 1889, p.
7

Winslow, Helen Maria
Salome Shepard, Reformer
Atlantic, 74:848, Dec 1894
Godey's, 127:621, Nov 1893
Picayune, 7 May 1893, p.
12

Winter, Alice (Ames)
Jewel Weed
Overland, 2d S, 49:185-6,
Feb 1907
The Prize to the Hardy
Overland, 2d S, 45:343, Apr
1905

Winter, Elizabeth C.
Spanish Treasure
Overland, 2d S, 21:662, Jun
1893
Picayune, 12 Feb 1893, p.
16

Winterburn, Florence Hull
Southern Hearts
Outlook, 65:136, 12 May
1900
Picayune, 27 May 1900, III,
7

Winthrop, Theodore
Cecil Dreeme

Winthrop, Theodore
Sewanee Review, 13:118,
Jan 1905
Mr. Waddy's Return
Nation, 79:441, 1 Dec
1904
Sewanee Review, 13:118,
Jan 1905

Wise, Daniel
Winwood Cliff
Godey's, 94:189, Feb
1877

Wise, Henry Augustus
Captain Brand, of the
Schooner 'Centipede'
Picayune, 23 Dec 1894,
p. 12
Nation, 41:140, 13 Aug
1885

Wise, John Sergeant
Diomed
Bookman (NY), 6:71-2,
Sep 1897
The Lion's Skin
Bookman (NY), 21:651-
52, Aug 1905
South Atlantic Quarterly,
4:193, Apr 1905

Wister, Owen
The Dragon of Wantley
Picayune, 4 Dec 1892,
p. 8
Saturday Review, 74:778-
79, 31 Dec 1892
How Doth the Simple Spell-
ing Bee
Overland, 2d S, 49:xvi,
Jun 1907
The Jimmyjohn Boss, and
Other Stories
Nation, 71:157, 23 Aug
1900
Lady Baltimore
Athenaeum, 4099:603,
19 May 1906
Atlantic, 99:121, Jan
1907

Bookman (London), 30:118,
Jun 1906
Bookman (NY), 23:296-7,
May 1906; 27:462-4, 466,
Jul 1908
Nation, 82:390, 10 May 1906
North American Review,
182:928, Jun 1906
Saturday Review, 101:794,
23 Jun 1906
Times Literary Supplement,
20 Apr 1906, p. 142
Lin McLean
Athenaeum, 3702:489, 8 Oct
1898
Bookman (NY), 7:254, May
1898
Nation, 66:407, 26 May 1898
Saturday Review, 85:335-6,
5 Mar 1898
Times Literary Supplement,
4 Jul 1902, p. 196
Philosophy 4
Athenaeum, 3945:716, 6 Jun
1903
Bookman (NY), 17:613-4,
Jul 1903
Sewanee Review, 11:503,
Oct 1903
Times Literary Review,
29 May 1903, p. 169
Red Men and White
Atlantic, 77:264-5, Feb 1896
Bookman (NY), 2:275-7, Dec
1895
Nation, 62:182, 27 Feb 1896
Times Literary Supplement,
4 Jul 1902, p. 196
The Virginian
Athenaeum, 3902:182, 9 Aug
1902
Atlantic, 90:277, Aug 1902
Bookman (NY), 15:569, Aug
1902; 27:458-61, 466, Jul
1908
Nation, 75:331, 23 Oct 1902
Saturday Review, 94:274, 30
Aug 1902
Sewanee Review, 10:504-5,
Oct 1902
South Atlantic Quarterly,

5:223, Jul 1906
Times Literary Supple-
ment, 4 Jul 1902,
p. 196

[Witherspoon, Orlando]
Doctor Ben
Cottage Hearth, 8:365,
Nov 1882
Nation, 35:447, 23 Nov
1882
Picayune, 21 Oct 1888,
p. 11
Saturday Review, 54:872,
30 Dec 1882

Woerner, John Gabriel
The Rebel's Daughter
Outlook, 63:1030, 30
Dec 1899

Wolf, Alice S.
A House of Cards
Nation, 63:180, 3 Sep
1896
Picayune, 6 Apr 1896,
p. 11
Poet-Lore, 8:619-20,
(No. 8) 1896

Wolf, Emma
Heirs of Yesterday
Bookman (NY), 13:78-9,
Mar 1901
The Joy of Life
Bookman (NY), 4:375,
Dec 1896
Overland, 2d S, 29:454,
Apr 1897
Picayune, 13 Dec 1896,
p. 16
Other Things Being Equal
Overland, 2d S, 20:661-
62, Dec 1892
Picayune, 4 Feb 1894,
p. 16

Wolfenstein, Martha
Idyls of the Gass
Outlook, 74:672, 11 Jul
1903

Saturday Review, 96:241, 22
Aug 1903
A Renegade, and Other Stories
Nation, 82:182, 1 Mar 1906

Wood, Anna Cogswell
Diana Fontaine
By Algernon Ridgeway
[pseud.].
Atlantic, 68:711, Nov 1891
Picayune, 28 Jun 1891, p.
12
The Westovers
By Algernon Ridgeway
[pseud.].
Saturday Review, 78:363, 29
Sep 1894
Westover's Ward
By Algernon Ridgeway
[pseud.].
Athenaeum, 3371:723, 4 Jun
1892
Saturday Review, 73:746, 25
Jun 1892

[Wood, Charlotte Dunning]
Cabin and Gondola
By Charlotte Dunning [pseud.].
Overland, 2d S, 7:321, Mar
1886
Picayune, 17 Jan 1886, p. 8
A Step Aside
By Charlotte Dunning [pseud.].
Cottage Hearth, 12:368, Nov
1886
Godey's, 113:593, Dec 1886
Harper's, 74:828, Apr 1887
Nation, 44:17, 6 Jan 1887
Overland, 2d S, 9:322, Mar
1887
Saturday Review, 62:656-7,
13 Nov 1886
Upon a Cast
By Charlotte Dunning [pseud.].
Nation, 41:159, 20 Aug 1885
Picayune, 5 Jul 1885, [p.
11]
Saturday Review, 61:548, 17
Apr 1886

Wood, Edith (Elmer)
The Spirit of the Service
Saturday Review, 97:177,
6 Feb 1904

Wood, Eugene
Folks Back Home
Nation, 86:287, 26 Mar
1908
Overland, 2d S, 51:487-
88, May 1908

Wood, Frances Hartson, and
Eva Paine Kitchel
Warp and Woof
Nation, 50:492, 19 Jun
1890

Wood, Henry
Edward Burton
Cottage Hearth, 16:225,
Jul 1890
Godey's, 121:172, Aug
1890
Overland, 2d S, 16:440,
Oct 1890
Picayune, 1 Jun 1890,
p. 10
Victor Serenus
Outlook, 58:980, 16
Apr 1898
Picayune, 24 Apr 1898,
p. 25
Saturday Review, 86:151-
52, 30 Jul 1898

Wood, Joanna E.
A Daughter of Witches
Athenaeum, 3801:276,
1 Sep 1900
Saturday Review, 90:432,
6 Oct 1900
Judith Moore
Nation, 67:264, 6 Oct
1898
A Martyr to Love
Picayune, 11 Apr 1897,
p. 25
The Untempered Wind
Nation, 60:426, 30 May
1895

Wood, John Seymour
College Days
Picayune, 8 Jul 1894, p. 7
Grammercy Park
Godey's, 125:518, Nov 1892
Picayune, 18 Sep 1892, p.
14
An Old Beau, and Other Stories
Picayune, 5 Mar 1893, p.
16
Yale Yarns
Godey's, 131:[546]-8, Nov
1895
Nation, 61:69, 25 Jul 1895

Wood, S. Ella
Shibboleth
Picayune, 11 Mar 1900, II,
3; 27 Nov 1898, p. 10

[Woodruff, Julia Louisa Matilda
(Curtiss)]
Bellerue
By W. M. L. Jay [pseud.].
Athenaeum, 3306:307-8, 7
Mar 1891
Saturday Review, 71:387-8,
28 Mar 1891
Holden with the Cords
By W. L. M. Jay [pseud.].
Atlantic, 35:108, Jan 1875
Harper's, 50:139, Dec 1874
Nation, 19:223, 1 Oct 1874
Shiloh
Nation, 12:45, 19 Jan 1871

Woods, George Bryant
Essays, Sketches, and Stories
Harper's, 46:776, Apr 1873
Saturday Review, 35:431, 29
Mar 1873

Woods, Katharine Pearson
From Dusk to Dawn
Nation, 56:202, 16 Mar 1893
Metzerott, Shoemaker
Nation, 50:225, 13 Mar 1890
Overland, 2d S, 15:318-20,
Mar 1890
Picayune, 27 Jul 1890, p.
10

A Web of Gold
　　Picayune, 7 Dec 1890,
　　　p. 8

Woods, Virna
　　An Elusive Lover
　　　Athenaeum, 3698:348,
　　　10 Sep 1898
　　　Saturday Review, 86:280,
　　　27 Aug 1898

[Wood-Seys, Roland Alexander]
　　Cut With His Own Diamond
　　　By Paul Cushing [pseud.].
　　　Bookman (London),
　　　1:148-9, Jan 1892
　　The Great Chin Episode
　　　By Paul Cushing [pseud.].
　　　Bookman (London),
　　　4:122, Jul 1893
　　　Saturday Review, 76:129-
　　　30, 29 Jul 1893
　　The Shepherdess of Treva
　　　By Paul Cushing [pseud.].
　　　Saturday Review, 81:82,
　　　18 Jan 1896

Woodville, Jennie [pseud.].
　　See Stabler, Mrs. Jennie
　　Latham.

Woolf, Philip
　　Who Is Guilty?
　　　Nation, 43:102, 29 Jul
　　　1886

Woolley, Celia Parker
　　A Girl Graduate
　　　Cottage Hearth, 15:272,
　　　Aug 1889
　　　Nation, 49:76, 25 Jul
　　　1889
　　　Overland, 2d S, 14:101-
　　　102, Jul 1889
　　Love and Theology
　　　Godey's, 115:429, Nov
　　　1887
　　　Nation, 45:485, 15
　　　Dec 1887
　　Rachel Armstrong
　　　Godey's, 118:180, Feb

1889

Woolsey, Mrs. Sarah C.
　　For Summer Afternoons
　　　By Susan Coolidge [pseud.].
　　　Harper's, 53:629, Sep 1876
　　The New Year's Bargain
　　　By Susan Coolidge [pseud.].
　　　Harper's, 44:781, Apr 1872
　　　Nation, 14:62-3, 25 Jan
　　　1872

Woolson, Constance Fenimore
　　Anne
　　　Atlantic, 50:111-3, Jul 1882
　　　Continent, 2:285, 6 Sep 1882
　　　Cottage Hearth, 8:263, Aug
　　　1882
　　　Harper's, 65:478, Aug 1882
　　　Nation, 35:182, 31 Aug 1882
　　　Picayune, 30 Jul 1882, [p.
　　　6]
　　Castle Nowhere
　　　Atlantic, 35:736-7, Jun 1875
　　　Harper's, 74:482, Feb 1887
　　　Picayune, 14 Nov 1886, p.
　　　11
　　Dorothy, and Other Italian Sto-
　　ries
　　　Nation, 62:181, 27 Feb 1896
　　East Angels
　　　Harper's, 73:477-8, Aug
　　　1886
　　　Nation, 43:396, 11 Nov 1886
　　　Picayune, 6 Jun 1886, p. 14
　　　Saturday Review, 62:395, 18
　　　Sep 1886
　　For the Major
　　　Atlantic, 52:119-20, Jul 1883
　　　Harper's, 67:317-8, Jul 1883
　　　Nation, 37:120, 9 Aug 1883
　　　Overland, 2d S, 2:211, Aug
　　　1883
　　　Picayune, 17 Jun 1883, [p.
　　　8]
　　The Front Yard, and Other
　　Italian Stories
　　　Atlantic, 77:129, Jan 1896
　　　Nation, 61:433, 12 Dec 1895
　　Horace Chase
　　　Atlantic, 73:705, May 1894

Woolson, Constance Fenimore
    Nation, 58:233, 29 Mar
        1894
    Saturday Review, 78:331,
        22 Sep 1894
    Jupiter Lights
        Atlantic, 75:126-8, Jan
            1890
        Nation, 50:225, 13 Mar
            1890
        Saturday Review, 69:234-
            35, 22 Feb 1890
    Rodman the Keeper
        Atlantic, 46:124-5, Jul
            1880
        Harper's, 74:482, Feb
            1887
        Nation, 30:313, 22 Apr
            1880; 44:299-300, 7
            Apr 1887
        Picayune, 5 Dec 1886,
            p. 8
        Saturday Review, 49:706,
            29 May 1880

Worden, A. T.
    See Arkell, William J.,
    and A. T. Worden.

Worth, Ellis [pseud.].
    See Ellsworth, Mrs. Lou-
    ise C.

Worth, Nicholas [pseud.].
    See Page, Walter Hines.

Wright, Annie L.
    Little Heartsease
        Godey's, 112:537, May
            1886

Wright, Harold Bell
    The Calling of Dan Matthews
        Bookman (NY), 30:189-
            90, Oct 1909
    The Shepherd of the Hills
        Athenaeum, 4278:489-90,
            23 Oct 1909
        Bookman (London),
            37:103, Nov 1909
        Overland, 2d S, 56:[613],

Dec 1910

Wright, Julia (McNair)
    Almost a Priest
        Godey's, 72:96, Jan 1871
    The Best Fellow in the World
        Godey's, 73:282, Sep 1871
        Harper's, 43:624, Sep 1871
    A Bonnie Boy
        Outlook, 63:510, 28 Oct 1899
    Patriot and Tory
        Saturday Review, 42:552, 28
            Oct 1876
    The Priest and the Nun
        Harper's, 40:299, Jan 1870
    A Wife Hard Won
        Godey's, 108:590, Jun 1884

[Wright, Mabel (Osgood)]
    At the Sign of the Fox
        By Barbara [pseud.].
        Athenaeum, 4065:397, 23
            Sep 1905
        Bookman (London), 28:211,
            Sep 1905
        Bookman (NY), 22:134, Oct
            1905
    The Garden, You, and I
        By Barbara [pseud.].
        Bookman (NY), 23:631-2,
            Aug 1906
        Saturday Review, 102:337,
            15 Sep 1906
    The Open Window
        By Barbara [pseud.].
        Nation, 87:265, 17 Sep 1908
    People of the Whirlpool
        Athenaeum, 3993:587, 7 May
            1904
        Nation, 77:55, 16 Jul 1903
        Sewanee Review, 12:122-3,
            Jan 1904
    Poppea of the Post-Office
        Nation, 89:278-9, 23 Sep
            1909
        Saturday Review, 108:508,
            23 Oct 1909

Wright, Mary (Tappan)
    Aliens
        Nation, 74:412, 22 May 1902

Overland, 2d S, 39:984,
Jun 1902
Saturday Review, 94:274,
30 Aug 1902
The Tower
Athenaeum, 4102:695,
9 Jun 1906
Bookman (NY), 23:628-
30, Aug 1906
A Truce, and Other Stories
Atlantic, 76:708, Nov
1895
Bookman (NY), 1:347-
48, Jun 1895
Nation, 62:61, 16 Jan
1896
Picayune, 2 Jun 1895,
p. 16

Wyatt, Edith Franklin
Every One His Own Way
Harper's, 103:822-3,
Oct 1901
True Love
North American Review,
176:735-9, May 1903

Wyckoff, Walter Augustus
The Workers
Nation, 66:211, 17 Mar
1898
Picayune, 30 Jan 1898,
p. 17

Wyman, Lillie Buffum (Chace)
Poverty Grass
Harper's, 74:482-3,
Feb 1887
Nation, 43:548, 30 Dec
1886
Overland, 2d S, 8:439,
Oct 1886

X., A.
See Mathews, Frances
Aymar.

[Yardley, Mrs. Jane Woolsey]
Little Sister
Continent, 3:189, 7 Feb
1883

A Superior Woman
Nation, 41:18, 2 Jul 1885

Yechton, Barbara [pseud.].
See Krausé, Lyda Farrington.

Yellott, George
The Funny Philosophers
Godey's, 84:192, Feb 1872
Saturday Review, 33:258, 24
Feb 1872

Yelverton, Thérèse
Zanita
Overland, 8:98, Jan 1872
Picayune, 5 Nov 1871, [p.
12]

Young, Fred Grant
Day-Dreams and Night-Mares
Picayune, 25 Nov 1894, p.
10

Young, Julia Evelyn (Ditto)
Adrift
Atlantic, 66:429, Sep 1890
Epoch, 6:758, 27 Dec 1889
Godey's, 120:96, Jan 1890

Young, Rose E.
Henderson
Atlantic, 93:852, Jun 1904
Sally of Missouri
Athenaeum, 3998:746, 11
Jun 1904
Nation, 78:134-5, 18 Feb
1904
Saturday Review, 98:22, 2
Jul 1904

Young, Virginia (Durant)
"Beholding as in a Glass"
Picayune, 10 Mar 1895, p.
14
A Tower in the Desert
Picayune, 18 Oct 1896, p. 9

Zearing, Marguerite
Hasta Leugo, Amigo Mio
Picayune, 17 Sep 1899, II,
10

Zogbaum

Zogbaum, Rufus Fairchild
Horse, Foot and Dragoons
Epoch, 2:477, 20 Jan
1888

Zollinger, Gulielma [pseud.].
See Gladwin, William
Zachary.

Titles Published Anonymously and Pseudonymously:

Authors' Nationality Not Determined

Ackroyd of the Faculty
 Overland, 2d S, 49:xiv,
  Jun 1907

Adam and Eve
 Picayune, 21 Nov 1880,
  [p. 5]

The Adventures of a Nice
 Young Man
 By Aix.
  Nation, 88:92-3, 28 Jan
  1909

The Adventures of Elizabeth
 in Rügen
  Atlantic, 93:852, Jun 1904

Aileen Ferrers
 Harper's, 50:599, Mar 1875

Alcestis
 Nation, 19:93, 6 Aug 1874

Alien
 Godey's, 130:431, Apr 1895

All for Him
 By * * * *.
  Picayune, 4 Nov 1877,
  [p. 12]

Almost a Duchess
 Godey's, 110:110, Jan 1885

American Coin
 Epoch, 5:405-6, 26 Jul
  1889

Andy Barr
 Overland, 2d S, 42:463, Nov
  1903

Anne Furness
 Harper's, 43:783-4, Oct 1871
 Picayune, 15 Oct 1871, [p. 14]

Anteros
 Harper's, 43:301, Jun 1871

Apples from Eden
 By Estelle.
  Picayune, 13 Jul 1890, p. 11

The Arab Wife
 Picayune, 22 Sep 1878, [p. 2]

Aristocracy
 Epoch, 4:154-5, 28 Sep 1888
 North American Review,
  147:594-5, Nov 1888

As It Should Be
 By Alex.
  Godey's, 79:93, Jul 1874

At the Red Stone
 Picayune, 21 Jun 1885, [p. 7]

At the World's Mercy
 Picayune, 23 Nov 1884, [p. 7]

Azalea
 Harper's, 54:618, Mar 1877

Azalem
 Overland, 2d S, 44:384-5, Sep

Appendix

Azalem
    1904

A Bachelor in Arcady
    Overland, 2d S, 43:426,
        May 1904

Baffled
    Harper's, 40:926, May 1870

Barrington's Fate
    Continent, 3:605, 9 May
        1883
    Nation, 36:152, 15 Feb
        1883

Bascobel
    Nation, 33:337, 27 Oct
        1881

The Battle of Moy
    Overland, 2d S, 1:654,
        Jun 1883

Beaulieu
    Picayune, 9 Jan 1881, [p.
        10]

Beautiful Edith
    Nation, 25:275, 1 Nov 1877

The Beautiful Miss Brooks
    Picayune, 26 Jul 1897, p.
        8

Beauty's Daughters
    Atlantic, 46:834, Dec 1880

Beneath the Wheels
    Harper's, 41:303, Jul 1870

Bird in the Bone
    Harper's, 42:931, May
        1871

The Blue Ribbon
    Harper's, 49:136, Jun 1874

Bound to John Company
    Harper's, 40:461, Feb
        1870

A Brave Lady
    Picayune, 17 Apr 1870, [p.
        12]

Brentford Parsonage
    Godey's, 92:94, Jan 1876

By the Marshes of Minas
    Picayune, 11 Feb 1900, II, 8

Camille's Tormentor
    Athenaeum, 2578:382-3, 24 Mar
        1877

The Case of Mohammed Benani
    Epoch, 3:237-8, 27 Apr 1888

The Caxtons
    Outlook, 58:639, 5 Mar 1898

Cecil's Tryst
    Harper's, 44:780, Apr 1872
    Nation, 14:410, 20 Jun 1872
    Picayune, 7 Apr 1872, [p. 10]

A Chelsea Householder
    Nation, 36:406, 10 May 1883

Cherry Ripe
    Picayune, 30 Dec 1877, [p. 15]

Children of Circumstance
    By Iota.
    Nation, 60:206, 14 Mar 1895

Christie Elwood
    Harper's, 42:623, Mar 1871

A Christmas Garland
    By H*nry J*m*s.
    Saturday Review, 102:702-3,
        8 Dec 1906

Clotilde
    Picayune, 12 Nov 1871, [p. 14]

The Clyffords of Clyffe
    Godey's, 73:570, Dec 1871

Clytie
    Picayune, 23 Jul 1882, [p. 2]

342

Colonel Dacre
Harper's, 49:443-4, Aug
1874

The Coming Race
Overland, 7:485, Nov
1871
Picayune, 10 Sep 1871,
[p. 5]

Confessions of Marguerite
Outlook, 76:710, 19 Mar
1904
Overland, 2d S, 43:424,
May 1904

Conjugal Amenities
By "Delta."
Picayune, 17 May 1896,
p. 15

The Country
Picayune, 1 Sep 1889,
p. 7

The Crime of Christmas Day
Nation, 40:285-286,
2 Apr 1885

The Curse of Intellect
Atlantic, 76:707, Nov 1895

Cyrilla
Picayune, 4 Feb 1877,
[p. 6]

Daisy Nichol
Harper's, 42:931, May
1871

A Dangerous Guest
Harper's, 41:935-6, Nov
1870

Daniele Cortis
Epoch, 1:542, 15 Jul 1887

The Danvers Jewels
Picayune, 13 Apr 1890,
p. 16

Daphne
By Rita.
Nation, 31:83, 29 Jul 1880
Picayune, 20 Jun 1880, [p. 6]

A Daughter of Heth
Harper's, 43:937, Nov 1871

David and Abigail
Picayune, 22 Jul 1894, p. 21

The Daysman
Overland, 2d S, 55:338, Mar
1910

The Delectable Duchy
By Q.
Overland, 2d S, 23:216-7, Feb
1894

Destinies
Times Literary Supplement, 23
Apr 1908, p. 135

Diane Coryval
Godey's, 108:590, May 1884
Nation, 38:195, 28 Feb 1884

A Discrepant World
Nation, 83:83, 26 Jul 1906

Dollarocracy
Picayune, 10 Apr 1892, p. 15

The Dominant Strain
Overland, 2d S, 42:366-7, Oct
1903

Don John
Nation, 32:173, 10 Mar 1881

Dorothy Fox
Nation, 12:114, 16 Feb 1871

Dot and Dime
Godey's, 95:175, Aug 1877
Picayune, 3 Jun 1877, [p. 12]

A Drama in Dutch
Atlantic, 75:566, Apr 1895

Appendix

The Earthly Purgatory
Times Literary Supplement,
24 Jun 1904, p. 197

Eglantine
Harper's, 51:602, Sep 1875

Emma Parker
Harper's, 42:931, May
1871

Endymion
By K. G.
Atlantic, 47:715-6, May
1881

Ersilia
Canadian Monthly and Na-
tional Review, 10:180,
Aug 1876
Godey's, 92:569, Jun 1876

Estelle Russell
Harper's, 42:141-2, Dec
1870

Ethel Midmay's Follies
Nation, 15:222, 3 Oct 1872

Every Day's News
Atlantic, 76:421, Sep 1895

Expatriation
Nation, 51:506, 25 Dec
1890

Expiated
Picayune, 10 Aug 1873,
[p. 10]

An Exquisite Fool
Godey's, 126:107, Jan
1893
Picayune, 20 Nov 1892,
p. 18

Fair Diana
By Wanderer.
Nation, 40:101, 29 Jan
1885

The Familiar Letters of Pepper-
mint Perkins
Cottage Hearth, 12:230, Jul
1886

The Flaw in the Marble
Bookman (London), 10:58, May
1896

For Percival
Picayune, 16 Feb 1879, [p. 11]

Fore and Aft
By Webfoot.
Saturday Review, 31:256, 25
Feb 1871

Fortune's Wheel
By Alex
Nation, 42:303, 8 Apr 1886

Four Irrepressibles
Godey's, 95:437, Nov 1877
Nation, 25:273, 1 Nov 1877

Fraternity
Nation, 47:299, 11 Oct 1888;
91:633-4, 29 Dec 1910

A Free Solitude
Times Literary Supplement,
5 Apr 1907, p. 111

Friday Night
Picayune, 22 May 1870, [p. 3]

From Darkness to Light
By Iota.
Picayune, 13 Apr 1873, [p. 10]

From Dreams to Waking
Harper's, 54:771, Apr 1877

Galana
Harper's, 47:131, Jun 1873

The Giant Killer
Harper's, 56:311, Jan 1878

Going and Son
By Monk.

Godey's, 80:196, Feb 1870
Harper's, 49:299, Jan
  1870

The Golden Butterfly
  Godey's, 94:462-3, May
    1877
  Harper's, 54:923-4, May
    1877

A Golden Sparrow
  Harper's, 45:785, Oct
    1872

Gray Mist
  North American Review,
    184:413-7, 15 Feb 1907

Grey Abbey
  Picayune, 17 Feb 1878,
    [p. 10]

Gwendoline's Harvest
  Nation, 11:127, 25 Aug
    1870

Harmonia
  Nation, 46:266, 29 Mar
    1888

Harold, An Experiment
  Picayune, 22 Nov 1891,
    p. 12

Heir Expectant
  Harper's, 42:142, Dec
    1870

The Heir of Malreward
  Nation, 19:10, 2 Jul 1874

Henry of Navarre
  Nation, 88:308, 25 Mar
    1909

The Hepworth's Millions
  Outlook, 59:690, 16 Jul
    1898

Her Brother's Letters
  Saturday Review, 104:241-2,

24 Aug 1907

Her Crime
  Nation, 36:42, 11 Jan 1883

Her Fortune Her Misfortune
  Picayune, 13 Feb 1898, p. 22

Hetty's Boarder
  Nation, 29:115, 14 Aug 1879

The High Road
  Bookman (NY), 19:513-5, Jul
    1904

Higher Law
  Picayune, 21 Apr 1872, [p. 13]

Hirell
  Picayune, 27 Feb 1870, [p. 5]

His Dear Little Wife
  Godey's, 97:172, Aug 1878

The Honorable Mrs. Farrard
  Picayune, 24 Mar 1878, [p. 3]

The House on the Marsh
  Godey's, 109:531, Nov 1884
  Nation, 34:464-5, 27 Nov 1884

How Much I Loved Thee
  Nation, 38:450, 22 May 1884

How to Make a Saint
  By "The Prig."
  Epoch, 2:35, 19 Aug 1887

Ida Craven
  Harper's, 54:150, Dec 1876

In a Silent World
  Picayune, 30 Mar 1896, p. 8

In Duty Bound
  Harper's, 42:400, Feb 1871

In Her Earliest Youth
  By Tasma.
  Picayune, 25 May 1890, p. 14

Appendix

In the House of Her Friends
  Bookman (NY), 23:632-3,
    Aug 1906
  Sewanee Review, 15:248,
    Apr 1907

In the Olden Times
  Nation, 36:553, 28 Jun
    1883

In the Shadow of the Hills
  Outlook, 60:920, 10 Dec
    1898

The Inner Shrine
  Atlantic, 104:681, Nov
    1909
  Bookman (NY), 29:526,
    Jul 1909
  Nation, 88:489, 13 May
    1909
  North American Review,
    190:119, Jul 1909

Irene
  Godey's, 72:573, Jun
    1871

Iseulte
  Harper's, 51:453, Aug
    1875

Isolina
  By E. G. T.
  Saturday Review, 34:837,
    28 Dec 1872

Iva
  Harper's, 43:458, Aug
    1871

Jack's Sister
  Harper's, 50:449, Feb
    1875

James
  Picayune, 3 Jan 1897,
    p. 17

The Jessica Letters
  Saturday Review, 98:85,

16 Jul 1904

A Jewel of a Girl
  Picayune, 17 Feb 1878, [p. 10]

John Schuyler's Millions
  Godey's, 112:426, Apr 1886

John Thompson, Blockhead
  Harper's, 44:780-1, Apr 1872

Johnny Ludlow
  Godey's, 91:569, Dec 1875
  Picayune, 3 Oct 1875, [p. 10]

Judith of the Plains
  Overland, 2d S, 43:259, Mar
    1904

Kate of Kate Hall
  Overland, 2d S, 45:xviii, Feb
    1905

Keith Deramore
  Atlantic, 72:126, Jul 1893
  Nation, 56:297, 20 Apr 1893
  Picayune, 19 Mar 1893, p. 10

Kempton-Wace Letters
  Saturday Review, 96:212, 15
    Aug 1903

Lapsed, but Not Lost
  Godey's, 96:83, Jan 1878

The Last of Her Line
  Harper's, 58:940, May 1879

The Last of the Haddons
  Harper's, 56:941, May 1878
  Library Table, 4:242, 11 May
    1878

Left-Handed Elsa
  Nation, 29:213, 25 Sep 1879

Life Is Life, and Other Tales and
Episodes
  By Zack.
  Nation, 67:299, 20 Oct 1898

Appendix

Tip Cat
  Godey's, 109:651, Dec
    1884

Torn Pippin's Wedding
  Harper's, 43:784-5, Oct
    1871

Toxas
  Epoch, 8:77, 5 Sep 1890

The Treasure Hunters
  Harper's, 50:449, Feb
    1875

Two Englishmen
  By "An American!"
    Saturday Review, 60:192-3,
    8 Aug 1885

The Two Miss Flemings
  Harper's, 60:152, Dec
    1879

Un Coin du Monde
  Atlantic, 39:381, Mar
    1877

Unawares
  Harper's, 45:942, Nov
    1872
  Nation, 15:319, 14 Nov
    1872

Under Foot
  Harper's, 40:774, Apr
    1870

Under the Greenwood Tree
  Harper's, 47:619, Sep
    1873

Unforgiven
  Atlantic, 25:762-3, Jun
    1870

An Unlaid Ghost
  North American Review,
    146:477, Apr 1888

Unsatisfied

Picayune, 16 Mar 1890, p. 16

Unveiling a Parallel
  By Two Women of the West.
    Picayune, 13 Aug 1893, p. 16

Veronica
  Harper's, 41:935, Nov 1870

A Very Young Couple
  Harper's, 48:498-9, Mar 1874

Ward or Wife?
  Harper's, 51:602, Sep 1875
  Nation, 21:105-6, 12 Aug 1875

Wheat in the Ear
  Outlook, 59:386, 11 Jun 1898

Which Is the Heroine?
  Harper's, 42:400, Feb 1871

The White Feather
  By Tasma.
    Picayune, 6 Nov 1892, p. 15

The White Witch
  Nation, 40:285, 2 Apr 1885

Why She Refused Him
  By Lorraine.
    Nation, 17:28, 10 Jul 1873

The Wild Olive
  Bookman (NY), 31:509-10, Jul
    1910
  North American Review,
    192:137-8, Jul 1910

Wild Times
  Picayune, 13 Apr 1873, [p. 10]

Wilfrede Cumbermede
  Harper's, 44:781, Apr 1872

Will Denbigh, Nobleman
  Library Table, 3:75, 22 Dec
    1877

The Wolf at the Door
  Library Table, 4:160, 2 Mar

1878
Picayune, 17 Feb 1878,
   [p. 10]
Sunday Afternoon, 1:288,
   Mar 1878

The Woman Errant
   Nation, 79:121-2, 11 Aug
   1904
   Saturday Review, 98:276,
   27 Aug 1904; 98:337-8,
   10 Sep 1904

The Woman in Black
   Godey's, 102:573, Jun
   1881

Womens' Husbands
   Nation, 29:444, 25 Dec
   1879

Won--Not Wooed
   Harper's, 43:623, Sep
   1871

The Wooing o't
   Atlantic, 33:618-9, May
   1874
   Nation, 17:277, 23 Oct
   1873

The Worldly Twin
   Picayune, 3 Dec 1893,
   p. 19

The Wreck of the Grosvenor
   Harper's, 56:941, May
   1878

Wrecked in Port
   Harper's, 40:299, Jan
   1870

A Yellow Aster
   By Iota.
   Nation, 58:369-70, 17
   May 1894

Young Mrs. Jardine
   Atlantic, 45:681-2, May
   1880

A Younger Sister
   Picayune, 12 Jun 1892, p. 12

Yourie Guardenin
   Overland, 2d S, 46:591, Dec
   1905